# FANTASY SPORTS AND THE CHANGING SPORTS MEDIA INDUSTRY

# FANTASY SPORTS AND THE CHANGING SPORTS MEDIA INDUSTRY

## Media, Players, and Society

**Edited by
Nicholas David Bowman,
John S. W. Spinda,
and Jimmy Sanderson**

**LEXINGTON BOOKS**
Lanham • Boulder • New York • London

Published by Lexington Books
An imprint of The Rowman & Littlefield Publishing Group, Inc.
4501 Forbes Boulevard, Suite 200, Lanham, Maryland 20706
www.rowman.com

Unit A, Whitacre Mews, 26-34 Stannary Street, London SE11 4AB

British Library Cataloguing in Publication Information Available

**Library of Congress Cataloging-in-Publication Data**
Names: Bowman, Nicholas David.
Title: Fantasy sports and the changing sports media industry : media,
    players, and society / edited by Nicholas David Bowman, John S. W. Spinda,
    and James Sanderson.
Description: Lanham : Lexington Books, [2016] | Includes bibliographical
    references and index.
Identifiers: LCCN 2015051315 (print) | LCCN 2016002334 (ebook) | ISBN
    9781498504881 (cloth : alk. paper) | ISBN 9781498504898 (Electronic)
Subjects: LCSH: Fantasy sports. | Mass media and sports.
Classification: LCC GV1202.F35 F35 2016 (print) | LCC GV1202.F35 (ebook) |
    DDC 793.93—dc23
LC record available at http://lccn.loc.gov/2015051315

    ISBN 978-1-4985-0490-4 (pbk : alk. paper)

∞™ The paper used in this publication meets the minimum requirements of
American National Standard for Information Sciences—Permanence of Paper
for Printed Library Materials, ANSI/NISO Z39.48-1992.

Printed in the United States of America

# CONTENTS

# ACKNOWLEDGMENTS

The inspiration for this volume came from a short e-mail conversation with representatives at Lexington Books who took an interest in our published research—that short e-mail led to longer phone calls and crowded hotel lobby conversations, and eventually a multi-national collaboration of editors and authors that I can truly call my friends. I sincerely appreciate: Lexington Books and their insistence that our project had some honest economic and social value (specifically Kasey Beduhn and Nicolette Amstutz, as well as Alison Pavan); my co-editors, for their friendship and hard work throughout the process (and for not blocking me on social media when I hounded them for book feedback); the many chapter solicitations that we received, which helped us refine the focus of the volume; the published authors, for their diligence and open-ness to our editorial comments on their work; our anonymous reviewer, for her or his sharp-but-sincere criticisms of the volume; my family (two- and four-legged ones), for their willingness to allow me to work in the living room while watching baseball.

—Nick Bowman
Morgantown, West Virginia

Working on this volume has been a pleasure. I would like to thank my co-editors, John Spinda and Nick Bowman for their work in putting this volume together. Nick, in particular has been the organizer and facilitator and kept everyone working within the timelines. Shaun Anderson, the editorial assistant, has been invaluable in handing the various administrative tasks required by this project. Without his assistance, this project would not have been able to be completed. The contributors to this volume have provided some excellent commentary and perspective on fantasy sport that will be influential in this emerging research agenda. I also would like to thank the team at Lexington Books for believing in this project and for the editorial team in their assistance in getting this project from conception to reality.

—Jimmy Sanderson
Phoenix, Arizona

**C**ompleting this edited volume took a lot of long work days and sacrifices, I would like to thank those that have been so vital in me being able to help bring this project to completion, my wonderful, supportive wife Shanna and my daughter, who always brings a big smile to my face, no matter what. I want to thank Nick Bowman, Jimmy Sanderson, and Shaun Anderson for all the support and patience they have had with me throughout my first book editing experience, it is greatly appreciated. Lastly, I want to thank all of our wonderful authors, who are truly the "stars of this show."

—John S. W. Spinda
Clemson, South Carolina

Finally, all three editors owe their deepest gratitude to Shaun Anderson for serving as the editorial assistant and head cat-wrangler of this project. Shaun volunteered his time with this book while completing his Ph.D. in Communication Studies at West Virginia University, and his efforts were nothing short of spectacular.

# INTRODUCTION

From amateur statistics tracking to augmented reality technology, fantasy sports play has established a prominent and promising foothold in the larger sports ecology. Often considered an isolated activity for the hardcore sports fan, fantasy sports play have since been incorporated into sports broadcasting and editorial coverage, sports marketing and promotions, and even into the very sports themselves—with athletes and teams using the activities to draw fans further into the sports experience. This edited volume collects emerging research and scholarship from leading scholars and sports professionals from several different fields to share historical and emerging perspectives on the importance of fantasy sports as an artifact of theoretical and empirical importance to larger issues of sport and society.

The volume is organized into five separate themes, all drawing from a different area of scholarship and each informing some of the various ways in which fantasy sports have permeated the larger Mediasport infrastructure. The first section historicizes fantasy sports by exploring its earliest roots in fan communities, both in the United States (the genesis of fantasy sports) and more recently in Europe and abroad. Chapters on the earliest fantasy sports games by Anderson and Bowman (chapter 1) and Spinda (chapter 2) provide a comprehensive review of fantasy sports from the mid-twentieth century to today, cumulating in a discussion by Wanatabe, Yan, and Wicker (chapter 3) of the fantasy sport's spread beyond the United States, and the costs and benefits of that spread.

The second section focuses on sports fans, and explores their usage of and motivations for engaging in the activity—examining the cooperative and competitive aspects of fantasy sports as a community-based activity (both online and offline), the risks and responsibilities adopted by fantasy sports players in terms of economic and social capital, and the unique role that gender plays in understanding fantasy sports play. Spinda and Havard (chapter 4) discuss the unique role that competition and *schadenfreude* play in how fans engage each other over fantasy sports, and Westerman, Boyan, and Daniel (chapter 5) provide a compelling argument for using fantasy sports play as a vehicle for understanding social presence—the sense of "being there" in a social interaction with others via computer. Baerg (chapter 6) provides a novel argument as to how fantasy sports play can be rhetorically understood through the lens of neoliberal capitalism by encouraging players to engage the space less as sports fans and more as entrepreneurs, and Lavalle (chapter 7) critically explores the ways in which women are positioned in fantasy sports spaces. This section is capped by Gearhart, Keaton, and Ruihley (chapter 8), who present data on the ways in which fantasy sports players self-disclose while engaged in the contests.

The third section examines fantasy sports through the lens of traditional and digital media organizations, including the manner in which legacy newspapers and broadcast stations have incorporated fantasy sports coverage into their daily operations and discussions about the role of social media in the larger fantasy sports discussion. This section will also include a discussion of how fantasy sports players select and attend to various media sources as a function of their fandom. Specifically, chapters by Hardin and Bien-Aime (chapter 9) discussion the intersection of legacy media and fantasy sports; Dwyer, Shapiro, and Drayer (chapter 10) explain fantasy players' broader media consumption habits; and Sanderson (chapter 11) explains the unique position that social media plays in the fantasy sports player's media repertoire.

The fourth section of the book takes a more global look at fantasy sports play by considering how the activity might impact sports organizations themselves. Specifically, Wanatabe, Wicker, and Yan (chapter 12) present original data showing how fantasy sports play can have a noticeable impact on how sports fans engage a major global sporting event: the 2014 FIFA World Cup. This discussion is followed by Grabowski (chapter 13) who offers a comprehensive primer on fantasy sports law, including historical and emerging issues faced by fantasy sports players and organizations related to legal issues ranging from copyright infringement to gambling, among others.

The fifth and final section of the book discusses the future of fantasy sports as an activity encompassing fans, athletes, institutions and media alike. Included in this section is a discussion by Ruihley and Billings (chapter 14) of the development of an international trade organization for fantasy sports (Fantasy Sports Trade Association), as well as a state-of-the-activity report by Miller (chapter 15) on the emergence of daily fantasy sports games. This section concludes with a capstone discussion by the volume's editors—Bowman, Sanderson, Spinda, and assistant Anderson (chapter 16)—that summarizes and synthesizes key arguments from the volume and gives a call for action to scholars and practitioners of fantasy sports.

Finally, as this book was a team effort between three editors and one editorial assistant, each with their own uses and motivations for the project, we have asked all four of these individuals to give a brief discussion of their vision for the volume.

So, I have to admit up front: I don't play many fantasy sports anymore, because I don't play them very well. It's not for a lack of interest or a lack of leagues or opportunities—indeed, it seems that my entire college fraternity regularly extends to me invitations to (re) join our Yahoo! Sports fantasy baseball and football leagues. For my NFL league, I believe my highest finish was seventh place (out of twelve teams), the season my 2007 London SillyNannies were led by quarterbacks Marc Bulger and Jeff Garcia, and Chicago Bears all-purpose offensive weapon Devin Hester paced my team to a 7–6 head-to-head record. I fared slightly better in fantasy baseball (after all, I'm a native St. Louisan and one of the "Greatest Fans in Baseball"), with my 2010 Hayesville Hicks earning me a third place finish (out of a league of twenty) behind the offense of Vladimir Guerrero and Hanley Ramirez and a 31-homer season from then-Milwaukee Brewer Corey Hart—the pitching of Bronson Arroyo (17 wins, 121 strikeouts) and Ubaldo Jimenez (19 wins, 214 strikeouts) along with Brandon Lyon (20 saves) certainly didn't hurt my cause. Why don't I play much anymore? Simply put, I'm a terrible general manager. I get sentimental about my favorite players and my favorite teams (I'm the guy who will draft his hometown heroes—in my case, St. Louis Rams and Cardinals players)—even when fantasy powerhouses are still available in the pool, and despite my rather deep knowledge of my favorite sports (I was a sports reporter in my former career, and I've constantly been around sports either as a spectator, sometimes participant and even college cheerleader), I don't have the ability to make the tough rational managerial decisions when called on.

In fact, this foolish(?) sentimentality is what first lead me to studying fantasy sports. During my time in Michigan (I did my Ph.D. at Michigan State University), my Cardinals were on a collision course with the Detroit Tigers for the 2006 World Series, and I found myself in a bit of a quandary: Do I want the Tigers playing my team? For that matter, did I want any other National League Central players on my club, given that their successful performances might hurt the Cardinals' (already weak, as an eventual wild-card contender) post-season chances? Right around this time, I noticed another anomaly in a league that I was playing in, as well as other leagues—at least from the stories friends were sharing with me—in that fantasy players seemed to be avoiding players such as then San Francisco Giants slugger Barry Bonds not as a feature of the player's performance (Bonds was in the midst of setting a new MLB record for season and career home run totals, albeit aided by performance-enhancing drugs), but rather out of spite. These observations led me to team up with colleagues Dr. Jessi McCabe (now with the Detroit Tigers front office) and Dr. Tom Isaacson (a professor at Marquette University in Wisconsin) to try to get a better understanding of the decisions fantasy sports players make when playing, and to see the role that dispositions toward favorite and rival players and teams might have in their fantasy sports play. Although the initial study (references in several chapters of this volume) was based on a small sample of players of fantasy baseball, we followed them around for several weeks and discovered that their reactions were very similar to mine: fantasy players' dispositions toward professional athletes played a biasing factor in whether or not they would select those players on their own teams! (Ed. note: it turns out that Dr. Brendan Dwyer and his colleagues had similar results related to this cognitive dissonance, and their research is outlined in chapter 10 of this volume). I suspect that the players we followed are not necessarily the most skilled or invested players of the forty-five million estimated to be playing in the United States today, but we might suggest that they are representative of the casual player: a sports fan looking for opportunities to get closer to her or his favorite sports.

For me, fantasy sports were a way to enhance and espouse my own fandom—which is why I couldn't (and still can't) break the habit of selecting my heroes despite their actual statistical fantasy value. Of course, no fantasy sports league would be complete without trash-talking among friends and loved ones (some of our authors cover this in chapter 5 of this volume), and there is a great deal of debate that goes down every time my name is on the draft board. Yet, the fun for me is less in the strategic choosing of the best athletes, and more in preparing for the ensuing barrage of questions that will eventually be hurled my way, pleading with me to justify my seemingly irrational draft picks. I wouldn't trade these interactions in for the world, even if it means not trading up for a hot shortstop or placekicker.

In this vein, my vision for this volume was to unpack the ways in which fans interact with and around fantasy sports, while getting a better appreciation for the complexity of fantasy sports—in particular, the industry and legal aspects of fantasy sports that we players often take for granted. By reaching out beyond my native communication and psychology colleagues, the following volume presents what I believe to be one of the most comprehensive collections of essays and original research studies on fantasy sports covering aspects of sports communication and psychology as well as cultural studies, economics, history, journalism, leadership studies, law, management, and recreation studies. Perhaps the one milestone that I am most proud of with this collective volume is the diversity of scholarship represented—such a diversity truly represents the multifaced nature of fantasy sports as a cultural and economic force in the contemporary professional sports scene.

Fantasy sports represent an incredible opportunity for fans to immerse themselves into the very sports that they love. Going back over my Yahoo! Sports rosters (Yahoo! players can log into their accounts and view any of their rosters; mine go back as far as the 2001 MLB and NFL seasons), I am less reminiscent over my (albeit mediocre) final rankings, but I have fond memories of the players on my rosters (Hines Ward and Priest Holmes in the NFL league, Tom Glavine, Chris Carpenter, and Brian Jordan in the MLB league) as well as the archived chats between players—and even the fantasy player names themselves. Fantasy sports play represents a chance to get a better understanding and appreciation of my favorite players, while serving as a fertile socialization space for friends whom I've lost contact with. In fact, after working on this volume, I think that I'll have to get the "Mountain Ears" up and running again in 2016: I've got a lot of friends to catch up with, and my "only pick Cardinals" strategy just might pay off now (as for my "only pick Rams" strategy, I am less hopeful here).

—Nicholas David Bowman
Associate Professor, Communication Studies
West Virginia University

Somewhat analogous to Nick's fandom for the St. Louis Cardinals, growing up in Pittsburgh (and being the first of my bloodline to not work in a steel mill or steel mill-related industry), I have been a lifelong Steelers fan. Additionally, I've always had a love for statistics within sports, so fantasy sports were a given once they became an online phenomena (that isn't to say I wouldn't have played offline if I was aware of it!). To my best recollection, I have played fantasy football for about a dozen years (primarily in one league with non-extended family and their friends), but I am not currently active in a "steady" fantasy football league. Despite all of the discussion about the Steelers above, my favorite sport is Penguins hockey, and has been since December 26, 1986, when I watched Mario Lemieux play live for the first time (I was four rows up just inside the blue line—I can remember this moment, and lots more from this game when I was eight years old, but cannot tell you something from yesterday . . .). I am still active in fantasy hockey and have been for about nine to ten years in one "keeper" league (where certain roster players can be "protected" from year to year and remain on a team). Although I have a deep fandom for the Penguins, I have held on to star winger Alexander Ovechkin for quite some time, despite him playing for a rival of my favorite team (the Washington Capitals). In fact, my long-time team name is "The Crosby Show," a play on words from the 80's sitcom, to honor the Penguins captain and star center Sidney Crosby. This irony is never lost on my opponents, who often refer to me as the "Crosby-less Show," as he has been "kept" on another team and not my team since the league began. Perhaps this incongruent relationship was a big part of my inspiration to co-author a chapter in this volume with Cody Havard about rival players and fantasy sports (chapter 4 of this volume).

Also, when I think about this project, it brings up some more memories, both from the academic realm and from my perspective as a fantasy sports participant. My first published work came in 2008 on the motivations of fantasy football players. Naturally, it was memorable for that reason, but it also had some bizarre elements that I've never been able to duplicate since. First, when collecting data, I was sending requests for websites to link to my online survey. It was about this time that I also discovered (the now much more popular) *Deadspin.com.* I went to bed August 14, 2007, with some low number of survey responses, and woke up the next day with a LOT more. I then saw that *Deadspin* (former editor Will Leitch) actually posted my survey link with the following entry: *"Some kid is doing a study on fantasy football for a grad paper. We encourage academia and all the gravity bongs that come with it, so help a tweed jacketer out."*

Going back and reading the comments make me laugh to this day. I will share just a few here (of the ones fit for this context):

- "Graduate paper in Communications Studies? Practice saying 'Double no-fat triple whip latte'"
- "Why did I choose engineering, when I could have studied fantasy football?"

- "This is a way better topic than MY grad paper on Mariah Carey's hit single 'Fantasy'"

As you can see, this wasn't a typical data collection experience! I was also informed years later that this rash of participants to the study also pushed over the limit of responses the departmental account had for the online survey tool they had at that time (to some expense). The year before, while obtaining narratives for why people play fantasy football, I rescued a brother and sister pair of cats on my way to go collect data with the co-author of that chapter, and my dissertation advisor, Paul Haridakis. It was a hot summer day and I couldn't stomach those little cats being in the heat. As it turns out, every shelter in Northeast Ohio I visited had no place for them. So they came with me, to collect data. They are still with me and always make me think of fantasy football, especially at times like this!

While this was all memorable in nature, the desire to do such a study (and this project as well) came from my curiosity about fantasy sports and its interesting array of effects, some more of which I can glean from my experiences. While the date wasn't as clear to me as my first NHL hockey game and had to be looked up, I remember back to (another) December 26, but this time it was in 2005. I was sitting with my cousin and his brother-in-law at a family gathering watching the New England Patriots and New York Jets on *Monday Night Football*. What some fantasy gamers refer to as "sweat time" was in high effect, as the brother-in-law and myself were facing off for the fantasy football league title. While this date was fuzzy, one thing that was less unclear was my recollection of Tom Brady connecting with Deion Branch (a wide receiver on my fantasy team and only active fantasy player remaining in the game). The pass officially went for twenty-two yards, from the New York Jets twenty-nine yard line to the seven yard line. However, Branch was *this close* to not being pushed out of bounds and would have walked in for a touchdown in a game between one team I am indifferent toward (Jets) and another I despised greatly (Patriots) that was already a two-touchdown lead for New England. So why did it matter so much? Why did I care? Because it was the difference between winning and losing the Smashmouth Football League Championship, that's why! My extended family teammate knew it was my last shot after the Patriots kicked a field goal a few plays later. They were up seventeen points and were likely done passing (and they were). He knew he had it in the bag and I had to hear about it with some good natured ribbing. This same football league also produced an interesting effect about six years later at my cousin's wedding. In this instance, I was able to quickly get along with all of his groomsmen, more so than other people I have met face-to-face for the first time. I can say without a doubt that this was due to being in the same fantasy football league. We had a built in "icebreaker" that is discussed in chapters 5 and 8 of this volume, developed from discussion board posts and live online drafts.

Lastly, I look back at my time in fantasy sports and see the role that the game has on the goodness of strangers that are barely known (and often not known face-to-face). In my fantasy hockey league that I noted above, I got started through an acquaintance I met at a restaurant job I had during summers/weekends in graduate school. He remains the only person I've ever met face-to-face in that league. However, about four years ago, when I was faced with a personal tragedy, the league commissioner offered to make me an extra championship trophy, which is a hockey puck with writing on it that sits on a modest display. While I was honored by the display, I politely declined (this situation reminds me of a similar narrative discussed in my chapter 2 of this volume). I wanted to win it the old-fashioned way. Unfortunately, I still haven't done it . . . but this year is MY year, I just know it . . .

—John S. W. Spinda
Assistant Professor, Department of Communication
Clemson University

I might be somewhat of an anomaly with this project as I am safely "retired" as a fantasy sports player. Indeed, my fantasy sports career might best be summed up by a term that characterizes much of the 1980s music that I cherish "one hit wonder." My first fantasy sports experience was 2005 during the NBA season. I played in a league with my brothers and several of our childhood friends and our participation was not so much about strategy as it was taking shots at one another, which while initially fun, quickly became unfulfilling. In 2009, I started playing fantasy football after one of my co-workers invited me to join this league. I came in a respectable third place that year and in 2010, found myself in the championship game in large part to just happening to check the waiver wire in Week 2 to find that one of the other competitors had dropped Drew Brees after two weeks of subpar performance. This happenstance was just one of several "breaks" that came my way that year.

I continued to play fantasy football each year and in 2013, found myself participating in three leagues. I think I felt social pressure to participate in these leagues, but finding myself on the tenure track with a wife and two kids at home, I quickly realized fantasy football (and fantasy sports at large) was just not going to be in my future. That being said, I was and still am greatly intrigued by fantasy sports and the hold it has on people. Thus, when the four of us were discussing an edited volume, when fantasy sports came up, I was a very enthusiastic advocate, and I am honored to have had a small part in this volume coming together.

I believe we have put together a very comprehensive collection of readings that will be a valuable resource for those who both have an interest in studying and playing fantasy sports. This volume brings together a collection of scholars whose interests and perspectives include (among others) economics, law, computer-mediated communication, social media, and psychology. While this volume has data-driven pieces, these are balanced out by theoretical essays that provide a diverse foundation on which fantasy sport scholarship can build.

I never cease to be amazed at the hold fantasy sport has on people. This year, as I've followed social issues in sport such as the Ray Rice and Adrian Peterson case, I was fascinated to see a good number of audience comments I read *not* talking about the moral aspects of these cases, but rather, the impact they would have on fantasy sports. This topic is addressed in this volume, along with compelling legal issues surrounding fantasy sports, such as sport leagues entering into agreements with fantasy sport operators, and I highly recommend checking out the website sportsjudge.com, that such a website possess a market in and of itself is fascinating.

Fantasy sports, then, really is just a moniker, for many participants, the only thing "fantasy" about fantasy sports is the name. For these individuals, the opportunity to "manage" a team is a very real task that carries with it significant implications for their personal identity, social relationships, and when aggregated with other fantasy participants, the fantasy sport industry. In that vein, I sincerely hope this volume helps spur research on fantasy sport that encompasses a variety of perspectives and add to a literature that has a very exciting future.

—Jimmy Sanderson
Director of Marketing, Communications, and Faculty Relations for Clemson Online
Clemson University

Sport to me has been fascinating ever since my youth. I could remember going to my hometown college's football games on Saturday afternoons and watch my uncle and his friends argue over who was the best player on each team. My uncle would further his arguments by saying if one team had the other's quarterback, they would be much better than they are. Of course, this was his excuse for every team that he liked.

Who knew that a few years later, the fantasy of swapping teams' top talents in order to gain a competitive advantage would become a reality; further propelling the popularity of major sports in our society. Thus, fantasy sports has grown from a local hobby that started over five decades ago to one of the most popular forms of entertainment today. This book explores the beginnings of fantasy sport, its growth, where it is currently, and where it is headed.

With my research, I have always been curious as to determine how sport can impact the way we view society. Given the fact that fantasy sport went from around 500,000 participants in 1988 to nearly 57 million participants in the U.S. and Canada as of 2015, I would say that it has a major in influence on how individuals view and participate in the enjoyment of sport.

—Shaun M. Anderson
Doctoral candidate, Department of Communication Studies
West Virginia University

As is discussed in chapter 16, fantasy sports have grown from being "one-off" paper-and-pencil contests in the basements of a few extreme sports and statistics aficionados to an activity embraced by a culturally, economically, and socially relevant market force. Fantasy sports have provided an activity that can both create and reinforce fan avidity, that encourages mediated social interactions, and that has global appeal among fans, sports, and media institutions alike. Of course, the book also discusses several barriers to fantasy sports growth, including the Western focus of most fantasy sports contests (focusing on sports popular in the United States, but with limited appeal elsewhere), and continued legal debates over the gambling and gaming status of many fantasy sports contests. While the costs and benefits of fantasy sports play are weighted—both in this volume and in practice (including the basements and bar stools used by fantasy sport players around the world), there is one unavoidable truth: Fantasy sports have emerged as a legitimate facet of larger sports culture. It is to this end that our volume attempts to highlight historical and emergent features of fantasy sports that might help all of us gain a better understanding of the games, as fantasy sports are anything but a fantasy.

# I

# ROOTS OF FANTASY SPORTS

# ❶

# THE ORIGIN OF FANTASY SPORTS

*Shaun M. Anderson and Nicholas David Bowman*

**W**hen asked what was the most important reason for becoming a professional sports team owner, Wall Street investor and current Tampa Bay Rays
principal owner, Stuart Sternberg, gave three reasons: "to win, to make
money, or to bask in the glow of being an owner" (Sullivan, 2012). Not to
be taken lightly, Sternberg's position as a professional sports team owner
can be considered one of the most challenging management positions in
the athletic and entertainment industry. Of course, the reality of being a
general manager of a sports team owner is quite different—and much less
glamorous—than that of the owner. For example, the 2014 movie *Draft
Day* gave an overview of the difficulties most team owners and managers
go through on a daily basis (Hamilton, 2014). The movie, starring Kevin
Costner as the general manager of the Cleveland Browns, takes place on
the morning of a fictitious 2014 National Football League (NFL) draft.
During this time, his character has to decide what to do when his team
acquires the number one draft pick: a scenario that is both exhilarating and
exhausting for any sports franchise. In addition to this, Costner's character
deals with issues such as salary cap disputes, disagreements with ownership,
the off-field behavior of the potential number one draft pick, and various
other football and non-football related issues. In short, the film shows some
of the sausage-making that goes into the NFL draft and, by extension, the
tribulations of the general manager's role in the process.

Given this, it might be difficult to imagine that many sport fans dream of becoming a professional sports team manager or owner, as these individuals often receive few accolades for a team's success and much of the vitriol for a team's failure. However, the growth of fantasy sports has provided a venue for the eager sports fans to become either and both of these positions—in fact, current (as of the 2015 writing of this chapter) Los Angeles Rams general manager Les Snead talks proudly of his fantasy sports hobby from his middle school days in an interview with the Associated Press:

> I'd get the bubblegum cards and I'd try to have my own draft, pick a team and figure out ways to do fantasy football before they had it. . . . So maybe I should have copyrighted the idea (Snead, as cited by Associated Press, 2012).

Although it is a consistently growing entity, fantasy sports players may share in the difficulties of ownership much like their live sporting event counterparts. Nonetheless, these games have increased in popularity since its inception and has increased in revenue generation. Therefore, this chapter will focus on the creation of fantasy sport, the motivations behind playing the sport, and the many facets of the sport.

## FUNDAMENTALS OF FANTASY SPORTS

For the purposes of this book, fantasy sports can be defined as "a sports-based Internet game in which collocated participants virtually manage teams of professional athletes in competition with each other" (Bowman, McCabe, & Isaacson, 2012; p. 257). Fantasy sport involves the selection and maintenance of fictional, or fantasy, teams made up of a selection of players from a particular sport league (Shipman, 2001). Carlson (2013) adds that fantasy sport play is an extracurricular activity in which sports fans serve as owner, manager, and/or coach of various players in a particular sport. Competitions are generally (but not historically) administered through an online or Internet medium and offer an additional level of interaction between sport and fans. Fantasy sport leagues allow participants to select teams of players drawn from all professional rosters and to have their fictional teams compete against other fictional teams. Typically either individual players or entire teams are drafted onto fantasy teams, making the initial draft a very important activity in the life of a league. Team performance is assessed by scoring the performance of players comprising each team based on actual match statistics. Fantasy sport, therefore, works best in sport domains where statistics are rigorously collected, easily understood, and widely available.

Fantasy sport represents a large industry, with its popularity evolving from that of an isolated, cult activity toward mass public appeal (Holleman, 2006). In the United States, annual growth as high as 7–10 percent (Klaassen, 2006) has resulted in an estimated forty-two million fantasy sport players, with competitions in this market generating economic activity between $4 and $5 billion annually (FSTA, 2014). The "stability and visibility of fantasy sport as a marketing platform is no longer questionable" (Roy & Goss, 2007, p. 105), While this is a positive step forward for fantasy sport, the game itself had much more humble beginnings.

## EARLY FANTASY SPORTS GAMES

While made popular by social networking and other digital technologies, fantasy sports predate the modern communication technology ecology—the earliest games were played similar to board games, using playing cards to emulate live games; others were nothing more than a long string of statistics hand-written from printed box scores. Fantasy sport can be traced back to 1962 (Esser, 1994). Fantasy football was developed by Bill Winkenbach, a businessman and limited partner with the Oakland Raiders, along with two writers of the *Oakland Tribune*, Scotty Stirling and George Ross. The initial development occurred during an East Coast road trip with the Raiders in New York of the Greater Oakland Professional Pigskin Prognosticators League (GOPPL). Notably, most other early football contests and leagues were also called GOPPPL until fantasy football became the accepted term.

After this, fantasy sports began transitioning into other sports such as fantasy baseball (Colston, 1996), which started in the basement of Harvard sociologist William Gamson in 1960, a game called the National Baseball Seminar that began nearly two years before GOPPPL's birth on the West Coast. Gamson's game was continued by one of his students Daniel Okrent, who coined the term rotisserie baseball from the name of a restaurant in Manhattan (La Rotisserie Francaise) where the idea for rotisserie baseball was first developed by Okrent, Glen Waggoner, and their colleagues in 1980. The charter members of Rotisserie League Baseball were in the publishing industry, which initially helped expose fantasy baseball to the rest of the world. Moreover, because Okrent was a member of the media, other journalists, especially sports journalists, were introduced to the game. Many early players were introduced to the game by these sports journalists, especially during the 1981 Major League Baseball strike as with little else to write about, many baseball writers wrote columns about Rotisserie league. A July 8, 1980, *New York Times* article titled "What George Steinbrenner Is to the American League, Lee Eisenberg is to the Rotisseries League" set off a media storm that led to stories about the league on CBS TV and other publications (Walker, 2006). Chapter 9 of this volume discusses the relationship between fantasy sports and traditional media in greater detail.

## FANTASY SPORTS 2.0: BROADER AND BIGGER

Fantasy sports have grown tremendously since the development of Rotisserie League Baseball (Lomax, 2006). Nearly thirty-two million people aged twelve and above are actively playing fantasy sports in the USA and Canada (Fantasy Sports Trade Association [FSTA], 2011). In Europe, the official Fantasy English Premier League game alone has more than two million players, and the site has grown year to year by 40 percent since its inception in 2002 (Montague, 2010). Fantasy Premier League has been estimated to be worth approximately $3 billion. Average fantasy players spend an average of $111 per year playing and three hours a week managing their teams (FSTA, 2014). According to FSTA (2014), fantasy sports have an over $3 billion annual impact for the fantasy sports industry in the form of publications, league fees, commissioner services, transaction fees, and the purchase of fantasy sport web content. This speaks to the popularity of fantasy sport, which has grown from 500,000 players in 1988 to over forty-one million currently (FSTA, 2014). From a sport consumer behavior perspective, fantasy sport provides a mixed experience of participatory sport and spectator sport. Given this, fantasy sport is quite different from more traditional sport consumption experiences.

Technological innovation, namely the Internet, has led to the rapid growth of fantasy sport. Instead of relying on word of mouth, the Internet enabled one to advertise electronically and find league participants around the globe. Most leagues have their own Web sites, and many Web sites include various amounts of information for online visitors (e.g., team information; player information such as ratings, contracts, and statistics; league standings; league statistics; transactions between teams; newsletters; and e-zines). To help manage all of this new growth, the Fantasy Sports Trade Association (FSTA) was established in 1999 to represent the interests of fantasy sports participants. The FSTA hosts a Web site (http://www.fsta.org) including articles, a message board, history and mission statements, committees, awards, a hall of fame, frequently asked questions, and advocacy news. In addition, the FSTA hosts two annual national conferences; chapter 14 has further information about the development of the FSTA.

Even as daily newspaper circulation and readership continues to decline (Barthel, 2015), many traditional media outlets, including newspapers and broadcast television as well as cable programming, are devoting substantial (and precious) space in their programming devoted to fantasy sports coverage (discussed further in chapter 9, this volume). The activity has grown to the point that even major sports leagues, such as the National Football League (NFL) now have entire operations completely devoted to fantasy sports (http://www.nfl.com/fantasyfootball)—surprising, given the historic animosity between professional sports leagues and fantasy sports competitions (cf. Schrotenboer, 2015). The activity has grown to the point that even independent fantasy sports operations—from large operations such as FanDuel to any number of private competitions between friends have grown online.

## DIFFERENT TYPES OF FANTASY SPORTS PLAY

As the activity grows, new types of fantasy sports games and leagues have evolved along with it. Fantasy sports competitions today are largely digitized and automated, cutting down significantly on the amount of work necessary on behalf of eager fantasy sports players to compile roster and statistics information by hand, and to track such changes on a constant basis. Accordingly, one of the more widely used formats of fantasy are Internet-based leagues. Internet leagues can be free, although some of them charge a nominal fee to join a league depending on the features available. Some leagues even offer prizes; from trophies to shirts to cash Internet-based leagues can handle unlimited numbers of participants. As a result, Internet participants generally are not involved in developing the rules or in running the league. The major Internet leagues have extensive Web sites including free content (e.g., player rankings, statistics, tips on strategy) and commissioner services (e.g., drafting tools, league software, statistic generation).

Most Internet games are really just emulations of the classic type of fantasy sports games: pool leagues whose results are based on current actual play. Players are drafted from a pool—usually the complete set of active athletes from a given professional sports league in a given live season—by general managers to each team. Teams compete against one another based on the statistics actually generated by the players during a week or so of real play (depending on how often the sport plays its contest, for example NFL games are weekly while Major League Baseball [MLB] games are almost daily). For example, in baseball the typical statistical categories include batting average, home runs, runs batted in, stolen bases, earned run average, wins, saves, and a composite ratio (usually some combination of other statistics, often varying from league to league).

Some leagues retain their teams and rosters for only a single season. Thus, each season involves new teams, new players, and new participants. Other leagues retain their teams and rosters over many seasons, and are known as keeper leagues. A keeper league can create a community of participants who are in constant communication via e-mail, discussion lists, and/or instant messaging, perhaps offering a more accurate simulation of managing a sports team through several seasons. However, these types of fantasy sports contests can still require a rather intensive time commitment on behalf of the player—FSTA (2014) suggest that the average player spends nearly nine hours per week with fantasy sports—and in response, many companies have begun offering daily fantasy sports leagues; chapter 15 details these daily games. Other fantasy-type contests, such as sports simulations in which players recreate or stage their own contests using attributes of real players and teams, are discussed in chapter 2.

Professional sports leagues once wary of fantasy sports now seem to embrace them, such as the NFL (mentioned earlier) and MLB (http://mlb .mlb.com/mlb/fantasy)—both sites prominently featuring news related to individual performance, trades, and injury news. Outside of the US, the Australian Football League (AFL) promotes one of the country's major national fantasy sport competitions. Early fears that fantasy sports would encourage fans to cheer for players over teams (thus diluting established team brands in team-based leagues such as the NFL and MLB) and would encourage insidious gambling effects seem to have been assuaged, given fantasy sports' potential to draw new fans and foster deeper fandom from existing ones (cf. Bowman et al., 2012).

## THE FANTASY SPORTS PLAYER ROSTER: WHO PLAYS, AND WHY?

Although the popularity of fantasy sport has been reiterated, it is time to focus on who plays the game. In this section, we will describe who plays fantasy sports and why they invest their time into playing. As fantasy sports continue to grow, it is imperative that we know who is involved so that we could possibly understand where it is going (which will be discussed in detail in the final chapter).

## Fantasy Sports Player Demographics

As of 2014, the FSTA reports a demographic profile of fantasy sports players that is rather singular. From their report, fantasy sports players tend to be male (80%), Caucasian (90%), single (52%), older (34 years), and educated (78 percent with a college degree), and report having played the games for nearly ten years on average. Beyond the FSTA data however, there is little knowledge about the nature or attraction of fantasy sport participation. Although some researchers forward that fantasy sports is gaining interest among individuals from diverse backgrounds (Lee, Kwak, Ryan, & Lin, 2007; Weekly, 2004), such claims seem to counter the actual player statistics provided by FSTA. It would be ideal for the phenomenon to be investigated into more detail. Pritchard & Funk (2006) suggested that while fantasy sport is assisting to develop and usher in the new age of the media-dominant sport consumer, researchers have yet to forward information regarding these important demographics. Additionally, the examination of gender roles has been explored, showing fantasy sport confirmed and reinforced hegemonic ideologies in sport spectatorship, knowledge, competition, and male bonding (Davis & Duncan, 2006). Work by Lavelle (see chapter 7, this volume) similarly argues that the role of females in fantasy sport seems to be treated more as a novelty niche than a legitimate consumer market.

## Motivations for Fantasy Sports Play

Studies within the sport marketing research have focused primarily on influences and motivations for choosing to participate in fantasy sport. Sport leagues have a vested interest in understanding the motives for fantasy sports because fantasy sport participation is related to more traditional sport consumption behaviors. For example, when compared with other fans, fantasy sport participants attend and watch more games, visit leagues' websites more often, and purchase more merchandise (FSTA, 2006). In this regard, identifying the motives of fantasy sport consumers would provide the sport leagues with a basis for developing an integrated marketing strategy that can leverage both traditional sport fanship and fantasy sport participation. At the micro level, the sport leagues can utilize the motives for fantasy sports to develop tailored marketing communication strategies for specific market segments.

Thus, motives for sport participation and sport spectatorship may provide useful starting points for exploring motivation to participate in fantasy sport. In addition, as both fantasy sport consumers and sport video gamers share a "fantasy" characteristic by doing something impossible in a real life, motives for sport video gaming may provide a basis for understanding of fantasy sport motivation (cf. Kim & Ross, 2006). Furthermore, since fantasy sport is mainly played online and its participants enjoy the sense of gambling, it may also be useful to investigate motives for sport online consumption and gambling (Davis & Duncan, 2006).

Roy and Goss (2007), for example, presented a conceptual framework which outlined the psychological, social, and marketer-controlled influences which were proposed to impact the consumption decision of whether to play fantasy sport or not. Similarly, other research has looked at the conceptualization of various motivations for fantasy sport play (Dwyer et al., 2008; Lee, Seo, & Green, 2008). Expanding on this work, Farquhar and Meeds (2007) used Q-methodology, and uses and gratifications within sport fan motivation scales, to develop a typology of five groups of fantasy sport players based on their motivations. Of these five groups, casual players, skilled players, and isolationist thrill-seekers emerged as the most common types, while trash-talkers and formatives were less common. Arousal and surveillance were found to be the two main motivations behind the types of different users, while entertainment, escape, and social interaction motivations were judged to be less important. Notably, Farquhar and Meeds (2007) did not expect social interaction to fantasy sports users in this study to be of minimal importance. Moreover, it implies that not all online communities build or maintain relationships. Overall, this area of work has increased knowledge of the motivations for playing fantasy sport, or the inputs of fantasy sport participation.

## FANTASY SPORTS AND THE SPORTS INDUSTRY

As far as fantasy sports from an economic standpoint is concerned, Nesbit and King (2010b) conclude that "anecdotal evidence and conclusions of numerous non-academic studies present a fairly convincing argument that fantasy sport has positively influenced the sport industry" (p. 11). The bulk of previous research has focused outside the consumer behavior or marketing consumption domain which is the subject of this research. Instead, the focus has been on the legal, sociological, and economic issues surrounding fantasy sport. For example, studies have focused on fantasy sport as a form of gambling (Bernhard & Eade, 2005, also discussed in chapter 3, this volume), including debate on the legal aspect of whether pay-to-play fantasy sport represents a form of illegal gambling (Holleman, 2006, also see chapter 13, this volume). Studies of fantasy sport players have been undertaken into the role of fantasy sport in bonding and social construction within groups of sport fans (Levy, 2005, also see chapter 5, this volume), which has implications for how sports teams and leagues might approach the activities as avenues to enhance fan avidity toward their brands (DeSarbo, 2009).

Regarding sports media, the executive vice president for ESPN's integrated media research arm explained that fantasy sports are among the heaviest users of media across platforms and a critical group for understanding media usage among consumers of information through television, radio, print, the Internet, and mobile devices (Enoch, 2010). Accordingly, many professional sport organizations now consider fantasy sport participants an attractive market segment, such as the aforementioned AFL, MLB, and NFL, to name a few. Compared to the general fan, fantasy sports players attend more games and watch more televised sport (FSTA, 2006). Moreover, for media companies (e.g., Yahoo!, ESPN), fantasy sport is a key financial resource, since they can sell fantasy sport participants premium fantasy packages. By offering free leagues, they draw more traffic and more advertising revenue to their websites; professional sports leagues also report similar secondary revenue streams from fantasy sports leagues they sponsor (cf. AFL, 2010). However, despite the popularity and economic impact of fantasy sports, few studies have been conducted to understand what motivates people to play and to continue to play fantasy sports. Nearly all of the literature on fantasy sports deals with either news, information, or basic survey research (Lomax, 2006, p. 388). Fantasy sport participants share some characteristics of traditional sport fans in that both groups follow televised sport contests (Smith, Synowka, & Smith, 2010). However, fantasy sport participants' viewing extends to players across an array of teams, rather than focusing on a single team, and they are actively engaged in choosing and managing the players on their team (Smith et al., 2010). It is possible that this level of active engagement may be more like active sport participation than passive spectation (Shipman, 2001).

## CONSUMER BEHAVIOR AND FANTASY SPORT

From a consumer behavior perspective, fantasy sport provides a mixed experience of participatory and spectator sport uniquely different from traditional sport consumption experiences (Lee et al., 2008; Lomax, 2006). As alluded to earlier in this chapter, fantasy sport allows the highly engaged sports fan an opportunity to compete and apply knowledge, while also building the interest and knowledge of participants with lower prior involvement in a sport. Further, fantasy sport provides additional social interaction between players. It can serve as an educational tool about the sport, teams, and players and can also serve to increase the commitment and interaction of consumers with a sport.

While these studies provide a foundation for the concept of fantasy sport and motivations for why people choose to play, there has been a small amount of research into how the virtual consumption of fantasy sport impacts upon real consumption of sport. For example, Nesbit and King, (2010a) and Nesbit and King (2010b) research which used survey data and regression modeling to show fantasy sport participation was positively related to television viewership and attendance at the subject sports events. Further, qualitative research by Drayer, Morse, Shapiro, Dwyer, and White (2007) and Drayer et al. (2010) used an attitude-behaviour framework (Fazio, Powell, & Herr, 1983) to investigate how fantasy sport participation changed attitudes toward the sport, the league, and its players which, in turn, was shown to impact on how and to what degree the traditional sport was consumed. Their findings suggest that playing fantasy sport led to a higher allegiance to players, increases in the use and forms of media consumption, consumers checking statistics online without watching games, and increases in consumers' overall league knowledge.

Given its popularity, a key question for sport administrators is the degree to which they should encourage consumers to participate in fantasy sport. On the one hand, it may be a valuable tool to increase education and involvement levels, thereby complementing the traditional consumption behavior related to the sport (e.g., game attendance and TV viewership). On the other hand, the activity may compete for consumers' time and playing fantasy sport may reduce other forms of sport consumption. Despite little empirical investigation, fantasy sport has widely been posited as a complementary activity (Nesbit & King, 2010b), which can increase consumer interest in a sport and broaden points of engagement. For example, fantasy sport could lead to more immersed and engaged consumers (Shipman, 2001) and is presented as an attractive marketing opportunity for sport leagues to attract fans from other sports, or to develop and retain current fan bases (Drayer, Morse, Shapiro, Dwyer, & White, 2010; Lee, Seo, & Green, 2008).

However, the rise of fantasy sport as a leisure product in its own right poses a potential problem. Consumers' time and resources are limited, so the possibility that fantasy sport participation could actually compete with other forms of sport consumption such as live game attendance or TV viewership, which is as yet unexamined, has the potential to impact negatively on important broadcast and match day revenue streams for sport organizations. Therefore, while fantasy sport may be a valuable tool to increase education and involvement levels, it may also drain consumers' time and resources to such an extent that it reduces other forms of sport consumption.

## MOVING FORWARD WITH FANTASY SPORTS

The widespread and rapid uptake of fantasy sport by both professional leagues and consumers has outpaced research in many regards. These questions are fundamental for sport managers, who rely upon traditional attendance and mass media rights and revenue to support their leagues, but need to adapt practice to incorporate the popular new digital forms of consumption. Fantasy sport is a prominent example of the new digital products. Its popularity dictates that sport managers engage with it, but how fantasy sport is best managed, commercially leveraged, and integrated with traditional sport consumption is poorly understood.

Although fantasy sports are a social phenomenon associated primarily with the United States, their potential for global growth and influence also has been noted (Boyle, 2005; Futterman, 2008; Hutchins, Rowe, & Ruddock, 2009; Thomas & Martin, 2010; also see chapter 2, this volume). While the 2009 Super Bowl drew 114.4 million viewers (Statistic, n.d.), soccer's 2014 World Cup championship match between Argentina and Germany attracted a cumulative television audience exceeding one billion viewers (Dassanayake, 2014). Despite the inability of fantasy providers to develop products to reach that particular audience, it is one that research shows is still a coveted one, as it will be discussed later in this book.

## CONCLUSION

As we navigated the terrain of fantasy sport, we have addressed how fantasy sport has grown from a watercooler hobby to a sophisticated and lucrative business for both players and sport managers. Throughout the rest of this volume, fantasy sport will be dissected even further to discuss the different intricacies of this gaming phenomenon. Such topics include the legal aspects of fantasy sport and the economics of fantasy sports. Additionally, the many perspectives of fantasy sport discussed in this volume will detail how this game has transcended the notion of being a sidekick to traditional sports, whether we like it or not. Moreover, fantasy sport has become a stand-alone entity; one in which players and non-players alike should not take for granted.

## REFERENCES

Andreff, W., & Staudohar, P. (2000). The evolving European model of professional sports finance. *Journal of Sports Economics, 1,* 257–276. doi:10.1177/152700250000100304

Associated Press. (2012, February 14). Rams hire Les Snead as general manager. Retrieved from http://usatoday30.usatoday.com/sports/football/nfl/rams/story/2012-02-14/les-snead-gm/53091692/1

Australian Football League. (2010). AFL membership. Retrieved from http://www.aflmembership.com.au.

Barthel, M. (2015, April 29). Newspapers: Fact sheet, from State of the News Media 2015. Washington, DC: Pew Research Center.

Bauer, H., Stokburger-Sauer, N. E., & Exler, S. (2008). Brand image and fan loyalty in professional team sport: A refined model and empirical assessment. *Journal of Sport Management, 22,* 205–226. Retrieved from http://fitnessforlife.org/Acu Custom/Sitename/Documents/DocumentItem/15596.pdf

Bernhard, B. J., & Eade, V. H. (2005). Gambling in a fantasy world: An exploratory study of rotisserie baseball games. *UNLV Gaming Research & Review, 9,* 29–43. Retrieved from http://digitalscholarship.unlv.edu/cgi/viewcontent.cgi?article=1165&context=grrj

Bowman, N., McCabe, J., & Isaacson, T. (2012). Fantasy sports and sports fandom: Implications for mass media research. In A. C. Earnhardt, P. M. Haridakis, & B. Hugenberg (Eds.), *Fandemonium: Explorations of Fan Power, Identity and Socialization* (pp. 255–273). Lanham, MD: Lexington.

Carlson, C. (2013). The reality of fantasy sports: A metaphysical and ethical analysis. *Journal of the Philosophy of Sport, 40,* 187–204. doi:10.1080/00948705.2013.785422

Dassanayake, D. (2014, July 13). One billion people set to tune in to watch Germany and Argentina battle for the World Cup. Retrieved from http://www.express.co.uk/news/world/488521/World-Cup-2014-Fans-gear-up-for-Germany-v-Argentina-final

Davis, N. W., & Duncan, M. C. (2006). Sport knowledge is power: Reinforcing masculine privilege through fantasy sport league participation. *Journal of Sport and Social Issues, 30*, 244–264. doi:10.1177/0193723506290324

DeSarbo, W.S. (2009, December 21). Measuring fan avidity can help marketers narrow their focus. *Sports Business Journal*. Retrieved from http://www.sportsbusinessdaily.com/Journal/Issues/2009/12/20091221/From-The-Field-Of/Measuring-Fan-Avidity-Can-Help-Marketers-Narrow-Their-Focus.aspx.

Drayer, J., Morse, A., Shapiro, S., Dywer, B., & White, J. (2007). The effects of fantasy football participation on NFL consumption: A qualitative analysis. *Sport Management Review, 13*, 129–141. doi:10.1016/j.smr.2009.02.01

Drayer, J., Morse, A., Shapiro, S., Dywer, B., & White, J. (2010). The effects of fantasy football participation on NFL consumption: A qualitative analysis. *Sport Management Review, 13*, 129–141. doi:10.1016/j.smr.2009.02.001

Dywer, B., Kim, Y., & Grey, D. (2008). *For love or for money: Exploring and developing a motivational scale for fantasy football participation.* Paper presented at North American Society for Sport Management Conference, Ontario, Canada.

Einolf, K. W. (2001). Turn fantasy into reality: Using fantasy football in an economics of sport course. Teaching economics: Instruction and classroom-based research. Irwin/McGraw-Hill Publishers.

Enoch, G. (2010, April). ESPN'S top 10 list for sports research. Broadcast Education Association Research Symposium, Las Vegas, NV.

ESPN. (2010, February 14). NFL attendances Retrieved from http://www.espn.com/nfl/attendance.

Fantasy Sports Trade Association. (2006). Fantasy Sports Trade Association National Customer Behaviour Survey Retrieved from http://www.fsta.org/.

Fantasy Sport Trade Association (2014). Industry demographics: At a glance. FSTA.org. Retrieved from http://www.fsta.org/?page=Demographics

Fantasy Sports Trade Association. (2010). Retrieved February 14, 2010 from http://www.fsta.org/index.php

Fabrigar, L. R., Wegener, D. T., MacCallum, R. C., & Strahan, E. J. (1999). Evaluating the use of exploratory factor analysis in psychological research. *Psychological Methods, 4*, 272–299. doi:10.1037/1082-989X.4.3.272

Farquhar, L. K., & Meeds, R. (2007). Types of fantasy sports users and their motivations. *Journal of Computer-Mediated Communication, 12*, 4, 1208–1228. doi:10.1111/j.1083-6101.2007.00370.x

Fazio, R. H., Powell, M. C., & Herr, P. M. (1983). Toward a process model of the attitude behavior relation: Accessing one's attitude upon mere observation of the attitude object. *Journal of Personality and Social Psychology, 44*, 723–735. doi:10.1111/j.1083-6101.2007.00370.x

Fink, J. S., Trail, G. T., & Anderson, D. F. (2002). Environmental factors associated with spectator attendance and sport consumption behavior: Gender and team differences. *Sport Marketing Quarterly, 11*, 8–19.

Gantz, W., & Wenner, L. A. (1991). Men, women and sports: Audience experiences and effects. *Journal of Broadcasting and Electronic Media, 35*, 233–243. doi:10.1080/08838159109364120

Gillentine, A., & Schulz, J. (2001). Marketing the fantasy football league: Utilization of simulation to enhance sport marketing concepts. *Journal of Marketing Education, 23*, 178–186. doi:10.1177/0273475301233003

Hamilton, J. (2014). Draft day: Why did the NFL-America's most obsessively image-conscious sports league-allow this catastrophe to happen? Retrieved from http://www.slate.com/articles/arts/culturebox/2014/04/draft_day_movie_kevin_costner_and_roger_goodell_star_in_the_nfl_s_version.html

*Herald Sun.* (2010). *Herald Sun* supercoach Retrieved September 14, 2010 from http://supercoach.heraldsun.com.au/.`

Holleman, M. C. (2006). Fantasy football: Illegal gambling or legal game of skill. *North Carolina Journal of Law & Technology, 8*, 59–80. Retrieved from http://ncjolt.org/fantasy-football-illegal-gambling-or-legal-game-of-skill/

Huberty, C. J., & Morris, J. D. (1989). Multivariate analysis versus multiple univariate analyses. *Psychological Bulletin, 105*, 302–308. doi:10.1037//0033-2909.105.2.302

Hutchins, B., Rowe, D. C., & Ruddock, A. D. (2009). "It's fantasy football made real": networked media sport, the internet, and the Hybrid reality of MyFootballClub. *Sociology of Sport Journal, 26*, 18–31. Retrieved from http://journals.humankinetics.com/ssj-back-issues/ssjvolume26issue1march/itsfantasyfootball-maderealnetworkedmediasporttheinternetandthehybridrealityofmyfootballclub

Karg, A. J., & McDonald, H. (2011). Fantasy sport participation as a complement to traditional sport consumption. *Sport Management Review, 14*, 327–346. doi:10.1016/j.smr.2010.11.004

Klaassen, A. (2006). That's real money—$1.5B—pouring into made-up leagues. *Advertising Age, 77*, 4–6.

Leary, M. R., & Altmaier, E. M. (1980). Type I error in counseling research: A plea for multivariate analyses. *Journal of Counseling Psychology, 27*, 611–615. doi:10.1037/0022-0167.27.6.611

Lee, S., Seo, W. J., & Green, B. C. (2008). Why do people play fantasy sports? Paper presented at North American Society for Sport Management Conference, Ontario, Canada.

Lee, W., Kwak, D. H., Ryan, J., & Lim, C. (2007, June). *Investigating the roles of personality and demographic variables in predicting the consumption of fantasy sport leagues.* Presented at the 2007 North American Society for Sport Management Annual Conference, Ft. Lauderdale, FL.

Levy, D. P. (2005). *Fantasy sports and fanship habitus: An investigation of the active consumption of sport, its effects and social implications through the lives of fantasy sport enthusiasts.* Unpublished doctoral thesis, University of Connecticut.

Lomax, R. G. (2006). Fantasy sports: History, game types, and research. In A. A. Raney & J. Bryant (Eds.), *Handbook of sports and media.* Mahwah, NJ: Lawrence Erlbaum Associates.

Madrigal, R. (1995). Cognitive and affective determinants of fan satisfaction with sporting event attendance. *Journal of Leisure Research, 27*, 205–227. Retrieved from http://js.sagamorepub.com/jlr/article/view/857

Mahony, D., Madrigal, R., & Howard, D. (2000). Using the psychological commitment to team scale to segment sport consumers based on loyalty. *Sport Marketing Quarterly, 9*, 15–25. Retrieved from https://business.uoregon.edu/files/media/madrigal-using-psychological-commitment_1.pdf

McDonald, H. J., & Adam, S. (2003). A comparison of online and postal data collection methods in marketing research. *Marketing Intelligence and Planning, 21*, 85–95. doi:10.1108/02634500310465399

Nesbit, T. M., & King, K. A. (2010b). The impact of fantasy football participation on NFL attendance. *Atlantic Economic Journal, 38*, 95–108. doi:10.1007/s11293-009-9202-x

Pritchard, M. P., & Funk, D. C. (2006). Symbiosis and substitution in spectator sport. *Journal of Sport Management, 20*, 299–321. Retrieved from http://digitalcommons.cwu.edu/cobfac/272

Roy, D. P., & Goss, B. D. (2007). A conceptual framework of influences on fantasy sport consumption. *Marketing Management Journal*, 96–108. doi:10.1016/j.smr.2010.11.004

Schrotenboer, B. (2015, January). Leagues see real benefits in daily fantasy sports. USAToday.com. Retrieved from http://www.usatoday.com/story/sports/2015/01/01/daily-fantasy-sports-gambling-fanduel-draftkings-nba-nfl-mlb-nhl/21165279/

Shipman, F. M. (2001). *Blending the real and the virtual: Activity and spectatorship in fantasy sports*. Paper presented at the Fourth International Digital Arts and Culture Conference, Providence, RI.

Statistic (n.d.) Superbowl tv ratings—viewership U.S. 1990–2015 Retrieved from http://www.statista.com/statistics/216526/super-bowl-us-tv-viewership/

Thomas, N. J., & Martin, F. (2010). Video-arcade game, computer game and Internet activities of Australian students: Participation habits and prevalence of addiction. *Australian Journal of Psychology, 62*, 59–66. doi:10.1080/00049530902748283

Trail, G. T., & James, J. D. (2001). The motivation scale for sport consumption: Assessment of the scale's psychometric properties. *Journal of Sport Behavior, 24*, 108–127. Retrieved from http://www.biomedsearch.com/article/Motivation-Scale-Sport-Consumption-Assessment/70935203.html

Trail, G. T., Robinson, M. J., Dick, R. J., & Gillentine, A. J. (2003). Motives and points of attachment: Fans versus spectators in intercollegiate athletics. *Sport Marketing Quarterly, 12*, 217–227. Retrieved from http://www.cabdirect.org/abstracts/20033210182.html

Weekly. (2004, September). Fantasy football numbers on the rise. *Charleston Gazette* p. 3.

# 2

# SIMULATIONS AND FANTASY SPORTS

## The Forgotten Element?

*John S. W. Spinda*

The historical development of fantasy sports (see Anderson & Bowman, chapter 1 of this volume) and game-based sports simulations (see Spinda, Wann, & Sollitto, 2012) both began in the early 1960s. A few decades later, sports video games were also introduced (see Donovan, 2010). Although each of these three forms of gaming illustrates a different means of repurposed competition through sports, in many ways, all three aim to achieve similar ends: a desire by their creators (and players) to repurpose sports through gameplay. Fantasy sports repurpose athletic competition through the compiled statistics of daily and weekly games during a season that are translated into a game format. Meanwhile, sports video games and game-based sports simulations use larger samples of compiled statistics (yearly/ career statistics) to create representations of athlete performance in their game formats. Previous research, to this point, has not considered how sports video games and game-based simulations can help scholars learn more about fantasy sports. However, given similarities in chronological development and/or expansive growth with Internet and gaming systems, it seems quite possible that scholars may learn a great deal about fantasy sports by framing it within the context of other forms of repurposed sports gameplay, such as sports video games and game-based simulations.

A second reason for examining these three forms of repurposed sports gameplay together is the significant cross-platform impact they have had on one another. For example, Guzzo (2005) noted that Daniel Okrent was highly motivated to develop Rotisserie Baseball (a popular form of fantasy baseball) with others because he no longer was able to find playing partners for Strat-O-Matic (SOM) baseball—a board, card, and dice-based simulation game that reflects nearly every conceivable variable associated with an actual baseball play, as well as a number of other professional sports (see Spinda et al., 2012). Likewise, Electronic Arts (EA) founder Trip Hawkins was largely inspired to create sports video games by SOM baseball as well, noting that "my personal desire to make authentic sports simulations was the primary reason that I founded Electronic Arts in the first place" (Donovan, 2010, p. 215). Since its founding by Hawkins in 1982, EA has gone on to develop a string of critically and economically successful sports video games, most notably the *Madden Football* franchise. This annually produced video game franchise is named after Hall of Fame National Football League (NFL) coach and continued franchise consultant to EA, John Madden. Beginning with its 1988 debut, the *Madden Football* series has generated over $4 billion dollars for EA (Paine, 2015).

Given this historically significant and understudied commonality between sports video games, game-based sports simulations, and fantasy sports, this chapter will aim to tie together three somewhat disparate bodies of literature relating to (a) the motives for fantasy sports participation, (b) the motives for sports video game play (e.g., *Madden Football*), and (c) the motives for game-based sports simulations (e.g., SOM games). Next, I will discuss themes of participant motives for playing the increasingly popular "franchise mode" of *Madden Football* online, derived through online focus group interaction. Much like SOM games, franchise modes in contemporary sports video games allow a user to control (or simulate) nearly every conceivable element of an NFL team's operation, strategy, and of course, on-field performance. While many scholars have examined the motives for fantasy sports participation, less have examined the motives for sport-based video game play or sports game-based simulations. Furthermore, research on franchise-based video gaming online has been absent to this point. This chapter will conclude with a discussion about how fantasy sports, sports video games, and game-based sports simulations may serve as functional alternatives to one another (Rosengren & Windahl, 1972, Rubin & Windahl, 1986) and how scholars could best move forward studying the significant role that a need for accurate simulation may play within fantasy sports.

## MOTIVES FOR FANTASY SPORTS, SPORTS VIDEO GAMES, AND SIMULATIONS

A large majority of the studies examining the motives for fantasy sports, sports video games, and sports simulations have utilized the uses-and-gratifications approach (U&G). Although U&G has been applied to very broad range of mediated and interpersonal communication phenomena (Rubin, 2009; Ruggiero, 2000) and new media (Sundar & Limperos, 2013), one consistent aim of U&G research has always been to explore "the social and psychological origins of needs" (Katz, Blumler, & Gurevitch, 1974, p. 510). The study of needs in U&G has been manifested in the exploration of motives, which has dated back to early U&G studies of media use. According to Rubin (2009), contemporary U&G research is grounded in five assumptions.

1. Communication behavior, including the selection and use of the media, is goal-directed, purposive, and motivated.
2. People initiate the selection and use of communication vehicles . . . to satisfy their felt needs or desires.
3. A host of social and psychological factors guide, filter, or mediate communication behavior.
4. The media compete with other forms of communication—or, functional alternatives . . . to gratify our needs or wants.
5. People are typically more influential than the media in the choice of communication media to satisfy needs (167).

Therefore, the motives for playing fantasy sports, sports video games (SVGs), and game-based sports simulations should provide guidance as to why *Madden Football* simulations are actively chosen by gamers to satisfy their felt needs.

## MOTIVES FOR FANTASY SPORTS PLAY

The motives for playing fantasy sport have received significant scholarly attention (Billings & Ruihley, 2014; see chapter 8, this volume). While many of these studies have found somewhat distinctive motives for fantasy sports participation, a great deal of commonality also has been found. Billings and

Ruihley (2014) have offered the most recent and comprehensive treatment of the motives found across extant research. Their analysis, involving both quantitative and qualitative data, provided evidence of ten motives associated with fantasy sports participation: self-esteem (sense of achievement from winning at fantasy sports), social sport (chat/share opinions about sports), control and ownership (actions associated with controlling/managing players and lineups), competition (enjoyment of competing and being better than others in league), camaraderie (getting along and staying in touch with others), arousal (stimulation/arousal from fantasy sport competition), surveillance (obtaining great deal of sports-related information and staying up-to-date with sports), pass time (occupying time and alleviating boredom), fanship (extension of passion for a particular sport, additional reason to follow sport closely), and escape (avoiding daily routines and forgetting about reality).

## MOTIVES FOR SPORTS VIDEO GAME PLAY

On the other hand, the motives specific to playing modern video games (Sherry & Lucas, 2003; Sherry, Lucas, Greenberg, & Lachlan, 2006) and sport video games (SVG) (Cianfrone & Zhang, 2013; Cianfrone, Zhang, & Ko, 2011; Kim & Kim, 2013; Kim & Ross, 2006; Kim, Ross, & Ko, 2007) have received less empirical investigation. Regarding overall video game play, Sherry and colleagues (Sherry & Lucas, 2003; Sherry et al., 2006) discovered six motives: competition (proving superior skill to other gamers, being upset at losing video game contests); challenge (positive feelings associated with solving or completing game levels/winning/game mastery), social interaction (video games as a reason to get together with others), diversion (avoidance of other tasks), fantasy (pleasure associated with doing something not possible in reality, assuming alter egos), and arousal (excitement, stimulation associated with video game play).

Using focus group interviews and some motive items from Sherry et al. (2006), Kim and Ross (2006) developed the sports video game motives scale (SVGMS), which contained seven motives specific to sports video game play: social interaction (opportunities to spend time with others), sports knowledge application (simulating strategies in SVG, using knowledge of players/teams), fantasy (pleasure associated with doing something not possible in reality, pretending to be star athlete/team member), competition (proving superior skill to other gamers, being upset at losing in sports video games), entertainment (fun, entertainment value of SVG), diversion (break from regular routines), and identification with sport (playing SVGs related to a favorite sport). Next, Cianfrone et al. (2011) created a modified version of the SVGMS that featured eight overall motives, six of which were similar/identical to Kim and Ross's (2006) original measure (social interaction, sports knowledge application, fantasy, competition, entertainment, diversion), but had renamed the identification with sport motive as a "sport interest" motive and added an existing measure of team identification (Trail, Robinson, Dick, & Gillentine, 2003). Recently, Kim and Kim (2013) studied SVG motives through segmentation, delineating two clusters of video game players, *fantasy seekers* (higher in knowledge application, fantasy, and competition motives) and *fun seekers* (higher in entertainment and love of sport motives). Overall, these two clusters indicated that fantasy seekers have a higher level of identification to the sport represented in the SVG and are more purposeful in their SVG uses, whereas fun seekers are more driven to fulfill hedonic needs through SVG play.

More specific to the current study, Kim et al. (2007) examined motives specific to *online* SVG play. Specific motives for online SVG play were developed from focus group responses and previous research (Kim & Ross, 2006; Sherry & Lucas, 2003) and were subsequently responded to by respondents from an online message board related to *Madden Football*. Kim et al. (2007) indicated that five motives are associated with playing *Madden Football* online. Four of these motives—knowledge application, competition, entertainment, and fantasy—were similar to the items noted in previous research (Kim & Ross, 2006; Sherry & Lucas, 2003). However, the socialization motive found in this study revealed some noteworthy differences. Specifically, online SVG gamers noted that they liked to "chat with others about sports through the SVG site" and "share opinions about sports teams and players through the online SVG sites" (Kim et al., 2007, p. 62). Therefore, this provides evidence of a gaming "community" element that may be beyond what most SVG motives studies have noted. Or, as Kim et al. (2007) noted: "it also seems likely that online gamers are seeking personal gratification . . . by sharing experience and knowledge with like-minded gamers in their peer group" (p. 54).

## MOTIVES FOR GAME-BASED SIMULATION PLAY

This idea of an active online community was also evidenced in a U&G study of online Strat-O-Matic (SOM) baseball players (Spinda et al., 2012). As described earlier, SOM games are precursors to modern SVG (particularly those from EA Sports, like the *Madden Football* series), although SOM and other game-based simulations are still played quite often, both online and offline. One anecdote that can further connect SVGs to game-based simulations (that relied primarily on dice rolling) came from a recent quote by *Madden Football* creative director, Rex Dickson, who stated that any interaction between two players in the game is "going to take several ratings and throw them into a formula and do a dice roll. The dice roll is how we get the randomness" (Paine, 2015, para. 54–55). Much like the continually expanding player ratings on *Madden Football* games, SOM and earlier game-based simulations are also designed to consider nearly every conceivable variable that impacts how a game could be decided. Thus, the most significant separation between game-based simulations and SVGs is simply the visual interface in which the game is delivered.

But unlike many sports video games, game-based simulations like SOM baseball, for instance, can be played with a near-infinite number of historical matchups. This may include any current-day Major League Baseball (MLB) players/teams facing MLB players/teams from decades past, or even Negro League Baseball players/teams (as was painstakingly recreated by two SOM baseball players). Overall, Spinda et al. (2012) found eight motives related to SOM baseball: nostalgia (relive memories of past players and teams, "puts you in control over boyhood idols"), knowledge acquisition (increased knowledge/baseball appreciation from play), social bonding (forming distant friendships, a sense of virtual community), enjoyment (fun and fulfillment of play), vicarious achievement (enjoyment of winning games/championships), game aesthetics (SOM baseball player cards and the game board, often recreated online from offline version, were seen as visually appealing), convenience (quick/easy/simple to play), and escape (diversion or escape from everyday life). Also, much like the previous research on SVG players (Kim & Ross, 2006), SOM baseball players indicated a strong identification with Major League Baseball teams and players, particularly those SOM baseball players that were motivated by knowledge acquisition and game enjoyment needs (see table 2.1).

## ONLINE SPACES IN SPORTS VIDEO GAMES

Beyond motivations for game play, research has also examined the specific elements associated with how SVG players manipulate and/or create social spaces in the quest for an accurate simulation of real-life sports. In a textual analysis of *Madden Football* related online message boards, Baerg

**Table 2.1. Complementary Motives for Fantasy Sports, Sports Video Games, and Strat-O-Matic Baseball**

| Fantasy Sports (FS) Motives (Billings & Ruihley, 2014) | Sports Video Game (SVG) Motives: Standard SVG (Kim & Ross, 2006) and Madden Football Online (Kim et al., 2007) | Strat-o-Matic Baseball (SOMB) Motives (Spinda et al., 2012) |
|---|---|---|
| Self-esteem (from FS victory) | Challenge (positive feeling with SVG mastery) | Vicarious Achievement (winning games in SOMB) |
| Social Sport (chatting and opinion sharing in FS) | Social Interaction (spending time with others in SVG) | Social Bonding (forming bonds with online SOMB community) |
| Control and ownership (of FS lineup/team) | Fantasy (doing something not possible in reality) | Nostalgia (being in control of "boyhood idols" and reliving memories) |
| Competition (defeating others in FS) | Competition (demonstrating superior skill in OSVG) | |
| Camaraderie (with fellow FS owners) | Social Interaction (spending time with others in SVG) | Social Bonding (forming bonds with online SOMB community) |
| Arousal (stimulation from FS play) | Entertainment (stimulation from SVG play) | Enjoyment (playing SOMB for the fun of the game) |
| Surveillance (staying up to date with sports and obtaining sports information) | Sports Knowledge Application (simulating strategies in SVG, using knowledge of players and teams) | Knowledge Acquisition (staying connected to sport of baseball) |
| Pass Time (alleviate boredom) | Diversion (break from regular routines) | |
| Escape (avoiding daily routines/reality) | Diversion (break from regular routines) | Escape (avoiding everyday routines/reality) |
| Fanship (extension of passion for a particular sport) | Identification with sport (playing SVG related to favorite sport) | Knowledge acquisition motive (staying connected to sport of baseball) |

(2008) found two main themes: a concern for the quantitative realism of the SVG in both games that are controlled by players and those simulated by the computer (related to how accurate statistics were as compared to actual NFL game statistics) and a online discourse described as being similar to scientific research and experimentation (with players collaborating and manipulating game sliders, or customizable options related to game play and simulated games). These themes are quite similar to motives that have been illustrated in studies of SVG players, fantasy sport players, and SOM baseball players, as all three games have been found to be driven by knowledge acquisition and are all seeking to simulate actual quantitative performance (which must be accurate as possible) as a basis for gameplay and/or simulation.

In sum, the research noted in this section has indicated that fantasy sports, online SVG play, and simulation games share a significant number of key similarities. Based on the findings from a number of studies (see table 2.1), all three games are motivated by a knowledge acquisition/application factor, a socialization/camaraderie factor, a feeling of vicarious control/management/ownership of athletes, the entertaining nature of the games, and the way that all three games allow for an escape or diversion from reality. Moreover, the research cited in this section implies that fantasy sports, SVG play, and sports simulations all fulfill needs and wants not gratified through actual sports viewing (Kim & Ross, 2006) and that frequent SVG players are highly identified sports fans that consume more sports than less frequent SVG players (Kim, Walsh, & Ross, 2008).

Therefore, one way in which fantasy sports can be better understood is to examine the nexus of fantasy sports, sports video games, and sports simulations. One example that provides such an interconnection is the "franchise mode" of *Madden Football*. However, no research at this point has directly examined the motives specific to franchise mode SVG play online. Therefore, a study was conducted that qualitatively examined the motives for why gamers choose to play this particular *Madden Football* game mode online with other gamers, which is consistent with uses-and-gratifications studies that have previously examined an initial set of motives for media activity (Greenberg, 1974) and for examining sports-relevant motives (Spinda & Haridakis, 2008; Spinda et al., 2012).

## INTERSECTIONS OF FANTASY SPORTS, SPORTS VIDEO GAMES, AND SIMULATION: A FOCUS GROUP INVESTIGATION

Online focus groups were conducted among groups of online *Madden Football* franchise mode players through message boards that were either developed and used for a self-contained "franchise simulation league" (FSL) or serve as a forum for FSL gamers to coordinate simulated league play. Message board administrators were asked for permission to pose questions and topics for elaboration to the forum. No compensation was provided for participation. Over the course of approximately ten days, participants were asked to provide their thoughts about the questions/topics related to experiences playing in the online franchise mode. This was done to come to preliminary understanding of specific motives that emerged for franchise league play and to determine how these preliminary motives were similar or different from the motives outlined in the earlier section concerning SVG play. Overall, twelve different gamers, all males, shared unique contributions to the focus group conversations.

Questions and topics that were posted for feedback included broadly asking how participants' FSLs operated (i.e., rules, roster building/trades, organization of games), asking participants how they felt the franchise leagues were similar/different to traditional fantasy football leagues, how long franchise teams are played within the FSL (i.e., how many seasons generally go by before the group decides to end and select new teams to manage), why they play in FSL (motives), and whether or not participants previously played franchise simulations before online franchise modes and FSLs (versus the game system offline). The aggregated text of the online focus group discussions was then analyzed using a qualitative software package (NVivo).

## RESULTS

Beyond providing clarification of the operation, rules, and management of FSLs, online forum responses indicated five broad motive themes related to motives for playing FSLs online: (1) sense of community and belonging, (2) creating a sense of realism, (3) management and development, (4) competition, and (5) eustress and game enjoyment. Below is a brief description of each of these motive themes along with selected quotes that provide further illustration.

### Sense of Community and Belonging

The most commonly mentioned motive theme revolved around *a sense of community and belonging*, specifically among the respondents in the self-contained FSL. In this motive theme, participants described how the FSL has grown beyond just a digital space where SVG enthusiasts just compete online, but rather has become a true community where members have established genuine and deep bonds. For example, respondents noted:

> There have been some tragedies in members lives that this community has actually donated not only a friend to talk to, but open there wallet as well to donate to families we do not know.

Other leagues just don't entice me, this group of strangers I joined to play Madden, have become my friends.

It's pretty uncommon to find a group of like-minded people and be able to speak very openly with them at virtually all hours of the night about anything, whether it's Madden, relationships, the NCAA, or anything else.

Within this motive theme, multiple respondents also acknowledged that this community has helped them feel like they belong, despite not being highly successful in FSLs. More specifically, respondents noted:

This league in particular isn't just about sim gameplay, being the better player, winning super bowls, or building the best team possible. We could all join many leagues with this same format and do well. The people in this particular league though are looking for a community, and we do a damn good job of providing that.

This in particular is the main reason I am still here. I'm not particularly a good player, but this community is fantastic.

A lot of the appeal of (the league) is the community. I personally am one of the worst players in the league, but I've never had a desire to leave and find somewhere where I could compete better.

Just sitting in the chat on any Sunday and discussing the games going on is as much fun as actually playing each other, in my opinion, but I'm biased because I'm constantly losing.

One respondent used an interesting metaphor from the 1987 war film *Full Metal Jacket* to elaborate on how he feels connected to this particular FSL as a community despite the fact that many other FSLs exist online:

To sum up what I quoted from (another contributor), I am reminded of a quote from *Full Metal Jacket*, "There are many like it, but this one is mine."

Lastly, and quite ironically given the nature of this chapter and book, a few respondents noted that the FSL community extends out into the fantasy football realm as well, with at least twelve of the league members having their own league. In sum, while this sense of community and belonging may have been unique to this particular FSL, or even a small fraction of leagues, it seems plausible that the highly active nature of a FSL (i.e., trading, strategy, simulated front office management duties, regular gameplay), combined with FSL tending to play out over multiple seasons with one franchise, could lead to an enhanced sense of community and belonging amongst its members. In this focus group analysis, this motive theme was the most frequently cited reason for playing in a FSL.

## Creating a Sense of Realism

The second most commonly acknowledged motive theme involved the FSL members' efforts to *create a sense of realism*. Baerg (2008) previously examined how online message boards were employed to achieve a more realistic gameplay, but especially simulation, in *Madden Football 2006*. In this study, gamers used a trial-and-error approach to manipulate game sliders to achieve quantitative realism. Likewise, some respondents noted a similar desire for quantitative realism to create a more genuine feel to the FSL. One respondents noted: "At the end of our games we want the final score and stats reflect what you might see on Sunday, and not look like you clearly just played a video game with crazy numbers."

However, responses in this study also elucidated a larger breadth of realism-seeking efforts. Multiple members of the self-contained FSL mentioned a sense of realism in gameplay as being vital. Specifically, they noted the creation of a set of written rules and regulations for the FSL that prohibited unrealistic play, noting that:

> emphasis is put on house-rules to ensure the game between two users doesn't devolve into a Head-to-Head/Unranked game that you world normally see against a random opponent online, where there is complete disregard for conventional football strategies and often times just comes down to who can abuse the same handful of formations/plays better than the other.
>
> Our commissioners have set up rules that allow this to happen like: you cannot go for it on fourth down unless you are down in the 4th quarter, and you must have various plays, etc.

Among these house rules were regulations that prohibited what was labeled "cheesy play," which was described in the following excerpt from the league rulebook:

> Cheesy play will be defined more specifically as we get further into Madden 15. For now, you are expected to use more than one play and more than the same route repeatedly (offense). While there will be no rule against running the same defense on every play, you should be aware that an offense may try to take advantage of a 1 play defense in a way that might become repetitive

and could lead to a dispute. For that reason, it is advisable that you mix up your plays on defense as well. The one firm rule regarding defensive playcall consistency is to refrain from blitzing every play or close to every play.

Beyond rules meant to prohibit human circumvention of realistic play. According to one respondent, the hallmark of the realism in gameplay was also achieved through playing another human in the FSL, as opposed to playing against the gaming system that uses artificial intelligence (AI): "I like the dynamics of playing another person because I think there is more strategy than playing AI, and learning to beat them and then learning how to repeat the same things over and over."

Overall, it was evidenced that realistic gameplay is quite important to FSL gamers, as it was the second most discussed motive theme in this analysis. However, these responses were informative in that realism is achieved in a multitude of efforts, whether that was the five-page description of league rules (complete with a FAQ section) to eliminate "cheesy play," or the gratification of playing a human opponent that captures "real life NFL situations within the gameplay."

## Management and Development

Next, *management and development* emerged as a motive theme in this analysis. Much like multiple studies in fantasy sports, as noted by Billings and Ruihley (2014), some FSL players indicated the importance of player and roster management. One respondent noted (responses unedited): "madden gives you the user the ability decide their fate. plus building up ur team n making them a SB (super bowl) contender is a good feeling. Like being a real player,coach an GM"

However, this fantasy sports inspired aspect of ownership and management made up a small portion of the overall discussion related to this motive theme. Much of the responses that touched on ownership and management described the vicarious satisfaction with franchise-related, team-related and individual player-related outcomes, as all three of these elements can help and FSL gamer improve their overall outcomes in the games. In other words, management and ownership functions were much more nuanced and pronounced, largely due to the capabilities and affordances given by the *Madden Football* games. One respondent clarified this by stating:

> We control every aspect of the game. We draft (players), set depth (charts), bid on free agents, call plays, run those plays, and use xp (experience points)

gained through the game to upgrade the players. On top of that, some of us also control pricing of tickets, food, and memorabilia in order to make our franchise more money to be able to offer bigger bonuses to prospective players.

Another difference between FSL play and typical fantasy football play, unless playing in a fantasy league with multiple "keeper" players, or players that remain on a team into the next season, seems to be how the two types of players think of the present (or near-future) outcomes versus longer-term future outcomes. While most fantasy football leagues involve play over one NFL season, or even one week/day games (see chapter 15, this volume), FSLs often run the course of multiple seasons that are not limited to the actual NFL schedule. So this leads some gamers to work with an eye to future seasons within the FSL. This was suggested in the following responses:

> By building for the future I mean trading away older players that will make a huge impact for 1–2 seasons for younger players or draft picks I can develop. For instance in this league I'm the broncos and traded Peyton Manning to the cardinals for (two players). In this instance it is clear that you would never do something like that in fantasy, or real life so that is one area when sim leagues can shy away from being a true sim league that mocks the nfl closely.

> Yes, developing players is a huge part of this. People love to get low rated players with physical talent and upgrade them over the course of a couple seasons.

> But with madden lg's its the control n building that has me hooked. You can draft ur team,game prep them through the season to add more xp to the xp already earned from season goals n make key players even better.

In sum, it is clear that controlling and managing of the franchise is enjoyable for some players, but for many players this also appears to be a means to an end; to build a better team by building up the attributes associated to key players. While it would seem likely that many FSL gamers very much enjoy having a favorite NFL player on their franchise within the league, the focus tends to be on sustaining long-term or future success as an integral part of the simulation.

## Competition

Next, *competition* was described as an important aspect of FSL play. This motive theme was relatively straightforward, with multiple respondents indicating that competition is why they started to play in Madden FSLs.

Respondents noted: "It started off being . . . the idea of building a team and competing against other human-controlled opponents was appealing" and "My motivation for playing in these leagues is the competition and interaction with other players."

However, some variations of the competitiveness motive theme began to take shape in some responses. For instance, one respondent noted the competitive aspect of FSL play comes from the high level of football knowledge many players have, while another suggested that "madden gaming is very confrontational at times because of competition."

### Eustress and Game Enjoyment

The fifth most discussed motive theme revolved around the fun and enjoyment associated with playing Madden FSL. This motive theme was expressed largely through statements that discussed the thrilling aspects of playing against others in the FSL. More specifically, respondents noted:

> I am not as big on the player development/acquisitions part of the game, that gets a bit tedious for me. I'm more of a strategist. I like the thrill of the game play, the chess match between you and the other player, the thrill of winning, and the agony of defeat.

> The kid in us comes out when we load that game in. I like making plays and winning games cuz of the gutsy calls I made.

Both of these narratives are closely associated to Wann's (1995) eustress motive (i.e., "positive stress" and stimulation associated with rooting for a sports team). Eustress also is similar to Billings and Ruihley's (2014) conceptualization of arousal as a motive for fantasy sport play.

### CONCLUSION: WHERE DO WE GO FROM HERE?

In this chapter, I examined the intersection of fantasy sports, sports video games (SVGs), and game-based simulations to provide an overview of how these three forms of gaming have both an overlapping, shared history and how they quite often parallel each other in need gratification at the present time. More specifically, I examined what motives emerged among online gamers that compete in *Madden Football* franchise simulation leagues (FSLs) to consider how they relate to motives for fantasy sports, SVGs and other game-based simulations, such as Strat-O-Matic (SOM) games. Using an online focus group method, five themes emerged for playing online in FSLs: (1) a sense of community and belonging, (2) creating a sense of realism, (3) management and development of teams/players, (4) competition, as well as (5) eustress and game enjoyment.

## WHY CONNECTIONS BETWEEN FANTASY SPORT, GAMING, AND SIMULATION MATTER: CHOOSING AMONG FUNCTIONAL ALTERNATIVES

In one form or another, all five of these motive themes can be related back to existing scholarship that has examined fantasy sports, SVGs, and game-based sports simulations. A sense of community was very evident in Spinda et al.'s (2012) analysis of online SOM baseball players (social bonding motive), online SVG play (Kim et al., 2007), and has been noted across studies of fantasy sports motives (Billings & Ruihley, 2014). Baerg (2008) previously detailed the thorough efforts that online gamers will undertake to create a sense of realism in *Madden Football*. Likewise, the passionate search for realism among SOM baseball fans led fans to painstakingly create Negro League Baseball player cards so that the players from this league may be used in gameplay to compete against the MLB players of their day (or even current day). While creating realism has not been explicitly noted as a motive in prior studies of fantasy sports, perhaps this motivation may have been unnoticed given that fantasy outcomes are driven by real statistical figures obtained by athletes.

Although developing players through increased attribute scores is something unique to FSLs, the gratification obtained from managing rosters well is something that has been found to be present in multiple fantasy sports motives studies (Billings & Ruihley, 2014). Similarly, the application of knowledge, which is an essential element of roster management, has been noted as a motive for SVG (Kim & Ross; Kim et al., 2007) as well as SOM baseball play (Spinda et al., 2012). The competition motive theme that emerged in this study was consistent with existing research that has found competition as a salient motive for playing fantasy sports (Billings & Ruihley, 2014), playing SVG, both offline and online (Kim & Ross, 2006; Kim et al., 2007), as well as in SOM baseball through the vicarious achievement motive, where a premium was placed on winning contests (Spinda et al., 2012). Lastly, the eustress and game enjoyment motive theme resembled the arousal motive for fantasy sports play (Billings & Ruihley, 2014), the entertainment motive for offline and online SVG play (Kim & Ross, 2006; Kim et al., 2007), and the enjoyment motive associated with SOM baseball (Spinda et al., 2012).

While further research is needed, it appears from the preliminary themes outlined in this study that the motives for playing in *Madden Football* FSLs are quite similar to overall SVG, which was anticipated, but also are very similar to participating in fantasy sports and game-based simulations. This begs an interesting question: If all of these forms of gaming satisfy similar motivations that sports fans have, what determines the eventual media choice to pursue fantasy sports, SVGs, or game-based simulations?

Returning to the assumptions of the U&G approach noted earlier, a useful way to consider how media is chosen for need gratification is the concept of *functional alternatives* (Rosengren & Windahl, 1972, Rubin & Windahl, 1986). Functional alternatives are individual media decisions based on the availability and utilization of particular media to satisfy needs. Further, the concept of functional alternatives assumes that there is more than one way of satisfying a need. In the case of whether to choose to play fantasy sports, sports video games, or a game-based simulation, a person will inevitably choose the media use that they feel most comfortable with, for "biological, psychological, or cultural reasons" (Rosengren & Windahl, 1972, p. 176).

For example, according to Rosengren and Windahl (1972), an individual who is highly extroverted may choose to have a face-to-face conversation to fulfill a socialization need. On the other hand, a highly introverted person may choose vicarious experience with a televised character to fulfill the same need. Or, as applied to the current study, an avid NFL fan who is highly extroverted may choose to play in a *Madden Football* FSL online to enjoy being a part of a stronger community of other avid gamers playing live than they otherwise may get playing in a fantasy football league that offers less socialization opportunities and/or static, time-delayed socialization through something like a league message board. At the same time, an introverted person may seek out an online FSL because he or she enjoy the vicarious nature of managing a franchise to success over the course of multiple FSL seasons more so than the camaraderie the league offers. In either instance, the media choice is often selected among a set of options.

But in today's growing marketplace for fan-based games, a multitude of functional alternatives exist. Or, as Rubin and Rubin (1985) stated: "The more functional alternatives available to an individual, in terms of both quantity and quality, the lesser is the dependency on and influence of a specific channel" (p. 39). Given both the quantity (the large number of fantasy and simulation game options for fans, such as the three examined in this study) and the quality (the large breadth of motives that these fantasy and simulation games have been found to satisfy), it may behoove fantasy sports scholars to consider a larger perspective moving forward. Such a perspective should aim to fully utilize the uses-and-gratifications model by more cogently linking motives to both the social and psychological factors that lead a user to make a media choice among many options as well as the consequences of those media choices. One illustration of such a linkage would be tying motives to the recent findings that have indicated that highly involved fantasy sports participants care more to see their fantasy team win over their favorite team (Lee, Ruihley, Brown, & Billings, 2013; see also, chapter 4 of this volume). While some motives for fantasy sports play emerge through reasoning, such as fantasy players who are more motivated to satisfy self-esteem needs also being likely to be those who may care more for a fantasy team, such connections are sorely lacking empirical support. Beyond this example, many consequences of participating in fantasy sports, sports video games, or game-based simulations need further examination and clarification. Given the growing number of options and how closely they appear to be in need gratification, this is an important step moving forward.

## MOVING FORWARD: HOW A NEED FOR ACCURATE SIMULATION RELATES TO FANTASY SPORTS

However, perhaps the most significant takeaway from this chapter comes back to simulation and its importance to the development of fantasy sport moving forward. A variety of options have emerged, or have been created, that allow fantasy sports to increase the perceived realism of fantasy games. One example would be fantasy league type, where fantasy owners can choose how many players are retained from year-to-year on team rosters. In some leagues, no players are kept (re-draft leagues), a few players are kept (keeper leagues), or all players are kept (dynasty league) from season to season. Some variation of these leagues can also occur, such as my personal experience where a fantasy hockey commissioner proposed an idea where the number of players kept gradually increased from zero to five players kept every six seasons, only to start again at zero players retained. Considering the current chapter, a natural parallel is implied between *Madden Football* FSLs and fantasy dynasty leagues. Miley (2013) noted such a similarity by stating: "when drafting in a new dynasty league, most people want to build a team composed of young players with upside" (para. 10), which would be quite similar to the narratives provided in this study about taking players in a FSL and hoping they develop (or be developed by the gamer) into top players later.

Also, some leagues offer a league draft that is "first come, first served" regarding players (often called a snake draft, which gets its name from the top-to-bottom reversal of draft order after every round). In a typical snake draft, once an athlete is selected, that athlete is not available for any other fantasy owner in that league to draft. On the other hand, auction leagues are also popular because they are very similar to North American sports that operate under a "salary cap" (e.g., NFL, NHL, NBA). In this instance, players are drafted in order, as with a standard draft, but each owner is given a set amount of fictional "dollars" to spend to draft a team. Premium players cost the most, all the way down to players expected to cost very little, and produce statistical performance to match. Lastly, depending generally on the fantasy platform and website chosen by fantasy players, game statistics and scoring are also able to be manipulated to increase perceptions of realistic scoring. Unfortunately, no data is available at this point to indicate what percentage of fantasy sports leagues employ customized scoring features, according to the Fantasy Sports Trade Association (FTSA; personal communication, June 22, 2015).

The point of the above overview on these emerging options is to clarify that fantasy sports are becoming more and more *customizable*. While some of this growth can certainly be attributed to the continued demand for fantasy sports in the consumer market, it would also seem quite likely much of this growth has been driven by the demand for more realistic fantasy sports action. This appears similar to the customization needs *Madden Football* gamers have within the sophisticated FSLs noted in this chapter and may also be why sports simulations, such as SOM (and other) continue to experience growth analogous to fantasy sports and SVGs. Because of this possibility, future researchers should also begin to examine the *need for accurate simulation* as a concept or variable to be researched when studying fantasy football, as well as SVG or simulation games for that matter. Researchers would then be free to focus on what motives are affiliated with simulation needs, and to then see how that need drives the choices between functional alternatives, such as fantasy sports, SVG, or simulation games.

Moreover, it could be argued, based on the concept of functional alternatives, that fantasy sports entities should be keenly aware of the options for accurate simulation available to fans. If one genre of gaming (e.g., SVGs, simulation games) is able to provide a more real-to-life "managerial experience" than fantasy football can offer, it may begin to lose market share, particularly if those other genres begin to aggressively push into the sports consumer marketplace. However, it is also possible that a true "saturation point" of realism does exist, as illustrated by Klosterman (2006) in discussing the EA Sports strategy game *NFL Head Coach*:

"NFL Head Coach" is—indeed—the most realistic sports simulation I've ever found. And it sucks. It is the dullest, most bureaucratic game ever created . . . "NFL Head Coach" is so real it's almost devoid of pleasure. I was drawn to this game because I wanted reality . . . which—as we all know—is repetitive and hard. This is why we play games in the first place. As is so often the case, what I "want" is the opposite of what I want. For whatever the reason, we have all been convinced that authenticity means everything (para. 7–9).

Perhaps "what we want" is what fantasy football delivers, but our need for accurate simulation is certainly worthy of further attention, even with its limitations.

## REFERENCES

Baerg, A. (2008). "It's (not) in the game": The quest for quantitative realism and the *Madden Football* fan. In L. W. Hugenberg, P. M. Haridakis, and A. C. Earnheardt (Eds.), *Sports Mania: Essays on Fandom and the Media in the 21st Century* (pp. 218–228). Jefferson, NC: McFarland & Company.

Billings, A. C. & Ruihley, B. J. (2014). *The Fantasy Sport Industry: Games within Games.* London: Routledge.

Cianfrone, B. A., & Zhang, J. J. (2013). The impact of gamer motives, consumption, and in-game advertising effectiveness: A case study of football sport video games. *International Journal of Sport Communication, 6,* 325–347.

Cianfrone, B. A., Zhang, J. J., & Ko, Y. J. (2011). Dimensions of motivation associated with playing sport video games: Modification and extension of the sport video game motivation scale. *Sport, Behavior, and Management: An International Journal, 1,* 172–189.

Donovan, T. (2010). *Replay: The History of Video Games.* Lewes, UK: Yellow Ant.

Greenberg, B. S. (1974). Gratifications of television viewing and the correlates for British children. In J. G. Blumler & E. Katz (Eds.), *The Uses of Mass Communication: Current Perspectives of Gratifications Research* (pp. 71–92). Beverly Hills, CA: Sage.

Guzzo, G. (2005). *Strat-O-Matic fanatics: The Unlikely Success Story of a Game That Became an American Passion.* Chicago: ACTA.

Katz, E., Blumler, J. G., & Gurevitch, M. (1974). Uses and gratifications research. *Public Opinion Quarterly, 37*(4), 509–524.

Kim, Y., & Kim, S. (2013). Segmenting sport video games by motivation: A cluster analysis. *Journal of Global Scholars of Marketing Science: Bridging Asia and the World, 23,* 92–108.

Kim, Y., & Ross, S. D. (2006). An exploration of motives in sports video gaming. *International Journal of Sports Marketing & Sponsorship, 8,* 34–46.

Kim, Y., Ross, S. D., & Ko, Y. (2007). Online sport video game motivations. *International Journal of Human Movement Science, 1,* 41–60.

Kim, Y., Walsh, P., & Ross, S. D. (2008). An examination of the psychological and consumptive behaviors of sport video gamers. *Sport Marketing Quarterly, 17,* 45–53.

Klosterman, C. (2006, July 27). Reality and fantasy don't mix. *ESPN.com.* Retrieved from http://sports.espn.go.com/espn/page2/story?page=klosterman/060727

Lee, J., Ruihley, B. J., Brown, N., & Billings, A. C. (2013). The effects of fantasy football participation on team identification, team loyalty, and NFL fandom. *Journal of Sport Media, 8,* 207–227. London: Routledge.

Lucas, K., & Sherry, J. L. (2003). Sex differences in video game play: A communication-based explanation. *Communication Research, 31,* 499–523.

Miley, A. (2013, August 26). Dynasty vs. keeper leagues: What's the difference? *USA Today.* Retrieved from http://www.usatoday.com/story/sports/fantasy/football/2013/08/26/dynasty-leagues-keeper-leagues--fantasy-football/2699177/

Paine, N. (2015, February 25). How Madden ratings are made: The secret process that turns NFL players into digital gods. *FiveThirtyEight.com.* Retrieved from http://fivethirtyeight.com/features/madden/#

Rosengren, K. E., & Windahl, S. (1972). Mass media consumption as a functional alternative. In D. McQuail (Ed.), *Sociology of Mass Communications: Selected Readings* (pp. 119–134). Harmondsworth: Penguin.

Rubin, A. M. (2009). Uses and gratifications perspective on media effects. In J. Bryant & M. B. Oliver (Eds.), *Media Effects: Advances in Theory and Research* (3rd Ed., pp. 165–184). London: Routledge.

Rubin, A. M., & Rubin, R. B. (1985). Interface of personal and mediated communication: A research agenda. *Critical Studies in Mass Communication, 2,* 36–53.

Rubin, A. M., & Windahl, S. (1986). The uses and dependency model of mass communication. *Critical Studies in Mass Communication, 3,* 184–199.

Ruggiero, T.E. (2000). Uses and gratifications theory in the 21st century. *Mass Communication & Society, 3*(1), 3–37.

Sherry, J. L., & Lucas, K. (2003, May). Video game uses and gratifications as predictors of use and game preference. Paper presented at the annual conference of the International Communication Association, San Diego, CA.

Sherry, J. L., Lucas, K., Greenberg, B. S., & Lachlan, K. (2006). Video game uses and gratifications as predictors of use and game preference. In P. Vorderer & J. Bryant (Eds.) *Playing Video Games: Motives, Responses, and Consequences* (pp. 213–224). London: Routledge

Spinda, J. S. W. & Haridakis, P. M. (2008). Development and construct validation of a fantasy sports motivation scale: A uses-and-gratifications approach (pp. 187–202). In P. M. Haridakis, L. W. Hugenberg, A. C. Earnheardt (Eds.), *Sports Mania: Essays on Fandom and Media in the 21st Century.* Jefferson, NC: Mc-Farland & Company

Spinda, J. S. W., Sollitto, M., & Wann, D. L. (2012). Cards, dice, and male bonding: A case study examination of Strat-O-Matic Baseball motives. *International Journal of Sport Communication, 5*(2), 246–264.

Sundar, S. S, &, Limperos, A. M. (2013). Uses and grats 2.0: New gratifications for new media. *Journal of Broadcasting & Electronic Media 57,* 504–525.

Trail, G. T., Robinson, M. J., Dick, R. J., & Gillentine, A. J. (2003). Motives and points of attachment: Fan versus spectators in intercollegiate athletics. *Sport Marketing Quarterly, 12,* 217–227.

Wann, D. L. (1995). Preliminary validation of the sport fan motivation scale. *Journal of Sport & Social Issues, 19,* 377–396.

**3**

# FANTASY SPORTS
# ACROSS THE POND

*Nicholas M. Watanabe, Grace Yan, and Pamela Wicker*

In their book *The Fantasy Sport Industry: Games within Games*, Billings and Ruihley (2013) note that focus is placed on fantasy sport within North America due to the relative size of the fantasy sport industry and participation in comparison to other parts of the world. While they provide a wonderful discussion of the potential for fantasy sport in the rest of the world, the focus of this chapter is to expand the knowledge and discussion in regards to fantasy sport outside of North America. As Billings and Ruihley (2013) argue, fantasy sport participation is currently higher around the world than it has been at any time in history. With this in mind, there seems to be a pertinent need to further consider the growth of the industry from a global perspective, especially as it evolves from the forms that are familiar to people in North America.

The Fantasy Sports Trade Association (FSTA, see also chapter 14 of this volume) estimates that around 500,000 people in North America were playing some type of fantasy sport in 1988. FSTA demographic research has shown that fantasy sport participation in North America has hit a record high of 41.5 million people (also see chapter 1, this volume). However, at the same time there has not been as large a growth in fantasy sport leagues and participation around the rest of the world. Thus, the question arises: Why has there not been similar interest in fantasy sport around the globe? In response to this, it can be argued that fantasy sport was naturally developed in North America, where there is not only a variety of mainstream professional sports, but that the keeping of statistics and scores has been an integral part of the viewership process in sports like baseball. Furthermore, the analysis and printing of statistics from sporting events in newspapers, almanacs, and books made it so that individuals could constantly keep track of players in their fantasy leagues.

This interest level also aligns with other behaviors which helped to build an affinity for quantitative interest in players such as simulation games and baseball trading cards (Spinda, Wann, & Sollitto, 2012; (also see chapter 2, this volume). Furthermore, it is also the case that the sports which were popular in North America—baseball, basketball, football and ice hockey—were all sports where it was easy to see the individual statistics which were accumulated across all players on a team. This is not necessarily the case with Europe and other regions of the world, where the primary sport of interest is often soccer. Research by Gerrard and Howard (2007) assessed the particular difficulties of using an analytical approach to soccer, as has been employed in baseball. While the difficulties of measuring individual performance in the sport of soccer are noted, they argue that perhaps the biggest issue for performing such analysis in Europe is the cultural barriers against using statistics to understand player performance (Gerrard & Howard, 2007). Finally, some argue that the relative lack of accessibility and/or popularity of broadcasts sports in Europe (compared to the USA) has made it so that there is less of a chance to be able to follow the performance of players in real time (Montague, 2010). Thus, the philosophical approach to sport and relative lack of access to electronic and digital live sport content in the past has made it so that Europe and other regions may not have been primed for growth in fantasy sport participation.

Outside of changes in viewership patterns and the philosophy of sport, there is also the fact that fantasy sport has been a relatively newer way for fans to be involved with sport leagues. Prior to fantasy sport, the consumption of sport occurred primarily through media channels. Outside of media channels, one of the ways in which a sport fan might be able to display their knowledge about sporting contests or be involved with the outcome or events of a game/match was through placing wagers. That is, wagering on sport has been pervasive in countries around the world, and whether legal or not, is still considered by many individuals as an exciting way to be involved with sport. Because sport betting has been a practice associated with the outcome of games and matches, it has thus evolved that there is competition between fantasy sport and gambling in many countries such as England and China. Additionally, it is important to note that while fantasy sport is not classified as gambling within North America (see chapter 13, this volume), it receives different treatment depending on the legal system of the country that the fantasy service is based in. Thus, in some European countries, fantasy sport is considered to be a form of gambling (Billings & Ruihley, 2013). This difference in classification is not only important in understanding the relationship between fantasy sport and gambling on a global scale, it also hints at the relationship between the two activities worldwide.

Considering issues including the lack of access, gambling laws, and different cultural/philosophical approaches to fantasy sport around the world, this chapter will examine the growth of fantasy sport in different regions of the world. Through analyzing fantasy sport from a global perspective, this chapter also will note the possibilities for growth, as well as the need for further research focused on the fantasy sport industry in international settings. Thus, while North America has received most of the attention from organizations and academics, the different contexts, meanings, and relationships that fantasy sport has with leagues and individuals across the globe warrants further investigation. From this, this chapter hopefully provides a step forward toward increased awareness and interest in the current state of fantasy sport in the rest of the world. In the rest of this chapter, we will cover a variety of contexts in which fantasy sport has grown around the globe, while considering factors that have caused either growth or constraint of fantasy sport participation on an international scale. Finally, we conclude with recommendations for the growth and improvement of access and participation in fantasy sport products and services around the world.

## FANTASY SPORT IN EUROPE

Much discussion has been placed on the issues surrounding why fantasy sport has not enjoyed great success in Europe (Montague, 2010). It is noted that the ability to analyze soccer statistically is much more difficult, and that there exists a philosophy that quantitative examination of individual player performances was not always looked upon positively as Gerrard and Howard (2007) noted in their research. Montague (2010) quotes Stefan Szymanski, author of the book *Soccernomics*, who argues that in Europe the focus is often placed on the beauty and poetry of sport, and that there has been backlash against trying to break down the sport into numerical analysis. Thus, it would seem that the difference in philosophy and approach toward sport which exists between Europe and North America could be one of the major reasons why fantasy sport has been slower to become mainstream around the globe.

However, it is just not the philosophy of how to watch and discuss sport which is behind these differences. There are many constraints which can be included in any discussion as to why fantasy sport has not picked up in certain regions. For some, the lack of access to internet and fan groups can be considered an important factor in getting involved in fantasy sport leagues. In considering the importance of the Internet in growing fantasy sport participation, research has noted that the existence of a "digital divide" also creates barriers for access to the Internet because of factors such as: Internet and telecommunications policies, the dominance of English language content, and the lack of technological support (Chen & Wellman, 2004).

Szymanski additionally argues in the Montague (2010) article that the amount of sport which has been broadcast live in England and other countries has greatly increased in recent years, creating more opportunities for consumers to be attracted to fantasy sport. With more live broadcasts, fans in England are able to follow more teams and see the range of players who are involved in a sport league. Additionally, the relatively recent increase in the supply (or access to) of broadband Internet in England (Chen, Tsai, & Tzeng, 2006) allows another channel of access for consumers to watch games/matches, as well as participate in fantasy sport. Thus, only in recent years have many sport fans been given access to a wide range of teams to view, and thus has in some sense changed the practice of viewership.

Outside of North America, fantasy sport has gained relatively widespread popularity in Europe when compared to the rest of the world. However, as has been noted in the discussion of betting laws and fantasy sport, there are still many countries within Europe that have established barriers which make participation in fantasy sport difficult for individual consumers, especially those who are not of legal gambling age. Billings and Ruihley (2013) note the gambling definitions are very important within Europe, and are found to be related to participation in fantasy sport in certain countries. Though soccer has been a natural place for fantasy sport to gain footholds in Europe because of the popularity the sport has across the continent, articles have noted that a wide variety of sports have been popular in a fantasy context, including baseball (Pfanner, 2004).

With the growing appeal of fantasy sport in Europe, there have been more organizations that have gotten involved in running and offering services to fans, with many organizations viewing leagues as great ways to promote and market their own brands. Thus, while major media outlets in North America have a tendency to offer the most popular leagues, there is a real mixture in Europe in regards to the belief of who should be in control of fantasy sport products and services (Pfanner, 2004). It also has been argued that there still exists a divide in the European sport market, with England representing one side of the equation that is heavily investing in the activity, and continental Europe considered to be less interested and developed in participating in fantasy sport. This divide is said to come because of a variety of factors, and is important to consider for the future of fantasy sport and its spread through Europe.

## ENGLAND

Fantasy sport made the jump to England in the early 1990s, where it was adapted to the game of football (soccer) in order to translate to the interests of fans in England and the rest of Europe. It is now estimated that around 10 percent of adults in the United Kingdom play fantasy sport, numbers which closely approximate fantasy sport use in North America (Werber, 2012). The flagship of the growth of fantasy sport in England, and much of the rest of Europe has been the English Premier League (EPL), the top flight of professional soccer in England. The EPL has been one of the most popular and viewed sport leagues/competitions in the world, and thus has been a natural place to build fantasy sport leagues. It is noted that because of the widespread appeal of the league, as well as the international composition of clubs in the league, that EPL fantasy leagues may be the most common type of league in the world. If one goes onto the respective Yahoo! websites for different countries, they are often able to find EPL fantasy leagues.

One of the leaders in fantasy sport in England has been the company *Fantasy League*, which offered a wide range of types of sport and leagues for users to be able to participate in. In 2012, Fantasy League was said to attract participants from ninety-nine countries in various fantasy competitions that it ran, the attraction most often being the EPL (Werber, 2012). In 2004, the number of individuals playing fantasy soccer in the UK was already over 1.5 million people, which led to intense competition between the leagues, media and other organizations involved in providing fantasy sport services to consumers (Pfanner, 2004). In 2004, the EPL demanded that they receive 7 percent of all fantasy related revenues in the country, as well as further control of publication and use of digital content created by papers. This came at a time when the newspapers in England were the ones who were predominantly in control of the fantasy soccer services for the EPL.

British newspapers not only helped to grow fantasy soccer in the country, they also were able to grow it into a larger part of their business, a practice which was similar to those used by digital media companies in the U.S. Not only did fantasy soccer serve as a way to increase readership and marketing of the brand of the newspapers, they also helped to adapt the papers to changes in consumer interest in fantasy sport and the EPL in England and beyond (Pfanner, 2004). The battle for control of fantasy revenues and digital content between the EPL and various media outlets reached such a height that there was even the threat that some newspapers would have their media credentials revoked for matches if an agreement was not put into place. As time progressed, eventually the EPL took charge of their ability to control fantasy sport by building their own fantasy soccer service to compete with all the other services provided by newspapers and broadcast media in the UK. These fantasy sport leagues run by media corporations have also been beneficial to them, as the organizations have allowed fans to join pay leagues, where the overall highest ranking winner are guaranteed large sums of prize money. In this manner, the newspapers and media have managed to use financial gains as a way to motivate fans to come to fantasy sport, rather than just put their income into sport gambling.

The fantasy sport market has continued to evolve in England and the rest of the UK Studies conducted in 2009 found that the number of individuals playing fantasy sport between the ages of 16 and 64 was above 5.5 million people (Fisher, 2009). Analysis of the UK market has shown that a significant number of the adult population is not just participating in fantasy sport leagues, but also show great interest in fantasy sport services and websites. When surveying the landscape of fantasy sport services that exist today, there are numerous organizations involved in offering leagues to fans, with a majority of them focused on soccer. More specifically, the major newspapers, sport leagues, and Internet/media providers in the country have built fantasy sport platforms, which not only continue to allow them to reach out and market to consumers, it also allows these organizations to boost their sales and value. However, it is still the case that organizations are still battling over who will be allowed to control fantasy sport products and platforms in England, with the professional leagues taking actions to try to regain more of a foothold in the realm of fantasy sport.

## FANTASY ON THE EUROPEAN CONTINENT

In Germany, fantasy sports started to grow at the time of the new millennium. Like in the UK professional soccer is the primary driving force of fantasy sport consumption. Specifically, the German Football Bundesliga attracts fantasy sports consumers to a variety of providers. Among these are, for example, Comunio, BILD Supermanager, Fußballmanager, Kicker, and also a platform from the German Football League (DFL). Similar to England, newspapers like BILD and Kicker provide opportunities to play fantasy sports to strengthen their position in the market. Probably the most prominent website for fantasy soccer is Comunio which was launched in 2000. It provides fantasy sports for several national leagues, the UEFA Champions League, Formula 1, and winter sports (e.g., alpine skiing, ski jumping, biathlon). Participation in fantasy sports is free, but fees may apply for users who desire extra content. The scarcity of academic literature about fantasy sports in Germany is surprising given the wide array of studies that have been conducted on professional soccer and specifically on the German Football Bundesliga. This lack of literature probably can be traced to a lack of reliable data on fantasy sport participation within Germany, as well as the relatively recent emergence of the activity in continental Europe.

Outside of the UK and Germany, the participation in fantasy sport has been rather mixed on the European continent. Like England and Germany, the big driving force in fantasy sport participation has been through soccer. While fantasy EPL leagues are popular across the continent, it is often the domestic and pan-continental competitions which bring fan interest to the sport product. In this, interest in fantasy sport in Europe thus revolves around competitions such as the UEFA Champions League or Europa League competitions. However, because these competitions limit the number of teams which are able to enter from each country, it is often the case that individuals are not able to pick their own local/favorite club teams. Thus, while the competition holds general interest and may get more individuals interested in watching large sporting events, there is lost potential for smaller domestic leagues throughout Europe. It is the case that fantasy sport leagues do exist for sports outside of soccer, such as European basketball, however they also fall into a similar situation as soccer, where the large pan-continental championships garner the most attention from fans and media.

As previously noted, fantasy sport has varying levels of governance and local laws placed upon it across Europe because of how gambling and related activities are governed. Because of this regulation, it is often difficult for leagues, media corporations, and other interested parties to start up fantasy sport leagues because of a large number of barriers which exist. Thus, in some cases the only form of fantasy sport can be found in "pick-em" games where individuals have to try to pick the winners of matches in a week. In many cases, this style of game may be popular, but do not hold high interest, and are often ancillary side products or services. For example, on the German television channel Deutsche Welle (DW) there is a soccer focused program called *Kick Off*. During the soccer season, this program has a weekly "pick the results" contest that viewers can play in, with one weekly winner having their name announced on air, and a seasonal winner getting the chance to be flown to Germany to watch a Bundesliga match.

Thus, it is the case in the European market that fantasy sport competitions also are sometimes run as sweepstakes or prize drawing competitions, with winners getting the chance to be drawn for a prize. In this manner, while it does generate interest, it does not necessarily drive fans to try to spend numerous hours consuming fantasy sport products. It may be because of this climate and general lack of large scale fantasy sport products that has caused the general lack of fantasy sport research in Europe. As prior noted, Germany has received a lot of attention in sport research, but has not received any attention in the examination of fantasy sport behavior, motivations, or consumption. Therefore, it is of no surprise that the rest of Europe has also received a similar level of attention when analyzing fantasy sport products and consumers. Thus, this paucity of research in Europe could present a new frontier for researchers, especially those who may be interested in examining fantasy sport leagues as they develop and are created in new markets.

## FANTASY SPORT IN ASIA

Possibly one of the toughest markets for fantasy sport has been Asia, where there are a number of constraints to participation throughout the region. Furthermore, the wide expansiveness of Asia also means that there are a range of consumer demographics and types of sport which are of interest to fan bases. The size and demographic differences which exist in Asia is both a constraint and opportunity at the same time. On the one hand, the Asian market, if properly managed, could be the biggest source of fantasy sport participation in the world. However, the size of the continent also means that being able to meet the demands of various consumer groups is very difficult. There also are economic imbalances between the wealth and purchasing power of nations/individuals throughout Asia, so it is often difficult to discuss sport fans specifically in the context of the entire continent. Because of these conditions, focus will be placed more on the East Asian countries of China and Japan. These countries are closely examined for multiple reasons: First, they all have a number of professional sport leagues which could potentially draw interest from large fan groups both domestically and internationally. Second, the market for professional sport is more established in these countries, with many of the leagues existing for several decades, including the Nippon Professional Baseball (NPB) league which has organized professional baseball in Japan for over sixty years. Finally, East Asia is an ideal choice because of the nature and type of sport which is played in the region. Though soccer is popular throughout the entire continent, East Asia has numerous professional baseball and basketball leagues. Thus, there are professional sport leagues in the region which are associated with sport that are more common in the fantasy sport market in North America.

## JAPAN

Fantasy sport is literally called *fantasy sport* in Japanese, with the word written in the katakana characters emphasizing that it is a foreign word (ファンタジースポーツ). The existence of fantasy sport in Asia can be traced back to 1995, when the company *Fantasy Sports Japan* was started. *Fantasy Sports Japan* (FSJ) is not only the oldest fantasy sport company within Japan, but also is the biggest (Fantasy Sports Japan, 2014). The company was able to partner with American fantasy sport corporation CDM Inc. to get access to the practices and technology used to deliver the best fantasy sport experiences. From this, FSJ offers over ten different fantasy sport leagues which individuals can play in, including baseball, American football, basketball, and ice hockey. Notably, the FSJ fantasy sports system is almost specifically focused on North American sport leagues, with the Japanese professional baseball league being one of the few domestic sport competitions in which fans are able to participate. FSJ is seen as the leader in fantasy sports in Japan, including in the development of websites and mobile version of fantasy sport for fans to use.

While FSJ has enjoyed some success in the fantasy sports market within Japan, there have been numerous other companies and media organizations which have also tried to get involved, mostly with limited success. Japanese media giant *Sports Nabi* joined in the world of fantasy sports in 2001 with a special fantasy baseball service. However, they found that despite the popularity of baseball, there was little interest in their product, and shut it down by the end of 2003. The lack of interest could potentially be traced to the fact that *Sports Nabi* did not use its resources in promoting the game to fans, and also did not have very much information introducing the concept of fantasy sport to the common consumer of sport media in Japan. Other companies also started privately operated fantasy sports companies in Japan like *Sports J*, which targeted mobile devices with a service called *Total Victory Baseball* through which individuals could play only fantasy baseball. *Sports J* was not successful, and they only were able to run the service from 2004 through the end of the NPB season in 2007.

Fantasy sport has gone through many attempts at bringing innovation to draw in new individuals in Japan, especially through the use of technology and mobile devices. There also was an attempt to get younger demographics interested in fantasy baseball by having an online game which used tradable cards for players which were drafted by participants. This idea has been somewhat successful, and has rebranded into a game called *Dream Baseball* which is still in existence today. While the game maintains some popularity among certain groups, the question exists as to whether fantasy sports can thrive in the Japanese marketplace.

In 1996, FSJ began their own version of MLB fantasy sports for fans to participate in Japanese. They were challenged in 2008 by the *Dream Stadium* Corporation who partnered with sport statistics companies in the U.S. to try to provide a more enhanced version of fantasy sport for fans online. Despite a successful initial launch of the *Dream Stadium* MLB fantasy league, the company was never able to get the product out of its beta testing stages, and was closed down after only one full season of operation. Thus, while the FSJ fantasy sport site exists, it is said there are no true fantasy sport sites that fans can use with online platforms similar to those found within North America.

In reality, fantasy sports is still rather non-existent within Japan, with FSJ the only organization which has been able to continuously operate a fantasy sports organization for several years in a row in Japanese. Outside of FSJ, the only chance for Japanese consumers to play fantasy sports is through accessing websites from the U.S. and other countries which offer fantasy sports in English or German. Thus, it is the case that there has been very little opportunity for consumers and sport fans in Japan to be fully exposed to the concept of fantasy sports. This lack of participation in fantasy sport in Japan can probably be traced to a variety of issues, especially considering the nature of media corporations in the country. While many websites and television companies cover sports, organizations like the Yomiuri Corporation (which is one of the largest television and newspaper corporations in Japan) have a stronghold over a large number of professional sporting events.

As the primary sporting events are either broadcast through the national NHK channels or Yomiuri, it is the case that these media groups do not offer fantasy sport leagues, and thus do not advertise them. Because of these conditions, it is often difficult for the common sport consumer in Japan to be able to learn about sport leagues, unless they are reading/watching information from secondary media sources. Additionally, as the fantasy sport media platforms used in Japan are not as advanced as those created and maintained by Yahoo!, ESPN, and other media groups in North America, it is the case that the fantasy sport services which are available are not very attractive to individuals. Thus, it is a mixture of media control over sport products/brands, a lack of user-friendliness, and general low-level of knowledge/interest which seems to contribute to low fantasy sport participation in Japan.

Another large issue which revolves around the growth of fantasy sports in Japan is the fact that even the most popular platforms are predominantly focused on sport leagues in North America. Outside of FSJ, the most successful organization in fantasy sports in Japan has been Yahoo! Japan's inclusion of fantasy NBA starting in 1996, as well as fantasy soccer in 2003. While the fantasy NBA continues to be somewhat successful, fantasy soccer was shut down in 2009, and had to be rebuilt and rebranded in their new *Fantasy Sakka* (literally fantasy soccer) system in 2011. As Yahoo! Japan has had more success in building fantasy products, they have moved forward toward trying to bring more fantasy content focused toward the Japanese consumer, including a new version of fantasy baseball focused on the NPB which began in 2013.

As with many countries, one of the large barriers which exist in getting fans to participate in fantasy sports in Japan is the wide availability and acceptance of sports wagering in the country. This barrier is not necessarily the case that the sport wagering systems are forcing fantasy sport out of the market, but rather that sport leagues directly promote the betting/lottery systems, but not fantasy sport participation. Thus, from the perspective of the consumer, the betting/lottery systems are seen as being directly linked to the sport league, while fantasy sport is a secondary activity that is not officially sanctioned by sport leagues. As the J-League, the country's professional soccer league, is one of the most popular sport leagues, it is curious that there have been no real attempts to build a fantasy sport system around the league. While professional baseball has enjoyed attention and success from several fantasy sport organizations, the J-League has been relatively ignored in regards to any type of fantasy sport. This also could be because of the different status that has been given to soccer in Japanese laws focused on sports betting.

In 1998, the Japanese government legalized gambling in the form of lotteries on soccer, with horse racing, powerboat racing, cycling and motorcycle racing the other sports which the country has allowed individuals to place wagers on in a legal manner (Asiabet, 2014). Wagering in Japan is done through a special lottery system which is branded as *Toto*, and has many forms which allows fans to pick the winners of the matches in a week, with having a proper number of picks allowing individuals to win large cash prizes. *Toto* launched in 2001 and is administered by a branch of the Japanese government known as the National Agency for Advancement of Sports and Health (Brasor & Tsukubu, 2010). Early forms of *Toto* allowed individuals to pick a series of outcomes for the matches, however this changed in 2006 when all picks were changed to an automated computer picking format. In this, *Toto* moved away from simply being a gambling wager system toward being a true lottery where individuals were only able to get tickets which were randomly generated by a computer. While the odds of winning are adjusted from one year to the next, *Toto* has continued to be a popular way for individuals to get involved with wagering in the context of soccer in Japan.

The *Toto* system is considered a beneficial gambling and lottery system in Japan, the profits of which go to the promotion and enhancement of sports and health across the country. However, from the standpoint of consumer interaction with sport matches, *Toto* is generally the only form of fantasy or gambling participation which exists in what is now the most expansive sport league in Japan. Clearly there is room for fantasy sport growth in Japan in regards to products which could be developed for popular sport leagues. The question remains as to whether fantasy sport would hold enough interest for consumers in Japan to be able to maintain a large market with several corporations and media organizations all involved. Though Japan has the financial resources and consumer purchasing power to maintain a healthy fantasy sport market, the relatively smaller population of the country and presence of betting and sport lotteries potentially causes competition over consumer dollars. The evidence displays that several fantasy sport corporations and mass media organizations have failed in being able to bring more fantasy sport products to the Japanese market. Thus, it remains to be asked as to whether the fantasy sport industry has reached its peak in Japan, or has there not been enough innovation and development of products to hold fan interest?

## CHINA

The formal introduction of fantasy sport into China has been a recent event, with the first licensed fantasy sport website and leagues in China formed in 2009 (Hotbox Sports, 2009). The development of fantasy sports, known as *FanTeXi* (范特西体育)—literally *fantasy sports*, was created through a partnership with Chinese company FTXSports (an acronym of FanTeXi) and American company Hotbox Sports (Hotbox Sports, 2009). Prior to the formation of this partnership, there was no officially licensed fantasy sport product in China, with sites running the sport either being unlicensed, or small scale operations. Additionally, Chinese consumers had the options to play fantasy sport on Western-based websites which were not blocked. Generally, fantasy sport sites have not been blocked because of the activity itself, but more often because of the ability to access information that is not considered acceptable by the central government. That is, it would seem that the Chinese government does not have a defined stance for or against fantasy sport, especially considering that new fantasy sport sites are beginning to take root in China in recent years. However, FTXSports and Hotbox were the first organizations on the market to provide a true fantasy sport platform and website that individuals could play in the Chinese language.

Currently, FTX sports runs a number of fantasy sports leagues, including National Basketball Association (NBA), soccer, as well as other games for consumers to play in that are not related to fantasy sport. In this, while the licensed NBA and soccer games that FTX has managed to run in the Chinese language on its website are of great importance, the company has also sought other products of interest to draw in consumers from a wide range of backgrounds. The sport sections of the website are predominantly in line with the sport consumer interests of China, with the two most popular and watched sports of soccer and basketball being the main product lines for FTX. In the early days of the launch of the FTXSports website, there was over 50,000 individuals in China who were registered to play in NBA fantasy leagues (Mullman, 2009). The website has shown that it appeals to various groups of Chinese sport consumers, however there has yet to be any publicly released information as to how quickly the FTX website has grown.

Like other countries, while FTX has managed to be the first mover, there have been other organizations which have also tried to enter the Chinese fantasy sport market. Probably the biggest competitor for FTX is the Chinese mass media corporation known as Sina Corporation. Sina Corporation runs four main products, Sina Mobile, Sina Online, Sina.net and Sina

Weibo. Weibo is a Chinese microblogging site similar to Twitter in the West, and is considered one of the most popular forms of communication in the world. Weibo is said to have over 100 million messages posted a day, and over half a billion registered users and growing (Ong, 2013). Through this, Sina Corporation has managed to start its own fantasy sport service focused around basketball, and has launched it through its Sina Online website, with marketing for the game also done through Weibo and its other media sites. Sina Corporation has not released the numbers of players which are registered or active in their fantasy sport leagues.

The Chinese market for fantasy sports is one that may have the largest potential moving into the future, especially when paired with growing population, wealth, and Internet/digital access, as well as the large market for sport products in the country. For example, the NBA's Chinese website registered over 4.5 billion page views in 2013, a 34 percent increase over 2012's numbers (Leavenworth, 2014). However, at the same time the companies and mass media organizations involved in fantasy sport in the country have never fully released any of their numbers, making it very hard to gauge the size and value of the Chinese fantasy market. At the same time, considering the total value of both legal and illegal betting in the country, it is clear that there is room for fantasy sport to grow, but that there is also conflict with the gambling and national lottery market. As fantasy sport leagues usually have no payout in China for winning, the ability to receive economic gains from participation is small when compared to the gambling industry.

## GAMBLING VS. FANTASY SPORT

In North America, the Fantasy Sports Trade Association (FSTA) has been adamant that participation in fantasy sport is not a form of gambling. The reasoning behind this statement probably relates to the stigmatization that goes along with gambling, as well as laws against sport gambling in many of the states within America. The gaming (gambling) industry around the world is probably the biggest competitor with the fantasy sport industry, as both gaming and fantasy sport require time and/or money from participants. Fantasy sport leagues often can be seen as approximating gambling in many situations, especially when individuals participate in pay leagues where individuals are required to pay entry fees to play. The United States has always been very careful in making the distinction between what is gambling and what is fantasy sport. This is evident even in the passing of national laws, such as the Unlawful Internet Gambling Enforcement Act of 2006 which was put into effect to stop individuals in the U.S. from illegally gambling online. Within the act, there is specific discourse which notes that fantasy sport is not the same as gambling, and that fantasy sport, horse racing, and special lotteries are not considered to be covered by this law. Notably, chapter 13 of the current volume offers a detailed primer of fantasy sports law.

So why is it so important to draw a distinction between gambling and fantasy sport? Not only is the difference crucial in regards to how fantasy sport is considered from a legal standpoint in North America, but it also has ramifications for the acceptance of the sport across the world. For example, in some European countries like Spain, legal definitions of fantasy sport do not separate the practice as markedly from gambling as is done in North America. Thus, there are more restrictions and potential stigmatizations placed on participation in fantasy sport in some countries. At the same time, an IPSOS research survey conducted on fantasy sport found that a large number of people who play fantasy sport did so without exchanging any monetary funds (FTSA, 2014). The FTSA thus argues very strongly that fantasy sport is not only different from gambling, but they also note that the practice of, participation in, and meanings of fantasy sport are different from gambling. A similar distinction can also be found in the research literature, and how it has generally approached both fantasy sport and gambling/gaming.

It is worth noting that there are some areas where there is overlap between gambling and fantasy sport participation. Not only do both have extensions into the realm of sport, but they may also get individuals to be more focused on certain sporting events because of the potential for either a payoff (for gamblers) or a win (for fantasy sport participants). Also, because of pay leagues that have cash prizes or fantasy sport websites like FanDuel. com, there has been a growing market for fantasy sport competitions which provide the chance of monetary gains from good performances. As more sites and leagues provide the potential for individuals to gain money from playing and participating, it is possible that the fine line between gambling and fantasy sport could be crossed. However, it is important to note, and is highlighted by the FSTA, that no fantasy sport company has ever been prosecuted for gambling charges in North America. Because many sport leagues place a high stigmatization on gambling, it is also vital for fantasy sport organizations to distance themselves from these practices so that they may be able to operate with less restrictions and negative publicity.

Considering the interrelated nature between the fantasy sport and gambling industries, it is important to examine the connection between these two leisure activities. While gambling has a long history, fantasy sport can be considered to be a relatively new activity which is still in development. It is exactly this evolving nature of fantasy sport that makes it so that the participation in leagues may differ greatly depending on the region of the world an individual lives in. As fantasy sport is poised to continue growing, there will also be a need for organizations involved in the activity to understand the importance of the global market. For example, the NBA has been strongly pushing its brand to an international market, especially Europe and China. In China, sport gambling is very popular, though the practice is made illegal by national laws.

However, the use of the Internet to place wagers on sporting contests is something which is constantly ongoing, with over a billion U.S. dollars thought to be wagered through illegal means in the country (Eimer, 2010). The total amount wagered on illegal sites is argued to be bigger than the economic output of Beijing, and another $1.6 billion U.S. dollars were expected to be legally bet online through special lotteries and gambling sites during the 2014 FIFA World Cup (China's betting laws, 2014). With the NBA working to develop its brand and fan engagement with their league and players, fantasy sport becomes one venue through which they can accomplish this goal. However, because fantasy sport has not been as fully adopted in other regions, it can be more difficult and face many constraints in trying to provide fans with a fantasy sport service. Thus, it is crucial for academics, practitioners, leagues, fantasy sport organizations, and other stakeholders to continue to study the importance of fantasy sport, as well as understand its development and positioning in the global sport market.

## CONCLUSION

Considering the regions and countries which have been discussed within this chapter, it is evident that fantasy sport is still poised to continue growing in many regions of the world. This growth potential is coupled from large populations starting to gain more access to computers and mobile devices which allow access to fantasy sport, as well as the relative lack of development of quality fantasy sport products in some areas. In this, it would be safe to say that fantasy sport will continue to grow and emerge around the globe; however this does not mean that there are not important issues which must be considered along with this process. The continued growth of leagues has the potential to bring more profits to fantasy sport operators, marketers, sport leagues/teams/players, media companies, and other stakeholders in the industry. At the same time, because of the prospective for growth, there is also the possibility that there will be more new and emerging fantasy products which could appear around the world. With the Internet potentially minimizing traditional barriers for access such as access and proximity to other participants, it may be that rival fantasy sport organizations in other countries could reduce the market share of existing powers. Furthermore, as fantasy sport continues its growth in terms of users, fees, and revenues, there is the potential that more countries will begin considering how to approach the governance of fantasy sport leagues and organizations from a policy perspective.

## EMERGING MARKETS AND THE FUTURE

For there to be continued growth in the fantasy sports industry, one of the key components will be to be able to grow participation numbers in emerging markets around the world. As noted, the English Premier League fantasy sports leagues have around 100 different countries which users participate from, a number which is bound to go up as the league expands its international brand and profile. However, this does not mean that fantasy sport has fully moved into many of the new and emerging markets around the world. Specifically, the growth of popularity and wealth in the Middle East has been an important target for the English Premier League (EPL) to continue developing their brand, including fantasy sport products (Fisher, 2009). With more EPL teams getting investment from Asia and the Middle East, it may be the case that there may also be more interest in fantasy sport leagues based on the EPL, as well as these markets understanding the importance fantasy has had for media companies.

China is naturally part of the discussion of emerging markets as well. This chapter discussed the development of fantasy sport within China, and how there is still a lot of competition with online gambling, as well as other types of online games. When considering that China has announced a national policy in 2014 focused on investing around $500 million US into the sports, recreation, and health industries in the country, there is clearly a lot of room for the growth of sport and related products (Goddard, 2014). As this national policy considers the importance of bringing foreign investment into the Chinese sport industry, media and fantasy sport stakeholders may want to consider the potential for building a bigger and more user friendly fantasy sport platforms. Not only would this provide stakeholders the chance to further break into the Asian market, which has been dominated by gambling, but it may also provide a way to provide more internationalization of existing fantasy sport services. In this manner, fantasy sport may provide a conduit through which to extend sports which are not common to China and other regions, and develop new consumer interest in both sport and fantasy related products.

Another important emerging market exists around the globe, and that is those countries and consumers with high interest in the game of cricket. Countries interested in cricket range from England, with a large existing fantasy sport market, to India, which has a large population and high consumer interest in the sport. Though fantasy cricket already exists and is played around the world, there is still great potential for the sport to be further marketed through fantasy sport services. Worldwide, cricket is said to have over one billion viewers, and the top league is the Indian Premier League (IPL), an organization which has strong financial backing for both players and teams (Humphreys & Watanabe, 2011). With broadband/Internet penetration continuing to grow through the world, it is believed that development of fantasy cricket, especially leagues focused on international test matches and the IPL, could be the next big thing in the global fantasy sport market. Thus, emerging markets present an opportunity to a large number of corporations, media outlets, and stakeholders that are seeking to grow and profit from the development of fantasy sport.

Exactly because of the high value that fantasy sport has, as well as the potential for it to be used for financial gains by a variety of organizations, the key question of organizational control of fantasy sport has risen to the forefront. While many of the media based fantasy sport leagues have created a strong foothold within the current market, many professional sport leagues are actively developing their own fantasy sport products to try to take back some of this control. Specifically, one can see organizations like the National Football League, the English Premier League, and even large governing bodies like FIFA and UEFA (which govern world and European football, respectively) creating fantasy leagues based around their competitions. Considering the wide reach that sporting events like the World Cup and Champions League have across the globe, the ability to control these brands in all facets, including fantasy sport, is important for organizations to be able to protect their brands and investment in these products. Thus, the trend of organizations trying to take more control of fantasy based sport products and services may continue to grow.

Considering the discussion in this chapter, it is evident that the growth of fantasy sport has been valuable to a large number of stakeholders worldwide. The number of participants, value of the industry, and its market share continue to grow in many countries, and remains poised to have rapid growth in a large number of markets. At the same time, there are still a lot of constraints and potential legal issues which could hamper the growth of fantasy sport, unless there is proper foresight and planning when dealing with these problems. Fantasy sport is not just a way to make money for organizations, but also a way to help market and enhance their brand. The growth of fantasy sport leagues across the globe coupled with increased access to broadband/high-speed Internet may also help to create linkage between different countries. Furthermore, as fantasy sport can help to develop further fan interest and involvement with sport competitions, there is a need for the management of products and services to continue to evolve to the wants and needs of consumers around the world.

## REFERENCES

Asiabet (2014). Betting in Japan. *AsiaBet*. Retrieved from: http://www.asiabet.org/japan/

Brasor, P., & Tsukubu, M. (2010, February 25). Soccer lottery BIG in Japan. *The Japan Times Blog*. Retrieved from: http://blog.japantimes.co.jp/yen-for-living/soccer-lottery-big-in-japan/

Billings, A. C., & Ruihley, B. J. (2013). *The Fantasy Sport Industry: Games within Games*. New York: Routledge.

Chen, W., & Wellman, B. (2004). The global digital divide–within and between countries. *IT & Society, 1*(7), 39–45.

Eimer, D. (2010, January 9). China's secret gambling problem. *The Telegraph*. Retrieved from: http://www.telegraph.co.uk/news/worldnews/asia/china/6942975/Chinas-secret-gambling-problem.html

Fantasy Trade Sports Association (2014). Industry Demographics. Retrieved from: http://www.fsta.org/?page=Demographics

Fisher, E. (2009, September 21). Fantasy players seen as big spenders in key consumer categories. *Sports Business Journal*. Retrieved from: http://www.sportsbusinessdaily.com/Daily/Issues/2009/09/Issue-6/Sponsorships-Advertising-Marketing/Fantasy-Players-Seen-As-Big-Spenders-In-Key-Consumer-Categories.aspx

Gerrard, B., & Howard, D. (2007). Is the Moneyball approach transferable to complex invasion team sports? *International Journal of Sport Finance, 2*(4), 214–230.

Goddard, E. (2014, October 20). China reveals multi-billion dollar investment plan for sport. *Inside the Games*. Retrieved from: http://www.insidethegames.biz/news/1023349-china-reveals-multi-billion-dollar-investment-plan-for-sport

Hotbox Sports. (2009, November, 17). Hotbox sports goes global. *Hotbox Sports*. Retrieved from: http://www.prweb.com/releases/2009/11/prweb3216814.htm

Humphreys, B. R., & Watanabe, N. M. (2011). Business and Finance of International Sport. In *International Sport Management* (Eds.) Ming Li, Eric Macintosh, and Gonzalo Bravo. Champaign, IL: Human Kinetics.

Leavenworth, S. (2014, October 12). NBA presses ahead with China expansion— and looks to India. *McClatchyDC*. Retrieved From: http://www.mcclatchydc .com/2014/10/12/243103/nba-presses-ahead-with-china-expansion.html

Montague, J. (2010, January 20). The rise and rise of fantasy sports. *CNN.com*. Retrieved from: http://www.cnn.com/2010/SPORT/football/01/06/fantasy.football. moneyball.sabermetrics/

Mullman, J. (2009, November 4). Hotbox hopes to turn fantasy sports into real profits. *Ad Age*. Retrieved from: http://adage.com/china/article/china-news/ hotbox-hopes-to-turn-fantasy-sports-into-real-profits/140292/

Ong, J. (2013, February 21). China's Sina Weibo grew 3 percent in 2012, passing 500 million registered accounts. *The Next Web*. Retrieved from: http://thenext web.com/asia/2013/02/21/chinas-sina-weibo-grew-73-in-2012-passing-500-mil lion-registered-accounts/

Spinda, J. S., Wann, D. L., & Sollitto, M. (2012). Cards, Dice, and Male Bonding: A Case Study Examination of Strat-O-Matic Baseball Motives. *International Journal of Sport Communication*, 5(2), 246–264.

Tsai, H. C., Chen, C. M., & Tzeng, G. H. (2006). The comparative productivity efficiency for global telecoms. *International Journal of Production Economics*, 103(2), 509–526.

Werber, C. (2012, October 16). Fantasy sports finds 'real' foreign markets. *Market Watch*. Retrieved from: http://www.marketwatch.com/story/fantasy-sports-finds -real-foreign-markets-2012-10-16

# FANS AND FANDOM

# "I WOULDN'T PICK THEM TO SAVE MY SEASON"

## The Impact of Rivalry on Fantasy Football

*John S. W. Spinda and Cody Havard*

**R**ivalry plays an important part in fan consumption of sport. It allows a fan to cheer for, and sometimes against teams, it can add to the excitement of watching a favorite team play, and even play a role in a person deciding how they want to consume their favorite team. With the popularity of fantasy sports growing (see chapter 1 of this volume), fantasy owners are often faced with difficult decisions on which players they want to fill their rosters. This chapter discusses the impact that rivalry can play on fantasy owners and their decision-making as it pertains to choosing players for their teams.

It is important to understand how rivalry impacts fantasy sport because the phenomenon can affect individual teams and leagues through understanding how rivalry impacts the strategic decisions owners make. For example, fantasy football represents an additional way for fans to consume the game while allowing them to make decisions they believe will lead to their competitive success. In order for fantasy football owners to be successful, they must draft the best players available, and in doing so, are faced with decisions on which players to pick and play throughout the season. When a fantasy owner is an avid fan of a team, he or she is faced with the additional pressure of showing favoritism toward a player from a rival team. In some instances, fantasy football owners may even choose to watch the players on their fantasy team play rather than their identified favorite team (Dwyer & LeCrom, 2013), even as they report high levels of attitudinal loyalty toward their favorite team (Dwyer, 2011). Because the identification they have with a favorite team, owners are faced with competing loyalties and have to find ways to cope with their decisions regarding which team (fantasy or favorite) and which players (from favorite team or from opposing/rival teams) to consume more. Further, other owners in the same fantasy league can use the internal struggle of drafting and playing rival players (whether from favorite NFL or intercollegiate teams) to try to persuade others from drafting the best players available.

When it comes draft time, fantasy owners find themselves culling over a plethora of information trying to choose the best player to fill their rosters. How productive will this player be this year? How productive was the player last year? Is the player hurt this season or has the player suffered a past injury that I should be worried about? Is the player too old, too young, or too inexperienced? Surely, many fantasy owners can empathize with those that have picked players involved in off-the-field trouble and kept them from competing for an extended period of time. Another decision that comes up for some fantasy owners is whether or not to draft players from rival teams. Fantasy owners are faced with difficult decisions when they find "the perfect player" only to find that they play for the rival team or maybe played for a rival school in college—Bowman, McCabe, and Isaacson (2012) reported similar struggles among Major League Baseball (MLB) fantasy players. When faced with whether or not to draft a rival player for their team or to choose a rival player for their lineup, it stands to reason that fantasy owners—and particularly fans that are highly identified with a favorite team—should experience internal conflict about this choice. Such a decision calls into question two competing tensions: (1) their loyalty and level of identification with a favorite team or (2) their desire to win as a fantasy owner. This decision becomes a more complicated one if the fantasy owner(s) are interacting with or have existing relationships with others in the league, as they may worry about their self-presentation and how the group perceives it. We will begin by discussing the current body of literature about rivalry in sport and how it interfaces with fantasy sports literature, moving on to the study conducted to test our research questions.

## WHAT THE RESEARCH SUGGESTS

To see how rivalry can impact decisions made regarding fantasy sport, we need to first look at rivalry. Havard, Gray, Gould, Sharp, and Schaffer (2013) define rivalry as "a fluctuating adversarial relationship existing between two teams, players, or groups of fans, gaining significance through on-field competition, on-field or off-field incidents, proximity, demographic makeup, and/or historical occurrence(s)" (p. 51). Further, Kilduff, Elfenbein, and Staw (2010) identified proximity and close historical competition as antecedents leading to the phenomenon, and recently, competition for personnel and perceived unfairness were identified as recurring events surrounding a rivalry (Tyler & Cobbs, 2015). In researching conference realignment in intercollegiate athletics, Havard and Eddy (2013) found fans have a fundamental need for rivalry.

The basis of rivalry in sport can be traced to the German term *schadenfruede*, which states that someone will rejoice in the demise of another person (Heider, 1958). Schadenfruede has been researched in professional and collegiate sport. Major League Baseball (MLB) fans responded positively to the failure of their rival team against a neutral third team (Cikara, Botvinick, & Fiske, 2012). Additionally, Cikara and Fiske (2012) found that the stereotypes people have of others, and the amount of envy toward others, can impact the amount of schadenfruede experienced. In sport, this means that the greater sense of rivalry a fan has, the more schadenfruede he or she will experience when the rival loses to a neutral team. Further, when fans of international soccer were presented with a defeat at the hands of a second party, they experienced schadenfreude when the second party and third neutral party were defeated (Leach & Spears, 2009). Further, the amount of envy and threat posed to the in-group impacted the pleasure German soccer fans experienced when a rival team lost in indirect competition (Leach, Spears, Branscombe, & Doosje, 2003). This means that after a loss, fans experienced joy when the team that beat them lost, along with a third team (rival that did not play favorite team) lost.

Extending schadenfreude, Disposition of Mirth explains that someone will rejoice when someone they dislike fails and experience sadness when the same person experiences success (Zillmann & Cantor, 1976). Applying mirth to a sport fandom context, the *disposition theory of sports spectatorship* (Zillmann, Bryant, & Sapolsky, 1989) implied that fans will cheer for the success of their favorite team and failure of their rival team in direct competitive situations; experiencing distress when defeated by a highly disliked opponent (rival) and euphoria when defeating a rival. At the intercollegiate level, schadenfreude has helped explain fan behavior and reaction to the failure of a rival team. In particular, Havard (2014) recently extended schadenfreude and the disposition theory of sports spectatorship by describing *Glory out of Reflected Failure* (GORFing), which is the enjoyment a fan gets when a rival team is defeated by someone other than their favorite team.

Additionally, the Sport Rivalry Fan Perception Scale (*SRFPS*; Havard et al., 2013) was developed and validated to measure four aspects of a rivalry: (1) *out-group indirect competition* (likelihood a fan will support rivals in competition versus other teams); (2) *out-group academic prestige* (amount of respect that a fan has for the prestige of a rival team and its fans); (3) *out-group sportsmanship* (perceptions of sportsmanship amongst rival fans); and the *sense of satisfaction* (satisfaction gained when a favorite team defeats that favorite team's rival). The SRPFS also was developed to provide an in-depth view of the animosity fans feel toward a rival team and has been used to test for fan group differences regarding favorite team identification (Wann et al., in press), favorite team sport consumption (Havard, Reams, & Gray, 2013; Havard, Shapiro, & Ridinger, 2015), and conference affiliation (Havard, in press; Havard & Reams; in press). Further, during the latest version of conference realignment, the measure was used to illustrate that fans displayed more animosity toward rival teams in the conference they were leaving than the one they were joining (Havard, Wann, & Ryan, 2013).

Beyond the perceptions of rivalry that may influence fantasy football decisions, *team identification*, or the level to which fans feel a psychological connection to a favorite sports team (Wann & Branscombe, 1993), may also influence how fantasy owners view decision-making. Highly identified fans are more likely to experience stronger feelings of dislike toward rivals because they view their associations with favorite sports teams as a salient social identity, as described by both social identity theory (*SIT;* Tajfel & Turner, 1979), and later by self-categorization theory (*SCT;* Turner, Hogg, Oakes, Reicher, & Wetherell, 1987). In SIT, the main motivation for fans is a self-enhancement, or making social comparisons that favor themselves (or the in-group) over those in the out-group. On the other hand, SCT implies that fans are motivated to self-categorize, where the group (team) identity overrides individual (fan) identity. Recent studies have concluded that when a social identity is made salient, such as team identification, self-enhancement motivations are overridden by self-categorization motivations (Reid & Hogg, 2005; Reid, Byrne, Brundidge, Shoham, & Marlow, 2007; Spinda, 2012; Zhang, 2010).

Behaviors associated with high levels of team identification have been illustrated in multiple studies, which have found that highly identified fans use positive traits when describing other fans of their favorite team, while using more negative terms in describing fans of rival teams (Franco & Maass, 1996; Wann & Branscombe, 1993), evaluate player performance differently based on whether a prospective athlete is believed to be a joining favorite team or a rival team (Wann, Koch, Knoth, Aljubaily, & Lantz,

2006), are less willing to offer assistance to others wearing rival team apparel (Levine, Prosser, Evans, & Reicher, 2005), and explain fan behavior of the favorite team as more acceptable than the rival team (Lalonde, 1992; Lalonde, Moghaddam, & Taylor, 2001). Taken together, this evidence suggests that a highly identified fan uses self-categorization to guide their perceptions and behaviors in a competitive situation, such as a rivalry. Or, as Duck, Hogg, and Terry (1999) noted: "'I' becomes 'we,' and 'me vs. you' becomes 'us vs. them'" (p. 1881).

Therefore, we might anticipate that higher levels of team identification would lead to more schadenfreude regarding the misery of rival teams, and would likely lead to highly identified fans being more reluctant to draft/utilize players for fantasy football from rival NFL teams. However, it is unclear at this point whether or not the self-categorization that is associated with highly identified fans simply overrides the desire to field the most competitive fantasy football team possible, which may include drafting players from rival teams. More specifically, Lee, Ruihley, Brown, and Billings (2013) found a nearly equal likelihood of a fantasy owner of drafting a player from a favorite NFL team (47.7 percent indicated they were likely to do so) versus drafting a player from a rival team (47.5 percent indicated they were likely to do so). In fact, fantasy football owners in our analysis reported being more *unlikely* to draft a player from a favorite NFL team (28.8%) than from a rival team (23.4%). Moreover, while an overall majority of fans in their sample preferred a win by their favorite NFL team over a win from their fantasy football team(s), many respondents noted the opposite, preferring a win for their fantasy team over their favorite NFL team. Next, Lee et al. (2013) indicated fans that preferred a favorite NFL team victory tended to root for winning NFL teams, and had significantly higher levels of NFL team identification, team loyalty, and overall NFL fandom.

In sum, this existing research suggests that the decision fantasy owners face regarding the drafting and playing of athletes from rival teams may be primarily impacted by three main factors: (1) the influence of perceptions associated with a rivalry and with rival teams; (2) the level of team identification a fantasy owner has regarding their favorite NFL team; and (3) the level of team identification a fantasy owner has regarding their fantasy football team(s). This leads us to the following research questions:

RQ1: How does rivalry perception impact selecting fantasy football athletes from rival teams?

RQ2: How does favorite NFL team ID impact selecting fantasy football athletes from rival teams?

RQ3: Will fantasy football owners indicate higher levels of identification with their favorite NFL teams or fantasy football teams?

## INVESTIGATING RIVALRY AND FANTASY FOOTBALL

### Sample

To address the research questions above, we recruited participants ($N$ = 123) via social media as well as online message boards and websites pertaining to professional football ($M_{age}$ = 33.02, $SD_{age}$ = 10.87, age range 18–87). In this sample, 88 percent of participants reported being male, while 11 percent of participants were female. Also, 1 percent of respondents declined to report sex. In this online survey, participants were prompted to choose the name of their favorite NFL team from a drop-down box containing the names of all thirty-two teams. Overall, twenty-nine of the thirty-two NFL teams were selected at least once as a favorite team (no fans reported Baltimore Ravens, New York Jets, or Kansas City Chiefs as a favorite team); with no one team representing more than 20 percent of the overall sample. This process of selecting a favorite team was utilized throughout the questionnaire by HTML text piping. Specifically, the favorite team selected by participants subsequently appeared in future scale items (e.g., "How important is it to you that the *team name* win?"). This choice is represented throughout the findings whenever "favorite NFL team" appears in parenthesis. Participants were also asked how many fantasy football teams they managed in the current season. Overall, 42 percent of participants reported managing just one fantasy team, 33 percent reported managing two teams, 11 percent reported managing three teams, and less than 10 percent reported managing four (8%), five to nine teams (4%), or more than ten fantasy football teams (2%).

## MEASURES

### Rival Teams

After selecting a favorite NFL team, participants were provided with another drop box with all thirty-two NFL teams again listed and were asked to select which NFL teams they believed are the biggest rivals of their favorite NFL team. Once more, HTML text piping was used to insert the team name of the rival team that was perceived to be the biggest rival of each respondent's favorite team. This choice was reflected in some

SRFPS scale items (e.g., "I feel I have bragging rights when the (favorite team name) defeats the (rival team name)").

## Sport Rivalry Fan Perception Scale

The SRFPS was used to measure the perceptions fans had of rival NFL teams. The measure consists of four subscales with three questions each, for a total of 12 questions. The scales utilized a seven-point Likert scale (e.g., 1 = *Strongly Disagree* to 7 = *Strongly Agree*), and with the exception of the items addressing support for the rival in indirect competition, higher scores indicate stronger negative perceptions of the rival team. The subscales (summed and averaged) asked fans to indicate (1) how likely they are to support their rival team when they are not playing their favorite team ($M$ = 2.06, $SD$ = 1.48, $\alpha$ = .90), (2) their perceptions of the prestige of the city in which the rival team plays ($M$ = 3.38, $SD$ = 1.37, $\alpha$ = .69), (3) fan behavior of the rival team ($M$ = 4.27, $SD$ = 1.52, $\alpha$ = .92), and (4) the sense of satisfaction felt when the favorite team beats the rival team ($M$ = 5.59, $SD$ = 1.30, $\alpha$ = .82). The SFRPS has been determined to be reliable for use in both the professional and intercollegiate sport setting in the United States.

## NFL TEAM IDENTIFICATION

NFL team identification was measured using the Sport Spectator Identification Scale (*SSIS;* Wann & Branscombe, 1993). This scale utilized seven items on eight-point semantic differential scales (e.g., 1 = *not important* and 8 = *very important*, 1 = *not at all a fan* and 8 = *very much a fan*, 1 = *do not dislike* and 8 = *dislike very much*, 1 = *never* and 8 = *always*, 1 = *never* and 8 = *almost every day*) that determine the level of psychological connection one feels with their favorite/most familiar team. The SSIS is a highly reliable measure of sport fan identification that has been applied in over 100 studies of sport fandom internationally (Wann, Melnick, Russell, & Pease, 2001). The seven SSIS items were summed and averaged to create the NFL team identification score ($M$ = 6.12, $SD$ = 1.60, $\alpha$ = .94).

## Fantasy Football Team Identification

Additionally, we sought to explore the differences between NFL team identification and fantasy football team identification. Because the last two items of the SSIS were not generally applicable to fantasy sports (e.g., public display of team name/insignia), a five-item version of the SSIS was also used to measure fantasy football team identification. The five remaining items were then matched to parallel-worded items measuring NFL team identification in a set of paired t-tests used in the forthcoming data analysis. Subsequently, the five remaining items were summed and averaged to create the fantasy football team identification score ($M$ = 6.45, $SD$ = 1.45, $\alpha$ = .90).

## Perceptions of NFL Team, Rival Team, and Fantasy Team Performance

In order to explore the potential impact of actual performance, three separate four-point items (1 = *low-performing*, 2 = *mediocre*, 3 = *successful*, 4 = *outstanding*) were employed to determine participants' perceptions of: (1) their favorite NFL team's on-field performance in recent years ($M$ = 2.27, $SD$ = 0.92), (2) the on-field performance of their favorite team's most important rival ($M$ = 2.84, $SD$ = 0.84), and (3) their fantasy football team's performance in recent years ($M$ = 2.84, $SD$ = 0.77).

## Choosing Rival Team Players for Fantasy Team

Because no current empirical measures could be identified that pertained to selecting rival team players for fantasy sports, the authors generated eleven Likert-scale items (1 = *strongly disagree* and 7 = *strongly agree*), in an attempt to create a measure that tapped fantasy sport participants' perceptions about drafting, acquiring, or placing rival players or groups of rival players (i.e., fantasy football team defense) in their fantasy lineups. An exploratory factor analysis (principal components) with varimax rotation was used to test the pool of eleven items. These items were found to be acceptable for factor analysis, as they were correlated, according to Bartlett's Test of Sphericity, $\div^2$ = 580.755, $df$ = 55, $p$ < .001 and were found to have good sampling adequacy, as Kaiser Normality was .86. An eleven-item, two factor solution emerged with no double loadings; explaining 58.20 percent of the total post-rotation variance in choosing a rival team player/group of players for a fantasy team (see table 4.1). The first factor, *comfort with choosing rival players* (eigenvalue = 4.74; 43.06 percent of the total post-rotation variance), consisted of eight items that indicated fantasy football players had a high comfort level with utilizing athletes from rival teams in fantasy football. This eight-item factor was summed and averaged to create the variable for choosing rival team players for fantasy team ($M$ =

4.68, $SD$ = 1.37, $\alpha$ = .90). Factor two, *rivalry perceptions in fantasy football play* (eigenvalue = 1.67; 15.14 percent of the total post-rotation variance), consisted of three items that indicated the development of a rivalry with other owners in a fantasy league, the development of dislike for certain NFL players due to being used by another successful fantasy team owner, as well as the enjoyment of defeating a fantasy football opponent that used rival players, or for certain NFL players or groups of players ($M$ = 4.94, $SD$ = 1.17, $\alpha$ = .52). However, due to inadequate reliability, this factor was omitted from subsequent analyses (see table 4.1).

**Table 4.1. Factor Loadings for Choosing Rival Team Players for Fantasy Team Measure: Principal Axis Factor Analysis with Varimax Rotation.**

| Factor | I | .2 |
|---|---|---|
| **Comfort with choosing rival players ($M$ = 4.68, $SD$ = 1.37, $\alpha$ = .90)** | | |
| I am comfortable drafting or adding players from rival teams for my fantasy team. | **.88** | .06 |
| I often avoid drafting or adding players from rival teams for my own fantasy teams.* | **–.83** | .10 |
| If it helps my fantasy team win, I will draft or add any player, regardless of how I feel about them or the team they play for. | **.81** | .14 |
| I set my own personal opinions of players and teams aside when drafting or adding fantasy players. | **.76** | .16 |
| I am comfortable drafting or adding players I do not like for my fantasy team. | **.75** | –.04 |
| If I believe two fantasy players will perform similarly, and can only draft one, I will not draft the player from a rival of my favorite team. * | **–.69** | .36 |
| I'd rather enjoy watching teams I dislike perform badly than to have to root for players on teams I dislike to earn my team fantasy points. * | **–.68** | .04 |
| If I believe two fantasy players will perform similarly, I will always bench the player (or groups of players, like a team defense) that plays for a rival team. * | **–.66** | .22 |
| **Rivalry perceptions in fantasy football play ($M$ = 4.94, $SD$ = 1.17, $\alpha$ = .52)** | | |
| I have found myself disliking certain players (or groups of players, like a fantasy defense) just because they are on a winning team in my fantasy league. | .09 | **.72** |
| When playing in fantasy football, I often feel a sense of rivalry with one or more of the other team owners in the league. | .08 | **.71** |
| It's especially gratifying when a fantasy opponent has disliked players on their roster (or groups of players, like a team defense) and I beat them in my fantasy matchup. | –.29 | **.64** |

*Note.* Factor Loadings ≥ .60 are listed in boldface. Factors are listed numerically in columns. Use of asterisk (*) indicates reverse-coded item for mean values and in final scale.

## RESULTS

Research question one sought answers for how sport rivalry perception impacted the selection and use of NFL players/groups of players from rival teams. Additionally, research question two pertained to how NFL team identification impacted the selection and use of NFL players/groups of players from rival teams. To answer both of these questions, a hierarchical regression analysis was employed. In both analyses, demographic variables served as the first step (age, gender), identification variables were added on the second step (NFL team identification, fantasy team identification), perceived performance variables were added in step 3 (perceived recent performance of favorite NFL team, most important NFL rival team, and fantasy football teams), and the fourth and final step of these equations included the four SRFPS subscales (out group indirect competition, out group city prestige, out group sportsmanship, and sense of satisfaction). The linear combination of these four steps of independent variables was then regressed on the eight-item measure related to choosing rival NFL players/groups of players for fantasy football play.

Overall, this linear combination of variables significantly predicted the selection of rival NFL players, $R = .55, R^2 = .23, F(11, 111) = 4.27, p < .001$. Specifically, as it relates to research question 1, the sense of satisfaction subscale ($\beta = -.32, p = .005$) significantly and negatively predicted the selection of rival NFL players for fantasy football, while the out-group city prestige subscale also approached significance in the overall model ($\beta = -.21, p = .055$). For research question two, fantasy football team identification ($\beta = .21, p = .026$) significantly and positively predicted the selection of rival NFL players for fantasy football. Table 4.2 provides an overview of model changes and final beta values for this hierarchical regression analyses.

Research question three pertained to whether fantasy owners would indicate higher levels of identification with their favorite NFL teams or their fantasy football team(s). Using the five-item, parallel-worded SSIS measures described above, we found that participants reported nearly identical levels of identification with fantasy football teams ($M = 6.45, SD = 1.45$) and favorite NFL teams ($M = 6.44, SD = 1.58$). Next, a series of paired t-tests were used to examine the mean differences between each of these five sets of parallel-worded items. The results of these analyses suggested that no significant difference was found between three of the five SSIS items: (1) importance of NFL team victory ($M = 6.53, SD = 1.75$) and importance of fantasy team victory ($M = 6.76, SD = 1.42$) $t(122) = -1.31, p = .191$; (2) how strongly participants see themselves as a fan of their favorite NFL team ($M = 6.76, SD = 1.53$) and how strongly participants see themselves as a fan of

Table 4.2. Hierarchical Multiple Regression Analysis Predicting Selection and Use of Players/Groups of Players from Rival NFL Teams from Demographic Variables, Identification Variables, Perceived Performance Variables, and Sport Fan Rivalry Perception Scale Measures.

| Predictor | $\Delta R^2$ | $\beta$ final |
|---|---|---|
| **Step 1—Demographic Variables** | .03 | |
| Age | | −.16 |
| Gender | | −.05 |
| **Step 2—Identification Variables** | .14** | |
| NFL Team Identification | | −.09 |
| Fantasy Football Team Identification | | .21* |
| **Step 3—Perceived Performance Variables** | .02 | |
| Favorite NFL Team Performance | | .12 |
| Rival NFL Team Performance | | .08 |
| Fantasy Football Team Performance | | −.03 |
| **Step 4—Sport Fan Rivalry Perception Scale** | .10* | |
| Out Group Indirect Competition Subscale | | .04 |
| Out Group City Prestige Subscale | | −.21 |
| Out Group Sportsmanship Subscale | | .03 |
| Sense of Satisfaction Subscale | | −.32* |
| Final Model | $F(11, 111) = 4.27,$ $R = .55, R^2 = .23**$ | |

Note., $R = .17$, $R^2 = .01$, $F(2, 120) = 1.74$, $p = .180$ for Step 1. $R = .41$, $R^2 = .14$, $F(4, 118) = 6.08$, $p < .001$ for Step 2. $R = .44$, $R^2 = .15$, $F(7, 115) = 3.99$, $p < .001$ for Step 3. Male = 0, Female = 1.
* $p < .05$, ** $p < .001$

their fantasy football team ($M = 6.47$, $SD = 1.73$), $t(122) = 1.48$, $p = .141$; and (3) how important is being a fan of your favorite NFL team ($M = 5.87$, $SD = 2.06$) and their favorite NFL team ($M = 5.91$, $SD = 2.12$), $t(122) = -0.18$, $p = .861$. However, two items significantly differed amongst the five SSIS items: (1) how strongly do your friends see you as a fan of your favorite NFL team ($M = 6.45$, $SD = 1.72$) and how strongly do your friends see you as a fan of your fantasy team ($M = 6.03$, $SD = 1.78$), $t(122) = 1.98$, $p = .050$; and (2) how closely do you follow your favorite NFL team in person/using media ($M = 6.70$, $SD = 1.72$) and how closely do you follow your fantasy football team in person/using media ($M = 7.14$, $SD = 1.37$), $t(122) = -2.69$, $p = .008$.

## CONCLUSION

In this chapter, we examined how fantasy football owners manage the predicament of drafting or playing athletes from rival NFL teams for their own fantasy team. Based on previous research, we tested whether this dilemma would be impacted by a few factors, such as the strength and impact of the rivalry as perceived by the fantasy owner, and the level of identification that fantasy owners had toward both his or her favorite NFL team and toward their fantasy football team(s).

Overall, our findings indicated fantasy football owners that were more willing to draft or play athletes from rival NFL teams had a higher level of identification with their chosen fantasy football team than their favorite NFL team and had less negative perceptions about their favorite NFL team's rival, particularly as it related to having "bragging rights" when a favorite NFL team defeats a rival. In short, the fantasy owners in our analysis chose not to self-categorize in two important ways; they demonstrated less out-group animosity toward rivals and viewed their fantasy football team as a more prominent social identity than their favorite NFL team by indicating a stronger level of identification for fantasy teams. This indicates that fantasy football owners find successful coping mechanisms for the internal, and sometimes external (from other team owners) conflict they experience when faced with drafting and playing teams from rival NFL (or college) teams by focusing more on the success of their fantasy football team.

It is also important to keep in mind that these findings accounted for the simultaneous impact of the perceived performance of each respondent's favorite NFL team, most important rival of that favorite team, and their fantasy football teams in the regression equations employed in our analysis. Recent success (or lack thereof) for favorite teams, rival teams, or fantasy teams significantly impacted the decision to draft/play athletes from rival NFL teams in fantasy football.

So if fantasy team success is not a powerful predictor of loyalty or identification with a fantasy team and willingness to select and use rival NFL players, what other factors may be more impactful on drafting and playing decisions? Future research should focus on identifying such factors. Experience may also play an important role in determining a fantasy owner's willingness to draft and play athletes from rival teams. For example, the more seasons a person has played fantasy football may make them more likely to draft the best player, regardless of NFL (or college) team affiliation, whereas a more novice fantasy owner may choose players from their favorite teams and avoid athletes from rival teams.

In addition to the contributions to the fantasy sport literature, findings from this chapter have important implications for fantasy team owners, and NFL organizations. For fantasy owners, knowing that the sense of satisfaction or bragging rights a person feels when their favorite team beats the rival can be very important when drafting players and interacting with other owners. For instance, if an owner is in a league with someone they know to be highly identified with their favorite NFL team, and strongly opposed to a rival team, they can use this knowledge to help influence draft selections of owners highly identified to NFL teams. The same can be said for experience, where an owner can use relative inexperience of other owners to gain a drafting advantage.

The NFL and teams can use findings from the chapter to promote players to fantasy owners. By providing statistics on how many players from rival teams are on fantasy rosters can create a sense of intrigue surrounding the NFL and fantasy football product. However, NFL and team officials should show caution when promoting rival players to fantasy owners to keep from diminishing the NFL on-field product. For example, the NFL should be careful promoting that a Washington Redskins player can help the fantasy team of an owner who is highly identified with the Dallas Cowboys, as this may negatively impact casual fans. Data from Bowman et al. (2012) suggested that when fantasy MLB owners drafted unliked players—or players from unliked team—the fantasy sports player's disposition toward those players significantly increased; such an effect suggests that mere exposure to "new" players might drive interest and fandom, which could translate to merchandising purchases or other economic benefits to professional athletes and sports organizations.

In sum, the findings from this chapter suggest that the impact of rivalry on fantasy sports appears more complex than originally estimated, based on the premises of self-categorization theory: It is not simply a matter of "us versus them" with favorite teams and rival teams. How fantasy owners strategically manage their favorite NFL team identity along with their allegiances to their fantasy football team(s) is a topic with much to be understood moving forward.

## REFERENCES

Bowman, N. D., McCabe, J., & Isaacson, T. (2012). Fantasy Sports and Sports Fandom: Implications for Mass Media Research. In A. C. Earnheardt, P. M. Haridakis, & B. Hugenberg (Eds.) *Fandemonium: Explorations of fan power, identity and socialization* (pp. 255–273). Lanham, MD: Lexington.

Cikara, M., & Fiske, S. T. (2012). Stereotypes and schadenfreude: Affective and physiological markers of pleasure at outgroup misfortunes. *Social Psychological and Personality Science, 3,* 63–71.

Cikara, M., Botninick, M. M., & Fiske, S. T. (2011). Us versus them: Social identity shaped neural responses to intergroup competition and harm. *Psychological Science, 22,* 306–313.

Duck, J. M., Hogg, M. A., & Terry, D. J. (1999). Social identity and perceptions of media persuasion: Are we always less influenced than others? *Journal of Applied Social Psychology, 29,* 1879–1899. doi:10.1111/j.1559-1816.1999.tb00156.x

Dwyer, B. (2011). Divided loyalty? An analysis of fantasy football involvement and fan loyalty to individual National Football League (NFL) teams. *Journal of Sport Management, 25,* 445–457.

Dwyer, B., & LeCrom C. W. (2013). Is fantasy trumping reality? The redefined National Football league experience of novice fantasy football participants. *Journal of Contemporary Atheltics, 7,* 119–139.

Franco, F. M., & Maass, A. (1996). Implicit versus explicit strategies of out-group discrimination: The role of intentional control in biased language use and reward allocation. *Journal of Language and Social Psychology, 15,* 335–359.

Havard, C. T. (2014). Glory out of reflected failure: The examination of how rivalry affects sports fans. *Sport Management Review, 17,* 243–253.

Havard, C. T. (in press). Rivalry among teams and conferences in intercollegiate athletics: Does a conference pride phenomenon exist? *Journal of Contemporary Athletics.*

Havard, C. T., & Eddy, T. (2013). Qualitative assessment of rivalry and conference realignment in intercollegiate athletics. *Journal of Issues in Intercollegiate Athletics, 6,* 216–235. Published online September 2013.

Havard, C. T., Gray, D. P., Gould, J., Sharp, L. A., & Schaffer, J. J. (2013). Development and validation of the Sport Rivalry Fan Perception Scale. *Journal of Sport Behavior, 36,* 45–65.

Havard, C. T., & Reams, L. (in press). Investigating differences in fan rival perceptions between conference in intercollegiate athletics. *Journal of Sport Behavior.*

Havard, C. T., Reams, L., & Gray, D. P. (2013). Perceptions of highly identified fans regarding rival teams in United States intercollegiate football and men's basketball. *International Journal of Sport Management and Marketing, 14,* 116–132.

Havard, C. T., Shapiro, S. L., & Ridinger, L. L. Who's our rival? Investigating the influence of a new intercollegiate football program on rivalry perceptions. *Manuscript under review.*

Havard, C. T., Wann, D. L., & Ryan, T. D. (2013). Investigating the impact of conference realignment on rivalry in intercollegiate athletics. *Sport Marketing Quarterly, 22*(4), 224–234.

Heider, F. (1958). *The psychology of interpersonal relations.* New York: Wiley.

Kilduff, G. J., Elfenbein, H. A., & Staw, B. M. (2010). The psychology of rivalry: A relationally dependent analysis of competition. *Academy of Management Journal, 53,* 943–969.

Lalonde, R. N. (1992). The dynamics of group differentiation in the face of defeat. *Personality and Social Psychology Bulletin, 18,* 336–342.

Lalonde, R. N., Moghaddam, F. M., & Taylor, D. M. (1987). The process of group differentiation in a dynamic intergroup setting. *Journal of Social Psychology, 127*, 273–287.

Leach, C. W., & Spears, R. (2009). Dejection at in-group defeat and schadenfreude toward second-and third-party out-groups. *Emotion, 9*, 659–665.

Leach, C. W., Spears, R., Branscombe, N. R., & Doosje, B. (2003). Malicious pleasure: Schadenfreude at the suffering of another group. *Journal of Personality and Social Psychology, 84*, 932–943.

Lee, J., Ruihley, B. J., Brown, N., & Billings, A. C. (2013). The effects of fantasy football participation on team identification, team loyalty, and NFL fandom. *Journal of Sport Media, 8*, 207–227.

Levine, R. M., Prosser, A., Evans, D., & Reicher, S. D. (2005). Identity and emergency intervention: How social group membership and inclusiveness of group boundaries shape helping behavior. *Personality and Social Psychology Bulletin, 31*, 443–453. doi:10.1177/0146167204271651.

Reid, S. A., & Hogg, M. A. (2005). A self-categorization explanation of the third-person effect. Human Communication Research, 31, 129–161. doi: 10.1111/j.1468–2958.2005.tb00867.x

Reid, S. A., Byrne, S., Brundidge, J. S., Shoham, M. D., & Marlow, M. L. (2007). A critical test of self-enhancement, exposure and self-categorization explanations for first and third person perceptions. *Human Communication Research, 33*, 143–162. doi:10.1111/j.1468-2958.2007.00294.x

Spinda, J. S. W. (2012). Perceptual biases and behavioral effects among NFL fans: An investigation of first-person, second-person, and third-person effects. *International Journal of Sport Communication, 5*(3), 327–347.

Tajfel, H., & Turner, J. C. (1979). An integrative theory of intergroup conflict. In W. G. Austin & S. Worchel (Eds.), *The social psychology of intergroup relations* (pp. 33–47). Monterey, CA: Brooks-Cole.

Turner, J. C., Hogg, M. A., Oakes, P. J., Reicher, S. D. & Wetherell, M. S. (1987). *Rediscovering the social group: A self-categorization theory*. Oxford: Blackwell.

Tyler, B. D., & Cobbs, J. B. (2015). Rival conceptions of rivalry: Why some competitions mean more than others. *European Sport Management Quarterly, 15*, 227–248.

Wann, D. L., Havard, C. T., Grieve, F. G., Lanter, J. R., Partridge, J. A., & Zapalac, R. K. (in press). Investigating sport rivals: Number, evaluations, and relationship with team identification. *Journal of Fandom Studies*.

Wann, D. L., & Branscombe, N. R. (1993). Sports fans: Measuring degree of identification with the team. *International Journal of Sports Psychology, 24*, 1–17.

Wann, D. L., Koch, K., Knoth, T., Fox, D., Aljubaily, H., & Lantz, C. D. (2006). The impact of team identification on biased predictions of player performance. *The Psychological Record, 56*, 55–66.

Wann, D. L., Melnick, M. J., Russell, G. W., & Pease, D. G. (2001). *Sports fans: The psychology and social impact of spectators*. London: Routledge.

Zhang, J. (2010). Self-Enhancement on a self-categorization leash: Evidence for a dual-process model of first- and third-person perceptions. *Human Communication Research, 36*, 190–215. doi:10.1111/j.1468-2958.2010.01373.x

Zillmann, D., Bryant, J., & Sapolsky, B. S. (1989). Enjoyment from sports spectatorship. In J. H. Goldstein (Ed.), *Sports, Games, and Play: Social and Psychological Viewpoints* (2nd ed., pp. 241–287). Hillsdale, NJ: Lawrence Erlbaum Associates.

# 5

# ROOTING WITH YOUR RIVALS

## Social Presence in Fantasy Sports

*Andy Boyan, David Westerman, and Emory S. Daniel*

**F**antasy sports are a unique place in the communication landscape that provide researchers with opportunities for several avenues of inquiry. The sheer volume of participation, the relationships between fandom and fantasy, and the perceptions of the players and teams are all worthwhile research pursuits. However, one untapped aspect of fantasy sports participation is the potential for computer-mediated communication (CMC) contexts to be examined. This chapter is written to explain how fantasy sports can be researched using communication models. As fantasy sport is often played in online environments, the CMC perspectives of research are used to provide guidance for scholars interested in integrating these two areas of inquiry.

In this chapter, we argue that fantasy sports are a communication phenomenon at their core. Fantasy sports are rife with potentially interesting interactions, and communication researchers have the opportunity to understand these more nuanced interactions and experiences that players have using the various lenses of communication theory. Sport communication research is in need of theoretical frameworks to help advance our treatment of phenomena, especially when it comes to social media contexts (Hardin, 2014). In this chapter, we present theories typically used in CMC research to encourage further examination of these fantasy sport and social media contexts in tandem with communication theory.

## FANTASY VS. REALITY IN SPORT

In live head-to-head sports competition, nearly half of all teams will lose (only "nearly" because sometimes they tie). This means that hundreds of thousands of fans crowd into arenas and stadiums each year and root for their favorite team while millions more watch at home. And they often watch their teams lose. When the game ends, the stadium closes, and the cameras turn off, many fans have to live with the agony of defeat, and it can leave people thinking to themselves, "I could manage a team better than our general manager." However, few people will ever have the opportunity to do so, at least when talking about managing a "real" sports team.

This is where fantasy sports come in. According to the Fantasy Sports Trade Association, it is estimated that forty-two million people over the age of twelve years old participate in fantasy sports (Fantasy Sports Trade Association, 2014, see also Ruihley & Billings, chapter 13 of this volume). For many fans, it is a way to stay connected to the games that they love. For example, an avid fan of the (US) National Football League's Green Bay Packers may be upset that the Packers lost last weekend, but some of those same fans may be elated by the loss if their fantasy quarterback played for the opposing team. Sure, their team may not have won, but they earned a personal victory because their fantasy player performed so well. With fantasy sports, there are now two games that occur simultaneously: the game that's played on the field, and the game that's played on the web.

The Internet seems like a perfect place for fantasy sports to play out. Although fantasy sports predate the mainstream proliferation of the Internet (see chapter 1, this volume, for details), the participatory, rather than simple (re: passive) consumption, model of the Internet today fits in with the participatory and social nature of fantasy sports. The nature of Web 2.0 as an online social infrastructure in particular provides users with various platforms of social interaction. This combined with the vast quantity and availability of information allows players to easily track, research, and compete with others. The result is a variety of systems where users connect with one another and use information in different ways. The topic of these interactions happen to be sports because the information about sport is recorded in detail and sports fans have access to online activities.

Research on fantasy sport participation shows that this type of gaming is a complement to typical sport consumption, such that those who participate in fantasy sports tend to consume more traditional sports media content and report higher levels of attachment and loyalty to teams and players than non-fantasy players (Karg & McDonald, 2011). Some findings (e.g. Drayer et al, 2010) indicate that results of fantasy participation can have an impact on fans' relationships with their favorite teams or players. This is interesting as fandom was generally thought to be unchanging in regard to fantasy sports. Those fans of losing teams might not be stuck rooting for "the same old letdowns" every season,[1] and instead are finding ways to make rooting for losers fun (Dwyer & Drayer, 2010; Brown, Billings, & Ruihley, 2012).

Fantasy sport does not just seem to be about sports viewing though. Research regarding the various motivations for play reveals multiple gratifications for fantasy sports use. A main motivation that has received little attention from the research literature is the social motivation. This may have the most value for communication scholarship because of the potential for examining communication in nontraditional channels.

## Fantasy Sports Are Communication-Rich Contexts

At their essence, fantasy sports are conducted with and through communication technologies. However, the structure of the activity itself provides more than simple message transfer. Fantasy sports are primarily played online, and much of the communication happens online, which provides CMC researchers an opportunity to examine communicators, relationships, and their interplay within the structured system.

Without the use of the fundamental communicative process, complex games such as fantasy sports are impossible to perform. First, fantasy sports are games with rules built to constrain the action of the players, assign benefits and penalties, and crown a champion. However games are also social in that players use them to connect with others, communicate with one another, and provide a common social experience to build relationships (Sherry et al., 2006). Therefore scholars can examine communication within games to understand how communication is used, how relationships function within the context of the games, and how game-related technologies impact communication of the participants.

Fantasy sport would not be the first place to research social communication interactions. Other digital game contexts have been examined as social platforms along with their entertainment media roots. For example, Steinkuehler and Williams (2006) argue that virtual worlds provide a "third place" for social interaction apart from home and work, and these social interactions rely on social capital just as much as nonvirtual social spaces. Numerous other studies show that social motivations for digital game play have important impacts on enjoyment outcomes (e.g., Frost & Eden, 2014), social comfort outcomes (Kowert & Oldmeadow, 2014), and friendships including life-long emotionally tied partners (Cole & Griffiths, 2007).

Communication research in social game contexts has focused on what messages participants use to achieve their goals and build or maintain relationships (e.g., Banks, 2013; Pena & Hancock, 2006). In fantasy sports games, Ruihley and Hardin (2011b) found that 62 percent of participants surveyed had participated in online message boards to communicate with other players. The researchers found the primary motivations for message board use were a) to plan out logistical strategies, b) socialize with others, c) surveil the competition, and d) to give and seek advice. The authors also reported that participants who used message boards had higher overall satisfaction of their fantasy sports experience. These findings suggest that socialization and basic interpersonal communication online in this context is a major function of fantasy sports.

## Relational Maintenance

Definitions differ within the literature, but at its most basic, relational maintenance is simply continuing the existence of a relationship (Duck, 1988). As such, relational maintenance has long been an area of study in interpersonal communication, and is growing as an area in CMC as well (Tong & Walther, 2011). Technology has been incorporated into maintenance of relationships. People use e-mail, blogs, social networking sites, text messaging, etc. for maintaining relationships (Tong & Walther, 2011). For example, 21 percent of cell phone/Internet users report feeling closer to their partner due to exchanges they had using these technologies. This percentage grows to 41 percent when considering only 18–29 year olds. Sexting has also increased since 2012 (Lenhart & Duggan, 2014). However, Tong and Walther suggest that most relational maintenance research has focused on romantic couples, largely ignoring other important relationships such as friendships and family members. This is one area where studying the relational maintenance uses of fantasy sports might come into play.

Another area of relational maintenance and technology that has received increased attention is long-distance relationships (Stafford, 2005; Tong & Walther, 2011). Again, this has largely been focused on romantic relationships. However, being physically separated from one's friends and family may be a key motivation for playing fantasy sports online. Communicators engaging in fantasy sports are not just doing it for themselves typically.

Families, friends, and even whole offices find themselves joining fantasy football pools and competing with their friends and colleagues. The social nature of fantasy sports might be a main draw for players. For example, it might be one method of keeping families connected, even though they live far away from each other. It might be a good way for old college friends to stay connected in each other's lives. According to the *Pittsburgh Post-Gazette*, it might also bring members of organizations together. The *Post-Gazette* suggests that managers should take a few moments to talk about the office fantasy league with employees, "[Managers] can turn the obstacles that come with fantasy football into a positive by finding out if [their] team is playing and finding out how they are doing" (Todd, 2014).

These studies provide the basis for understanding the landscape of fantasy sport, but the real interactions within the game are a place where human communication happens at a more interpersonal level. In some cases these interactions have received mainstream press. For example, in the *Mandel v. UBS/Painwebber Inc.* case in 2004, two employees alleged sexual and religious harassment during the fantasy football season, claiming that some of their colleagues suggested that the season was "the Gentiles versus the Jews" and that "the plaque should never hang in anybody's office that doesn't celebrate Christmas." Despite the allegation presented, the court upheld the judgment in favor of the employer (*Mandel v. UBS/Painwebber Inc.*, 2004).

Participants in the fantasy sports CMC context also provide researchers with an opportunity to examine a variety of relationships as they play out in CMC. Participants could range in relationship closeness from very close friends and family members all the way through complete strangers. More notably, the interactions the participants have are within a specified, agreed-upon context. That is, there is not necessarily small talk or relational maintenance, but the situation is fundamentally task-oriented. In an effort to find natural communication situations, other CMC research has examined social support contexts such as cancer support forums (e.g. Wright, 2002). Fantasy sport provides a task-oriented online communication context in a natural environment, and allows participants to socially engage with one another within a structured situation.

Because fantasy sports are primarily played out online, much of the communication is recorded online. This provides researchers with a CMC context that has an established basis for online data collection. Additionally, the ability to alter one's persona when online may lead to communication that can be difficult to recreate in a lab setting (e.g., flaming, trash talking, etc).

## Communication as a Process

Perhaps the most intriguing aspect of fantasy sports from a communication research perspective is how time is a measurable, and relevant part of the fantasy sports process. Whereas time is crucial element in the entire communication discipline, only recently have there been renewed calls to examine the role of communication as a process over time in more depth now that the tools for data collection and analysis using complexity mathematics are readily available (Sherry, 2014). The nature of fantasy sport as a season-long progression of multiple participants in a common, competitive task, all within an accessible recorded form, provides researchers with the opportunity to gather time-relevant data and assess outcomes of communication as process.

## FANTASY SPORTS AND SOCIAL MOTIVATIONS

Although previously mentioned above, the social dynamics of fantasy sports cannot be overstated. Other research relevant to the study of communication in fantasy sport provides a backdrop of understanding how participants interact with and through fantasy sports. This research focuses on a uses and gratifications paradigm, wherein fantasy sports are used for particular outcomes. Understanding player motivations is key in developing practical research designs within fantasy sport (see chapter 2, this volume, for details).

## Interpersonal Motivations

Motivations to play fantasy sports include at least three social factors. Ruihley and Hardin (2011a) distinguished between camaraderie and social sport motivations, where camaraderie is a reason to be interested in sports in order to build or maintain relationships with other people, and social sport is the use of sport to be able to talk to "multiple societal constituencies" (Billings & Ruihley, 2014). A third motivation is competition, which Ruihley and Hardin (2011a) found to be ranked second in importance of involvement in sports only behind general sports fanship.

Billings and Ruihley (2014) found that competition, social sport, and camaraderie were ranked in the top five of ten overall motivations for participation in fantasy sport. It is unknown how the motivations for play will impact the types of communication that users engage in in fantasy sports, however, research in other online gaming contexts has shown that the verbiage players use to describe their play experiences is related to the types of play they report engaging in (Banks, 2014). Thus, it seems likely that social reasons for playing fantasy sports will drive how people communicate in them.

## Competitive Motivations

Social interaction is not the only social element of fantasy sports motivation. Many players report the competitive nature of the game being highly motivating (Billings & Ruihley, 2014). This is notable in the context of understanding fantasy sports as a locus for field data in CMC research, as the type of information that participants reveal is likely to be skewed by additional motivations. In the case of fantasy sports, competition is not just friendly, it is also often for money.

Gambling via fantasy sport is one important element of the fantasy sport landscape. A subset of fantasy players enters their leagues with the understanding of a monetary entry fee and a cash prize payout. The Fantasy Sports Trade Association (2014) estimated that on average players spent $111 annually on the game through gambling, access to information and media, and other related expenses (see also Watanabe, Yang, and Wicker, chapter 3 of this volume).

Because of the competitive nature of fantasy sports, and also the often-financial incentives for success, the situation for online communication becomes based in how success in the game is achieved. Essentially, to be successful in fantasy sports a player must have information about a player or team that will provide that player with an advantage over his or her opponent. This is one reason for the amount of time spent with media in fantasy sports. The quest for information to have an advantage over one's opponent is the controllable element in a game that is somewhat determined by chance. Therefore, the communicative interactions that occur in the competitive fantasy space are frequently in regards to hiding information, but still trying to gain what one wants.

For example, if one author of this chapter has a hot tip that his typically good player's wife and kids have the flu, then he might try to trade the player to another author for the week without losing value in the trade. In this way the first author could hedge his potential losses as well as stick his competition with a potentially poor performer. The potential for sensitive and valuable information in the fantasy context is heightened by the competitive nature of the game.

Lee et al. (2013) examined how individual differences locus of control and perceived football knowledge were related with attitudes toward fantasy sports. The findings do suggest that people with higher knowledge of sports use their knowledge to outperform competitors in fantasy games, and those with higher knowledge had more positive attitudes toward fantasy games. Also, players who preferred a greater locus of control had more positive attitudes toward fantasy sports. The authors argue that this is because of the high level of control in the fantasy sport structure, unlike other games that are more heavily weighted toward chance.

## FANTASY AS REALITY? COMPUTER-MEDIATED COMMUNICATION (CMC) PERSPECTIVES

Fantasy sports provide a very unique outlet for computer-mediated communication to occur. But how do we examine this communication phenomenon? This next section will provide an overview of some prominent CMC theories and concepts that we think are important for study of fantasy sports. We will provide some thoughts on how these can be incorporated into research in this area, but we hope that reading this chapter provides a muse for readers to apply fantasy sport contexts to other areas of theory building as well.

### Social Presence

Although many people are unable to afford tickets to a game, they can watch games on TV. Indeed, TV companies have advertised that their television sets bring the game to you and make you feel like you are at the game. This is an example of the first concept to discuss: telepresence.

Telepresence is a concept that cuts across many fields, including, but certainly not limited to: psychology, engineering, communication, robotics, and philosophy. Very simply defined, it is the "illusion of non-mediation" (Lombard & Ditton, 1997), although Tamborini and Skalski (2006) suggest that "perception of non-mediation" may be a better way to think of telepresence. The International Society of Presence Research (2000) has defined "Presence (a shortened version of the term 'telepresence') as a psychological state or subjective perception in which even though part or all of an individual's current experience is generated by and/or filtered through human-made technology, part or all of the individual's perception fails to accurately acknowledge the role of the technology in the experience," and suggests that telepresence is not equated with a technology, but varies across people, time, and degree.

Thus, telepresence can be thought of as a combination of three things: content, channel, and user (Pettey, Bracken, Rubenking, Buncher, & Gross, 2010). When the right user gets the right content through the right channel, telepresence goes up. Importantly, user expectations matter greatly for telepresence to occur. Telepresence is a general concept, but scholars in the area generally note different kinds of telepresence (e.g., Lee, 2004). Of particular interest to this chapter is the concept of social presence. As a concept, social presence goes back at least to Short, Williams, and Christie's (1976) social presence theory (SPT). This conceptualization of it suggests social presence as salience in another person and of a relationship, and is dependent upon the number of cue systems that a channel provides. However, similar to thought on telepresence as a whole, social presence is now more thought of as a psychological concept (Nowak & Biocca, 2003). Briefly stated, social presence can be summed up as "a sense of being with another" (Biocca, Harms, & Burgoon, 2003, p. 456) without noticing the technological means (Lee, 2004). A related concept called electronic propinquity (Walther & Bazarova, 2008) has been defined as "electronic presence" (Korzenny, 1978, p. 7) and "the psychological feeling of nearness that communicators experience using different communication channels" (Walther & Bazarova, 2008, p. 624).

As mentioned above, SPT (Short, Williams, & Christie, 1976) suggests that social presence is a technologically determined concept. That is, at best, it would be very difficult to feel a sense of connection and salience in another person through a channel that provides few cue systems. However, research on the topic has found that people can in fact feel present with another person using technology, even with very "lean" channels that provide few cue systems, like instant messaging.

Another theory that can help account for these issues with SPT is Walther's (1992) social information processing theory (SIPT; see also, Walther & Parks, 2002). SIPT (Walther, 1992) is a theory that was formulated originally in an era of limited cues. Things other than text largely did not exist online. Today, we have many more cues (although text still remains abundant), but SIPT still remains a useful theory for understanding the social dynamics of much CMC.

Why?

First, it begins with the idea that people largely have the same goals in communicating with others no matter the channel used. It also suggests that when the nonverbal and other cues we might normally use to help accomplish these goals are lacking, we use what is available (Walther, Loh, & Granka, 2005). In SIPT, cues are not equivalent to functions (Walther

& Parks, 2002), and functions largely do not change. This combined with the notion that we can and do use the cues that are available suggest the continued utility of SIPT, even as CMC becomes less text only.

So, how do people overcome the things that CMC can sometimes lack? One potential method is by being more skilled at using the channel (Walther & Bazarova, 2008). This may seem like common sense, but some people are more skilled at using certain channels to accomplish their communication goals than others. Furthermore, skepticism about the interpersonal potential of CMC also seems to limit the potential for using media in this way (Utz, 2000). So next time you hear someone say that people cannot form relationships online, it may be more of a case that the sender of that message is not able to do so. But just like the authors of this chapter cannot dunk a basketball, it does not preclude other people who are more skilled from doing so.

Second, one of the key components of SIPT is that goals can be accomplished, but they take more time to do so through CMC (Walther, 1992; Walther & Burgoon, 1992; Walther, Anderson, & Park, 1994). Fewer cue systems being utilized at any given time in CMC means less information may be flowing at any given time. Furthermore, it takes longer to type and read than to speak and listen while also watching the communicator. There may be things that jump-start goal accomplishment online (Westerman, 2007) but it still generally takes longer online.

Third, people are able to rely more strongly on what the channel does provide them and circumvent the lack of things like nonverbals. People can use things like chronemics (Walther & Tidwell, 1995), emoticons (Walther & D'Addario, 2001), and lurking (Ramirez, Walther, Burgoon, & Sunnafrank, 2002) to learn about others and help manage relationships. They also may use a very simple thing and ask more questions and disclose more when interacting online (Tidwell & Walther, 2002). Anticipating (and perhaps desiring) future interaction (Walther, 1994) with the other person can help motivate a person to put forth the time and effort necessary for online communication goal fulfillment. Fourth, there may be times when the "limitations" of CMC can be strategically utilized by communicators. For example, O'Sullivan's (2000) impression management model suggests a strategic use of channel limitations for sharing news to help people manage impressions and save face. Another perspective that fits into the strategic use of channel "limitations" perspective is Walther's (1996) hyperpersonal perspective.

SIPT is a theory designed in part to explain findings that were inconsistent with earlier theories of online social interaction (Walther, 1992;

Walther & Parks, 2002). One such theory is social presence theory (Short, Williams, & Christie, 1976), which suggests that social presence, defined as salience in another person and relationship, is a function of the number of cue systems that a channel provides. Although SIPT points out and helps explain problems with SPT, a recent idea suggests ways that SIPT can help explain the experience of social presence.

If social presence is a psychological concept, and not technologically determined, SIPT (Walther, 1992) is well articulated to account for the experience of social presence. SIPT logic would suggest that if establishing a feeling of social presence is a goal in social interaction, then it is one that people will be able to accomplish regardless of the channel used to interact. This would be accomplished in part by utilizing circumventions that allow users to overcome the limitations of the channel used (Westerman & Skalski, 2010).

Research on the related concept of electronic propinquity has also shown that propinquity, again, defined as "electronic presence" (Korzenny, 1978, p. 7) and a "psychological feeling of nearness" (Walther & Bazarova, 2008, p. 624) has shown that it can especially be felt when electronic options are the only options for communication (like might occur for fantasy sports players) and when the communicators are higher in skills (Walther & Bazarova, 2008). In order to feel present, based on the logic of SIPT, one may have to be both willing and able to do so.

## Hyperpersonal Model

SIPT suggests that people can accomplish interpersonal goals at levels similar to face-to-face, if given enough motivation, abilities, and time. However, sometimes relationships can go above and beyond what they would face-to-face. One explanation for how these might occur is Walther's (1996) hyperpersonal model.

This model suggests a sort of "perfect storm" of source, receiver, channel, and feedback (the four horsemen of hyperpersonal) that can come together to lead to more personalness than would happen face-to-face. First, sources can sometimes better selectively self-present themselves to look really good online due to the lack of nonverbal cues (Walther, 2007). Second, receivers may start to idealize the sender of a selectively self-presented message who appears to look really good, especially when the receiver wants a relationship. Third, the breaking from normal FtF interaction rules (disentrainment) that CMC can allow gives people more time to think and edit their messages, and also can help eliminate attention to distracting cues that are filtered out of the CMC environment. Finally, feedback can help lead to a self/other-fulfilling prophecy for the sender. As the receiver idealizes the sender, and responds favorably to them in kind, the original sender may start to actually become better. For example, if a receiver sends feedback to a sender suggesting that they are interested in conversing more, the sender might actually become more confident in communicating with the sender, and might start having more fun, be more positive, outgoing, etc.

## MOVING FORWARD WITH A FANTASY SPORT CMC RESEARCH AGENDA

Fantasy sports provide communication researchers with fertile ground for experimental research that generalizes to real world behaviors. Additionally, CMC theories within the fantasy sports context open doors for sports communication research to further the systematic understanding of sports-related communication phenomena. The application of CMC theories to fantasy sports participation provides researchers with the opportunity to move beyond the descriptive tendency of sport and social media research, and to extend CMC theories by providing unique, generalizable contexts for different types of communication to occur.

A research agenda for fantasy sports CMC should use existing descriptive work to understand the fantasy sports experience and contexts fully in order to contextualize the communication that may occur in research. Researchers can then determine which types of online forums are more or less helpful for collecting data.

Past research has found salience of participants interacting through mediated communication has an effect on subsequent interpersonal relationships (Pena & Hancock, 2006). If this finding were applied to fantasy sports, then communication in this context should have an impact on relationships started, maintained, and dissolved within this context.

One especially interesting area to test in fantasy sports is how relationships occur. An especially useful theory to help drive research in this area is SIPT (Walther, 1992). Utz (2000) applied SIPT to relational development in MUDs, a semi-social context similar to fantasy sports (task combined with social), and found that friendships were developed largely in line with SIPT suggestions. Fantasy sports, as another overtime, semi-social sphere, would likely see similar results. If people are willing and able to do so, they will very possibly form friendships through fantasy sports if given enough time. They will find ways to manage and overcome the limitations of the channel in order to build these relationships as well. A future line of research can use SIPT as a driving mechanism to organize how relationships develop through fantasy sports.

## HYPER-PERSONAL AND HYPERNEGATIVITY IN FANTASY SPORTS RESEARCH

Fantasy sports might also be a place for very deep (and potentially very fast) relationships to develop. Walther's (1996) notion of hyperpersonal communication may apply especially well to fantasy sports. First, people may be selectively self-presenting themselves, both as skilled fantasy players but also as fans of particular players or teams. This could possibly lead to others idealizing those self-presenters, especially if they are also fans of those same players or teams. Given the relative lack of information to go on, and the channel's ability to filter out other distracting information, this may lead to a sense of increased similarity and liking toward the other person. Finally, there could be especially strong feedback in play here helping to solidify the hyperpersonal experience. For example, if the receiver of the original message is also a fan of the sender's favorite team or player, this may embolden the sender to continue discussing this fandom, adding to their mutual liking. This feedback about a shared like is not necessarily what hyperpersonal was designed to encompass, but could be an interesting addition to the hyperpersonal idea.

Hyperpersonal relationships are typically considered as those that are more "positive" (personal, close, liked, etc.) than they would be under FtF conditions. Walther and Parks (2002) also suggest the possibility of "hypernegative" effects online. This idea of hypernegative effects seems understudied (perhaps because they are unlikely), but fantasy sports seem like a possible place for this phenomenon to occur. Although positive hyperpersonal relationships seem possible in fantasy sports, hypernegative may be an even more likely possibility. A hypernegative effect would occur when someone felt incredibly negatively about someone else, more so than they would FtF, because of the perfect storm of the four horsemen of hyperpersonal communication. So, if a person selectively self-presents themself to appear like a huge fan of a team, or tries to make themself appear like the greatest fantasy sports manager of all-time, or regularly beats the other players, taking their money and/or pride, and this causes a receiver to not idealize that person, but instead to abhor them, because the channel allows the person to edit extra-angry responses, then this might lead to a hypernegative relationship.

Finally, if the receiver abhors and talks trash back to the original sender, it is possible that the original sender may start to act even more in line with the way they are being treated, thus creating a sort of self/other-fulfilling feedback prophecy as well. In most situations, this kind of interaction would be unlikely because the people would likely just stop interacting. However, in a fantasy sport league, the participation, and often money, is on the line for the entire season. Competitive vitriol is also a part of the attraction to playing. Future research can examine how (and if) hypernegative relationships occur, as it may be a space for working through them scientifically.

## SOCIAL PRESENCE IN FANTASY SPORTS RESEARCH

Fantasy sports might also be an especially powerful way for players to maintain a sense of social presence with people they already know. For example, one of the authors of this chapter plays in a fantasy football league that has been going for twenty-plus years. He remembers getting together with the other players in the clubhouse in one player's backyard to hold the first draft, and also remembers calculating scores by checking the newspaper on Monday morning (this league started before the Internet was widespread). Now that this author has moved away from these other players, he continues to play in this league (that has now moved online), mostly to still feel connected to his friends. Examining how fantasy sports can be an important part of establishing a sense of social presence would be a useful and important addition to thinking about mixed-mode relationships (Walther & Parks, 2002) as well, especially the kind that begins face-to-face and then moves to be mostly/entirely online.

## CMC OVER TIME

The experimental nature of CMC research has not focused very much on the length of effects, and how those effects might compare to FtF interactions. Many fantasy sports have a season-long interaction time. These interactions are recorded and tracked along with levels of success and failure, quantity and quality of participation in the activity. This situation could be leveraged to test a variety of SIPT and social presence outcomes over multiple time points.

How would relational closeness with members of the fantasy league change over time? Do relationships form between winners and losers? Or does that reduce the relational closeness? How might that impact mixed-mode relationships that were established offline first, but then moved online into the fantasy format?

## CONCLUSION

Do more vitriolic interactions demonstrate the proposed hyper-negativity effect? How do groups that talk trash build or break down relationships as compared to those who use more supportive language? What are the types of language used in supportive competitive language versus trash talking? Does trash talking increase relationship building? How do competitive success or failure impact relationships over time? What do financial risk and loss contribute to hyper-negative or hyper-personal CMC interactions? These questions demonstrate the rich opportunity for fantasy sport and CMC researchers to build an agenda of research that incorporates both areas of study. Sport communication scholars will benefit from CMC perspectives because the rigor of theoretical and experimental tradition that informs CMC theories, while CMC scholars will benefit from the fantasy sports context because the nature of the activity provides controllable conditions for extending theory in novel ways.

## NOTE

1. The authors mean no offense to those who root for teams that do not regularly win. The authors have personally experienced being fans of letdown teams. However, according to the authors, their so-called letdown teams are going to turn it all around next year. Go (NCAA, Washington State) Cougars, Go (NFL, Buffalo) Bills, Go (NHL, Buffalo) Sabres, Go (NFL, Detroit) Lions!

## REFERENCES

Banks, J. (2013). Human-technology relationality and self-network organization: Players and avatars in World of Warcraft. Unpublished dissertation. Colorado State University: Fort Collins, CO. Retrieved from https://www.academia.edu/4528351/Human-technology_relationality_and_Self-network_organization_Players_and_avatars_in_World_of_Warcraft

Banks, J. (2015). Object, me, symbiote, other: A social typology of player-avatar relationships. *First Monday.*

Berry, M. (2013). *Fantasy life: The outrageous, uplifting, and heartbreaking world of fantasy sports from the guy who's lived it.* New York: Penguin Books.

Billings, A. C. & Ruihley, B. J. (2014). *The fantasy sport industry: Games within games.* Routledge. New York.

Biocca, F., Harms, C., & Burgoon, J. K. (2003). Toward a more robust theory and measure of social presence: Review and suggested criteria. *Presence, 12*(5), 456–480. doi:10.1162/105474603322761270

Brown, N., Billings, A. C., and Ruihley, B. (2012). Exploring the change in motivations for fantasy sport participation during the life cycle of a sports fan. *Communication Research Reports, 29*(4), 333–342. doi:10.1080/08824096.2012.723646

Cole, H. & Griffiths, M.D. (2007). Social interactions in massively multiplayer online role-playing gamers. *Cyberpsychology and Behavior, 10*(4), 575–583.

Drayer, J., Shapiro, S. L., Dwyer, B., Morse, A. L., & White, J. (2010). The effects of fantasy football participation on NFL consumption: A qualitative analysis. *Sport Management Review, 13*(2), 129–141. doi:10.1016/j.smr.2009.02.001

Dwyer, B., & Drayer, J. (2010). Fantasy sport consumer segmentation: An investigation into the different consumption modes of fantasy football participants. *Sport Marketing Quarterly, 19,* 207–216.

Duck, S. (1988). *Relating to others.* Milton Keynes, UK: Open University Press.

Fantasy Sports Trade Association (2014). "Industry Demographics." Retrieved on November, 17, 2014 from http://www.fsta.org/?page=Demographics

Frost, J.H. & Eden, A.L. (2014). The effect of social sharing games and game performance on motivation to play brain games. In B. Schouten et al (Eds.) *Games for Health 2014.* Springer Fachmedien Weisbaden.

Hardin, M. (2014). Moving beyond description: Putting Twitter in (theoretical) context. *Communication and Sport, 2*(2), 113–116. doi:10.1177/2167479514527425

International Society for Presence Research. (2000). *The concept of presence: Explication statement.* Retrieved from htpp://ispr.info/

Karg, A. J., and McDonald, H. (2011). Fantasy sport participation as a complement to traditional sport consumption. *Sport Management Review, 14*(4), 327–346. doi:10.1016/j.smr.2010.11.004

Korzenny, F. (1978). A theory of electronic propinquity: Mediated communications in organizations. *Communication Research, 5,* 3–24. doi:10.1177/009365027800500101

Kowert, R. & Oldmeadow, J. A. (2014). Playing for social comfort: Online video game play as a social accommodator for the insecurely attached. *Computers in Human Behavior.* doi doi:10.1016/j.chb.2014.05.004

Lee, K. M. (2004). Presence, explicated. *Communication Theory, 14,* 27–50. doi:10.1111/j.1468-2885.2004.tb00302.x

Lee, J., Ruihley, B. J., Brown, N, & Billings, A. C. (2013). The effects of fantasy football participation on team identification, team loyalty and NFL fandom. *Journal of Sports Media, 8*(1), 207–227. doi:10.1353/jsm.2013.0008

Lenhart, A., & Duggan, M. (February 11, 2014). Couples, the internet, and social media. *Pew Research Center.* Retrieved from http://www.pewinternet.org/
2014/02/11/couples-the-internet-and-social-media/

Lombard, M., & Ditton, T. B. (1997). At the heart of it all: The concept of presence.
*Journal of Computer-Mediated Communication, 3*(2). doi:10.1111/j.1083-6101.1997
.tb00072.x

Mandel v. UBS/Painewebber Inc., 860 A.2d 945 (Nj. 2004).

Nowak, K. L., & Biocca, F. (2003). The effect of the agency and anthropomorphism
on users' sense of telepresence, copresence, and social presence in virtual environments. *Presence, 12,* 481–494. doi:10.1162/105474603322761289

O'Sullivan, P. B. (2000). What you don't know won't hurt me: Impression management functions of communication channels in relationships. *Human Communication Research, 26*(3), 403–431. doi:10.1093/hcr/26.3.403

Pena, J., & Hancock, J. (2006). An analysis of socioemotional and task communication in online multiplayer video games. *Communication Research, 33*(1), 92–109.
doi:10.1177/0093650205283103

Petty, G., Bracken, C. C., Rubenking, B., Buncher, M., and Gress, E. (2010).
Telepresence, soundscapes and technological expectation: Putting the observer
into the equation. *Virtual Reality, 14*(1), 15–25. doi:10.1007/s10055-009-0148-8

Ramirez, A., Walther, J. B., Burgoon, J. K., & Sunnafrank, M. (2002). Information-
seeking strategies, uncertainty, and computer-mediated communication: Toward a conceptual model. *Human Communication Research, 28*(2), 213–228.
doi:10.1093/hcr/28.2.213

Ruihley, B. & Hardin, M. (2011a). Beyond touchdowns, home runs, and 3-pointers:
An examination of fantasy sports participation motivation. *International Journal
of Sport Management and Marketing, 10*(3/4), 232–256.

Ruihley, B. & Hardin, M. (2011b). Message boards and the fantasy sport experience. *International Journal of Sport Communication, 4*(2), 233–252.

Sherry, J. L. (2014). Media effects, communication, and complexity science insights
on games for learning. In F. C. Blumberg (Ed.). *Learning by playing: Video gaming in education.* Oxford University Press. New York, NY.

Sherry, J., Greenberg, B., Lucas, S., & Lachlan, K. (2006). Video game uses
and gratifications as predictors of use and game preference. In P. Vorderer &
J. Bryant (Eds.), *Playing computer games: Motives, responses and consequences.*
Mahwah, NJ: Erlbaum.

Short, J., Williams, E., & Christie, B. (1976). *The social psychology of telecommunications.* London: Wiley.

Stafford, L. (2005). *Maintaining long-distance and cross-residential relationships.*
Mahwah, NJ: Erlbaum.

Steinkuehler, A.C. & Williams, D. (2006). Where everybody knows your (screen)
name: Online games as "third places." *Journal of Computer-Mediated Communication, 11*(4), 885–909.

Tamborini, R., & Skalski, P. (2006). The role of presence in the experience of electronic games. In P. Vorderer & J. Bryant (Eds.), *Playing video games: Motives, responses, and consequences* (pp. 225–240). Mahwah, NJ: Erlbaum.

Tidwell, L. C., & Walther, J. B. (2002). Computer-mediated communication effects on disclosure, impressions, and interpersonal evaluations: Getting to know one another a bit at a time. *Human Communication Research, 28,* 317–348. doi:10.1111/j.1468-2958.2002.tb00811.x

Todd, D. (2014, August 24). Workzone: Fantasy leagues powering into offices. *Pittsburgh Post-Gazette.* Retrieved from http://www.post-gazette.com/business/2014/08/24/Workzone-Fantasy-leagues-powering-into-offices/stories/201408240100

Tong, S. T., & Walther, J. B. (2011). Relational maintenance and computer-mediated communication. In K. B. Wright & L. M. Webb (Eds.), *Computer-mediated communication in personal relationships* (pp. 98–118). New York: Peter Lang.

Utz, S. (2000). Social information processing in MUD's: The development of friendships in virtual worlds. *Journal of Online Behavior, 1.* Retrieved from http://www.behavior.net/JOB/v1n1/utz.html

Walther, J. B. (1992). Interpersonal effects in computer-mediated interaction: A relational perspective. *Communication Research, 19,* 52–90. doi:10.1177/009365092019001003

Walther, J. B. (1994). Anticipated ongoing interaction versus channel effects on relational communication in computer-mediated interaction. *Human Communication Research, 20,* 473–501. doi:10.1111/j.1468-2958.1994.tb00332.x

Walther, J. B. (1996). Computer-mediated communication: Impersonal, interpersonal, and hyperpersonal interaction. *Communication Research, 23,* 3–43. doi:10.1177/009365096023001001

Walther, J. B. (2007). Selective self-presentation in computer-mediated communication: Hyperpersonal dimensions of technology, language and cognition. *Computers in Human Behavior, 23,* 2538–2557. doi:10.1016/j.chb.2006.05.002

Walther, J. B., Anderson, J. F., & Park, D. (1994). Interpersonal effects in computer-mediated interaction: A meta-analysis of social and anti-social communication. *Communication Research, 21,* 460–487. doi:10.1177/009365094021004002

Walther, J. B., & Bazarova, N. N. (2008). Validation and application of electronic propinquity theory to computer-mediated communication in groups. *Communication Research, 35,* 622–645. doi:10.1177/0093650208321783

Walther, J. B., & Burgoon, J. K. (1992). Relational communication in computer-mediated interaction. *Human Communication Research, 19,* 50–88. doi:10.1111/j.1468-2958.1992.tb00295.x

Walther, J. B., & D'Addario, K. P. (2001). The impacts of emoticons on message interpretation in computer-mediated communication. *Social Science Computer Review, 19,* 323–345. doi:10.1177.089443930101900307

Walther, J. B., Loh, T., & Granka, L. (2005). Let me count the ways: The interchange of verbal and nonverbal cues in computer-mediated and face-to-face affinity. *Journal of Language and Social Psychology, 24,* 36–65.

Walther, J. B., & Parks, M. R. (2002). Cues filtered out, cues filtered in: Computer-mediated communication and relationships. In M. L. Knapp & J. A. Daly (Eds.), *Handbook of interpersonal communication* (3rd ed., pp. 529–563). Thousand Oaks, CA: Sage.

Walther, J. B., & Tidwell, L. C. (1995). Nonverbal cues in computer-mediated communication, and the effects of chronemics on relational communication. *Journal of Organizational Computing, 5,* 355–378. doi:10.1080/10919399509540258

Westerman, D. (2007). Comparing uncertainty reduction in face-to-face and computer-mediated communication: A social information processing theory perspective. Unpublished dissertation. East Lansing, MI: Michigan State University

Westerman, D. & Skalski, P. D. (2010). Computers and telepresence: A ghost in the machine? In C. C. Bracken and P. D. Skalski (Eds.), *Immersed in media: Telepresence in everyday life* (pp. 63–86). New York: Routledge.

Wright, K. (2002). Social support within an on-line cancer community: An assessment of emotional support, perceptions of advantages and disadvantages, and motives for using the community from a communication perspective. *Journal of Applied Communication Research, 30*(3), 195–209.

# 6

# DRAFT DAY

## Risk, Responsibility, and Fantasy Football

*Andrew Baerg*

In the spring of 2014, a group of high school boys at Corona del Mar High School in Newport Beach, California, came together to decide how best to plan for the school's upcoming prom. However, rather than planning anything related to theme, food, or music, the boys united around what they perceived to be a responsible way to deal with the question of their dates. Their solution? The boys decided to hold a "prom draft." Each boy would randomly pick a number out of a bowl. The boy with the lowest number would then be given the first pick in the draft, and conceivably, the best chance of gaining the prom date of his choosing (Chen, 2014; Steussy, 2014). One report even suggested that boys were selling top picks to others who had a greater interest in an earlier selection. According to one student, as much as $140 was exchanged for the apparent privilege of a high draft pick (Flores, 2014).

At a glance, any connection between proms and sports beyond the clichéd quarterback-homecoming queen pairing would seem obtuse. However, the story of the prom draft speaks to how discourses surrounding sport and culture can easily bleed into one another. As a consequence, it becomes important to explore these discourses and their roots to better understand what this discursive intermingling means. This essay aims to more deeply examine one of these discourse mixes, the phenomenon of fantasy sports and its connection with neoliberal notions of risk and responsibility.

I begin by reviewing the limited scholarly work on the subject. This essay then situates the popularity of fantasy football in its contemporary context by discussing some of the key tenets of neoliberalism and risk before linking these tenets to a qualitative textual analysis of fantasy football strategy articles from sports media websites. This analysis reveals how the discourses on these sites naturalize a neoliberal subjectivity oriented around risk and responsible risk management.

## FANTASY SPORTS: WHO IS PLAYING? WHAT DOES IT MEAN?

Online fantasy football participants would appear to be prime examples of the active sports fan fostered by new media sport (Boyle & Haynes, 2002; Real, 2006). To this point, the minimal scholarly attention paid to fantasy sports has focused primarily on these active participants and their reasons for participation, especially in the context of new media. For example, although his work preceded the widespread popularity of the World Wide Web, Kaplan (1990) noted how computers were changing participants' experiences of fantasy baseball. Even as labeling Kaplan's work a participant study might be suspect, his informal interviews with fantasy baseball participants appear to be the first academic work to focus on participants' motivations. Hiltner and Walker (1996) used fantasy baseball as their critical example in studying how people communicate online. Other more recent fantasy sports participant studies have focused on reasons for participation (Brown, Billings, & Ruihley, 2012; Farquhar & Meeds, 2007; Lee, Kwak, et al., 2011; Ruihley & Billings, 2012; Ruihley & Hardin, 2013; Spinda & Haridakis, 2008), effects on participants' media usage (Comeau, 2007; Nesbit & King, 2010b; Nyland & Randle, 2008), influence on fan relations to real sport (Corrigan, 2007; Drayer, Shapiro, et al., 2010; Nesbit & King, 2010a), processes of fantasy team selection (Smith, Sharma, & Hooper, 2006), participant winning expectancy (Kwak, Lim, et al., 2010), and perceived ease of use of fantasy sports websites (Kwak & McDaniel, 2011).

Even as these studies examined fantasy sports participation uncritically, some scholars have considered the more pernicious side of fantasy sports participation. Participant online discourse has linked fantasy sports activity to pathological gambling (Bernhard & Eade, 2005). Carlson (2013) critiques fantasy sports for the way it moves participants to bisect their rooting interests between favorite teams and their fantasy teams. Carlson also sees fantasy sports generating the problem of its participants attending strictly to the more statistically productive events in sport, those that typically generate points for their fantasy teams. Therefore, fantasy sports implicitly deny the value of teamwork in favor of individual performance. Davis and Carlisle Duncan's (2006) critical feminist reading of participant discourse suggests that fantasy sports have become another venue in which the reinforcement of hegemonic white masculinity may occur and argue for this reinforcement as an additional motivation for participation.

Like Davis and Carlisle Duncan (2006), Oates (2009) and Begley (2014) also address aspects of the ideological side of fantasy sports. As part of a broader argument about what he terms "vicarious management" (p. 31), Oates argues that fantasy sports aligns its participants with the authority structures of the National Football League rather than with the athletes who prop up this institution. In fantasy sports, participants are thereby positioned to perceive athletes as disposable commodities. Oates subsequently argues that fantasy sports operate within the larger historical and intertwined trajectories of hegemonic masculinity and white supremacy, a conjunction he labels "racialized androcentrism" (p. 33). Begley's (2014) look at the cultural discourses of fantasy football speaks to how some of its accompanying texts, like her primary example, the fantasy sports themed television series *The League*, affirm a specific type of neoliberal citizen/ subject in contemporary capitalism. Within this cultural discourse, Begley sees the themes of individualism, entrepreneurialism, a focus on knowledge for the sake of control, power fantasies, and inclusion fantasies. These types of fantasies have been parodied by the online satire magazine, *The Onion*, in their series, "Tough Season" (viewable at http://www.theonionco/ fantasyfootball/?video=189).

This essay aims to contribute to this relatively meager body of research by analyzing an aspect of fantasy sports that has yet to be considered, the media texts produced by the fantasy sports industry. A few industry studies have engaged the way mainstream mass media have responded to the growth of fantasy sports more broadly (Woodward, 2005) and addressed the question of intellectual property with respect to the use of Major League Baseball player names and images in fantasy baseball (Bolitho, 2006–2007; Evans, 2008; Gelchinsky, 2008; Grady, 2007; Massari, 2007; Mead, 2007; Stohr, 2008). However, the populist media texts produced for consumption by fantasy sports participants have yet to be analyzed. It is these texts that discursively position participants in particular ways.

Where Oates (2009) asserts fantasy sports positions its players within the frame of racialized androcentrism and Begley (2014) understands fantasy sports to perpetuate specific forms of neoliberal citizens/subjects, this chapter concentrates on another theme resident in these cultural discourses. This theme is that of risk and risk management. As discourses of risk and risk management become prominent in fantasy sports discourses, they subsequently position fans in new ways. These fans are no longer passive. These fans are not even merely active in making meaning from their sport consumption. Rather, fantasy sports participants are positioned to become overtly responsibilized fans in their fantasy sports activity. This essay takes up the texts produced by one segment of the fantasy sports industry as evidence of this positioning work. By looking at the way fantasy football is discussed on various sports websites, I argue that these representations of fantasy football incline their audiences to think about their fandom as a fandom intimately tied to responsibility, i.e., a responsibilized fandom. This responsibilized fandom mirrors other aspects of a broader neoliberal worldview (see below), a worldview that encourages people to practice risk management. Fantasy sports thereby have the potential effect of rendering a risk management approach to decision-making as common sense when what is represented as common sense is grounded in this neoliberal worldview.

## AN EMPIRICAL LOOK AT FANTASY FOOTBALL PREVIEWS

The study employs critical qualitative textual analysis to examine the texts in the data set. This project analyzes texts that guide fantasy players about the choices they will need to make ahead of the impending fantasy season (i.e., the content produced by the fantasy sports media who produce advice for participants). Rather than try to address these preview articles across several sports, this chapter concentrates specifically on preseason preview articles related to the most popular fantasy sport, football. It also further narrows this set of articles from those related to all aspects of fantasy football ahead of the 2014 season to those specifically focused on draft strategies. To zero in on draft strategy makes this project potentially more applicable to fantasy sports media discourses more broadly given the draft's prominence in fantasy sports.

The selected articles in the data set were derived from mainstream sports media websites and the NFL's own website. These sites included: *usatoday.com*; *si.com*; *rotowire.com*; and, *NFL.com*. The articles in this data set were subsequently coded for common themes. To be sure, this data set may not be representative of fantasy sports generally, however, its findings can and should be taken up by others who might use this work and apply it to other sports like baseball, basketball, and hockey.

Before beginning the analysis proper, it is important to contextualize these fantasy football discourses and their positioning of participants within a more theoretical framework. Foucault's notion of governmentality and the way governmentality theory has been applied to an examination of neoliberalism serves as the guiding theoretical backdrop for this study. The next section briefly explains governmentality and its relation to neoliberalism in contemporary culture.

## NEOLIBERALISM, SPORT, AND LEISURE PRACTICE

The notion of governmentality has its roots in Foucault's conceptualization of the term in his broader project on the explication of power. Foucault considered governmentality as a way of thinking about how rule functions, who rules, and to what purposes rule is directed within the context of government. He defined governmentality as a means of thinking about power and its concern with the conduct of conduct (Foucault, 1991) in arguing that governmentality serves as the node where techniques of power and techniques of the self coalesce. Subjects have the ability to act freely, but this freedom operates within boundaries and parameters established by government for governmental objectives. Governmentality studies have been primarily interested in how these processes work within neoliberalism (Dean, 1999; Rose, 1996, 1999).

As neoliberalism has served as the guiding governmental rationality of late twentieth and early twenty-first century democracies (Harvey, 2005), its prominent features have shaped other cultural domains as well. Sport would appear to be no exception. In recent years a developing body of literature has arisen linking various aspects of sport to governmentality and neoliberalism. Sport studies scholars have applied Foucauldian-inflected governmentality theory to areas of sport and social policy (Burke & Hallinan, 2008; Green & Houlihan, 2006; Law, 2001; McDermott, 2007; Park, 2005; Ralph, 2006; Scherer and Jackson, 2004), citizenship (Lee, Jackson & Lee, 2007), the spaces of sport (Fusco, 2005) and fitness discourses (Jette, 2006; Markula, 2004; Smith Maguire 2008).

It would seem that the majority of these types of governmentality studies have concentrated on how political rationalities shape the formation of the free self of neoliberal professional and institutional life (Binkley, 2006).

However, aside from the aforementioned scholarship on fitness discourses, this work has yet to more broadly consider popular leisure practices that would appear to be outside the realms of professional and institutional sport. Considering leisure practices unhinged from these more formally structured zones of activity enables an examination of what governmentality theorists call translation. Translation involves "processes which link up the concern elaborated within rather general and wide-ranging political rationalities with *specific* programmes for government of this or that problematic zone of life" (Rose, 1999, p. 50, emphasis in original). Translation mechanisms move political rationalities around to different sites as they link the macro to the micro. In doing so, translation mechanisms enable rule at a distance such that the values of the governing become enmeshed with the standards of conduct of the governed (Rose, 1999). These translation mechanisms might be akin to Bennett's (2002) concern about "the varying ways in which different kinds of cultural knowledge are translated into the varying technical forms through which new realities are produced and sustained, and brought to bear on the regulation of conduct" (p. 30). Attending to the discourses produced by the fantasy football sports media provides insight into the workings of these translation mechanisms.

Given the relative lack of attention paid to how governmentality functions in leisure practice and more specifically, to the texts produced by the fantasy football industry, this essay asks the following questions. What kinds of political rationalities does fantasy football discourse naturalize for its participants? What macro level values do micro level fantasy football discourses encourage as they position fantasy team owners? By critically examining the discourses of the fantasy football industry, I argue that these texts naturalize a subjectivity associated with neoliberal risk management and its attendant responsibilization. Discourses produced by the fantasy football industry further the potential for the activity to serve as a translation mechanism linking authority's objectives to the aspirations of the free subjects of government.

## NEOLIBERAL RISK MANAGEMENT
## AND RESPONSIBLE SUBJECTS

Although the neoliberal person is multifaceted, one of its most important characteristics concerns that of responsibility. In a neoliberal context, the subject is constructed through "a whole series of interventions aimed at producing the human being as a moral creature capable of exercising responsible stewardship and judgment over its own conduct" (Rose, 1999, p. 42). In a neoliberal context, to become this moral creature is to exercise responsibility by acting entrepreneurially in maximizing one's resources to greatest effect. If the good entrepreneur is one who makes maximum use of the resources, then that subject is also accorded the moral value of being responsible as well.

How is the subject encouraged to adopt this position of responsibility? One of the ways this responsibilization occurs is through the circulation of discourses invoking the notion of risk management. In drawing on the work of Ulrich Beck (1992, 1999), Kenny (2005) argues that neoliberal society's approach to risk has changed as he reflects on how "our contemporary understandings of risk, and the ways in which risk assessments permeate both the choices we make in our everyday lives and public policy" (p. 50). Unlike the period before neoliberal hegemony, risk management now no longer sits only under the purview of institutions, but also falls upon the self in the practice of daily life. O'Malley (1996) discusses a similar idea in using the term "prudentialism" which he defines as "a technology of governance that removes the key conception of regulating individuals by collectivist risk management, and throws back upon the individual the responsibility for managing risk" (p. 197). Via this prudentialism, citizens are coaxed into risk management in a variety of cultural domains in calculating future possibilities and responding to the outcome of these calculations. O'Malley goes on to assert that risk management techniques have become privatized in the context of prudentialism such that the rational and responsible individual becomes the one who not only desires to minimize risk, but who also actively pursues this management as well.

Identifying and managing risk becomes a way for the neoliberal subject to categorize the real and to render what cannot be seen visible. In minimizing invisibility, risk management aims to make that which is to be governed transparent and subject to a field of visibility so that future circumstances can be predicted and risk minimized. In a neoliberal context, failing to adopt this type of strategy may be deemed irresponsible (Rose, 1999, Kenny, 2005).

In much the same way as the responsible risk-managing subject appears in other cultural domains, so too does this subject appear in sport and leisure discourse. This project examines these discourses as they are produced by the fantasy football media industry. This neoliberal approach to risk management was expressed in a variety of ways in this discourse as fantasy football websites prepared participants for the coming season. Among these expressions of addressing risk included the drafting strategies writers encouraged owners to deploy in managing risk, how owners were positioned to perceive football players as embodying varying degrees of risk, and how owners were positioned to ideally behave during the draft. All of these discourses came together to encourage a responsibilized fandom oriented around the successful management of risk.

## RISK MANAGEMENT AND FANTASY FOOTBALL ADVICE

The multiple pieces of advice provided fantasy owners in this media discourse portray a clear interest in positioning them as risk managers. Risk ends up being the frame through which the draft process occurs and the object toward which it is directed, the players being drafted. As a consequence, risk becomes a property of both operating within the draft process and positioning the athletes who are drafted. Risk also ends up becoming a way in which owners are positioned to see themselves through these discourses.

### Draft Strategy and Risk Management

First, several articles overtly referenced the broader problem of risk in their advice to fantasy football participants about the draft process. Some of these overt references to risk represented it as a threat to the owner's potential success as part of the general set of guidelines to which owners ought to adhere. Bonini's (2014) second principle for draft success encouraged owners to, "Identify risk before pulling the trigger. . . .Even the most daring owners assess a player's risk-reward ratio" (para. 3). Heaney (2014b) explained how refusing to draft a running back in the first four rounds, contrary to conventional wisdom, becomes a strategy designed "to fight the increasing risk in drafting stud running backs early" (para. 2). Liss (2014) implied the dangers of taking too much risk in asserting, "If you draft a top running back early, it's important that you get their backups. Spending a late middle round pick is necessary to reduce your risk" (para. 21). Fabiano (2014a) noted the challenges involved in drafting some risky players, but stated that these challenges could be offset with a careful draft pick, "You are also allowing yourself to minimize some of the risk with players such as C. J. Spiller or Trent Richardson (among others) because you can draft them as flex starters rather than No.2s" (Fabiano, 2014a, para. 8). In each of these examples, risk was deemed a threat that needed to be directly addressed. As owners participated in their fantasy drafts, risk had to be identified, fought, reduced, and minimized.

Other writers were concerned about undue risk that could accrue from poor strategy as a draft unfolded. Liss (2014) warned that, "if the 10th one gets picked right before your turn, and you know that there's not a lot of difference between the 11th and 19th, then you'd be wise to choose a player at another position where there's more risk of a dropoff before your next pick" (para. 20). In an analysis of a mock draft, Gelhar (2014a) justified an owner's selection by saying that, ". . . the drop from Rodgers to the next quarterback was too large a risk losing him over that same span" (Gelhar, 2014a, para. 10). As with the citations above, risk is again deemed something to be avoided if at all possible. Making the selection with the least risk prevents owners from facing a drop or dropoff to a player who will be riskier.

Risk was not only addressed via explicit invocation, but also implicitly through the lens of the related economic concepts of opportunity cost and scarcity. Beller (2014c) explained opportunity cost thusly,

> . . . despite what you've heard, the time-honored tradition of waiting on a quarterback still makes sense. The reason? Opportunity cost. You pay for every pick you make in a fantasy draft in two ways. There's the seen cost, the overall pick in the draft, and the unseen cost, what you pass up to take your guy. For my money, that latter price tag is far too high to take a quarterback early. Let's say you have the 11th pick in a 12-team draft, and take Brees with your first pick and LeSean McCoy with your second at 14th overall. The opportunity cost you've paid by taking Brees comes in the form of a second-tier back (think Ray Rice) or elite wide receiver (think Brandon Marshall or A. J. Green) (para. 1–3).

Opportunity cost becomes one of the ways in which owners can evaluate various levels of risk. More opportunity cost means greater risk in that the owner has sacrificed a more valuable asset for one that will likely not be as productive. In another article, Beller (2014g) again raised the notion of opportunity cost in encouraging owners not to take non-elite quarterbacks too early in their drafts, "This should be obvious from the statistics above, but the opportunity cost associated with any highly ranked quarterbacks not named Peyton Manning, Aaron Rodgers or Drew Brees is simply too great" (para. 13). Refusing to account for opportunity cost would put an owner's overall draft strategy at risk and could lead to fantasy failure.

Along the same lines as opportunity cost, risk was also implicitly discussed in terms of scarcity within the draft, particularly with respect to positions. As part of his now decade old, but still posted, fantasy football strategy guide, Liss (2004) evoked concerns about running back scarcity reminding owners that, "starting running backs will go at least 20 deep—

and often deeper as savvy fantasy owners often draft three or more running backs in the early rounds, knowing that the position is so scarce" (para. 8). This positional scarcity was noted by others who reasoned that, "Because there is such a shortage of bona fide 'bell cow' running backs, it's hard to pass up one of them if you have one of the first four . . . selections in your draft" (Grant, 2014, para. 4) and, "The supply of featured running backs does not meet the demand of a fantasy football lineup, so you could be in dire straits if you pass on the position" (Fabiano, 2014b, para. 3). In another article, Fabiano (2014a) justified his selection in a mock draft on the basis of scarcity, "I went with Bush because of his immense skills as a pass catcher in Detroit along with the fact that the running back position was starting to thin out" (para. 5). Gelhar (2014a) noted the ongoing trend in this direction, one that contrasted a recent wide receiver boom, saying, "That's a far cry from years past, and speaks to both the scarcity of top-tier running backs and the wealth of bonafide studs at wide receiver" (para. 12). Running back scarcity was also joined by other types of scarcity in different types of drafts. Liss (2011) commented on the dearth of quality quarterbacks available as the draft might unfold for larger leagues. "In a 14-team league (or deeper), the position typically becomes far more scarce, as the waiver wire is usually fairly barren during the year, and owners are therefore inclined to draft backup QBs earlier" (para. 6).

As with opportunity cost, the notion of positional scarcity relates to the risk issue for the way it must be addressed in an owner's draft. Without careful assessment of the paucity of excellent running backs, owners could find themselves risking missing out on the most productive option once their pick arose. Acknowledging scarcity also becomes a strategy by which risk can be managed by having it pushed into the future rather than engaged in the immediate present. When faced with scarcity, owners can address it by snapping up a scarce resource like a top tier quarterback and leave a more difficult, riskier decision that might derive from ignoring scarcity for a later round. Kicking the risk can down the road as a consequence of scarcity becomes a viable risk management option for fantasy football owners.

## FOOTBALL PLAYERS AND DEGREES OF RISK

Perhaps even more pervasive than the theme of risk and the draft process, a second theme these discourses revealed identified risk as an inherent property of potential draftees. Football players were frequently overtly positioned as bearing various degrees of risk. O'Brien (2014) urged owners considering quarterbacks to, "Secure one of those veteran studs. It's a low-risk, high-reward investment" (para. 2). Evidently, going with a more experienced quarterback meant selecting one who possessed less risk than a trendier younger player. Similar sentiments were echoed by other writers. In addressing early round draft strategy, Liss (2014) advised, ". . . maybe snag a top-tier quarterback over a risky running back with a late first round ADP [average draft position]" (para. 5, inclusion mine). To affirm this point, later in the article, Liss addressed the issue of safety and risk in the early rounds of the draft saying, "Stick with a safe and steady player over one who could be great, but who carries more risk" (para. 12).

On the obverse, choosing an older running back like Marshawn "Beast Mode" Lynch, would mean balancing that risk with a second safer pick. "Beast Mode likely has at least one more great year in him, but backing up that risk . . . is a smart and safe way to go" (Gelhar, 2014a, para. 7). Risk was also a factor when considering injury issues as well. Gelhar's (2014a) discussion of running backs also saw him note that the Cowboys' Demarco "Murray comes with a little risk this year, as he has a sizeable injury history . . ." (para. 5). When risk was unavoidable, owners were encouraged to leverage a perceived safer choice as a hedge against problems that might arise with that risk. In the previously cited article, Gelhar (2014a) goes on to say that, ". . . pairing the high-upside but potentially risky Bernard with the fantasy point monster Charles is a savvy move" (para. 9). To look at these sources was to see risk explicitly counterbalanced by notions of high reward, safety, steadiness, smarts, and savviness.

Where risk was not mentioned directly, this positioning of athletes as bearers of risk was invoked more subtly via discourses of prudentialism associated with safety and insurance. Beller (2014d) noted how a group of top tier wide receivers were a wiser selection in a particular draft slot than their potentially equally productive running back counterparts, "All six of those receivers have safer, higher floors than running backs being selected in the same range" (para. 4). Later in the same article, Beller reiterated this point declaring that football is "a sport that has been proven to be fraught with peril for running backs. Why even mess with that when the receivers are so rock-solid?" (para. 5). Safety and solidity were clearly preferable than the risks associated with peril. Where risk would need to be taken, insurance would need to be acquired to offset that risk. This was especially important in considering running backs for, "The chances that your starting running back makes it through 16 games will be slim. Make sure you have insurance" (Grant, 2014, para. 10). Even specific types of insurance were advocated by some writers. Liss (2014) spoke against the alleged benefits

of the "handcuff strategy," one in which an owner selects a player and his
backup just in case the starter is injured. "Only rarely should you concern
yourself about getting your stars' real life backups as insurance" (Liss, 2014,
para. 28). Insurance needed to be found outside of an owner's star's team
rather than in the star's potential substitute.

This prudentialism was also expressed in a desire for consistent rather
than volatile fantasy production. Consistent players carried considerably
less risk than those whose performance had the capacity to fluctuate wildly.
Running backs were typically thought to be the most consistent point
producers. Liss (2011) noted that, "given their higher volume of touches,
their scoring is less volatile than that of receivers, i.e., you can count on
more consistent week-to-week production from them than you can from
receivers" (para. 14). Liss (2011) commented on the difficulty in forecast-
ing receiver performance saying that, "they see fewer than half the touches
that comparable backs do and their production is more volatile, i.e., it's less
consistent on a weekly basis" (para. 16). Similarly, Gelhar (2014b) spoke
to the volatility of most wide receivers urging owners to instead select the
Detroit Lions', Calvin Johnson, because "He's the most consistent receiver
in fantasy, with the potential to lead his position in scoring every year. He's
the only no-brainer first-round pick" (para. 3). Elsewhere, Gelhar (2014a)
favorably assessed a mock drafter's selections by pointing to the virtue of
consistency, "I like Money's selection of Thomas, who is about as consistent
as wide receivers come" (para. 5) before complimenting another drafter's
choices declaring that, "This might not be the sexiest fantasy tandem, but
these two will produce as consistently as any other duo in these first two
rounds" (para. 7). Grant (2014) contrasted selecting a consistent player with
one who might end up being taken far too early in the draft by rhetorically
asking, "Why reach for a running back that you're not sure about in favor of
a player that can consistently post 13–15 fantasy points per week?" (para. 7).

With this advice, subjects were encouraged to avoid unwise decisions
that rolled the proverbial dice on players who had yet to demonstrate the
ability to perform consistently. A riskier strategy was only to be deployed in
later rounds of the draft when the participant's draft pick resources did not
have the same value as those picks used to select players who would be on
the participant's starting team each and every week. Given this perspective,
the best players were those who could be trusted to produce for an owner
on a consistent basis. Consistent production was equated to minimal risk.
All of these examples clearly positioned players as bearers of risk and subsequently in need of careful, maximally responsible risk management from
owners interested in drafting them.

## THE FANTASY OWNER AT RISK

If consistency was to be treasured and volatility to be avoided in the draft selections, fantasy owners were also warned about the dangers of falling into a different form of volatility. This volatility to be avoided speaks to a third theme resident in the data. Throughout these articles, owners were not only advised about how to consider risk responsibly in their assessment of how to draft and who to draft, but this advice was also extended to the owners themselves. Owners were warned about the pitfalls of an emotional and/or mental volatility that might come from a lack of preparation or from being unable to make the choice one wanted to make. To possess this kind of personal volatility would yield a draft characterized by failure. Those who could avoid the experience of this volatility and manage the risk that was the self would be in the best position to succeed. Several articles characterized the type of person who best manages this form of risk.

In most cases, these media discourses assumed their readers were invested in being adequately prepared for their impending drafts. However, in some instances, this assumption was overtly stated, "Don't show up without knowing what you're getting into. You have some sort of stakes riding on this, be it pride or whatever. Act like it" (Heaney, 2014a, para. 2). The successful managing of risk was to be something taken seriously, in whatever form it took.

The owner who could manage risk successfully also was represented as never being compelled to make an undesirable decision out of hurried desperation. "If there are six picks before you're up next, have seven guys ready. Otherwise, you'll face the dreaded panic pick and lose control of the board" (Heaney, 2014a, para. 8). To yield control of the board to one's fellow competitors, and even worse, making "the dreaded panic pick" would be highly problematic. To be panicked also was related to being hurried in that, "You don't want to be frantically looking over your cheat sheet in the fifth or sixth round after Rounds 1–4 unfold in unexpected fashion" (Beller, 2014b, para. 4). Later in the same article, Beller raised a similar concern about inadequate preparedness urging owners to select a solid quarterback before they were gone or face the problem of being "forced to spend two picks on fringe starters, and that's a recipe for disaster" (para. 5). To be placed in a position where one would panic, act frantically, or be forced into a pick would betray a lack of preparation unbefitting of the responsible risk manager.

This panicked and frantic activity could place an owner in the unenviable position of lacking options. As a way to avoid panic and its dire consequences, Beller (2014f, 2014g) appeared particularly appreciative of a tiered player ranking strategy in which players are divided into groups based on their fantasy point potential. Tiers mitigate the possibility that an owner would need to make a risky pick out of a lack of choice. The strategy promised to "allow fantasy owners to easily find the best available players, rather than forcing themselves to take a player at a specific position" (Beller, 2014g, para. 6). Beller (2014f) argued that, "Without tiers, I might fall into a trap and force myself into taking the next wideout in my rankings . . ." (para. 5). Heaney (2014a) affirmed the tier strategy's facility in preventing an unwise selection in advising, "Don't feel pressured into taking someone too soon just because others are grabbing the same position. Set your value tiers and stick to them" (para. 9). In each of these quotations, fantasy owners were implicitly told that they should never find themselves in a position where they were forced to make a selection they might not want to make.

Whether it be a general failure to prepare, preparation that inadequately placed an owner in the unenviable position of being forced to make an unwanted selection, or, even worse, preparation that was so incomplete that it yielded panicked or frantic behavior, these discourses positioned fantasy owners to responsibly manage risk and thereby avoid undesirable outcomes.

## IMPLICATIONS

In looking at the ways in which fantasy football owners were positioned by these media discourses, they become subject to translation mechanisms that move neoliberal ideas about responsibility and risk into the generally non-productive zone that is leisure space. By promoting an approach to decision-making that appears entirely dominated by the presence of risk and managing said risk, fantasy football media discourse naturalizes a particularly neoliberal emphasis on how subjects make responsible choices. To choose is to necessarily address risk. To choose responsibly is to address risk in a prudent manner.

Failing to see the process of decisions as conjoined to risk, like the draft process, is to make decisions irresponsibly. Failing to see the objects of decisions as bearers of risk, like the athletes being drafted, is to assess the objects of risk irresponsibly. Failing to see oneself as subject to risk, like the owners making draft picks, is to irresponsibly place the self at risk. This irresponsibility inevitably leads to a lost season. By contrast, a fantasy football league's potential winner has theoretically embraced this neoliberal approach to decision-making and been rewarded with a much greater chance of victory. In these discourses, the best owners are implicitly given the stamp of moral approval for maximizing resources and minimizing the risks attached to navigating the uncertainty of fantasy football.

However, as a translation mechanism, these media discourses and their capacity to position fantasy football participants resonate beyond the immediate confines of the activity. Even as these discourses promise subjects the freedom to make choices and construct the fantasy team they have always wanted, they simultaneously naturalize governmental rationalities associated with responsibility through risk management. The ways in which this responsibility is represented in this media discourse speaks to the potential effects of fantasy football participation. As others in this volume suggest, fantasy sports participation is often motivated by control (see chapters 2, 5, and 10; see also Billings & Ruihley, 2014). However, control is not an ideologically neutral term within these fantasy sports media discourses. A common sense understanding of control is directly related to managing others (one's fantasy team), resources (one's draft picks), and the self (one's demeanor) through the lens of responsible risk management. If fantasy sports operates as a translation mechanism, it may have the effect of moving participants to perceive other decisions that need to be made through this neoliberal, risk-oriented perspective. Others may come to be understood through the lens of risk, everyday decision-making may be subject to a risk calculus, and the self may be understood as subject to risk. Although there may be many alternative ways to think about the self, others, and decision-making, fantasy sports privileges and encourages this type of risk-saturated approach.

This perception also relates to the dynamic between work and play. Being responsible is an expected part of functioning as a good employee within the context of production. One might expect that leisure time away from work would allow for some relief from the pressures of this responsibility. However, rather than representing fantasy football as an escape from the responsible risk managing self of production, the discourses found here encouraged the extension of this type of neoliberal subjectivity in leisure space. As a consequence, in applying Rose's (1999) argument more narrowly here, if subjects have notions of responsibility via risk management reinforced within the apparent freedom and informality of leisure space, they may be more likely to align themselves with more formal mechanisms of neoliberal institutional and political power. Following Begley (2014), these discourses and the way they position subjects subsequently provide another demonstration of what it means to be a responsible neoliberal citizen, albeit in a context not overtly linked to citizenship. The most responsible, moral citizens are ultimately those who recognize risk and make decisions in a way that best manages it with respect to self and other. Participation in fantasy sports encourages this expression of what it means to be a productive, well-adjusted citizen in our twenty-first century neoliberal context. As a consequence, fantasy sports participation may have much more far-reaching social and cultural effects than we might imagine.

## CONCLUSION

This chapter has argued that fantasy football discourses produced by the sports media industry naturalize a particularly neoliberal approach to the activity. This neoliberal approach is characterized by an emphasis on responsible risk management. These discourses position fantasy football owners to adopt a risk management strategy that recognizes the risks inherent in the draft process, the varying degrees of risk resident in players, and risks that, without careful planning and preparation, might appear in owners themselves.

Reading and analyzing these fantasy football discourses through the lens of governmentality theory enables a fuller understanding of its ubiquity in the contemporary historical moment while acknowledging how this activity positions subjects in relation to neoliberal power. Attending to how neoliberal ideas may shape practices like fantasy football discourses and those who are positioned to adopt them also furthers additional insight into the ways in which the extension of subjectivities tied to the professional and the institutional traverse leisure space.

## REFERENCES

Beck, U. (1992). Risk society: Towards a new modernity. London: Sage.

Beck, U. (1999). World risk society. Cambridge: Polity Press.

Begley, M. M. (2014). Coaching neoliberal citizens/subjects, fulfilling fundamental fantasies: Cultural discourses of fantasy football. In B. Brummett & A. W. Ishak (Eds.), *Sports and Identity: New Agendas in Communication* (pp. 280–304). New York and London: Routledge.

Beller, M. (2014a, May 28). Fantasy football strategies: Going RB/RB at the top. *Si.com*. Retrieved July 24, 2014 from http://www.si.com/fantasy/2013/07/24/fantasy-football-draft-strategy-two-running-backs.

Beller, M. (2014b, May 28). Fantasy football draft strategies: Navigating the middle rounds. *Si.com.* Retrieved July 24, 2014 from http://www.si.com/fantasy/2013/08/07/fantasy-football-draft-strategy-middle-rounds.

Beller, M. (2014c, May 28). Fantasy football draft strategies: Waiting to draft quarterbacks. *Si.com.* Retrieved July 24, 2014 from http://www.si.com/fantasy/2013/07/18/fantasy-football-draft-strategy-waiting-quarterbacks.

Beller, M. (2014d, August 12). Fantasy football 2014 draft strategies: Late first round picks. *Si.com.* Retrieved August 22, 2014 from http://www.si.com/fantasy/2014/08/12/fantasy-football-2014-draft-strategies-late-first-round-picks.

Beller, M. (2014e, August 14). Fantasy football 2014 strategies: Targeting great offenses. *Si.com.* Retrieved August 22, 2014 from http://www.si.com/fantasy/2014/08/13/fantasy-football-2014-draft-strategies-targeting-great-offenses.

Beller, M. (2014f, August 14). Fantasy football 2014 strategies: Tiered player rankings. *Si.com.* Retrieved August 22, 2014 from http://www.si.com/fantasy/2014/08/14/fantasy-football-2014-draft-prep-tier-strategy.

Beller, M. (2014g, August 15). Fantasy football 2014 draft preview: Tips and advice for PPR leagues. *Si.com.* Retrieved August 22, 2014 from http://www.si.com/fantasy/ 2014/08/15/fantasy-football-2014-draft-preview-ppr-strategy.

Bernhard, B. J., & Eade, V. H. (2005). Gambling in a fantasy world: An exploratory study of rotisserie baseball games. *UNLV Gaming Research & Review Journal,* 9(1), 29–42.

Binkley, S. (2006). The perilous freedoms of consumption: Toward a theory of the conduct of consumer conduct. *Journal for Cultural Research, 10*(4), 343–362.

Bolitho, Z. C. (2006–2007). When fantasy meets the courtroom: An examination of the intellectual property issues surrounding the burgeoning fantasy sports industry. *Ohio State Law Journal,* 1–49.

Bonini, C. (2014, August 22). 9 tips to hack your draft like a pro. *Fantasy.usatoday.com.* Retrieved August 22, 2014 from http://fantasy.usatoday.com/2014/08/football-more-draft-tips.

Boyle, R., & Haynes, R. (2002). New media sport. *Culture, Sport, Society,* 5(3), 95–114.

Brown, N., Billings, A. C., & Ruihley, B. (2012). Exploring the change in motivations for fantasy sport participation during the life cycle of a sports fan. *Communication Research Reports,* 29(4), 333–342. doi:10.1080/0882

Burke, M., & Hallinan, C. (2008). Drugs, sport, anxiety and Foucauldian governmentality. *Sport, Ethics and Philosophy,* 2(1), 39–66.

Carlson, C. (2013). The reality of fantasy sports: A metaphysical and ethical analysis. *Journal of the Philosophy of Sport, 40*(2), 187–204. doi:10.1080/00948705.2013.785422.

Chen, T. (2014, May 7). California high school students accused of using a "prom draft" to find date. *Abcnews.com.* Retrieved May 12, 2014 from http://abcnews.go.com/blogs/headlines/2014/05/calif-high-school-students-accused-of-using-a-prom-draft-to-find-date

Comeau, T. O. (2007). Fantasy football participation and media usage. Unpublished doctoral dissertation, University of Missouri-Columbia.

Corrigan, T. F. (2007). Fantasy fans? Comparing team identification among fantasy football players and non-fantasy football players. Unpublished Masters Thesis, Florida State University, Tallahasee, FL.

Davis, N. W., & Carlisle Duncan, M. (2006). Sports knowledge is power. *Journal of Sport & Social Issues, 30*(3), 244--264.

Dean, M. (1999). *Governmentality: Power and rule in modern society*. London: Sage Publications.

Drayer, J., Shapiro, S. L., Dwyer, B., Morse, A. L., & White, J. (2010). The efffects of fantasy football participation on NFL consumption: A qualitative analysis. *Sport Management Review, 13*(2), 129–141. doi:10.1016/j.smr.2009.02.001.

Evans, S. B. (2008). Whose stats are they anyway? Analyzing the battle between Major League Baseball and fantasy game sites. *Texas Review of Entertainment & Sports Law, 9*, 335–351.

Fabiano, M. (2014a, July 14). 20 things fantasy owners should know before drafting. *NFL.com*. Retrieved July 23, 2014 from http://www.nfl.com/fantasyfootball/story/0ap2000000363811/article/20-things-fantasy-owners-should-know-before-drafting.

Fabiano, M. (2014b, August 19). The perfect round-by-round fantasy draft strategy. *NFL.com*. Retrieved August 22, 2014 from http://www.nfl.com/fantasyfootball/story/0ap1000000373849/article/the-perfect-roundbyround-fantasy-draft-strategy.

Farquhar, L. K., & Meeds, R. (2007). Types of fantasy sports users and their motivations. *Journal of Computer-Mediated Communication, 12*, 1208–1228.

Flores, A. (2014, May 7). Talk of "prom draft" at O.C. high school spurs note from principal. *Los Angeles Times*. Retrieved May 12, 2014 from http://www.latimes.com/local/la-me-0507-prom-draft-20140507-1-story.html.

Foucault, M. (1991). Governmentality. In G. Burchell & e. al. (Eds.), *The Foucault effect* (pp. 87–104). Chicago: University of Chicago Press.

Fusco, C. (2005). Cultural landscapes of purification: Sports spaces and discourses of whiteness. *Sociology of Sport Journal, 22*, 283–310.

Gardner, S. (2014a, August 19). 5 important tips when preparing for your draft. *Fantasy.usatoday.com*. Retrieved August 22, 2014 from http://fantasy.usatoday.com/ 2014/08/football-5-draft-tips.

Gardner, S. (2014b, August 19). One underused way to hack your draft, maximize your scoring potential. *Fantasy.usatoday.com*. Retrieved August 22, 2014 from http://fantasy.usatoday.com/2014/08/football-draft-stacking.

Gelchinsky, J. M. (2008). Publicity rights: A home run for fantasy leagues. *Journal of Intellectual Property Law & Practice, 3*(3), 161–162.

Gelhar, A. (2014a, August 19). Fantasy football draft strategies: Is RB-RB outdated? *NFL.com*. Retrieved August 22, 2014 from http://www.nfl.com/fantasy football/story /0ap3000000380027/article/fantasy-football-draft-strategies-is-rbrb-outdated.

Gelhar, A. (2014b, August 21). Draft day strategies: Stockpile stud WRs. *NFL.com*. Retrieved August 22, 2014 from http://www.nfl.com/news/story/0ap 3000000381135/article/draft-day-strategies-stockpile-stud-wrs.

Grady, J. (2007). Fantasy stats case tests limits of intellectual property protection in the digital age. *Sports Marketing Quarterly, 16*, 230–231.

Grant, M. (2014, August 20). Running back strategy reflects shifts in on-field use. *NFL.com*. Retrieved August 22, 2014 from http://www.nfl.com/fantasyfoot ball/story/0ap3000000381230/article/running-back-strategy-reflects-shift-in -onfield-use.

Green, M., & Houlihan, B. (2006). Governmentality, modernization, and the "disciplining" of national sporting organizations: Athletics in Australia and the United Kingdom. *Sociology of Sport Journal, 23*, 47–71.

Harvey, D. (2005). *A brief history of neoliberalism*. New York: Oxford University Press.

Heaney, T. (2014a, August 17). 10 mistakes to avoid in your fantasy football draft. *Fantasy.usatoday.com*. Retrieved August 22, 2014 from http:// fantasy.usatoday .com/2014/08/football-draft-tips.

Heaney, T. (2014b, August 13). How to hack your draft by avoiding running backs. *Fantasy.usatoday.com*. Retrieved August 22, 2014 from http://fantasy.usatoday .com/ 2014/08/rb-draft-strategy.

Hiltner, J. R., & Walker, J. R. (1996). Super frustration Sunday: The day Prodigy's fantasy baseball died; an analysis of the dynamics of electronic communication. *Journal of Popular Culture, 30*(3), 103–117.

Jette, S. (2006). Fit for two? A critical discourse analysis of Oxygen fitness magazine. *Sociology of Sport Journal, 23*, 331–351.

Kaplan, J. (1990). Universal baseball madness: The effect of rotisserie play on psyche and social life. *Play & Culture, 3*, 11–17.

Kenny, S. (2005). Terrify and control: The politics of risk society. *Social Alternatives, 24*(3), 50–-54.

Kwak, D. H., Lim, C., Lee, W.-Y., & Mahan III, J. (2010). How confident are you to win your fantasy league: Exploring the antecedents and consequences of winning expectancy. *Journal of Sport Management, 24*, 416–433.

Kwak, D. H., & McDaniel, S. R. (2011). Using an extended Technology Acceptance Model in exploring antecedants to adopting fantasy sports league websites. *International Journal of Sports Marketing & Sponsorship* (April), 240–253.

La Canfora, J. (2006, August 13). Beating yourself takes new meaning; Reality of fantasy football touches lives of NFL players in some way. *Washington Post*, p. E.1.

Law, A. (2001). Surfing the safety net: "Dole bludging," "Surfies" and governmentality in Australia. *International Review for the Sociology of Sport, 36*(1), 25–40.

Lee, N., Jackson, S. J., & Lee, K. (2007). South Korea's "glocal" hero: The Hiddink syndrome and the rearticulation of national citizenship and identity. *Sociology of Sport Journal, 24*, 283–301.

Lee, W.-Y., Kwak, D. H., Lim, C., Pedersen, P. M., & Miloch, K. (2011). Effects of personality and gender on fantasy sports game participation: The moderating role of perceived knowledge. *Journal of Gambling Studies, 27*, 427–441. doi:10.1007/s10899-010-9218-9.

Liss, C. (2004). 10 basic fantasy football strategy tips. *Rotowire.com*. Retrieved July 23, 2014 from http://www.rotowire.com/football/101/basic_strategy.htm.

Liss, C. (2011). Fantasy football draft strategy: 10 things you need to think about. *Rotowire.com*. Retrieved July 23, 2014 from http://www.rotowire.com/football/101/draft-strategy.htm.

Liss, C. (2014). Fantasy football draft strategy. *Rotowire.com*. Retrieved September 25, 2014 from http://www.rotowire.com/football/101/draft-strategy.htm.

Massari, M. G. (2006). When fantasy meets reality: The clash between on-line fantasy sports providers and intellectual property rights. *Harvard Journal of Law & Technology, 19*(2), 443–465.

Markula, P. (2004). "Tuning into one's self": Foucault's technologies of the self and mindful fitness. *Sociology of Sport Journal, 21*, 302–321.

Mead, D. (2007). C.B.C. Distribution and marketing v. major league baseball advanced media, L.P.: Why major league baseball struck out and won't have better luck in its next trip to the plate. *Minnesota Journal of Law, Science and Technology, 8*(2), 715–736.

McDermott, L. (2007). A governmental analysis of children "at risk" in a world of physical inactivity and obesity epidemics. *Sociology of Sport Journal, 24*, 302–324.

Nesbit, T. M., & King, K. A. (2010a). The impact of fantasy football participation on NFL attendance. *Atlantic Economics Journal, 38*, 95–108.

Nesbit, T. M., & King, K. A. (2010). The impact of fantasy sports on television viewership. *Journal of Media Economics, 23*, 24–41. doi:10.1080/08997761003590721.

Nyland, R., & Randle, Q. (2008). Participation in internet fantasy sports leagues and mass media use. *Journal of Website Promotion, 3*(3/4), 143–152. doi:10.1080/15533610802077180.

Oates, T. P. (2009). New media and the repackaging of NFL fandom. *Sociology of Sport Journal, 26*, 31–49.

O'Brien, P. (2014, August 4). Fantasy football myths: What to avoid in 2014. *Fantasy.usatoday.com*. Retrieved August 22, 2014 from http:// fantasy.usatoday.com/2014/08/top-five-fantasy-football-myths.

O'Malley, P. (1996). Risk and responsibility. In A. Barry, T. Osborne & N. Rose (Eds.), *Foucault and political reason: Liberalism, neo-liberalism and rationalities of government* (pp. 189–208). Chicago: University of Chicago Press.

Park, J.-k. (2005). Governing doped bodies: The World Anti-Doping Agency and the global culture of surveillance. *Cultural Studies<=>Critical Methodologies, 5*(2), 174–188.

Ralph, M. (2006). "Le Senegal qui gagne": Soccer and the stakes of neoliberalism in a postcolonial port. *Soccer & Society, 7*(2–3), 300–317.

Real, M. R. (2006). Sports online: The newest player in mediasport. In J. Bryant & A. A. Raney (Eds.), *Handbook of Sports and Media* (pp. 171–184). Mahwah, NJ and London: Lawrence Erlbaum Associates.

Rose, N. (1996). Governing "advanced" liberal democracies. In A. Barry, T. Osborne & N. Rose (Eds.), *Foucault and political reason: Liberalism, neoliberalism and rationalities of government* (pp. 99–122). Chicago: University of Chicago Press.

Rose, N. (1999). *Powers of freedom: Reframing political thought.* Cambridge: Cambridge University Press.

Ruihley, B. J., & Billings, A. C. (2012). Infiltrating the boys' club: Motivations for women's fantasy sport participation. *International Review for the Sociology of Sport, 48*(4), 435–452. doi:10.1177/1012690212443440.

Scherer, J., & Jackson, S. J. (2004). From corporate welfare to national interest: Newspaper analysis of the public subsidization of NHL hockey debate in Canada. *Sociology of Sport Journal, 21*, 36–60.

Smith, B., Sharma, P., & Hooper, P. (2006). Decision making in online fantasy sports communities. *Interactive Technology & Smart Education, 4*, 347–360.

Smith Maguire, J. (2008). Leisure and the obligation of self-work: An examination of the fitness field. *Leisure Studies, 27*(1), 59–75.

Spinda, J. S. W., & Haridakis, P. M. (2008). Exploring the motives of fantasy sports: A uses-and-gratifications approach. In L. W. Hugenberg, P. M. Haridakis & A. C. Earnheardt (Eds.), *Sports mania: Essays on fandom and the media in the 21st century* (pp. 187–199). Jefferson, NC: McFarland & Company.

Steussy, L. (2014, May 7). High school boys hold "draft" to pick prom dates. *Orange County Register.* Retrieved May 12, 2014 from http://www.ocregister.com/articles/draft-612766-prom-school.html.

Stohr, G. (2008, June 2). MLB rebuffed by U.S. Supreme Court on fantasy rights. Retrieved June 21, 2008 from http://www.bloomberg.com/apps/news?pid=2060 1079&sid=a.5jCrvS31Uo&refer=home.

Woodward, D. F. (2005). A whole new ballgame: How fantasy sports has evolved in the mass media. Unpublished Masters Thesis, University of Texas at Arlington, Arlington, TX.

# 7

# A CLUSTER CRITICISM OF JUSTIFICATIONS OF FANTASY SPORTS FOR WOMEN

*Katherine Lavelle*

Increasingly, women are playing fantasy sports, but they are a relatively new demographic to participate. Sport media platforms, such as Yahoo! and ESPN provides a range of options for participation. ESPN, one of the most popular sources for sport news and programming, struggles with its coverage of women's sports (Adams & Tuggle, 2004; Mean, 2011; Turner, 2013), the role and power held by its female reporters and anchors (Deitsch, 2014), and its relationship to female fans (Mean, 2011). In 2009, Turner (2013) found that 3.3 percent of all *SportsCenter* coverage featured female athletes, and that 5.2 percent of reporters on *SportsCenter* were female. In 2010, ESPN introduced espnW, a site which attempts to "serve women as fans and athletes" and "provide(s) an engaging environment that offers total access to female athletes" ("About espnW," 2014, para. 1). While espnW was created with good intentions, it has been criticized for being a "pink ghetto" (Stableford, 2010, Para. 12) allowing ESPN to provide minimal coverage of women's sports (Messner, 2013).[1] On August 29, 2014, espnW launched a partnership with *Her Fantasy Football* (HFF), a website developed and maintained by three football loving sisters (the Williams sisters), who proclaim that, "Fantasy Football isn't just a guy's game!" ("About Us," n.d., para. 1). The Williams sisters use a relationship-based system for evaluating players, arguing that "sometimes it feels like fantasy analysis ends up competing over who can apply the most obscure statistic to each player's projection" (Kirby, Lee,

& Williams, 2014a, Para. 16). HFF uses statistics to evaluate players, but frames fantasy football as a way to build community and friendship.

Previous scholarship has found that fantasy football leagues can be difficult spaces for women to navigate, especially with their emphasis on competition and forms of male domination (Davis & Duncan, 2006). Women are participating in fantasy football in higher numbers, but still constitute a fraction of all players ("Industry Demographics," 2014). In order to study how female participants are represented on espnW's coverage of "women's" fantasy football, this essay analyzes *HFF's* initial espnW blog post, "Her Fantasy Football's Top 200 Rankings for 2014," which grouped NFL players into categories similar to how women might rank potential romantic partners. While *HFF* represents a small sample of women's participation in fantasy sports, because it was hosted by ESPN, it is critical to examine how ESPN attempts to engage and market to potential female fantasy sport fans.

Since recent scholarship has found that male and female fantasy sports participants have similar motivations to participate (Billings & Ruihley, 2014), does the *HFF* relationship-based system of fantasy football reinforce hegemonic femininity? In this context, "Hegemonic femininity . . . describes the form of femininity that supports the dominance of men" (p. 361), and suggests that if women are deemed to be unfeminine, they are seen as the "other" and separate from men. Conversely, Connell (1995) described the phenomenon of "hegemonic masculinity," which suggests that men are the standard for evaluation of sports, and women are judged in relation to men, not as independent entities. These concepts are critical to understanding how male/female fans are represented in fantasy sports coverage. In order to evaluate how *HFF* characterizes the female fantasy sport participant, this essay uses a cluster criticism analysis to evaluate key terms in *HFF's* espnW posts. By reviewing the relevant contextual factors in fantasy sports, and the scholarly literature from communication and sport, this analysis aims to uncover how women are represented in *HFF*.

## A NEW SPIN ON FANTASY SPORTS

By 2014, 8.2 million women participated in a fantasy sports league (Industry Demographics, 2014). In response to this increasing trend, espnW launched its own coverage of fantasy football in August of 2014 using the independent website, *Her Fantasy Football*. HFF debuted on espnW on August 29, 2014, with a series of introductory posts and a pre-season ranking of players for fantasy participants. The original ranking of players had no disclaimer. Instead, it posited that, "Fantasy football is all about relationships" (Kirby et al., 2014a, para. 1). The post ranked the top 200 NFL football players, which included comments about the players' appearance, dateability, and *HFF*'s "love" for them. The introductory post explains how the Williams sisters joined a fantasy football league. Their families watched Denver Broncos games together and their shared fandom eventually translated into their interest in participating in fantasy leagues (Kirby et al., 2014a).

On September 2, 2014, espnW placed a disclaimer on "Her Fantasy Football's Top 200 Rankings for 2014," which stated that the bloggers used humor to help "supplement ESPN's existing coverage" (para. 1). This editor's note seemed to respond to potential criticisms about espnW's approach to female fans. espnW was designed for an audience under covered by ESPN (Turner, 2013). ESPN does not focus on women's sports coverage, on its website or news coverage (Turner, 2013). Ideally, espnW would serve as a forum to feature female athletes, but not in a way that overemphasizes traditional definitions of femininity. If espnW attended to the underserved female sports fan, one would hope that the fantasy sports coverage also would be more inclusive of female fantasy sports participants. But *HFF*'s fantasy football rankings use hegemonic femininity to uphold versions of women, and outside of the disclaimer, the rest of the article remains intact, instructing participants to categorize fantasy football players based on relationship labels, such as "Friends with Benefits" and "One Night Stands."

The debut of "women's" fantasy sports coverage on espnW justifies study because it is the first time that espnW developed its own fantasy coverage to compliment ESPN's traditional coverage of fantasy leagues (Kirby, Lee, & Williams, 2014b). This tactic is not surprising. Billings and Ruihley (2014) found that ESPN's fantasy sport growth strategy attempts to convert fans of ESPN coverage into playing on the website. There are a number of other sites that promote fantasy play, such as Yahoo! Sports, so by promoting fantasy sports to new users, espnW can recruit new players, instead of trying to convert fans of other sites (Billings & Ruihley, 2014). Considering that previous research has found that male and female fantasy sports participants have similar motivations (Billings & Ruihley, 2014), it is noteworthy that espnW uses a relationship strategy to recruit women. In order to contextualize this issue, it is critical to discuss the scholarly literature on this issue.

## WOMEN AND FANTASY SPORTS

### Masculinity

Football is linked to a masculine culture (Spandler & McKeown, 2012). Masculinity and femininity are complicated terms that often appear in communication and sport literature (Bruce, 2012; Connell & Messerschmidt, 2005; Hardin, 2013; Hargreaves, 1994; Kane, LaVoi, & Fink, 2013). Trujillo's (1991) landmark article identified mediated sport as a critical site for reinforcing masculinity and making these features part of "cultural values" (p. 292–293). Consequently, most of the major professional coverage focuses on men's sports (Cooky, Messner, & Hextrum, 2013; Kane, 2013). Because there is so much focus on male athletes, women's sports are often not part of the sports conversation (Bruce, 2012).

The focus on male sports is reflected in fantasy football leagues (Billings & Ruihley, 2014). In their study of motivations and the demographics of fantasy sports, Billings and Ruihley (2014) found that most fantasy sports leagues were focused on men's sports, which "reinforces masculinity" (p. 54). The most popular sport to play in fantasy leagues is professional football (Billings & Ruihley, 2014), which is the favorite male sport of American women (Brady, 2012). Unlike basketball and baseball, which require daily monitoring, football has weekly games, but enough statistics to allow for different structures of fantasy games. Fantasy sports provide a unique environment to observe theoretical issues surrounding representations of women and culture because fantasy sport participation is not restricted by age, location, or athletic ability (Billings & Ruihley).

### FANTASY SPORTS

Fantasy sports have been studied from a variety of perspectives. A number of scholars have studied how fantasy sports change the way that fans perceive sports (Billings & Ruihley, 2014; Bowman, McCabe, & Isaacson, 2012; McGuire, et al., 2012), and scholars have attempted to identify larger demographic trends surrounding fantasy sports participants (Bowman et al., 2012). Participation is often correlated with higher investment in sports viewership (Billings & Ruihley, 2014). For instance, Billings and Ruihley (2014) have found that typical fantasy sports participants watch nearly twenty-four hours of ESPN media per week. Media conglomerates like ESPN want to expand participation because if more people are participating in fantasy sports, more people are watching their programming (Billings & Ruihley).

Recent scholarship has isolated motivations for a person to participate in a fantasy sports league (Billings & Ruihley, 2014; McGuire, Armfield, & Boone, 2012). Spinda and Haridakis (2008) found that there are a variety of motivations, where the most salient ones are "ownership, achievement/ self-esteem, bragging, rights, and amusement" (p. 196). Billings and Ruihley (2014) found that the top three motivations for fantasy sports participation were self-esteem, social sport, and camaraderie. Billings and Ruihley's findings are particularly valuable because they reviewed the most recent scholarship on fantasy motivations, and explored motivations for a variety of demographic characteristics, including race, sex, and age. Scholarship on women in fantasy sports has been limited in part because participant numbers were so low until recently.

## Women in Fantasy Sports

Fantasy sports are often associated with young, White, men (Billings & Ruihley, 2014). As explained in the 2014 "Industry Demographics" report generated by the Fantasy Sports Trade Association, 80 percent of fantasy sports participants are male and 90 percent are White. Davis and Duncan (2006) identified a number of reasons why women felt alienated in fantasy leagues. They argued "fantasy sport is another way in which men symbolically bolster their superiority over women in the sport domain" (p. 251). Davis and Duncan noted that calling a participant a "woman" is frequently used as an insult in fantasy games and players "attempt to emasculate [each other] by ridicule or taunts" (p. 260). In their analysis, they found that women were often seen as "placeholders for men" (p. 261) and often seen as second-class participants to men in fantasy leagues. Women who love sports find themselves in a tough place because unlike men, who might get the benefit of the doubt about their interest level in sports, women must prove their loyalty to sports in order to participate in fantasy leagues (Davis & Duncan, 2006). Burr-Miller (2011) discussed the importance of "community ties" in fantasy sports leagues. Individuals who participate must have some sort of connection to the league prior to joining. Women might not have those natural connections from friends, family, or other social groups (Davis & Duncan, 2006), and thus, might have to actively seek out leagues.

Despite the concerns discussed by Davis and Duncan's (2006) study, more recent scholarship has found that women's status in fantasy sports have improved. Ruihley and Billings (2012) found that women who participated in fantasy sports are invested in their fantasy leagues, even if they are part of a "perceived 'second class' status" (p. 16) that is frequently faced by female participants. More specifically, Billings and Ruihley (2014) found that when women participated in fantasy sports, their participation mirrored men's. In fact, Ruihley and Billings concluded their discussion of gender and sport, noting, "While the group may be small in numbers, they have similar characteristics and motives for the activity" (pp. 56–57). Given these findings, it reinforces the view that female fantasy sports participants aren't a special case or group. If they are fans, they just want to participate without special treatment based on self-identified sex.

## SPACES FOR FANTASY SPORTS

The platforms used for fantasy sports participation are critical to evaluating coverage about fantasy sports. Oates (2009) and Billings and Ruihley (2014) have found that since fantasy sports are played online, a league hosted by a sports news site, such as ESPN, is more attractive than leagues that require users go to other places to find out information about players. Ruihley and Hardin (2013) found that because of the increase in the popularity of fantasy sports, sponsor sites need information about players to help make picks and determine trades.

In addition to supporting fantasy sports, many of these sports news sites also support blogs and other forms of sports discourse. In previous communication and sport scholarship, blogs have been described as "interpretive communities" (Mean, Kassing, & Sanderson, 2010, p. 1595) because participants share their love of sports and want to talk to others with similar interests (McCarthy, 2012). McCarthy (2012) has noted that this love "creates an intimacy with the sport that traditional sports journalism, even with its myriad firsthand quotes and access to information does not" (p. 3). Sports blogs allow for more participation and more communication than other types of mediasport, which may be limited in scope and content (Antunovic & Hardin, 2012). If *Grantland*[2] has taught sports fans anything, blogs provide an almost infinite way to write about particular nuances of sports, and connections that would be limited by traditional sports media operating on a deadline with space limitations.

Despite the hope that online communities are more inclusive for women (Antunovic & Hardin, 2013), recent scholarship doesn't support this assertion (Hardin, Zhong, & Corrigan, 2012; Lisec & McDonald,

2012; Pope, 2012). There are a number of reasons for this situation, in-cluding; few women participate in sports blogging (Hardin et al., 2012), few blogs focus on female sports (Clavio & Eagleman, 2011), and in some cases, blogs promote sexism (Lisec & McDonald, 2012). For instance, in their study of the sports website *Deadspin*, Lisec and McDonald (2012) found that many of the website's blog posts contained "blatant sexist and homophobic references to female athletes" (p. 174). Even if women are given the opportunity to blog, often times, they are not featured in blog posts (Antunovic & Hardin, 2013). One of the unique features of espnW is not only are women's sports covered; there are a number of female columnists who regularly write and contribute to discussion about sports. In fact, during the recent Ray Rice/NFL domestic violence controversy, ESPN television used espnW columnists to contextualize and provide more comprehensive perspective on the crisis ("espnW addresses domes-tic," 2014, August 5).

Sports websites that focus on female fans, such as espnW, are a good idea in theory, but can result in deemphasizing women's sports content on mainstream news sites (Markovits & Albertson, 2012, as cited in Antunovic & Hardin, 2012). Hardin, et al. (2012) found that even with the presence of female sportswriters and fans, these blogs reproduced roles and representa-tions of women that were complicit with stereotypical notions of women. Consequently, this research raises the question: Will espnW's fantasy foot-ball blogs also reinforce stereotypical representations of women?

## HER FANTASY FOOTBALL AND PORTRAYALS OF FEMALE FOOTBALL FANS

In order to evaluate the espnW blog *Her Fantasy Football*, I conducted a cluster criticism of the debut blog posts from late August/early Septem-ber 2014. In cluster criticism, Burke (1950) emphasized the importance of identification and division, arguing that humans are always separated from each other and use language and consubstantiality to come together. Consubstantiality means that a rhetor or speaker tries to be persuasive by highlighting common ideas or attitudes they share with their audience (Burke, 1950). Foss (2009) has argued that the identity of the rhetor is critical to creating consubstantiality in persuasion. Attempts at identi-fication can be created by evaluating language, framing, and words in a rhetorical text (Foss, 2009). Identification can focus on demographic characteristics such as sex (Foss, 2009).

In identifying these areas of related terms, the critic can determine how particular terms are used together to make meaning (Foss, 2009). As Foss explains, "the meanings that key symbols have for a rhetor are discovered by charting symbols around those key symbols in an artifact" (p. 65). For instance, the term "lady" is given meaning by other terms around it, such as "The Lady Volunteers" in college basketball. In isolation, the term "lady" is neutral. But it becomes significant in a world where the men's team doesn't have a sex descriptor, such as the "Gentleman," thus suggesting that women's basketball needs explanation that the men's team does not (Cralley & Ruscher, 2005).

Cluster criticism provides insight into espnW's coverage of "women's" fantasy football. In their debut post on espnW, the *HFF* team introduces themselves, claiming, "we specifically aimed it at the people—oftentimes women—who feel intimidated by the sheer volume and presumed complexity of the game" (Kirby et al., 2014b, September 2, para. 4). The positioning of this coverage suggests that women are intimidated by numbers, a.k.a., traditional fantasy football. HFF makes it clear that people who would read their blog would focus on a different (and possibly read as, inferior), approach to making decisions about choosing players.

For my analysis, I chose the inaugural posts from *Her Fantasy Football* posted prior to the start of the 2014–15 NFL regular season. While *Her Fantasy Football* continues to contribute to espnW, the inaugural posts are important to examine because they attempt to persuade readers to participate in fantasy leagues. The initial post also establishes tone on the website, especially since fantasy football league membership occurs prior to the start of the season (the weekly post provide support for individuals' participation). By evaluating the debut posts, we can have a better sense of how these posts function to reinforce hegemonic femininity.

## TERMINISTIC SCREEN "RELATIONSHIP"

The introductory post of "Her Fantasy Football's Top 200 Rankings for 2014" characterizes fantasy sports participation as like being in a relationship. *HFF* argues that people play fantasy sports to stay "connected with family and friends" (Kirby et al., 2014a, August 29, para. 1). The term "relationship" appears, where HFF discusses the "relationship" with their parents, and identify fantasy sports as a potential dating opportunity for participants. They discuss how two of the three sisters "MARRIED" people they met in fantasy leagues, and discuss how fantasy football has helped keep their family connected (para. 2). By using the term "relationship," it reinforces the discussion of fantasy sports away from traditional statistical analysis. This type of commentary is similar to other approaches involving women and football, as discussed by Brady (2012), including the concept of "surviving" football, by focusing on character development of the players on the field (Brady), and treating football as something that women can't understand without translation (Duncan & Davis, 2006).

Not only is relationship part of evaluating on field performance, but so is the way that players are contextualized for fantasy participants. This contextualization is similar to how female athletes are often discussed. Daddario and Wigley (2007) have argued that women on the athletic field are often portrayed as in a relationship, such as a wife, daughter, or mother. *HFF* characterizes male athletes as having interpersonal relationships with each other. For instance, New England Patriots quarterback Tom Brady is described as the person "we all want him to be our real-life husband" (Kirby, et al., 2014b, August 29, Para. 68) In real life, Tom Brady is married to supermodel Gisele Bundchen and is known for his interest in fashion, and making frequent media appearances, such as hosting *Saturday Night Live* (Hanzus, 2012, August 3). Unlike many football players who are relatively anonymous, the quarterback is a high profile position and Tom Brady in particular has been savvy about parlaying his success on the field to other ventures (Leitch, 2008). In this case, *HFF* emphasizes a previously established connection that female fans might already have to make fantasy sports more interesting. Considering Brady's (2012) argument that football broadcasts are changing commentary to be more inclusive of women, it would make sense that fantasy sports might be positioned similarly.

Three days after the Top 200 Rankings appeared (September 2, 2014), espnW posted a disclaimer with the *HFF* rankings. It is unclear why this editor's note appeared. There were few posts in the comments section that are critical of the article, there was very little coverage of any controversy in the media, but it is clear from its tone and an apology on the *HFF* podcast (Kirby, Lee, & Williams, 2014, September 4), that there was significant criticism about the appropriateness of ranking football players using a relationship-based system. In the editor's note on September 2, 2014, the term "relationship" is framed as a joke. The editors explain that it is "all in the spirit of having fun with the game and having a good laugh" (para. 1). The apology continues explaining that the "relationship category . . . was misunderstood as perpetuating the very stereotypes we intended to have fun with" (para. 1). It is unclear if espnW is completely rejecting the relationship framing, and if so, are they rejecting Her Fantasy Football? The note concludes with the statement "we look forward to working with Her Fantasy Football this season to develop their voices with espnW" (para. 1).

EspnW is eliminating the term "relationship," but maintains the blog post in its entirety. This decision puts both espnW and *HFF* in a difficult position. As Roberts-Miller (2009) explained in her discussion of persuasion and identity, in-group and out-group identity often operate on the assumption that all members are homogenous. In other words, if espnW assumes that all of its fan base was offended, does the fantasy sports coverage need to include humor? This editor's note leaves the tone of the *HFF* coverage clear. If espnW wants to involve more women in fantasy football, but it is only approaching it from a humorous standpoint, its stance on women-centered fantasy football coverage about relationships and marriage reinforces stereotypical views about female athletes.

This approach positions relationships with players, or more specifically, players' abilities to form relationships with teammates is more important than traditional metrics. Despite the focus on relationships status, the ranking is attached to traditional metrics. For instance, Green Bay Packers (running back) Eddie Lacy is described as having a rough season because quarterback Aaron Rodgers missed a significant portion of the 2013–14 season due to injury. "We're confident he (Lacy) can match his running numbers from last year (1,178 yard, 11 touchdowns). With a legitimate passing game in place with Rodgers, look out for Lacy" (Kirby, et al., 2014b, Para. 10). Another example is Dallas Cowboys' Dez Bryant (wide receiver) analysis, who is described as catching "25 touchdowns" because of the "deep balls from Quarterback Tony Romo" (para. 13). Despite framing their rankings as deemphasizing traditional metrics, traditional metrics help define relationships.

## TERMINISTIC SCREEN "LOVE"

The *HFF* crew creates emotional connections with NFL players by framing them through love. These comments are examples of what Daddario (1998) describes as sports coverage with a "tendency toward emotion, intimacy, and dialogue" (p. 106). Daddario emphasizes the importance of character as a way to involve female fans. By focusing on love, celebrity culture and direct discussion of physical attractiveness of players, these blog posts reinforce gender roles. Arguing that women would be interested in athletes because they want to date them suggests that women enjoy football because it can be considered similar to a romantic relationship.

There are several players that *HFF* encourages participants to "love." In terms of "love" expressed toward players, participants are encouraged to "start dating" Seattle Seahawk Marshawn Lynch (Kirby et al., 2014b, para. 15), and if Chicago Bears quarterback Jay Cutler "loves" his teammate, wide receiver Brandon Marshall, "you'll love him too" (para. 19). Another Chicago Bears player, running back Matt Forte is described as "Mr. Dependable" (para. 9). Finally, HFF declares "we LOVE Jordy Nelson (Green Bay Packers wide receiver)" (para. 22). These comments are made without much context. If the target audience for this blog is women who have been intimated by the high stakes world of fantasy sports, is "loving" a player enough to choose him for the fantasy team? Despite these characteristics, *HFF* does use statistical analysis in their rankings. For instance, the Philadelphia Eagles (running back) LeSean McCoy is described as "What's not to love? Last year McCoy rushed for 1,607 years and nine touchdowns. Tack on to that his 52 receptions for 539 years and another two touchdowns" (Kirby, et al., 2014b, para. 5). These comments illustrate what Davis and Duncan (2006) criticized as reinforcing gender dynamics in fantasy football.

Celebrity culture is also part of *HFF*'s framing of NFL players. *HFF* describes Detroit Lions running back Reggie Bush (the former boyfriend of reality television superstar Kim Kardashian) as, "Players who date reality starts never play well while they date them" (Kirby, et al., 2014b, August 29, para. 48), suggesting that off-field romantic relationships are important criteria for evaluating player performance. New Orleans Saints tight end Jimmy Graham is described as "the Ryan Gosling of fantasy football" (para. 12), referencing the popular actor known for his association with the "Hey, Girl" memes and popularity among rabid female fans who want him to be their boyfriend (Silman, 2014, May 29). Without much context about the players' on field performance, would someone who is willing to invest the time in fantasy sports (and read espnW) going to make a decision based on the "Ryan Goslingness" of a player? Instead, this is an example of what Daddario (1997) described as the "viewers' collective memory" (p. 110). While first time fantasy football players might not have collective memories about football, they probably do have some connection to Ryan Gosling because he is famous and frequently in entertainment news. Using this reference makes football seem more relatable to new participants, especially potential female fans.

Finally, there is discussion about the physical attractiveness of the players. The most explicit descriptor of physical attractiveness is awarded to Green Bay Packers quarterback Aaron Rodgers. He's called a "stud" (Kirby et al., 2014b, para. 10; which is typical fantasy football discussion), and "totally healthy, dependable, and uh, he's not so hard on the eyes, either. He'll look good in your fantasy team colors" (para. 32). Rodgers meets many of the expectations of conventional heterosexual male attractiveness: He is tall, with blue eyes and brown hair, and even has a conventionally beautiful celebrity girlfriend (at least, at the time), Olivia Munn (Carson, 2014, September 24). Rodgers has done work to uphold his heterosexual image. In fact, when rumors circulated that Rodgers was dating his male assistant, Rodgers responded on his radio show that he "really, really like[d] women" (Richardson, 2013, December 31). Davis and Duncan (2006) discussed the importance of reinforcement of traditional gender roles in fantasy sports. It is interesting that Rodgers is the only player out of 200 who is explicitly discussed as physically attractive. Others are described favorably, but no other player is explicitly judged on his physical appearance.

## IMPLICATIONS

While there are a number of women who blog about sports (Antunovic & Hardin, 2013; Hardin et al., 2012), and entire websites are devoted to the female perspective in sports (Clavio & Eagleman, 2011), it is critical to evaluate how espnW articulates women's participation in fantasy sports. EspnW attempts to develop a unique voice for female athletes and fans. Turner's (2013) longitudinal analysis of *SportsCenter* suggests that how ESPN covers women and minorities is crucial. EspnW hosts a Women's Sports Summit where topics include "How women are using social media to innovate," and "The WNBA: A story of commitment, passion innovating" ("Women + Sports," 2014). Because ESPN is the self-described "worldwide leader in sports," and is such an industry leader in sports information (Turner, 2013), it is critical to examine how they market to fans. In its first direct attempt to attract women to fantasy football, espnW fails to make a persuasive case to its potential audience. This coverage helps establish the tone and perception of female fantasy sports participants by espnW. Focusing on good-looking male players who might function as imaginary boyfriends and partners does not fit within the expectations women have of fantasy sports coverage, if they have similar motivations to male participants (Billings & Ruihley, 2014). As Whiteside and Hardin (2011) found in their study of women's sports television viewing patterns, women are often pulled away from uninterrupted sports viewing due to domestic responsibilities, not lack of interest or knowledge in sports. The relationship based framing represents a misunderstanding by espnW about women's perception of participating in fantasy sports.

A rhetorical/critical perspective on women in fantasy sports can help illuminate questions about identification and representations that have not been previously been explored. Given the role of fantasy sports in everyday practices and the increasing importance in media texts, understanding how female participants are discussed is critical. Considering the audience of espnW readers, individuals who are interested in women's sports, and given the content of espnW (which often criticizes the coverage of women's athletics) (Wolter, 2014), the partnership with *HFF* seems out of sync with other coverage on the website. Even though the purpose of this coverage is humorous, because there is so little coverage of women's sports or women on ESPN (Cooky, et al., 2013; Kane, 2013), it magnifies the impact of this coverage. Focusing on relationship with players, their physical appearance, and the idea that fantasy sports is about friendship and marriage reinforces stereotypical views about women. This approach diminishes the importance of female participation in fantasy football because they don't have serious coverage immediately. Creating high profile coverage that reinforces stereotypical notions of women prevents espnW from moving forward as a network that is reflective of women's experience. Even in the text of *HFF*, they distinguish themselves from other (read male) fantasy sports coverage by labeling their coverage as different. Consequently, previous stereotypes about female athletes are reinforced.

Further research should be conducted to explore the role of fantasy sports within the context of female sports bloggers. As sports media platforms continue to devote more time and resources to fantasy coverage, evaluating how other marginalized or underrepresented groups are represented is important. This study focuses on one set of coverage, but exploring the percentages, themes, and approaches to participation is critical as we continue to explore fantasy sports as a communication phenomenon.

## NOTES

1. On the ESPN main website (accessed on September 21, 2014), there is a link to espnW, but viewers have to click "More Sports," to see regular coverage of any women's sports.

2. Grantland is a sports website (hosted by ESPN) that includes blogs and long form stories.

# REFERENCES

About espnW. (2014). *espnW*. Retrieved from http://espn.go.com/espnw/about

About Us. (n.d.). *Her Fantasy Football*. Retrieved from http://herfantasyfootball.com/about-us/

Adams, T., & Tuggle, C. A. (2004). ESPN's SportsCenter and coverage of women's athletics: "It's a Boys' Club." *Mass Communication & Society, 7*, 237–248.

Antunovic, D. & Hardin, H. (2012). Activism in women's sports blogs: Fandom and feminist potential. *International Journal of Sport Communication, 5*, 305–322.

Antunovic, D. & Hardin, M. (2013). Women bloggers: Identity and the conceptualization of sports. *New Media & Society, 15* (8), 1374–1392. doi:10.1177/1461444812472323

Billings, A. C. & Ruihley, B. J. (2013). Why we watch, why we play: The relationship between fantasy sport and fanship motivations. *Mass Communication & Society, 16*, 5–25. doi:10.1080/15205436.2011.635260

Billings, A. C. & Ruihley, B. J. (2014). *The Fantasy Sport Industry: Games within games*. New York, NY: Routledge.

Bowman, N. D., McCabe, J., & Isaacson, T. (2012). Fantasy sports and sports Fandom: Implications for mass media research. In A. C. Earnheardt, P. M. Haridakis, & B. S. Hugenberg (Eds.) *Sports Fans, Identity, and Socialization: Exploring the Fandemonium* (pp. 255–273). Lanham, MD: Lexington Books.

Brady, K. (2012). Football Fans *Do* Wear Pink: Game Day Broadcasts, Female Football Fans, and Their NFL. In A. C. Earnheardt, P. M. Haridakis, & B. S. Hugenberg (Eds.) *Sports Fans, Identity, and Socialization: Exploring the Fandemonium* (pp. 221–236). Lanham, MD: Lexington Books.

Bruce, T. (2012). Reflections on Communication and Sport: On women and femininities. *Communication & Sport, 1*(1/2), 125–137. doi:10.1177/2167479512472883.

Burke, K. (1950). *A Rhetoric of Motives*. Berkeley: University of California Press.

Burr-Miller, A. C. (2011). What's your fantasy? Fantasy baseball as equipment for living. *Southern Communication Journal, 76*, 443–464. doi:10.1080/10417941003725299.

Carson, D. (2014, September 24). Green Bay Packers fans blame Olivia Munn for Aaron Rodgers' poor play. *Bleacher Report*. Retrieved from http://bleacherreport.com/articles/2209671-green-bay-packers-fans-blame-olivia-munn-for-aaron-rodgers-poor-play

Clavio, G. & Eagleman, A. N. (2011). Gender and Sexually Suggestive Images in Sports Blogs. *Journal of Sport Management, 7*, 295–304.

Connell, R.W. (1995). *Masculinities*. Berkeley: University of California Press.

Connell, R. W. & Messerschmidt, J. W. (2005). Hegemonic Masculinity: Rethinking the concept. *Gender & Society, 19* (6), 829–859. doi:10.1177/0891243205278639

Cooky, C., Messner, M. A., & Hextrum, R. H. (2013). Women play sport, but not on TV: A longitudinal study of televised news media. *Communication & Sport, 3*, 1–28. doi:10.1177/2167479513476947

Cralley, E. L., & Ruscher, J. B. (2005). Lady, girl, female, or woman: Sexism and cognitive busyness predict use of gender-biased nouns. *Journal of Language and Social Psychology, 24*, 300–314. doi:10.1177/0261927X05278391

Daddario, G. (1997). Gendered sports programming: 1992 Summer Olympics coverage and the feminine narrative form. *Sociology of Sport Journal, 14*, 103–120.

Daddario, G. (1998). *Women's Sport and Spectacle: Gendered Television Coverage and the Olympic Games.* Westport, CT: Praeger Publishers.

Daddario, G. & Wigley, B. J. (2007). Gender marking and racial stereotyping at the 2004 Athens Games. *Journal of Sports Media, 2*, 31–54.

Davis, N. W. & Duncan, M. C. (2006). Sport knowledge is power: Reinforcing masculine privilege through fantasy sport league participation. *Journal of Sport & Social Issues, 30 (3)*, 244–264. doi:10.1177/0193723506290324

Deitsch, R. (2014, June 16). Debating role of women in sports media; Marino's balancing act; more. *Sports Illustrated.* Retrieved from http://www.si.com/nfl/2013/11/24/media-circus-women-sports-media-espn-nfl-network

espnW addresses domestic violence in wake of Ray Rice suspension. (2014, August 5). *ESPN MediaZone.* Retrieved from http://espnmediazone.com/us/press-releases/2014/08/espnw-addresses-domestic-violence-wake-ray-rice-suspension/

Finley, N. J. (2010). Skating femininity: Gender maneuvering in women's roller derby. *Journal of Contemporary Ethnography, 39 (4)*, 359–387. doi:10.1177/0891241610364230

Foss, S. J. (2009). *Rhetorical Criticism: Exploration and Practice.* Long Grove, IL: Waveland Press.

Hanzus, D. (2012, August 3). Tom Brady is game for another "SNL" hosting gig. *NFL.com.* Retrieved from http://www.nfl.com/news/story/09000d5d8297338d/article/tom-brady-is-game-for-another-snl-hosting-gig

Hardin, M. (2013). Want changes in content?: Change the decision makers. *Communication & Sport, 1(3)*, 241–245. doi:10.1177/2167479513486985

Hardin, M., Zhong, B., & Corrigan, T. F. (2012). The funhouse mirror: The blogosphere's reflection of women's sports. In T. Dumova & R. Fiordo (Eds.), *Blogging in the Global Society: Cultural, Political, and Geographical Aspects* (pp. 55–71). Hershey, PA: Information Science Reference.

Hargreaves, J. (1994). *Sporting Females: Critical Issues in the History and Sociology of Women's Sports.* New York: Routledge.

Industry Demographics (2014). *Fantasy Sports Trade Association.* Retrieved from http://www.fsta.org/?page=Demographics

Kane, M. J. (2013). The better sportswomen get, the more the media ignore them. *Communication & Sport, 1(3)*, 231–236. doi:10.1177/2167479513484579

Kane, M. J., LaVoi, N. M., & Fink, J. S. (2013). Exploring elite female athletes' interpretations of sport media images: A window into the construction of social identity and "selling sex" in women's sports. *Communication & Sport, 1* (3), 269–298. doi:10.1177/2167479512473585

Kirby, C., Lee, B. M. & Williams, A. (2014, August 29). Her Fantasy Football's Top 200 Rankings for 2014. *espnW.* Retrieved from http://espn.go.com/espnw/news-commentary/article/11415434/her-fantasy-football-top-200-rankings-2014

Kirby, C., Lee, B. M., & Williams, A. (2014a, September 2). Hey Fantasy rookies, we can help you crush your league. *espnW.* Retrieved from http://espn.go.com/espnw/news-commentary/article/11417728/hey-fantasy-rookies-help-crush-your-league

Kirby, C., Lee, B. M. & Williams, A. (2014b, September 2). Her Fantasy Football's Top 200 Rankings for 2014. *espnW.* Retrieved from http://espn.go.com/espnw/news-commentary/article/11415434/her-fantasy-football-top-200-rankings-2014

Kirby, C., Lee, B. M., & Williams, A. (Producer). (2014, September 4). *Her Fantasy Football Podcast* [Audio podcast]. Retrieved from http://espn.go.com/espnw/news-commentary/fantasy/

Leitch, W. (2008, January 30). Athlete or celebrity? Brady doesn't have to choose. *The Fifth Down.* Retrieved from http://fifthdown.blogs.nytimes.com/2008/01/30/athlete-or-celebrity-brady-doesnt-have-to-choose/?_php=true&_type=blogs&_r=0

Lisec, J. & McDonald, M. G. (2012). Gender inequality in the new millennium: An analysis of WNBA representations in sport blogs. *Journal of Sports Media, 7* (2), 152–178.

McCarthy, B. (2012). A sports journalism of their own: An investigation into the motivations, behaviours, and media attitudes of fan sports bloggers. *Communication & Sports,* 1–15. doi:10.1177/2167479512469943

McGuire, J. P., Armfield, G. G., & Boone, J. (2012). Show me the numbers! Media dependency and fantasy game participants. In A. C. Earnheardt, P. M. Haridakis, & B. S. Hugenberg (Eds.) *Sports Fans, Identity, and Socialization: Exploring the Fandemonium* (pp. 275–290). Lanham, MD: Lexington Books.

Mean, L. J. (2011). Sport, identity, and consumption: The construction of sport at ESPN.com. In A. C. Billings (Ed.), *Sports Media: Transformation, Integration, Consumption* (pp. 162–180). New York, NY: Routledge.

Mean, L. J., Kassing, J. W., & Sanderson, J. (2010). The making of an epic (American) hero fighting for justice: Commodification, consumption, and intertextuality in the Floyd Landis defense campaign. *American Behavioral Scientist, 53* (11), 1590–1609. doi:10.1177/0002764210368087

Messner, M. (2013). Reflections on communication and sport: On men and masculinities. *Communication & Sport, 1,* 113–124. doi:10.1177/2167479512467977

Oates, T. P. (2009). New media and the repackaging of NFL fandom. *Sociology of Sport Journal, 26,* 31–49.

Pope, S. (2012). "The Love of my life": The meaning and importance of sport for female fans. *Journal of Sport and Social Issues,* 1–20. doi:10.1177/0193723512455919

Richardson, A. S. (2013, December 31). Packers quarterback Aaron Rodgers says he's not gay and "I really, really like women." *Yahoo! Sports.* Retrieved from http://sports.yahoo.com/blogs/shutdown-corner/packers-quarterback-aaron-rod-gers-says-not-gay-really-231000585--nfl.html

Roberts-Miller, P. (2009). Dissent As "Aid and Comfort to the Enemy": The rhetorical power of naïve realism and ingroup identity. *Rhetoric Society Quarterly*, *39* (2), 170–188. doi:10.1080/02773940902766763.

Ruihley, B. J. & Hardin, R. (2013). Meeting the informational needs of the fantasy sport user. *Journal of Sports Media, 8 (2)*, 53–80. doi:10.1353/jsm.2013.0013.

Silman, A. (2014, May 29). The complete history of Ryan Gosling, from child star to heartthrob to movie director. *Vulture*. Retrieved from http://www.vulture.com/2014/05/illustrated-comprehensive-history-bio-biography-ryan-gosling.html

Spandler, H. & McKeown, M. (2012). A critical exploration of using football in health and welfare programs: Gender, masculinities, and social relations. *Journal of Sport and Social Issues, 36*, 387–409. doi:10.1177/0193723512458930

Spinda, J. S. W., & Haridakis, P. M. (2008). Exploring the motives of fantasy sports: A uses-and-gratifications approach. In L. W. Hugenberg, P. M. Haridakis, & A. C. Earnheardt (Eds.) *Sports Mania: Essays on Fandom and the Media in the 21st Century*, 187–199. Jefferson, NC: McFarland.

Stableford, D. (2010, October 1). ESPN to launch women's brand 'ESPNW' and some women are not pleased. *The Wrap*. Retrieved from http://www.thewrap.com/media/column-post/espn-launch-women-brand-espnw-21374/

Trujillo, N. (1991). Hegemonic masculinity on the mound: Media representations of Nolan Ryan and American sports culture. *Critical Studies in Mass Communication, 8*, 290–308.

Turner, J. S. (2013). A longitudinal analysis of gender and ethnicity portrayed on ESPN's *SportsCenter* from 1999 to 2009. *Communication & Sport, 1*, 1–25. doi:10.1177/2167479513496222.

Wolter, S. (2014). "It just makes good business sense": A media political economy analysis of espnW. *Journal of Sports Media, 9*, (2), 73–96. doi:10.1353/jsm.2014.0011.

Whiteside, E. & Hardin, M. (2011). Women (not) watching women: Leisure time, television, and implications for televised coverage of women's sports. *Communication, Culture, & Critique, 4*, 122–143. doi:10.1111/j.1753-9137.2011.01098.x.

Women + Sports Summit. (2014). espnW. Retrieved from http://espn.go.com/espnw/summit/

# 8

# THE ROLE OF SELF-DISCLOSURE IN FANTASY SPORT LEAGUE SATISFACTION

*Christopher C. Gearhart, Shaughan A. Keaton, and Brody Ruihley*

Identified in the research are many motivations driving fantasy sport play (see chapter 1, this volume, for details) including frequently cited motives such as arousal, passing time, surveillance, escape, enjoyment, and ownership (e.g., Farquhar & Meeds, 2007; Roy & Goss, 2007; Ruihley & Hardin, 2011a; Spinda & Haridakis, 2008). Most fantasy sport researchers also acknowledge that a general class of motivations can be ascribed to social interaction among members (see also chapter 5, this volume, for details), including communication acts such as conversations involving the logistics of the league, seeking advice or opinions about fantasy players, engaging in friendly banter, discussing non-fantasy related issues, and the sharing of sports information (Davis & Duncan, 2006; Roy & Goss, 2007; Ruihley & Hardin, 2011a; Spinda & Haridakis, 2008). Although the focus of this chapter is maintaining previously existing relationships online through fantasy sport message board interaction, as mentioned in the introduction of this volume there is also the ability for fantasy sport league message boards to build rapport and provide "icebreaker" discussions for fantasy players meeting face-to-face for the first time.

Roy and Goss (2007) describe fantasy sport consumption as partly a function of social influences, comprising two major categories of community and socializing. Socializing most notably involves elements such as "talking smack" or "trash talking," which are opportunities to chide and ridicule fantasy opponents, whereas community is the ability to interact with others having shared interests and further developing one's identity. In this chapter we examine camaraderie with attention to the factors that influence a fan's participation on fantasy sport league message boards. We set to specifically investigate the conditions that relate to more or less personal self-disclosures on fantasy league message boards. From a fan's perspective, fantasy leagues offer not only arenas for competition but also for the maintenance of close, personal relationships.

Ruihley and Hardin (2011a) divided fantasy sport users' (FSUs) social motivation into two similar areas: social sport and, again, camaraderie. Social sport focuses on fantasy sport as a platform for sharing and discussing sport-related material (akin to sport spectatorship), whereas camaraderie concerns relationship maintenance in the fantasy sport environment. Using these two categories, a survey of 1,201 FSUs ranked social sport and camaraderie as, respectively, the second and fifth greatest motivations for fantasy sport play (Billings & Ruihley, 2013a). When examining the sole top motive of the participants, social sport and camaraderie were, respectively, ranked second (top motive for 34.7 percent) and third (top motive for 28.3 percent). As this empirical evidence demonstrates and as chapters 1 and 5 affirm, the social nature of participation in a fantasy sports league (FSL) is a prevalent motivation amongst FSUs. Roy and Goss (2007) go as far to suggest that the social connections in FSLs can even "outweigh" (p. 102) sport interest for some FSUs.

Fulfilling social motivations likely entails, to some degree, FSUs' interpersonal engagement on fantasy league message boards. Using fantasy league message boards (LMBs) is a popular part of the fantasy sport experience, with about two-thirds of FSUs reporting using them at least once a season and 20 percent posting to them on a daily basis (Ruihley & Hardin, 2011b). These readily accessible LMBs allow players to "socialize informally and to learn about or get to know one another" (Ruihley & Hardin, 2011b, p. 245). Given that FSUs endorse camaraderie motivations—the belief that FSLs facilitate relational maintenance—then it follows that LMBs are a possible vehicle for the satisfaction of this motivation. Therefore, LMBs serve as important sites for understanding the frequency and content of online interactions between members, as posts to LMBs containing personal information facilitate friendship and camaraderie through the process of self-disclosure (Altman & Taylor, 1973; Berger & Calabrese, 1975).

## SELF-DISCLOSURE IN ONLINE CONTEXTS

A body of research investigating interpersonal relationships in online groups provides evidence that Internet communities such as online games

(Utz, 2003), newsgroups, discussion forums (McKenna, Green, & Gleason, 2002), and blogs (Bane, Cornish, Erspamer, & Kampman, 2010) all offer computer-mediated arenas for individuals to maintain relationships. Being primarily located online, fantasy sport leagues would seem to be no exception. Indeed, personal accounts by fantasy sport users indicate use of the fantasy sport medium in maintaining relationships (see Kepner, 2006) and scholarly research finds these leagues are often comprised of members with relational connections established before their involvement in the FSL. In fact, Ruihley and Hardin (2011a) report that FSUs mention family, friends, church groups, and roommates as people who invited them to join a fantasy league. Thus, FSLs serve as sites for online and offline friends to interact and maintain relationships (also see chapter 5, this volume).

Although FSUs personally report maintaining relationships through their leagues, it remains unclear how these social connections are sustained. Ruihley and Hardin (2011b) provide evidence that FSLs are similar to other online group relationships whereby familiar members, especially those who are geographically separated, use message boards as vehicles to reminisce about past experiences, keep others updated on their lives, and strengthen ties with one another over the course of the season; essentially, these online forums foster the sharing of personal information between FSUs (Parks & Floyd, 1996a). Social motivations for fantasy sport participation are commonplace in the fantasy literature, including terms such as camaraderie (Ruihley & Hardin, 2011a) and bonding (Davis & Duncan, 2006) that imply the presence of some form of interpersonal self-disclosure or sharing of personal information. However, despite these apparent social motivations, it is possible that key features of FSLs actually deter personal self-disclosures among FSUs.

This chapter investigates the nature of self-disclosure in FSLs with an appreciation for the influence of two prominent characteristics: the primarily male participation and subsequent hypermasculine atmosphere (Davis & Duncan, 2006). To better understand FSU relational communication, a sample of 190 participants that is vastly male (88%) ranging from eighteen to sixty-three years of age ($M = 26.1$; $SD = 7.68$) and predominately self-described as White or Caucasian (80.1%) is used to explore the frequency with which FSUs disclose personal information, how league members perceive and respond to disclosures of other players, and any relation between self-disclosure and league satisfaction. The young, White, male representation of this sample resembles research by Davis and Duncan (2006) profiling the prototypical FSU as occupying "the most privileged rung on the social ladder" (p. 247).

## GLOBAL CHARACTERISTICS OF
## FSLS INFLUENCING SELF-DISCLOSURE

The extent to which LMB use includes the sharing of personal information or is limited to "talking smack" and other sport-related talk is contested. Studies cited previously indicate that bonding, camaraderie, and relationship maintenance are commonplace in FSLs. However, at least one study, Farquhar and Meeds (2007), reports that among FSUs, social interaction was "ranked quite low by most of the participants," even venturing out to suggest that FSLs are arenas that may deteriorate or deter relationship building (p. 1224). Although the authors acknowledge their finding is contrary to previous research regarding online gaming motivations (e.g., Utz, 2003), these provocative claims beg the question if FSUs actually engage in personally revealing conversations to maintain relationships.

Two characteristics of FSLs may inhibit the sharing of personal information on LMBs. First, as noted by Farquhar and Meeds (2007), the competitive environment of FSLs shift a focus away from relationally-focused communication like self-disclosure to superficial "trash talk" or banter. Davis and Duncan (2006) highlight how interaction in FSLs can become competitive exchanges of sport knowledge, with FSUs battling to be the most well-informed. These researchers describe a strong conformity to masculine gender norms, which includes a hyper-competitive/aggressive component inherent in fantasy leagues and the interactions of FSUs, a sentiment reiterated by Billings and Ruihley (2013b). This type of environment is not surprising given the majority male composition of FSLs, which is the second prominent influence on disclosure behavior.

A fantasy sport trade study provides figures that estimate FSLs of all sport types are comprised of predominantly males with a male-female ratio of almost 9:1 (Fantasy Sport Trade Association, 2011). This discrepancy is not without communicative consequences. As men are notoriously different than women regarding self-disclosure (see Dindia & Allen, 1992 for a review), the vast gender difference evident in FSLs presupposes that disclosure would be lower among groups (i.e., leagues) of male friends. It is consistently acknowledged that, in general, women and men value different aspects of their same-sex friends (Caldwell & Peplau, 1982; Parks & Floyd, 1996b); essentially, women tend to place greater emphasis on conversational and emotional expressiveness, whereas men's friendships focus on shared activities and interests (specifically, competition and sports [Fehr, 1995]). This norm accompanies online environments as well. Indeed, research conducted with online disclosers finds males are less open and tend

to self-disclose less online (Bond, 2009) and they are less likely to recipro-
cate another's self-disclosure (Barak & Gluck-Ofri, 2007). Comprised of a
high majority of males, one could expect FSLs to follow masculine gender
norms whereby the expectation of men involved in a competitive, hyper-
masculine environment is that self-disclosure is avoided.

Responding to a series of forced-choice questions (*No—Yes*), the 190 respondents were asked if they had ever 1) posted personal information to the
league message board (*Yes* = 150 [78.9%] / *No* = 40 [21.1%]); 2) witnessed
other FSUs post personal messages (*Yes* = 132 [69.5%] / *No* = 58 [30.5%]);
and 3) responded to another member's post of personal information (*Yes*
= 37 [19.4%] / *No* = 44 [23.2%] / 109 missing). These frequency counts,
which are presented in table 8.4, support beliefs that self-disclosure among
fantasy participants on LMBs is limited.

## INDIVIDUAL DIFFERENCES INFLUENCING
## SELF-DISCLOSURE

Although these general characteristics of FSLs do influence self-disclosure, it should also be acknowledged that individual differences among
leagues and FSUs are pertinent as well. In particular, the closeness of
relationships between disclosers (i.e., FSUs) contributes meaningfully
to the presence of personal self-disclosures (Altman & Taylor, 1973).
Communication researchers have found that relational development in a
virtual setting such as a newsgroup forum is a function of time and experience with the online group (Parks & Floyd, 1996a). Related to fantasy
sport, research comparing message board users versus nonusers finds that
message board users report being involved longer in fantasy leagues (7.5
years, compared with 6.8 years for nonusers; Ruihley & Hardin, 2011b). If
FSUs who have been active in the league for a longer time are more likely
to post messages to LMBs, and if they already have previous relationships
with others in the league, then it is probable they are more willing to disclose more private information about themselves and their relationships,
regardless of general characteristics of FSLs.

Using the sample of 190, bivariate correlations and planned contrast
analyses illustrate relationships between years in a fantasy league and
reports of personal self-disclosures and depth of self-disclosure. First,
crosstab analysis was utilized to depict the relationship between disclosing
personal information and amount of time spent in the league. Respondents
were classified into three groups based on the amount of time spent in the

league—one to four years ($n$ = 106), 5–9 years ($n$ = 49), 10+ years ($n$ = 35)—and then compared for whether they reported posting personal details to LMBs, where the longer one participate in leagues, the more likely they are to post (at least, the likelihood of them not posting personal details decreases over time; $\chi^2$ = 12.05, $p$ < .01).

Next, self-disclosure depth was positively related to the amount of time involved in the league, supported by a small but statistically significant bivariate correlation, $r$ = .15, $p$ = .05. This indicates that as league members spent more years in their primary FSL they were more likely to report deeper self-disclosures. This correlation was followed with a planned contrast analysis that examined the sample classified into one of three groups again based upon their amount of time in the league: one to four years ($n$ = 106), 5–9 years ($n$ = 49), 10+ years ($n$ = 35). Results of *a priori* linear (polynomial) planned comparisons (–2, +1, +1) indicated that the specified contrast weights were not appropriately related to each group's reported levels of disclosure depth, $t(187)$ = 1.33, $p$ = .19. A means plot illustrates that disclosure depth does not increase in a linear pattern as predicted but instead means plots indicate substantially deeper disclosures only amongst the longest tenured group of FSUs (see figure 8.1).

Overall, it appears that the competitive, hyper-masculine environment of FSLs deters the sharing of personal information on LMBs; however, when personal self-disclosures do occur, they generally happen when users have spent a significant amount of time in the league.

## PERCEPTIONS OF PERSONAL SELF-DISCLOSURES AND LEAGUE SATISFACTION

A tenant of self-disclosure is that not all disclosures are similar in content and context. Among other characteristics, self-disclosures vary according to the depth (i.e., intimacy level of information disclosed) and valence (i.e., positive or negative) of the message (Altman & Taylor, 1973). In terms of the depth of disclosure, information can range from superficial details like attitudes about movies and music to high intimacy topics such as personal beliefs, needs, fears, and values. Deeper disclosures are considered more private and thus increase the trust between individuals (Rubin, 1975) and they are typically shared between people who are more familiar with one another (Altman & Taylor, 1973; Taylor, 1968). With respect to valence, messages are categorized as those which share positive information such as getting a new job or negative information like going to prison. Notably,

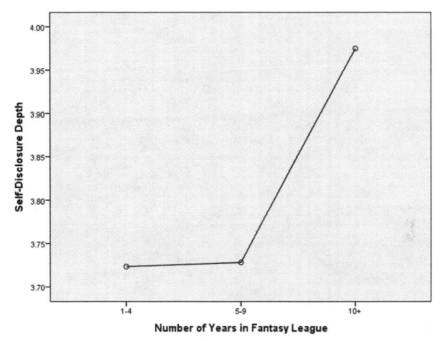

**Figure 8.1.**

judgments regarding disclosure depth and valence range across contexts and consequently are perceived differently according to the norms and expectations of the setting.

For example, Caltabiano and Smithson (1983) report on two relevant findings regarding the appropriateness of self-disclosures in dyadic conversation with respect to variables of disclosure depth and valence. First, they indicate that positive disclosure in contrast to negative disclosure is considered most appropriate. They speculate that this is the case because negative disclosures violate norms for presenting oneself in a positive light and reduce desires for future communication (Blau, 1964). Second, intimate disclosures between same-sexed persons are negatively sanctioned, particularly in male-male interactions (Caltabiano & Smithson, 1983; Lewis, 1978). Given the majority male participation in FSLs, it is likely that many of the personal disclosures would be male-male.

In addition to characteristics of disclosure messages, the public context of LMBs likely negatively influences appropriateness judgments of FSUs. Disclosures (regardless of positive or negative valence) are considered less appropriate when they occur in a public rather than a private context (Bazarova, 2012). In a group context such as a college classroom, negatively valenced disclosures are considered especially inappropriate as compared to positive disclosures because they violate the norms of classroom behaviors (Frisby & Sidelinger, 2013).

The studies mentioned previously indicate unspoken rules regarding self-disclosure in dyads and groups both public and private; because these rules regulate who can disclose what information, where, and to whom, expectancy violations theory is a theoretical framework to explain patterns in FSUs' self-disclosures. Expectancy violations theory (Burgoon & Hale, 1988) labels these disclosure rules as *expectations* and predicts that these expectations may or may not be met. Communicative violations of an individual's expectations, whether positive or negative, lead the individual to experience arousal, to evaluate the event, and then to respond accordingly. Given an understanding about perceptions of self-disclosure among men in a public group context, positive self-disclosures are likely rated as more appropriate than negative self-disclosures and more intimate self-disclosures are likely rated as less appropriate than less intimate self-disclosures.

Data from the 190 respondents supports these assumptions. The perceived appropriateness of self-disclosures was measured using two sets of disclosure topics, Positive and Negative. Sixteen negative topics (e.g., "The death of a family member [grandparent, parent, sibling, cousin]"; "Loss of a job") and fourteen positive topics (e.g., "The birth of a child"; "Getting married / starting a new dating relationship") were each rated by participants on a Likert-type scale ranging from 1 (*not very appropriate*) to 5 (*very appropriate*). Items were averaged for a total appropriateness score in each category, Positive ($M$ = 3.14; $SD$ = .93) and Negative ($M$ = 2.60; $SD$ = .84). A follow-up test for significant differences between means indicates a statistically significant difference, $t(180)$ = –5.79, $p$ < .01, suggesting negative disclosures are rated as less appropriate (see table 8.1).

These thirty messages also varied with respect to their level of depth. Messages of greater depth were those more personal in nature (i.e., "Getting diagnosed with a sexually transmitted disease" [negative], "Celebrating recovery from major illness" [positive]) and those more superficial (i.e., "Getting into a minor car accident" [negative], "Attending special activities like a football game" [positive]). Items were averaged for a total appropriateness score in each depth category, High-intimacy ($M$ = 3.28; $SD$ = .87) and Low-intimacy ($M$ = 3.38; $SD$ = .83). A follow up $t$-test for significant differences between means does not indicate a statistically significant difference, $t(180)$ = –1.07, $p$ > .05, suggesting that high- and low-intimacy disclosures are both moderately appropriate.

Although not specific to the context of FSLs, the presence of intimate self-disclosure has been found to increase satisfaction with other online

**Table 8.1. Means and Standard Deviations of Message Appropriateness**

| Factors | M | SD | α | Sample Item |
|---|---|---|---|---|
| **Valence*** | | | | |
| Positive | 3.14 | .93 | .96 | Getting a new job |
| Negative | 2.60 | .84 | .95 | Going through a divorce |
| **Depth** | | | | |
| High Int. | 3.28 | .87 | .86 | The illness of a family member |
| Low Int. | 3.38 | .83 | .84 | Taking a vacation |
| **Combinations** | | | | |
| NH | 3.01 | .98 | .80 | Diagnosis of a sexually transmitted disease |
| PH | 3.56 | .94 | .80 | Overcoming a major illness |
| NL | 3.12 | .96 | .78 | Getting into a car accident |
| PL | 3.64 | .87 | .72 | Going to a special event like football game |

Note. Int. = Intimacy; NH = Negative/High-intimacy; PH = Positive/High-intimacy; NL = Negative/Low-intimacy; PL = Positive/Low-intimacy.
* Statistically significant difference (p < .05 or higher).

groups (Parks & Floyd, 1996a). When self-disclosure is considered to be an appropriate norm in online communities, members are more pleased with their participation (Dietz-Uhler, Bishop-Clark, & Howard, 2005). If reciprocated, disclosures strengthen the ties that bind people together (Jourard, 1971); for example, in electronic support groups, personal disclosures can enhance the bonds of trust between group members, legitimize group membership, and strengthen group identity (Galegher, Sproull, & Kiesler, 1998). Admittedly, these contexts are much different than the competitive environment of fantasy sports.

Regarding FSLs, research finds increased sharing and participation in fantasy league message boards relates to a greater sense of satisfaction and a higher level of commitment to the league (Ruihley & Hardin, 2011b). Given that social interaction is a popular motive for FSUs, when such motives are fulfilled, members are more likely to return to the league; thus, recidivism is partially a function of self-disclosure because FSUs are able to satisfy social motivations partly by maintaining relationships via self-disclosure (see table 8.2).

**Table 8.2. Independent t-tests Comparing Scores on Motivation Factors, Satisfaction Variables, and Self-Disclosure Depth**

| | Disclosers (n = 40) | | Non-Disclosers (n = 150) | |
|---|---|---|---|---|
| Factors | M | SD | M | SD |
| Satisfaction | 6.53 | .91 | 6.32 | 1.01 |
| Future Intent | 6.60 | .87 | 6.31 | 1.04 |
| Depth* | 4.10 | .87 | 3.68 | .92 |

Note. * Significant difference between groups at p < .05 or greater.

**Table 8.3.   Bivariate Correlations between Variables of Interest**

|              | Years | Per.  | Resp. | Depth | Cam.  | Sat.  | Fut.  | Age |
|--------------|-------|-------|-------|-------|-------|-------|-------|-----|
| Years        | —     |       |       |       |       |       |       |     |
| Personal     | .22** | —     |       |       |       |       |       |     |
| Respond      | .33** | .52***| —     |       |       |       |       |     |
| Depth        | .15*  | .18*  | .20*  | —     |       |       |       |     |
| Camaraderie  | .19** | .02   | .37** | .32***| —     |       |       |     |
| Satisfaction | .29** | .09   | .28*  | .19*  | .51***| —     |       |     |
| Future       | .34***| .12   | .27*  | .18*  | .48***| .67***| —     |     |
| Age          | .55***| .26***| .32** | −.03  | .16*  | .29***| .33***| —   |

Note. Years = Number of years in primary fantasy sport league; Personal = Personal self-disclosures; Respond = Respond to other league members self-disclosures; Depth = Depth of self-disclosures; Satis = League Satisfaction; Future = Future intentions to participate in one's primary fantasy sport league.
* = $p < .05$; ** = $p < .01$; *** = $p < .001$

Participant data were separated into two groups: those who reported disclosing personal information on message boards ($n = 40$) and those who did not ($n = 150$). Then, scores on satisfaction were compared between these two groups (see table 8.3). The independent samples $t$-tests did not identify any differences in satisfaction or future intent to participate between disclosers and non-disclosers. This is expected given that many FSUs would not continue to participate in their primary leagues if they were not satisfied. To further investigate the social factors that might influence league satisfaction, correlations between league satisfaction and self-disclosure depth were investigated. There were positive associations suggesting deeper disclosures related to greater league satisfaction ($r = .19$, $p < .05$) and future intent to participate ($r = .18$, $p < .05$) (see table 8.4). FSUs who felt they could share more deep information within their league were more pleased with their FSL experience and more likely to continue participation in the league.

**Table 8.4.   Crosstab Analysis of Reports of Personal Disclosures * Amount of Time in an FSL**

|                        | Years Participating in Primary League | | | |
|------------------------|-------------|-------------|-------------|--------------|
| Post personal details? | 1–4         | 5–9         | 10+         | Total        |
| No                     | 93 (62%)    | 35 (23.3%)  | 22 (14.7%)  | 150 (78.9%)  |
| Yes                    | 13 (32.5%)  | 14 (35%)    | 13 (32.5%)  | 40 (21.1%)   |
| Total                  | 106 (55.8%) | 49 (25.8%)  | 35 (18.4%)  | 190          |

## DATA IMPLICATIONS

This chapter sought to investigate the influence of global FSL characteristics on frequency and perceptions of self-disclosure, certain individual difference variables that contribute to the disclosure of personal information on FSL message boards (e.g., age), and the subsequent influence on league satisfaction and commitment. Overall, findings are three-fold and indicate that 1) despite research acknowledging social interaction as a motivation for participation in FSLs (Davis & Duncan, 2006; Roy & Goss, 2007; Ruihley & Hardin, 2011a; Spinda & Haridakis, 2008), a majority of FSUs do not disclose personal information on message boards but do respond to the messages of others; 2) frequency and depth of self-disclosures are related to longer duration of FSL involvement as well as desire to continue participation; and 3) negatively valenced messages were considered most inappropriate by FSUs.

## NON-DISCLOSURE AS NORMATIVE

The first finding is not surprising given the context and characteristics of FSLs and their members in general, and aligns with previous conceptualizations of fantasy sport interaction that suggest fantasy sport LMBs are spaces for "online interactions and competition that may be *non-* or even *anti*-social" (Farquhar & Meeds, 2007, p. 1224). Comprised of mostly young, White men, FSLs are a competitive environment in which sharing of feelings is seen as counter-productive to the goal of winning. According to some scholars, FSLs serve as sites for men to reaffirm their masculinity through actions such as competition, displays of sports knowledge (Davis & Duncan, 2006), and even aggression (i.e., trash-talking banter on LMBs). Consequently, this often excludes feminine behaviors such as emotional and personal sharing. FSLs are sites for men to display masculine gender role norms or colloquially to show "what it is to be a real man" (Davis & Duncan, 2006, p. 247) which, according to extant research, is a person that avoids or limits self-disclosure (Dindia & Allen, 1992) particularly in online contexts (Bond, 2009). FSUs—who are predominantly male—seem to view fantasy message boards as inappropriate venues for sharing personal feelings likely due to contextual factors such as the competitive purpose of the group and its public nature (Bazarova, 2012).

Relationship maintenance through sharing of personal details is not a feature of most fantasy sport LMBs (especially younger leagues); what is more
probable is that men (and women) maintain their relationships through the
shared activity of participating in fantasy sport. This is expected given sport
spectatorship is a basis for many male friendships (Branscombe & Wann,
1991; Fehr, 1996). From the fan's perspective, the data presented in this
chapter are not unique, as an absence of personal sharing in FSLs is similar
to other small groups centered upon sport spectatorship (of which FSLs
are an extension) such as fan clubs for fans geographically separated from
their team. In an ethnographic account of a Pittsburgh Steelers football fan
club in Fort Worth, Texas (which is an oddity in Dallas Cowboys country),
Kraszewski (2008) notes that viewing games and cheering on the team is the
main purpose of time spent in the club and that sharing personal information is not the norm. He states, "People at the Steelers bar did not socialize
with other members when we were not watching football" (p. 149), and he
further describes most members as being unaware of the social standing
and personal beliefs of fellow group members. The benefit of shared activity and lack of self-disclosure associated with other sport-centric spectatorship groups like fan clubs is reflected in FSLs as well.

## ADDITIONAL CONTRIBUTING FACTORS

Given the differences between face-to-face and online group communication, there are likely additional reasons for why self-disclosure is not the
norm in online FSLs. One possible explanation for the lack of sharing may
be the number of leagues that FSUs participate in during the year. Subjects in this sample reported participating in four leagues per year which,
especially if in the same sport, would require large amounts of time devoted simply to competition not to mention extra time for maintaining
relationships with potentially thirty or more other members. Moreover,
most individuals do not belong to four different face-to-face sport fan
clubs, partly because the convenience that online group membership af-
fords is absent. Additionally, access to other online social networks like
Facebook, which is purposely devoted to users sharing personal information, allows for FSUs to engage and interact in a more appropriate venue
than FSL message boards. As a majority of the sample was twenty-five
years or younger, the proliferation and popularity of social networking
sites such as Twitter and Facebook likely have replaced the relational

management function of many LMBs. This might not be the case for older FSUs who might not be pervasive social media users.

While it may be speculated that general characteristics of FSLs discourage self-disclosure, one significant individual difference that fosters self-disclosure is time. FSUs who report offering personal disclosures on LMBs are more likely to have been involved with the league for longer. To wit, for league members who have participated in their league between one to four years only 12 percent report posting personal details on LMBs as compared to 37 percent of FSUs participating for ten-plus years. A greater duration in the league also relates to deeper disclosures by FSUs. Taken together, greater experience in the online environment and presumed closer relational ties to league members both contribute to a greater willingness to express more intimate, personal life details. This finding is consistent with literature concerning online self-disclosure, which finds that individuals' depth of disclosures grows as the depth of their involvement increases (Parks & Floyd, 1996a). More intimate, personal sharing happens when participants become better acquainted and feel more comfortable within the group, which can explain what occurs in FSLs in this study (see figure 8.1). It may also be related to age as those who are older are more likely to report responding to and sharing personal information (see table 8.4).

It seems that self-disclosures naturally happen over time as involvement grows (and presumably as participants age), but solely the presence of self-disclosure is not associated with feelings of satisfaction. This finding is also likely a reflection of the purposeful and competitive nature of FSLs, and it suggests that through acts such as trash-talking and friendly banter FSUs are able to satisfactorily fulfill needs for social interaction. In general, FSUs report being satisfied with their leagues and do not deem it as essential that they share their lives to be content with their primary FSLs. But, those who share deeper levels of personal information report greater satisfaction. It is unclear if satisfaction comes before, after, or along with an increased depth of sharing. Future research may be committed to investigating the turning points at which league conversations deepen into sharing personal details (i.e., the death of a family member, loss of a job, or birth of a child) in an FSL.

Finally, the third finding indicates negative disclosures are considered the most inappropriate by FSUs. This is not surprising given that previous research has identified negative disclosures as inappropriate in both face-to-face (Caltabiano & Smithson, 1983) and online contexts (Bazarova, 2012). Negative disclosures violate norms for presenting oneself in a positive light and, as a result, decrease likelihood of seeking future communication. The most appropriately viewed disclosures were those that were low-intimacy and positively valenced followed closely by high-intimacy, positively valenced disclosures.

## LIMITATIONS

As with much self-report research, a number of limitations inhibit the generalization of the findings in this chapter to larger populations. First, this research presents only a cross-sectional examination of FSUs and message board use, and does not investigate differences in self-disclosure over time. While results do suggest time is related to greater disclosure, without a longitudinal study it cannot be certain that time is an explanatory mechanism accounting for variance in reports of self-disclosure. Second, it is uncertain that FSUs are thinking of only one primary fantasy league as the majority of respondents reported participation in multiple leagues and sports. Respondents may be providing general impressions about self-disclosure in their various experiences across leagues. Next, claims regarding differences between men and women self-disclosing in a FSL are speculative, because this study was unable to compare the sexes due to a scarcity of female participants. Future research may be interested in specifically examining female FSUs for differences in personal self-disclosures as women tend to share more information about themselves than do men (Dindia & Allen, 1992). Also, it may be possible that the presence of women in a FSL might increase the amount of personal sharing.

## CONCLUSION

This chapter examined personal self-disclosure among fantasy sport players with respect to the amount, perceived appropriateness, and impact on fantasy league satisfaction. From a fan's perspective, although participation in a fantasy league partly serves a social function it is not typically one of relational sharing. That is, the maintenance of social relationships does not usually occur through the sharing of personal information as evidenced by the fact that the majority of respondents reported not self-disclosing personal details. Although social motivations are a part of the fantasy experience (Davis & Duncan, 2006; Roy & Goss, 2007; Ruihley & Hardin, 2011a; Spinda & Haridakis, 2008; chapter 5, this volume), it appears that individual attributes are influential in decisions to self-disclose, namely time. FSUs involved in fantasy leagues for longer durations are more likely to self-disclose. In sum, the competitive environment of fantasy leagues appear to deter self-disclosure but may continue to promote relationship maintenance through shared activity and competition as FSUs report being satisfied with their leagues. There is caution that it remains unknown the extent to which self-disclosure on LMB is a function of fantasy sport characteristics or individual differences.

## REFERENCES

Altman, I., & Taylor, D. A. (1973). *Social penetration: The development of interpersonal relationships.* New York: Holt, Rinehart & Winston.

Bane, C. M. H., Cornish, M., Erspamer, N., & Kampman, L. (2010). Self-disclosure through weblogs and perceptions of online and "real-life" friendships among female bloggers. *Cyberpsychology, Behavior, and Social Networking, 13*(2), 131–139. doi:10.1089/cyber.2009.0174

Barak, A., & Gluck-Ofri, O. (2007). Degree and reciprocity of self-disclosure in online forums. *CyberPsychology & Behavior, 10*(3), 407–417. doi:10.1089/cpb.2006.9938

Bazarova, N. N. (2012). Public intimacy: Disclosure interpretation and social judgments on Facebook. *Journal of Communication, 62*(5), 815–832. doi:10.1111/j.1460-2466.2012.01664.x

Berger, C. R., & Calabrese, R. J. (1975). Some explorations in initial interaction and beyond: Toward a developmental theory of interpersonal communication. *Human Communication Research, 1*(2), 99–112. doi:10.1111/j.1468–2958.1975.tb00258.x

Billings, A. C., & Ruihley, B. J. (2013a). *The fantasy sport industry: Games within games.* New York: Routledge.

Billings, A. C., & Ruihley, B. J. (2013b). Why we watch, why we play: The relationship between fantasy sport and fanship motivations. *Mass Communication and Society, 16*(1), 5–25. doi:10.1080/15205436.2011.635260

Blau, P. M. (1964). *Exchange and power in social life.* New York: Wiley

Bond, B. J. (2009). He posted, she posted: Gender differences in self-disclosure on social network sites. *Rocky Mountain Communication Review, 6*(2), 29–37.

Branscombe, N. R., & Wann, D. L. (1991). The positive social and self concept consequences of sports team identification. *Journal of Sport & Social Issues, 15*(2), 115–127. doi:10.1177/019372359101500202

Brown, N., Billings, A. C., & Ruihley, B. J. (2012). Exploring the change in motivations for fantasy sport participation during the life cycle of a sports fan. *Communication Research Reports, 29*(4), 333–342. doi:10.1080/08824096.2012.723646

Burgoon, J. K., & Hale, J. L. (1988). Nonverbal expectancy violations: Model elaboration and application to immediacy behaviors. *Communication Monographs, 55*(1), 58–79. doi:10.1080/03637758809376158

Caldwell, M. A., & Peplau, L. A. (1982). Sex differences in same-sex friendship. *Sex Roles, 8*(7), 721–732. doi:10.1007/BF00287568

Caltabiano, M. L., & Smithson, M. (1983). Variables affecting the perception of self-disclosure appropriateness. *The Journal of Social Psychology, 120*(1), 119–128. doi:10.1080/00224545.1983.9712017

Collins, N. L., & Miller, L. C. (1994). Self-disclosure and liking: A meta-analytic review. *Psychological Bulletin, 116*(3), 457. doi:10.1037//0033-2909.116.3.457

Davis, N. W., & Duncan, M. C. (2006). Sports knowledge is power reinforcing masculine privilege through fantasy sport league participation. *Journal of Sport & Social Issues, 30*(3), 244–264. doi:10.1177/0193723506290324

Dietz-Uhler, B., Bishop-Clark, C., & Howard, E. (2005). Formation of and adherence to a self-disclosure norm in an online chat. *CyberPsychology & Behavior, 8*(2), 114–120. doi:10.1089/cpb.2005.8.114

Dindia, K. (2000). Sex differences in self-disclosure, reciprocity of self-disclosure, and self-disclosure and liking: Three meta-analyses reviewed. In S. Petronio (Ed.), *Balancing the secrets of private disclosures* (pp. 21–36). Mahwah, NJ: Lawrence Erlbaum.

Dindia, K., & Allen, M. (1992). Sex differences in self-disclosure: A meta-analysis. *Psychological bulletin, 112*(1), 106. doi:10.1037/0033-2909.112.1.106

Fantasy Sport Trade Association. (2011). FSTA press releases. Retrieved 9 September, 2011, from http://www.fsta.org/blog/fsta-press-release

Farquhar, L. K., & Meeds, R. (2007). Types of fantasy sports users and their motivations. *Journal of Computer-Mediated Communication, 12*(4), 1208–1228. doi:10.1111/j.1083-6101.2007.00370.x

Fehr, B. (1996). *Friendship processes.* Thousand Oaks, CA: Sage.

Frisby, B. N., & Sidelinger, R. J. (2013). Violating student expectations: Student disclosures and student reactions in the college classroom. *Communication Studies, 64*(3), 241–258. doi:10.1080/10510974.2012.755636

Galegher, J., Sproull, L., & Kiesler, S. (1998). Legitimacy, authority, and community in electronic support groups. *Written Communication, 15*(4), 493–530. doi:10.1177/0741088398015004003

Jourard, S. M. (1971). *Self-disclosure: An experimental analysis of the transparent self.* New York: Krieger.

Kepner, T. (2006, October 6). League is a fantasy; friendships are not. *The New York Times.* Retrieved from http://www.nytimes.com/2006/10/08/sports/baseball/08cheer.html

Kraszewski, J. (2008). Pittsburgh in Fort Worth: Football bars, sports television, sports fandom, and the management of home. *Journal of Sport & Social Issues, 32*(2), 139–157. doi:10.1177/0193723508316377

Lewis, R. A. (1978). Emotional intimacy among men. *Journal of Social Issues, 34*(1), 108–121. doi:10.1111/j.1540-4560.1978.tb02543.x

McKenna, K. Y. A., Green, A. S., & Gleason, M. E. J. (2002). Relationship formation on the Internet: What's the big attraction? *Journal of Social Issues, 58*(1), 9–31. doi:10.1111/1540-4560.00246

Parks, M. R., & Floyd, K. (1996a). Making friends in cyberspace. *Journal of Communication, 46*(1), 80–97. doi:10.1111/j.1083-6101.1996.tb00176.x

Parks, M. R., & Floyd, K. (1996b). Meanings for closeness and intimacy in friendship. *Journal of Social and Personal Relationships, 13*(1), 85–107. doi:10.1177/0265407596131005

Roy, D. P., & Goss, B. D. (2007). A conceptual framework of influences on fantasy sports consumption. *Marketing Management Journal, 17*(2), 96–108.

Rubin, Z. (1975). Disclosing oneself to a stranger: Reciprocity and its limits. *Journal of Experimental Social Psychology, 11*(3), 233–260. doi:10.1016/S0022-1031(75)80025-4

Ruihley, B. J., & Hardin, R. L. (2011a). Beyond touchdowns, homeruns, and three–pointers: An examination of fantasy sport participation motivation. *International Journal of Sport Management and Marketing, 10*(3), 232–256. doi:10.1504/IJSMM.2011.04479

Ruihley, B. J., & Hardin, R. L. (2011b). Message board use and the fantasy sport experience. *International Journal of Sport Communication, 4*(2), 233–252.

Spinda, J. S. W., & Haridakis, P. M. (2008). Exploring the motives of fantasy sports: A uses-and-gratifications approach. In L. W. Hugenberg, P. M. Haridakis & A. C. Earnheardt (Eds.), *Sports mania: Essays on fandom and the media in the 21st century* (pp. 187–199). Jefferson, NC: McFarland.

Taylor, D. A. (1968). The development of interpersonal relationships: Social penetration processes. *The Journal of Social Psychology, 75*(1), 79–90. doi:10.1080/00224545.1968.9712476

Utz, S. (2003). Social identification and interpersonal attraction in MUDs. *Swiss Journal of Psychology, 62*(2), 91–101. doi:10.1024//1421-0185.62.2.91

# FANTASY AND SPORTS MEDIA

**9**

# LEGACY MEDIA AND FANTASY SPORTS

*Steve Bien-Aimé and Marie Hardin*

For sport media companies, fantasy sport is currently an important feature of their editorial offerings and appears to be a significant part of their long-term strategies. Shapiro, Drayer, and Dwyer (2014) opined on the future of fantasy sport, saying, "As the industry continues to mature, fantasy participants are becoming a highly valued segment of the sport consumer population" (p. 85). Because young fans have grown up consuming sport while also participating in fantasy sport, fantasy sport-related products should continue to thrive and grow (Billings & Ruihley, 2014). The industry's own figures support such predictions. In 2004, 13.5 million people in the United States and Canada played fantasy sport (Fantasy Sports Trade Association, n.d). By 2014, more than forty-one million people participated in fantasy (Fantasy Sports Trade Association, n.d). From an economic standpoint, the explosion of fantasy sport gamers have equated addition millions of dollars for media companies. From 2009 to 2014, Yahoo! Inc.'s fantasy sport revenue jumped from $127 million to $250 million (Edwards, 2014). In the same period, ESPN went from about $99 million to $180 million, and CBS from $60 million to $92 million (Edwards, 2014).

For media companies, the appeal of fantasy sport is not limited solely to the gaming component. ESPN set a record for most unique visitors to a sports website in August 2014 (Fisher, 2014). The figure, 82.4 million visitors, surpassed the 80.7 million visitors reached in June 2014 during the men's World Cup soccer tournament. Fantasy football was attributed as one of the reasons for the record figure (Fisher, 2014).

FoxSports.com recognizes the importance of fantasy football fans, according to the company's lead fantasy sport editor Ryan Fowler (personal communication, November 10, 2014). Fowler said that from 2013 to 2014 the company has seen a "significant" increase in video streams for fantasy content. For example, Fowler indicated that the fantasy football waiver wire video always ranks in website's the top 20 video offerings. Fowler said a strong case can be made that fantasy sport fans are perhaps the most desired group to reach. He explained that casual fans "might flip a few pages," but fantasy team owners might "flip 15 pages" because they care so much about researching their rosters. He noted that this trend "shows you that the fantasy owner is more valuable than the person coming for general information."

Research from Ruihley and Hardin (2013) buttress Fowler's observation. More than 66 percent of the fantasy players the authors questioned said they leave the website where their respective fantasy game is played in order to seek out additional information. Ruihley and Hardin (2013) surmised: "Possible explanations for surveying the fantasy sport landscape could be to confirm host site opinions, gather diverse viewpoints, seek out information from multiple outlets, or just satisfy the need to obtain as much information as possible" (p. 69). The need for a great deal of data appears to be a paramount reason. According to 2014 data, fantasy sport participants are heavy sport news consumers, as almost 75 percent read four or more news websites and spend almost nine hours a week acquiring fantasy sport news (Fantasy Sports Trade Association, n.d). To provide some context, Americans average spending 70 minutes a day or 8.2 hours per week consuming news (Pew Research Center for the People & the Press, 2010).

## FANTASY SPORTS AND DIGITAL MEDIA

The boom in fantasy sport coincided with the rise of the Internet (see also Anderson & Bowman, chapter 1, this volume). In fact, some would posit that the Internet as perfect medium for fantasy sport (Edwards, 2014). Fowler agreed with that sentiment, saying, "The Internet made everything easier" (personal communication, November 10, 2014). While traditional media—such as television, radio, and newspapers—have not had the easiest time adapting to new technology, seeing its workforce shrinking about 20 percent from 2003 to 2013 (U.S. Bureau of Labor Statistics, 2004; U.S. Bureau of Labor Statistics, 2014), the fantasy sport industry has thrived during this same period. This could possibly be attributed to the advent of the Internet. With information across the World Wide Web being transferred within seconds, it makes sense that more traditional platforms of media would struggle to keep a viable workforce—as much as been suggested by FoxSports.com's Fowler (personal communication, November 10, 2014). IBISWorld, a business that analyzes U.S. industries (IBISWorld, n.d.) predicts that improvements in Internet access coupled with more people on the Web will only help the fantasy sport industry (Edwards, 2014). Newspapers might have been ill-suited for the Internet era starting in the mid-1990s (Billings and Ruihley, 2014). Newspapers such as *USA Today* had been a great resource for fantasy sport players, especially baseball, because such newspapers provided box scores for every game. However, Billings and Ruihley (2014) noted a change in news consumption habits:

> When fantasy participation migrated to the Internet, the statistics naturally moved with the games, as websites would automatically enter the statistics and determine scores, outcomes, and standings. . . . As a result, participants would no longer turn to newspapers and magazines for statistics; the Internet was a virtually instant leader in that regard (p. 62).

In addition, the economic woes of many U.S. newspapers have forced publishers to cut back as companies have been reducing and/or eliminating sections (Edna, 2013; Pew Research Center's Journalism Project staff, 2008). Sports sections have not been immune, said Ron Fritz, senior editor for sports at the *Baltimore Sun*. "One of the things most newspapers trimmed were stats packages," he said in an interview (personal communication, November 11, 2014). During his tenure at the *Sun*, which began in 2006, there was a fantasy baseball segment, but it was short-lived. Overall, Fritz does not run much fantasy content, and his readers do not seem to mind. He said, "There's so many outlets to get that information." Academic research indicates that fantasy sport players do not rely on newspapers, either (Ruihley & Hardin, 2013).

However, having a robust fantasy sport presence could help increase fandom for media companies and sport leagues. Brian Rolapp, a NFL vice president, told the *Tampa Tribune* that fantasy football players watch at least two more hours a week of football than those who do not play fantasy football (Snel, 2005). Media companies that pay billions of dollars to acquire sport broadcasting rights factor fantasy sport into their bids. ESPN pays the NFL $1.8 billion per season to broadcast *Monday Night Football*, and ESPN executive Jason Waram told the *Hollywood Reporter*, "A lot of fantasy games come down to Monday night . . . and even if you don't care about the teams, you'll stay up late to watch if one of your players is playing" (Bond, 2011, para. 22). NBC, CBS, ESPN, and FOX are supporting their multi-billion dollar investments in football by producing television shows dedicated to fantasy gamers. Satellite television provider DirecTV went a step further by dedicating a channel solely to fantasy football: "The Fantasy Zone channel will focus solely on how the live action is affecting the day's fantasy stats, with up-to-the-minute game analysis, stats and on-screen tickers that offer projections and key player updates" (Strauss, 2014, para. 3). Anthem Media Group trumped that move by creating the first twenty-four-hour channel dedicated to fantasy sport, the Fantasy Sports TV Network (Marketwired, 2014). The viewers for fantasy sport programming are highly desirable, given that the audience tends to be older, educated, and financially lucrative (Fantasy Sports Trade Association, 2014; see also chapter 1, this volume)

Research by Billings and Ruihley (2013) indicates that fantasy sports participants are generally traditional sports fans, too. Playing fantasy sports might also lead to consumers learning more about a particular sport and the players in that sport (Lee, Ruihley, Brown & Billings, 2013). Anecdotally, female fantasy football participants told the *New York Daily News* that fantasy football taught them about the actual sport and the players in the NFL. In U.S. professional sport, player movement between teams is frequent, and that movement could impact fandom, according to Lee et al. (2013): "The popularity of fantasy football and the high player turnover rate in the NFL, because of free agency, make it easier for fantasy football owners to cheer for their fantasy team players rather than an actual team" (p. 223). Lee et al. (2013) posit that traditional sport fans and fantasy sport participants are perhaps "siblings" on the fandom continuum. There is a relationship between traditional and fantasy sports fans, but that relationship does not appear to be one that can be defined simply. To this end, Nesbit and King report that fantasy football participants are more likely to attend NFL games than are non-fantasy football participants. It could also be for media companies that fantasy sport leads to increased web traffic and viewership by taking casual or even non-sport fans and increasing their level of sport fandom.

Fantasy sport companies generally follow two models for participation: charging users to play in leagues or allowing participants to play in free leagues (Miller, 2005). The free option is most popular with media companies; independent leagues whose players want to feel closer to gambling might choose a "pay to play" model. While most fantasy sport leagues are dedicated to season-long play, there has been an explosion of leagues centered on daily games (Brustein, 2013; Drape, 2014; Matuszewski, 2014). Companies such as FanDuel and DraftKings allow participants to pay a fee for the opportunity to make thousands of dollars in a day. However, Drape (2014) notes that prognosticating on players' performances is perilously close to gambling (see also chapter 3 and 13, this volume) an area U.S. sport leagues seek to avoid:

> Major League Baseball especially has taken daily fantasy sports under its wing. It has a partnership with DraftKings, which offers a daily contest on MLB. com in which prizes include tickets to games rather than cash.That stance may be surprising for a league that barred Pete Rose for life for betting on games, but baseball executives see daily fantasy sports as an increasingly important part of their future (para. 4).

In fact, Robert Bowman, the chief executive of Major League Baseball Advanced Media, the league's Internet company, said it was exploring a larger partnership with DraftKings and did not rule out the possibility of cash tournaments or other formats in which money is at stake. Drape (2014) explained his reasons as to why he felt that professional team media managers like Bowman are becoming more apt to accepting online daily fantasy sports leagues:

> Season-long fantasy is a war of attrition. The cleverness here is that it's over quickly, and for a younger generation, it's more appropriate. It's where the people are. It drives traffic. It's not to make extra bucks for MLB.com. It is evolving, and we are continuing to evolve (para. 8).

However according to the Unlawful Internet Gambling Enforcement Act signed by President George W. Bush in 2006, fantasy sport for the most part is not recognized by the federal government as gambling if, "all winning outcomes reflect the relative knowledge and skill of the participants and are determined predominantly by accumulated statistical results of the performance of individuals (athletes in the case of sports events) in multiple real-world sporting or other events" (Legal Information Institute, n.d., para. 22). The legality of daily fantasy sport games has allowed the NBA to partner with FanDuel (Rovell, 2014) and the NHL to partner with Draft-Kings (Heitner, 2014b) . . . with both deals being announced in the same week. In fact, sport teams themselves are reaching deals with fantasy sport providers in what *Forbes* called "a type of 'gold rush' between the fantasy giants in securing partnerships with major professional sports leagues and the teams situated therein" (Heitner, 2014b, para. 4).

The deals with the sport leagues must be viewed under a traditional media lens. While MLB, the NFL, NHL, and NBA—widely considered the big four sports in the United States—sell the broadcast rights to their respective events to make the bulk of their revenue, each sport league also has its own television network and website that must mesh journalistic operations with the financial goals of the sport league and the owners of each league's respective franchises.

## IMPORTANCE OF SYNERGY

The rise of daily fantasy sport games has extended to traditional media companies looking for new revenue streams as traditional sources of income dry up. In summer 2014, both *USA Today* and *Sports Illustrated* created their own daily fantasy sport platforms (Business Wire, 2014; Heitner, 2014a; Willens, 2014). In exploring the case of *USA Today*, one must also account for corporate synergy. *USA Today* is owned by Gannett Co. Gannett television stations are available to about 30 percent of Americans, and the company owns eighty-two daily newspapers (Gannett, n.d.). Gannett's range extends pretty far in the United States, and company executives said they are seeking to use that clout for the company's new fantasy sport venture. Gannett's current integration plan stands in contrast to the company's philosophy about fantasy sport in the mid-1990s. *USA Today's* Howard Kamen told Billings and Ruihley (2014) that there was very little coordination between the physical news operations of *USA Today* and the newspaper's online operations, and that the company overall did not see fantasy sport as a robust revenue stream.

The success of *Sport Illustrated's* and *USA Today's* ventures might rest in how other members of the company embrace fantasy sport. ESPN.com has a very successful fantasy gaming platform, and James Quintong, a fantasy sport editor for ESPN.com, said he has seen attitudes regarding fantasy sport change both within ESPN and throughout the broader sport landscape over the years (personal communication, November 10, 2014). Speaking about fantasy sport, Quintong said, "It's become a lot more mainstream. . . . It seems more integrated into the coverage." To explain his point, Quintong referenced the ESPN television show *Fantasy Football Now*. He said it started as a web-only program, but the show's popularity attracted the attention of management, leading to *Fantasy Football Now* being a key part of ESPN's Sunday morning NFL pregame package.

This appetite has changed how football is viewed. While the score ticker (and information ticker for twenty-four-hour news networks) appears to be an indelible part of watching sport contests on television, fantasy sport fans need the ticker to provide more than the scores of all the "professional" games. Recall from Lee et al. (2013) that fantasy football players might care little about the outcomes of "real" games. Fantasy sport fans, however, must stay abreast of the latest statistical developments in the NFL, and so in recent years, the statistics of key performers are mentioned in the sport tickers as well as mentions to play the respective network's fantasy game.

Even in traditional news, journalists are acknowledging the presence of fantasy sport fans, Quintong said (personal communication, November 10, 2014). He said that in ESPN's NFL programming, some reporters, in addition to talking about a specific development such as a player injury or team signing, will describe the subsequent fantasy impact

Sport blogs, while newer than traditional media, cannot be ignored by mainstream news organizations, and bloggers do not ignore fantasy sport. SB Nation, which reports forty-eight million unique visitors annually (Vox Media, n.d.), has a partnership with FanDuel for one-week fantasy football and daily fantasy baseball. Cursory examination of SB Nation's website reveals that synergistic relationships appear healthy between its journalism unit and fantasy gaming business interests. In support of its dealings with FanDuel, SB Nation offers its readers advice specifically tailored to building rosters for SB Nation's fantasy games. Thus, instead of providing tips for building season-long fantasy players, SB Nation provides guidance for constructing teams for one-week stints for its own fantasy football game and for daily play in fantasy baseball.

For a successful fantasy sport offering, coordination must not be restricted to those who handle programming decisions; the actual fantasy sport games must work well and be in tune with fan interests and patterns for accessing such games, FoxSports.com's Fowler said (personal communication, November 10, 2014). While some companies such as Fox Sports and ESPN create and entirely run their own fantasy games, others work with corporate partners. *Sports Illustrated's* FanNation will be supported by TopLine Game Labs (*Business Wire*, 2014). Fowler said at Fox Sports, the company's engineering team works feverishly to keep pace with newer technology, and the changes force he and his content team to always conceive of fresh ways to present fantasy-sport related news and information. "We try to evolve with the technology, and we evolve the content," he said.

The synergistic relationships are not limited to content providers and engineering teams, either; perhaps most effective is when sponsors are integrated into the content. In 2013, Volkswagen and CBS Sports partnered to create Coach's Corner (Chudgar, 2013; Volkswagen, 2013). In this offering, fantasy football players "compete with CBS Sports personalities to see whose team does better, and the CBS personality will then heckle or praise his opponent with a custom video response embedded in a VW banner" (Chudgar, 2013, para. 9). CBS Sports leveraged its web and broadcast platforms to enhance both its fantasy football game and its relationship with a sponsor.

## FIGHT FOR MARKET SHARE

The moves by both Time, Inc., which owns *Sports Illustrated*, and Gannett also signal a change in the arms race that is fantasy sport. Nonetheless, prospective operators face barriers to success due to the widespread dominance of major providers. Yahoo, ESPN, and CBS provide fantasy sports services across a range of sports and are complemented by a host of information and other media coverage that makes them a favorite webpage for consumers. Therefore, although barriers to entry are low, new industry players may find it very difficult to succeed against incumbent players (Edwards, 2014, p. 20),

Daily fantasy games could be a way for both companies to gain more than a foothold in the burgeoning fantasy sport market. A quick glance at some of the current industry leaders shows that Gannett and Time, Inc. have work to do to catch up to their competitors. Perhaps surprisingly, the top media company in the fantasy sport industry is not a sport entity or a traditional media firm. Yahoo! Inc. controls about 18 percent of the fantasy sport market through its Yahoo Sports entity, according to IBISWorld, a business that analyzes U.S. industries (Edwards, 2014; IBISWorld, n.d.). Most of Yahoo's fantasy games are free, but there are some add-ons that high-end fantasy players can purchase; the company derives most of its income from advertisements (Edwards, 2014). The fantasy platform has also benefited from the fact that millions of people use Yahoo's e-mail services; that alone offers the company millions of potential customers for its fantasy games. For instance, IBISWorld predicted that more than four million people would play fantasy football through Yahoo (Edwards, 2014).

ESPN, dubbed "The Worldwide Leader in Sports," is second in market share at 12.9 percent (Edwards, 2014). Similarly to Yahoo!, ESPN's fantasy offerings are mostly free as the company makes the majority of its revenue from advertising (Edwards, 2014). However IBISWorld notes that ESPN employs its strength in multiple media to sell premium data procured by its huge staff of journalists while also being "able to leverage its role as a sports broadcaster to drive users to its fantasy sites." ESPN broadcasts fantasy football programming and offers advice to players through its magazine, radio shows, and podcasts, among other points of contact with players (Edwards, 2014, p. 22).

CBS is next at 7.3 percent (Edwards, 2014). CBS Sports makes most of its fantasy sport revenue from subscriptions and seeks new revenue streams by partnering with outside companies to develop apps to power CBS's fantasy games. The reason for the revenue strategy is underpinned by the network's high subscription rate. "Since a majority of the company's user base already pays for subscriptions, it is expected these particular consumers will be more likely to spend additional money on value-added applications" (Edwards, 2014, p. 23–24).

While IBISWorld predicts fantasy sport to grow steadily, but not at the fevered pitch experienced earlier in the 2000s, fantasy sport experts expect daily games to be perhaps the next wave of growth within the industry; hence, the 2014 moves by Time, Inc. and Gannett. If fantasy game players need more advice to play daily games, then the content fantasy experts produce will shift to accommodate the audience, he said.

Women represent another unrealized market for the fantasy game industry (Edwards, 2014, also discussed in chapter 7 of this volume). IBISWorld reported that women compose about 31 percent of fantasy sport players, but that number is expected to grow (Edwards, 2014). However, fantasy sport operators might not be able to cater to female fantasy sport fans in the same way they cater to men. In analysis of male and female fantasy sport players, Ruihley and Billings (2013) found statistically significant differences between the two groups. For instance, women were seemingly late adopters of the fantasy sport movements, as the male respondents were playing for 5.8 years on average compared to 3.2 for women. Also, men devoted more time to their fantasy teams, 3.1 hours a week while the sport was in season, compared to 1.5 a week for women. Despite these differences, Ruihley and Billings (2013) note "the levels at which motivations for men's and women's fantasy sport play are different (as they tend to be heightened for men), the priorities and primary aims that men and women exhibit when deciding to play are remarkably similar" (p. 447). Those aims were entertainment, surveillance, and enjoyment.

## CONTENT PROVIDERS OR JOURNALISTS?

Billings and Ruihley (2014) indicated there is a tension around the question of whether fantasy sport experts are journalists or just analysts. Even the trade association for fantasy sport professionals, the Fantasy Sports Writers Association, does not appear to side one way or another. On its website, the association said it "was founded to be a voice for writers in the arena of fantasy sports" (Fantasy Sports Writers Association, n.d.). Quintong, who is a Hall of Fame member of the Fantasy Sports Writers Association, said there is no consensus in the industry as to whether fantasy analysts are actually journalists (personal communication, November 10, 2014). He added, "I think we end up using [the term] writers because people might be more comfortable with that." While fantasy sports analysts do not need to interact with traditional journalistic sources such as players, coaches, and team executives (Loop, 2013), Quintong said some current fantasy writers are former sports beat writers. He went on to say that having access to "real" players and coaches can yield insights that standard fantasy analysts might not be able to obtain. Quintong and Fowler, both of whom were trained as traditional journalists, make their careers creating fantasy sport content, but both stress that having journalism backgrounds can only help current and aspiring fantasy writers stand out (personal communications, November 10, 2014). Quintong said there is "a lot of opinion and analysis" in fantasy writing, which is "less about reporting straight-up facts." Loop (2013) explains further:

> One distinctive element of fantasy reporting is its emphasis on Subjectivism over Objectivism because the subjectivist epistemology includes the interpretive nature of the field; reporters are making educated judgments. Analytical journalism doesn't require its practitioners in fantasy to be neutral. In fact, writers are engaged and playing the fantasy sports they cover, another distinctive element and, in most cases, a requirement (p. 17).

What exactly is analyzed in fantasy sport coverage can create problems for fantasy sport experts. ESPN fantasy expert Matthew Berry (2014) touched on the tension that occurs when fantasy sport intersects with real life in a September 2014 column. Berry asked on Twitter whether fans would drop Minnesota Vikings running back Adrian Peterson from their rosters after a grand jury indicted Peterson on a charge of abused his four-year-old son and the NFL moved to prevent Peterson from playing.[1]

The responses focused primarily on Peterson's potential fantasy impact, not the moral questions raised by keeping Peterson on their fantasy teams. Berry, who called himself "a complete and total hypocrite" (para. 1) in the beginning of his column for drafting players of dubious character in previous years, said he was removing Peterson from one of his eight fantasy teams. Berry explained his reasoning, "I don't know if it's possible to win at fantasy and still have a conscience, but I'm looking forward to finding out" (para. 12).

At times, sport finds itself in a gray area, Fowler said (personal communication, November 10, 2014). He said people follow sport, especially fantasy sport, seeking an "escape." Fowler said he understood the unease of fans regarding Adrian Peterson's legal issues, but he said fantasy sport is not the place to locate one's "moral compass." "We're working in a game/entertainment content-producing site," Fowler said. "When people come to our site, they are looking to escape the day-to-day rigors of life." At times that would mean analyzing the fantasy football merits of Adrian Peterson, notwithstanding people's feelings on corporal punishment.

Judging Peterson's perceived fantasy value does highlight another fissure between fantasy and traditional sport fans. Actually interviewing people is not necessary to conduct a fantasy sport analysis. Fantasy sports experts' disconnect with human sources could lead to dissatisfaction with some news consumers as mainstream media continues to embrace fantasy content (Billings & Ruihley, 2014) The conflict stems from fantasy sports experts being given a perceived equal platform to traditional journalistic accounts, despite the fact that the fantasy analysts cannot provide expert commentary on the tangible game (Billings & Ruihley, 2014). This conflict with older, traditional sport fans was described, perhaps tongue-in-cheek, by a *Washington Post* reader in 2003:

> Let me be perfectly blunt on this, so there can be no misunderstanding:
> Fantasy football is destroying the very fabric of this nation.
> Indeed, if this fad continues unchecked, I wouldn't be surprised if America were not under Communist or fascist control by 2010, or certainly no later than Super Bowl XLVIII (Chad, 2003, para. 5–7).

Another fear of sport consumers is that media's providing additional fantasy content might come at the expense of media focusing on the games on the field or court (Billings & Ruihley, 2014). This appears to have come to fruition at some level. For example, Loop (2013) analyzed the Twitter feeds of ESPN fantasy sports journalists and found that most of the journalists' tweets were dedicated toward answering questions (43%). The next highest percentage was retweets at 16 percent. Quintong and Fowler both acknowledge that fantasy sport fans care little about general fantasy sport news;

these fans care about information related only to their fantasy sport teams (personal communications, November 10, 2014). Generalizing the nature of the requests, Quintong said team owners want to know which players should be on their fantasy teams' active rosters: "Hey, pick X or Y for me?" He surmised that Sunday live chats before NFL games follow this format "95 to 99 percent" of the time. In addition, these types of interaction make it possible for outlets such as Sirius XM's twenty-four-hour fantasy sport station. People can call in to the show, get the advice they need and then go about their day.

Fowler said the brevity of fantasy sport content might not appeal to traditional journalists, but it resonates with his fantasy sport audience (personal communication, November 10, 2014). He went on to say that audiences have a short attention span because of their busy schedules. He also said that this technological innovation has allowed fantasy sport players the convenience to make quicker game transactions. "It's not a slap across the face to say our audience has a short attention span," he said. "People are a lot busier." He said the speed of the Internet, coupled with the numerous devices capable of accessing the Web, allows for fantasy sport fans to gather loads of information quickly. But the information they want is limited to which players will perform well, which players should be acquired, and which players should be dropped. Quintong said fantasy sport analysis is not some huge outlier either because one cannot ignore the game occurring in real life (personal communication, November 10, 2014). "It's still about wins and losses. But how they get [wins] makes a big difference."

## NEWSPAPERS AND FANTASY SPORT

There could also be disconnect between the needs of fantasy sport participants and newspapers. A little more than 20 percent of participants used radio sources and about 25 percent used newspapers to help them with their fantasy sport gaming while almost 80 percent of fantasy sport players watched television shows to gain information (Ruihley & Hardin, 2013). And newspapers' embrace of fantasy sport has been uneasy at best. A LexisNexis search for "fantasy baseball" or "fantasy football" for the year 2003 yielded fifty articles among major newspapers in the United States. The articles provided little content for fantasy sport, save for scant references to *USA Today's* online fantasy baseball offerings. In fact, the articles often commented on fantasy sport in a derisive manner:

Come fall, what's the toughest job in America? Try NFL offensive coordinator. With the league's popularity, the public's zest for high-scoring games and the addiction known as fantasy football, offensive coordinators often find themselves the target of criticism.

Fans are convinced they can call a better game, produce better scores and secure better fantasy numbers for their players (Mills, 2003, para. 1–3).

However, the same search for 2013 produced 133 results (mainly for fantasy football), with the articles providing far more robust coverage from two national newspapers, the *New York Times* and the *Washington Post*.

Staff at newspapers have been shrinking for a decade. According to a 2003 census by the American Society of News Editors, there were 54,200 daily newspaper journalists working full time (American Society of News Editors, 2004). That number fell to 36,700 by 2013 (American Society of News Editors, 2014). The decrease in journalists cannot solely be explained by the closing of fifteen daily newspapers between 2007 and 2011 (Mitchell & Rosenstiel, 2012). To put that figure in perspective, there are more than 1,300 daily newspapers in the United States (Edmonds et al., 2013). Revenue streams for newspapers have also suffered in recent years. Revenue for newspapers' print advertising in 2003 was $44.9 billion compared to $1.2 billion for online advertising (Edmonds et al., 2012). A dramatic decline was seen by 2011 when print advertising revenue fell to $20.7 billion; online advertising revenue increased to $3.2 billion (Edmonds et al., 2012). In fact, the physical size of newspapers have declined as well (Edna, 2013; Pew Research Center's Journalism Project staff, 2008). This forces editors to make tough decisions as they increasingly have fewer staff to cover beats and less space in which to place the stories. the *Baltimore Sun's* Ron Fritz said he rejects the pitches he receives from freelance fantasy writers partly because there is not enough space in his section to run their content (personal communication, November 11, 2014). He said the paper's focus is to dominate its region in terms of coverage and expertise about the sports and real-time leagues at play each week. Local and regional news outlets are increasingly cutting back on national and international stories and are marshaling resources to reporting on stories in their circulation areas (Glaser, 2008; Tornoe, 2013). As Fritz mentioned earlier, readers can acquire fantasy sport information from myriad sources; thus, the *Sun's* obligation is to provide coverage readers cannot find elsewhere.

## CONCLUSION

Fantasy sport has penetrated all aspects of traditional media, with varying success. While companies with strong national print Internet, television, and radio holdings, such as ESPN, CBS, and Fox, have been able to leverage their respective media might to make their fantasy sport holdings extremely lucrative, other media giants have struggled to do the same. Clearly, attaining a commitment from all corporate corners is vital to make a successful fantasy sport product. The new daily fantasy gaming phenomenon will test media companies' efforts to coordinate disparate entities in order to either grow or maintain their revenue streams from fantasy sport.

A focus on revenue leads to one of the predominant questions for the immediate future of fantasy sport: whether the market has achieved full saturation. IBISWorld (Edwards, 2014) predicts solid growth for fantasy sport, and based upon the attention given to daily fantasy sport games, it appears that media companies and sport leagues see the industry trending upward. However, the difference between fantasy sport and gambling, though legally different, is not so clear to all relevant parties. A day after the NBA's Adam Silver (2014) wrote in the *New York Times* that sports betting should be more widely legalized, Dallas Mavericks owner Mark Cuban supported the sentiment made by his league's commissioner. His sentiments were summarized:

> In an email exchange with CBSSports.com, Cuban said he believes Silver realizes that it's "hypocritical" of sports leagues to reward and endorse fantasy sports but oppose sports betting. Silver's op-ed was published online a day after the NBA announced a fantasy sports partnership with FanDuel, a CBS Sports sponsor.
> "We all know leagues benefit from the interest in our leagues that [gambling and fantasy sports] create," Cuban said. "In the past for PR reasons, we have put up token resistance to them. I agree with Adam that now is the time to take sports betting out of the shadows and deal with it like the huge business it is" (Berger, 2014, para. 7–9).

From the looks of it, there could be an ethical issue for media companies to address, either currently or in the future, depending on how the government and courts address sport betting. If media outlets are currently going to promote daily fantasy games and charge people money for the chance to win larger sums of cash, then this is perilously close to gambling. In their quest to increase revenue, sport leagues and media companies might be departing from the realm of harmless fun and venturing into spaces where problem behavior can occur—an area of future research and discussion for those interested in the role of fantasy sports in the larger sports media ecology.

## NOTE

1. In November 2014, Peterson pleaded no contest "to a misdemeanor count of recklessly injuring his 4-year-old son" (Olson, 2014).

## REFERENCES

American Society of News Editors (2004, April 14). 2004 census: Newsroom employment drops again; diversity gains. Retrieved from November 11, 2014 from http://asne.org/content.asp?pl=121&sl=157&contentid=157.

American Society of News Editors (2014, July 29). 2014 Census: Minorities in newsrooms increase; 63 percent of newspapers have at least one woman among top-three editors. Retrieved from November 11, 2014 from http://asne.org/content.asp?pl=121&sl=387&contentid=387.

Berger, K. (2014, November 14). Cuban: Silver "exactly right" on sports betting. *CBSSports.com*. Retrieved November 15, 2014 from http://www.cbssports.com/nba/writer/ken-berger/24806648/cuban-silver-exactly-right-on-sports-betting.

Berry, M. (2014, September 18). Adrian Peterson: Fantasy's fallen star. Retrieved September 10, 2015 from http://espn.go.com/fantasy/football/story/_/id/11548711/matthew-berry-fantasy-football-reaction-adrian-peterson.

Billings, A. C., & Ruihley, B. J. (2013). Why we watch, why we play: The relationship between fantasy sport and fanship motivations. *Mass Communication and Society*, *16*, 5–25. doi:10.1080/15205436.2011.635260

Billings, A. C., & Ruihley, B. J. (2014). *The Fantasy Sport Industry: Games within Games*. New York: Routledge.

Bond, P. (2011, August 10). What fantasy football means to Hollywood. *The Hollywood Reporter (Hollywoodreporter.com)*.

Drape, J. (2014, July 28). Lost a fantasy game? Try again tomorrow: Pro leagues warm to online daily fantasy leagues. *New York Times*.

Brustein, J. (2013, March 12). Fantasy sports and gambling: Line is blurred. *New York Times*, p. B9.

Business Wire (2014, July 14). Time Inc.'s *Sports Illustrated* launches FanNation. *MarketWatch*. Retrieved October 26, 2014 from http://www.marketwatch.com/story/time-incs-sports-illustrated-launches-fannation-2014-07-14.

Chad, N. (2003, October 27). Roto-rooters' draining pursuit. *Washington Post*, p. D2.

Chudgar, S. (2013, August 12). Fantasy football players are dream demographic—if you can get their attention. *Advertising Age*. Retrieved from November 13, 2014 from http://adage.com/article/media/fantasy-football-players-a-dream-dem ographic/243585/.

Drape, J. (2014, July 29). Daily fantasy sites draw real world's attention. *International New York Times*, Sports p. 13.

Edmonds, R., Guskin, E., Rosenstiel, T., & Mitchell, A. (2012). The state of the news media 2012: An annual report on American journalism; Newspapers: By the numbers. Pew Research Center's Project for Excellence in Journalism. Retrieved August 20, 2012 from http://stateofthemedia.org/2012/newspapers-building-digi tal-revenues-proves-painfully-slow/newspapers-by-the-numbers/.

Edmonds, R., Guskin, E., Mitchell, A., & Jurkowitz, M. (2013). The state of the news media 2013: An annual report on American journalism; Newspapers: By the numbers. Pew Research Center's Project for Excellence in Journalism. Retrieved November 30, 2014 from http://www.stateofthemedia.org/2013/newspapers -stabilizing-but-still-threatened/newspapers-by-the-numbers/.

Edna, J. (2013, October 8). In print, newspapers cut opinion. Pew Research Center. Retrieved November 11, 2014 from http://www.pewresearch.org/fact -tank/2013/10/08/in-print-newspapers-cut-opinion/.

Edwards, J. (2014). IBISWorld industry report OD4577: Fantasy sports services. *IBIS World*.

Fantasy Sports Trade Association (2014). Industry demographics: At a glance. FSTA.org. Retrieved from http://www.fsta.org/?page=Demographics

Fantasy Sports Writers Association (n.d.). Homepage. Retrieved October 23, 2014 from http://www.fswa.org/

Fisher, E. (2014, September 15). NFL training camps, fantasy football helps ESPN set another ComScore record. *Sports Business Daily*. Retrieved November 12, 2014 from http://m.sportsbusinessdaily.com/Daily/Issues/2014/09/15/Media/ Comscores.aspx.

Gannett (n.d.). Our company. Retrieved October 27, 2014 from http://www.gan nett.com/article/99999999/WHOWEARE/100427016.

Glaser, M. (2008, March 17). Newspapers should focus on local news—but not forget bigger picture. *PBS Media Shift*. Retrieved November 10, 2014 from http://www.pbs.org/mediashift/2008/03/newspapers-should-focus-on-local-news -but-not-forget-bigger-picture077/.

Heitner, D. (2014a, August 13). Daily fantasy sports expands with *USA Today* joining the party. *Forbes*. Retrieved October 26, 2014 from http://www.forbes.com/ sites/darrenheitner/2014/08/13/daily-fantasy-sports-expands-with-usa-today-join ing-the-party/.

Heitner, D. (2014b, November 14). FanDuel and DraftKings dueling over team and league partnerships. *Forbes*. Retrieved November 14, 2014 from http://www .forbes.com/sites/darrenheitner/2014/11/14/fanduel-and-draftkings-dueling -over-team-and-league-partnerships/.

IBISWorld (n.d.). About IBISWorld: The largest provider of industry information in the U.S. Retrieved November 13, 2014 from http://www.ibisworld.com/about/default.aspx

Lee, J., Ruihley, B. J., Brown, N., Billings, A. C. (2013). The effects of fantasy football participation on team identification, team loyalty and NFL fandom. *Journal of Sports Media*, 8(1), 207–227. doi:10.1353/jsm.2013.0008

Legal Information Institute (n.d.). 31 U.S. Code § 5362—Definitions. Cornell University Law school. Retrieved November 12, 2014 from http://www.law.cornell.edu/uscode/text/31/5362.

Loop, M. (2013). Twitter usage in fantasy sports journalism. *The International Journal of Sport and Society*, 3, 17–29. doi:

Marketwired (2014, January 14). World's first fantasy sports TV network set to launch. *Yahoo! Finance*. Retrieved October 19, 2014 from http://finance.yahoo.com/news/worlds-first-fantasy-sports-tv-135500088.html.

Matuszewski, E. (2014, January 12). Fantasy sports league show up on bottom line. *Pittsburgh Post-Gazette*, p. C3.

Miller, S. (2005, December 12). The real revenue in fantasy sports: The statistics, players and profits are authentic; just the teams aren't. *Multichannel News*, p. 38.

Mills, R. (October 12, 2003). XXX, OOO? Not for coordinators. *St. Petersburg Times*, p. 11C.

Mitchell, A., & Rosenstiel, T. (2012). The state of the news media 2012: An annual report on American journalism. Retrieved July 24, 2012 from http://stateofthemedia.org/2012/overview-4/major-trends/

Nesbit, T. M., & King, K. A. (2010). The impact of fantasy football participation on NFL attendance. *Atlantic Economic Journal*, 38, 95–108. doi:10.1007/s11293-009-9202-x

Olson, R. (2014, November 5). Peterson's status unclear after plea. *Star Tribune*, p. 1C.

Pesce, N. L. (2014, September 3). Fantasy women: Running mock NFL teams is female turf, too—and these New Yorkers are game. *New York Daily News*, p. 35.

Pew Research Center for the People & the Press (2010, September 12). Americans spending more time following the news. Retrieved from October 21, 2014 from http://www.people-press.org/2010/09/12/americans-spending-more-time-following-the-news/.

Pew Research Center's Journalism Project staff (2008, July 21). The changing newsroom. Pew Research Center Journalism Project. Retrieved November 11, 2014 from http://www.journalism.org/2008/07/21/the-changing-newsroom-2/.

Rovell, D. (2014, November 12). NBA partners with FanDuel. *ESPN*. Retrieved November 13, 2014 from http://espn.go.com/nba/story/_/id/11864920/nba-fanduel-reach-4-year-exclusive-daily-fantasy-deal.

Ruihley, B. J., & Billings, A. C. (2013). Infiltrating the boys' club: Motivations for women's fantasy sport participation. *International Review for the Sociology of Sport*, 48, 435–452. doi:10.1177/1012690212443440

Ruihley, B. J., & Hardin, R. (2013). Meeting the informational needs of the fantasy sport user. *Journal of Sports Media, 8*, p. 53–80. doi:10.1353/jsm.2013.0013

Shapiro, S. L., Drayer, J., & Dwyer, B. (2014). Exploring fantasy baseball consumer behavior: Examining the relationship between identification, fantasy participation, and consumption. *Journal of Sport Behavior, 37*. 77–93.doi:

Silver, A. (2014, November 14). Legalize sports betting. *The New York Times*, p. A27.

Snel, A. (2005, September 13). Fantasy leagues make real cash. *The Tampa Tribune*. Moneysense, p. 1.

Strauss, C. (2014, July 8). DirecTV goes all-in on fantasy. *USA Today*, p. 3C.

Tornoe, R. (2013). Honing in on hyperlocal. *Editor & Publisher, 146*(3). 44-48

U.S. Bureau of Labor Statistics (2004, May 7). Occupational Employment and Wages, May 2003: 27–3020 Reporters and Correspondents. Retrieved October 30, 2014 from http://data.bls.gov/cgi-bin/print.pl/oes/2003/may/oes273020.htm.

U.S. Bureau of Labor Statistics (2014, April 1). Occupational Employment Statistics: May 2013 National Occupational Employment and Wage Estimates. Retrieved October 30, 2014 from http://www.bls.gov/oes/current/oes273022.htm.

Vox Media (n.d.). SB Nation. Retrieved November 11, 2014 from http://www.vox media.com/brands/sbnation.

Willens, M. (2014, August 12). *USA Today* to launch daily fantasy sports gaming site. *Advertising Age*. Retrieved October 26, 2014 from http://adage.com/article/ media/usa-today-launch-daily-fantasy-sports-gaming-site/294531/.

# 10

# FANTASY SPORTS AND MEDIATED FANDOM

*Brendan Dwyer, Stephen L. Shapiro, and Joris Drayer*

**T**oday's sports fan has never had it better. On any given Sunday in the fall, one has the ability to watch eight live National Football League (NFL) games at once on his or her 70" flat screen High Definition television while streaming four others to his or her tablet via DirecTV's NFL Sunday Ticket To-Go. At the same time, he or she could listen to the in-car audio of the NASCAR race, digitally record a National Hockey League (NHL) game while following and being part of the World Series conversation on Twitter. Meanwhile, there is still the ability to stream live coverage of the one-hole Ryder Cup playoff directly to his laptop while also texting vigorously back and forth with his fantasy football opponent about a controversial touchdown.

Enhancements in technology and a plethora of new media outlets have provided today's sports fans with options, a lot of options. With all these options, mediated sport fans have several choices to ensure they make the most of their limited amount of disposable time and money. What to watch? What to listen to? What platform to use? What to subscribe to? What package to pay for? Who to communicate with? What to say and with what medium to say it? The list could go on and on. At heart of this burgeoning sport media age has been the growth and proliferation of fantasy sport participation. Its impact on the attitudes and behaviors of millions sports fans has been nothing short of a phenomenon.

The following chapter highlights fantasy sport participant motives, perceptions, gambling associations, social interactivity, favorite team loyalty, game outcomes, and media consumption. In particular, our chapter relies on empirical research in the area of fantasy sport consumer behavior to validate the tremendous effect fantasy sports has had on traditional sport fandom. We aim to underscore the potential opportunities for sport teams, leagues, and broadcast administrators looking to effectively communicate and engage this highly-lucrative segment of sports fans.

To begin, it is important to introduce a framework that explains the fantasy sport participant experience. This framework (see figure 10.1), titled the *fantasy sport consumption model* (FSCM), was created in 2010 and provides a foundation for why and how fantasy sport participation impacts favorite team fandom, perceptions of professional sport, and ultimately, media consumption in the form of time and money spent and even platform selection (television, cell phone, computer, etc.).

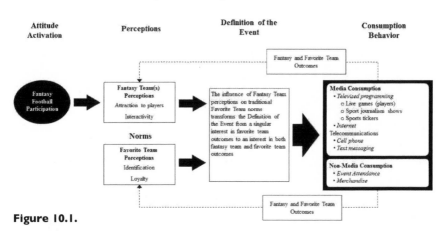

**Figure 10.1.**

Drayer, Shapiro, Dwyer, Morse, and White (2010) created the FSCM. It was guided by the application of Fazio, Powell, and Herr's (1983) attitude-behavior relationship framework that explains the significance of positive and negative attitudes toward an object (or activity) in predicting direct and indirect consumer decisions. The model was grounded in the context of fantasy football and was supported by three propositions. First, fantasy sport activates new attitudes within participants to create a redefined professional sport product. That is, one's relationship with professional sport (i.e., NFL, NBA, or MLB) changed given the added interest of individual players and their statistics. Interesting to note, these new fantasy sport-specific attitudes do not replace one's normative attitudes toward a favorite team, but simply added to one's evolving relationship with professional sport. Second, the redefined version of professional sport broadens one's consumption behavior of associated products and services, specifically media services. Lastly, the authors found that the outcomes of both fantasy and favorite team competition continually influenced both a participant's favorite team norms and fantasy team perceptions so as to keep the redefinition process in play. In all, the results supported previous research that fantasy sport participation has created a new, highly-engaged sport fan with a broader, yet stronger interest in professional sport (Farquhar & Meeds, 2007; Shipman, 2001; Spinda & Haridakis, 2008) (see also Wicker, Grace, & Watanabe, chapter 12, this volume).

The FSCM was tested empirically and upheld by Dwyer and Drayer (2010) and Dwyer (2011b). It was then amended by Dwyer and LeCrom (2013) through the inclusion of novice participants (see figure 10.2), and then once again by Dwyer (2013) through the examination of team outcomes and media consumption (see figure 10.3).

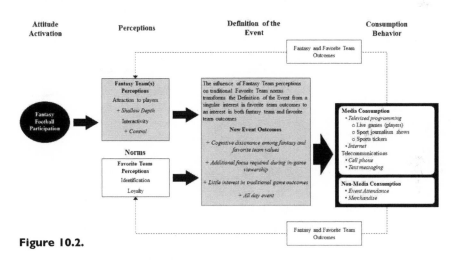

**Figure 10.2.**

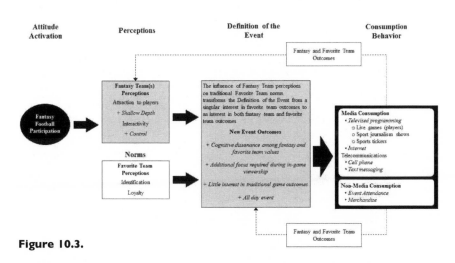

**Figure 10.3.**

The following sections will highlight the distinct factors and components of the above frameworks to explain the unique process of fantasy sport consumption.

## FANTASY SPORTS AND ATTITUDE ACTIVATION

As the FSCM model suggests, participating in fantasy sports activates a second set of attitudes toward the sport. This aspect of the model is one of the key distinguishing features of fantasy participation for a number of reasons. First, this second mode of engagement with a sport creates a new set of perceptions and attitudes toward the sport. Second, these multiple points of engagement lead to radically altered consumption behaviors. Third, these new attitudes and behaviors appear to be complementary in nature, meaning that they can coexist and create a heightened interest in the sport overall. The following section will explore the creation of a new set of attitudes toward professional spectator sports resulting from participation in fantasy sports. The second and third points will be explained later in the chapter.

## WHY DO PEOPLE PLAY FANTASY SPORTS?

In order to understand the attitudes and behaviors that emerge upon participation in fantasy sports, it is perhaps best to understand why people engage in this activity to begin with. The FSCM model presented by Drayer et al. (2010) suggested that most, if not all, fantasy participants have some existing connection to the sport to begin with. From here, they are using fantasy sports as a means to increase their involvement with the sport. But why? From the research on these reasons for participation, two key concepts have emerged: interactivity and controllability.

### Interactivity

One of the aspects of fantasy football that is so attractive to participants is the interactivity that is inherent in the activity. Fantasy participants often cite social interaction as one of the primary reasons for their participation (Dwyer & Kim, 2011; Farquhar & Meeds, 2007; Spinda & Haridakis, 2008). In other words, people like playing fantasy sports because it gives them an opportunity to connect with family, friends, and coworkers. Whether it is in the form of trash-talking or merely a discussion of the week's events, fantasy sports is considered a "pro-social" activity among participants (Drayer, Dwyer, & Shapiro, 2013; Dwyer & Kim, 2011; Farquhar & Meeds, 2007). This interaction is especially high early in the season when the draft occurs (the major community event for each fantasy season) and when each participant's level of commitment is usually highest, as one participant's level of commitment may wane based on poor performance. This phenomenon will be discussed in detail later in this chapter. Each of the primary fantasy sports websites, such as Yahoo!, CBS Sports, and ESPN.com, includes a message board, chat room, and/or other interactive tools in order to provide people with an opportunity to engage in conversations with other individuals with in each league. These "communities" are an integral part of the fantasy sport experience, in that they facilitate the social interaction that motivates many to continue to engage in fantasy sports (see also chapters 5 and 8, this volume).

What is not yet clear is how participation in fantasy sports affects relationships outside of the fantasy sports leagues. Fantasy participants often spend many hours engaging in conversation, watching games, and doing research in an effort to ensure a winning performance. While these activities are all great for engagement with the sport, they may have a negative effect on relationships outside of fantasy sports environment. To date, proof of such outcomes are largely anecdotal or represented humorously in popular culture (for example, in the popular show called *The League*).

## Controllability

One of the other primary aspects of fantasy sports that is central to peoples' enjoyment of the activity is the controllability of outcomes. Sports fans spend hours supporting their favorite team, but in the end, they have little, if any, effect of the outcome of the game. On the other hand, the outcomes related to fantasy sports are based on the decisions made by the participant related to the draft, trades, signing/releasing players, and setting lineups. Fantasy sports leagues invest substantial resources in giving participants access to all of the information necessary to give them the greatest sense of control. Draft kits, research tools, customizable statistical analyses, expert commentary, and other informational resources are provided by all fantasy sports websites in order to give people the sense that they have the greatest competitive advantage when it comes time to make decisions related to their fantasy team (see also, chapter 6 of this volume).

## GAMBLING AND FANTASY SPORTS

A key piece of this discussion from a legal point of view is the notion of gambling. Playing fantasy sports for money remains a key aspect of the activity for some participants. Concurrently, legislators have debated whether or not playing fantasy sports for money represents an illegal form of gambling. The scope of this debate is far too complex for this chapter; however, a discussion of how money influences participants' perceptions of fantasy sports is warranted.

The discussion of gambling can be connected to the previous sections in this chapter. First, the research indicates that the potential for financial gain is not one of the primary reasons that people participate in the activity (Drayer, Dwyer, & Shapiro, 2013; Dwyer & Kim, 2011). Second, problem gambling is often associated with anti-social tendencies (Holleman, 2006; Pietrzak & Petry, 2005); research has found that fantasy sports may be more of a pro-social activity, suggesting that there are features of the activity that make it distinct from traditional forms of gambling (Holleman, 2006; Drayer, Dwyer, & Shapiro, 2013). Finally, by definition, gambling involves an element of luck; however, fantasy participants are primarily motivated to play because through careful research, they have some element of control of the outcome. Again, while playing for money is a feature of the game that some participants find appealing, it is not considered a form of illegal gambling and is not cited as a primary motivation for participating (see also chapters 3 and 12, this volume).[1]

Some sites have a page designed to track league finances but this has not been an emphasis for most fantasy platforms. This may be due to the fact that gambling is not a primary reason that most fantasy participants partake in the activity and may also be a strategy to minimize the perception that fantasy sports may be a form of sports betting, which would make it illegal in most states. Currently, it appears as though the daily fantasy leagues are more focused on the gambling aspects as the quick turnaround from the time of the bet until the time of the payout is significantly shorter than a standard fantasy sports league.

## ATTRACTION TO PLAYERS

Now that the reasons for participation have been explained, it is time to understand the nature of the new set of perceptions of the league that are created as a result of this participation. The traditional sports fan is fiercely loyal to his or her favorite team. However, once that fan begins participating in fantasy sports, he/she develops an attraction to individual players around the league. In fact, the initial critiques of fantasy sports was that the activity would have a negative impact on the traditional, passionate, team-centered attitudes by creating a more fragmented definition of the league. Indeed, the nature of fantasy sports is that it forces participants to follow a group of individual players scattered throughout the league. As a result, fantasy participants develop an attraction to these individual players.

Should sports leagues and teams be concerned that this attraction to individual players may cannibalize the traditional team-centric fan loyalty? To date, the research suggests that this fantasy sports participants' attachment to individual players is shallow and does not endure past a single season (Drayer et al., 2010; Dwyer & LeCrom, 2013). However, the fantasy consumer is an important part of the sport spectator experience in today's environment. As a result, television networks and sports websites are providing more information about individual players than ever before. From statistical details of games scrolling along the bottom portion of a telecast to detailed information about player injuries, media entities are attempting to appease both types of consumers. The introduction of the NFL Red Zone Channel is another example of the league making an effort to provide information and highlights to inform the fantasy user. On this channel, the league focuses on games where scoring plays are imminent. These plays have the greatest impact on fantasy results and are therefore of great interest to the fantasy participant.

## FAVORITE TEAM NORMS

A woman had tickets to Game 7 of the Stanley Cup Finals right at center ice. As she sits down, a man comes down and asks if anyone is sitting in the seat next to her. "No," she says, "the seat is empty."

"This is incredible," said the man. "Who in their right mind would have a seat like this for the Stanley Cup and not use it?"

She says, "Well, actually, the seat belongs to me. I was supposed to come with my husband, but he passed away. This is the first Stanley Cup we haven't been to together since we got married in 1967."

"Oh . . . I'm sorry to hear that. That's terrible. But couldn't you find someone else—a friend or relative, or even a neighbor to take the seat?"

The woman shook her head. "No. They're all at the funeral" (Yi, 2011).

Team loyalty in sports is a defining characteristic for fans. Sport fans have a connection with their favorite teams that is unique and generally stronger than affiliations with other products or services. Many sport fans remain committed to consuming their favorite teams, even in environments where the team is underperforming or muddling through challenging circumstances on and off the field. The Chicago Cubs have not won a World Series in 106 years, and yet they continue to have a loyal fan base that spreads beyond the city of Chicago (Savage, 2011).

Fans tend to connect themselves emotionally with their favorite team. If the team succeeds, fans are in a more positive mood and are motivated to align themselves with their team. If the team loses, the fan feels a sense of loss and, for a period of time, may disassociate themselves from the team. This loyalty and behavioral commitment was demonstrated in a series of experiments. Cialdini et al. (1976) coined the term BIRGing (Basking in Reflected Glory), where fans are more likely to increase association when their favorite teams are successful. Later, Snyder, Higgins, and Stucky (1983) examined the process of CORFing (Casting off Reflected Failure) to explain fans tendency to disassociate with their favorite teams, when those teams were unsuccessful.

Sport identification and loyalty has been examined extensively in the sport management literature. Research has focused on the dynamics and magnitude of spectator attachment to team (Madrigal, 1995; Trail, Anderson, & Fink, 2000; Wakefield, 1995; Wann & Branscombe, 1993), the evolution of identification (Funk & James, 2001, 2004), and various facets of attachment beyond the team perspective (Robinson & Trail, 2005; Trail, Fink, & Anderson, 2003; Woo, Trail, Kwon, & Anderson, 2009). The literature has evolved to provide a better understanding of how identification leads to sport consumption (James & Trail, 2008; Lock, Taylor, Funk, & Darcy, 2012; Shapiro, Ridinger, & Trail, 2012; Trail et al., 2003). Attachment to a team or various facets of a team (i.e., coaches, the sport itself, and/or individual players) has a significant influence on type and magnitude of sport consumption. Interestingly, research has shown that highly identified fans have stronger BIRGing behavior when their favorite teams are winning and are less likely to display CORFing behavior when their favorite teams are unsuccessful (Spinda, 2011). The role identification plays within the context of fan loyalty and consumption should not be understated.

The relationship between fan commitments to their favorite teams and sport consumption has translated into significant revenue within the context of commercialized sport. The total market value of the four major professional sports leagues in North America are estimated at $74 billion, with generated revenues above $24 billion. At the collegiate level sport programs have an estimated value of $9 billion (Howard & Crompton, 2014). With enhanced channels for consumption, the sport fan has a multitude of sources for consuming sport. These sources include traditional forms of consumption, such as attendance, television viewership, and licensed merchandise purchased, and new mediated consumption, such as Internet, live streaming of events, mobile devices, and social media. All of these sources increase the opportunity for sport organizations to generate additional revenue.

In fact, it can be argued that new forms of mediated consumption have changed the landscape for sport fans. Traditionally team identification and loyalty was developed through strong geographic connections, as traditional forms of consumption are limited to local or regional areas (Gladden & Funk, 2001). With the development of new forms of mediated consumption, the sport consumption experience has evolved. Presently, teams and leagues are building team identification and loyalty outside their local area by catering to the "displaced" fan (Fain, 2013). Out of market sport packages through cable networks, live streaming of events online, and social media allows teams to interact and build loyalty across the globe. Additionally, it is easier for fans to consume multiple events at the same time through television, mobile applications, and social media. This is becoming more commonplace for younger generations that are growing up with newer technology.

Within the FSCM, traditional team norms play a significant role. In many cases these norms are the foundation of an individual's sport fandom. As the Stanley Cup example at the beginning of this section, the Chicago Cubs, and the growing population of hardcore displaced fans demonstrate, attitudinal loyalty is a deep-seeded construct, not easily altered. In order to understand the impact of fantasy participation on sport consumer behavior it is imperative to integrate traditional team norms.

Since sport consumption through fantasy participation involves consuming multiple players playing on various teams throughout a league, a sport consumer could face the dilemma of divided loyalty between one's favorite team and fantasy team (Dwyer, 2011). As Dwyer (2011) noted, sport fans tend to select products and services based on specific needs and not just loyalty to team. There is a growing body of literature to support the notion that fantasy outcomes are more important than favorite team outcomes for subset of the sport fan population (Lee, Ruihley, Brown, & Billings, 2013; see also chapter 4, this volume). However, given the competing interests of the two foci and the importance of building fan loyalty from an organizational perspective, it will remain imperative to understand how fantasy related behaviors impact traditional, favorite team fandom.

## IMPACT OF FANTASY PERCEPTIONS
## AND FAVORITE TEAM NORMS

The next step in the FSCM is the integration of the favorite team norms and fantasy team perceptions. This step is intriguing as it requires a participant to make decisions based on the confluence of favorite team focused beliefs (traditional and enduring, yet passive) and fantasy team focused attitudes (controlled, revolving, and interactive). For example, where the favorite team attitudes have familial or regional ties that endure beyond a single season, fantasy football related beliefs are most often associated with individual players that a participant may only manage for one week. This relationship with a player could be equally intense as favorite team attachment because of the short term consequences of a fantasy matchup, but most often the relationship does not last as long. However, when you multiply a participant's attachment to his/her players by the number of players on his/her team, a fantasy participant has a platform for higher engagement.

For example, a typical participant manages up to twelve players on his/her own team. Each week, this participant competes against another fantasy football team with an average of ten different activated players (with non-activated players remaining on a team's bench). As a result of this competition, a certain level of attraction is awarded to the participant's own players as well as an awareness of the players on his/her opponent's team. With ownership not limited to any specific player on any specific team, the combination of these non-traditional interests can ultimately result in a competitive curiosity in nearly every NFL game played each weekend. According to Dwyer and LeCrom (2013), this dramatic change has led to the following new phenomena for sport fans: (1) cognitive dissonance among fantasy and favorite team values, (2) additional focus required during in-game viewership, (3) little interest in traditional game outcomes, and (4) interest in NFL games and programming became an all-day event.

Cognitive dissonance is a term used to explain psychological discomforts or a state of disequilibrium in one's values, beliefs, and/or attitudes that stems from the inflow of conflicting messages, events, or experiences (Festinger, 1957). As it relates to fantasy sports, imagine a participant who is a San Francisco Giants fan, yet also has Los Angeles Dodgers pitcher, Clayton Kershaw, on his fantasy baseball team. In most fantasy baseball leagues during the 2014 MLB season, Clayton Kershaw was considered the best pitcher in the game, and in most cases also the best overall player in fantasy baseball. In other words, if this participant wanted to do well in his fantasy league, having Kershaw on his team was extremely beneficial.

During the season, he faced the Giants four times pitching an average of eight dominant innings resulting in thirty-six strikeouts, a 1.50 earned run average, and most importantly, three wins for the arch-rival Dodgers. For a participant in this situation, cognitive dissonance between fantasy and favorite team values is logical.

While this may sound like a unique situation, it happens in every form of fantasy sports. As a result, participants with strong favorite team loyalties are forced to either avoid fantasy players from certain teams or be left with a tortuous experience cheering for both teams in the same contest. This results in cognitive dissonance among fantasy participants, and according to Dwyer and LeCrom (2013), this phenomenon is not limited to within game situations. It also impacted viewership, draft day selections, and lineup decisions. For instance, when one's favorite team was playing at the same time as other fantasy players, participants were torn between which games to watch. In addition, choosing which player to draft or put in one's lineup can be difficult as there is often an opportunity cost to selecting the wrong player. Where these decisions add to the interactivity and controllability of the game, there are also consequences for participants (see also chapter 6, this volume).

Another occurrence exhibited during this step of the FSCM is a heightened level of focus during in-game viewership (Dwyer & LeCrom, 2013). The quest to find individual player statistics is obviously the most apparent change in behavior exhibited as player statistics is the basis for fantasy participation. The focus does not end there, however, since fantasy participants have been known to fixate on minute details beyond traditional game situations (i.e., the score and time remaining). For instance, possession, which players are on the field of play, and even their alignment have been found to be important factors (Dwyer & LeCrom, 2013).

Despite an enhanced focus during individual games, Dwyer and LeCrom (2013) also found that fantasy participants had little interest in traditional game outcomes when their favorite or favorite team's rival was not playing. In fact, at times participants could not identify which team actually won the game they watched less than seventy-two hours earlier. In a survey of the 280 non-favorite NFL team games logged and questioned, the correct team was selected only 148 times (52.9%). If the participant's favorite NFL team was playing in the game (ninety-six occurrences), however, the game outcome was recalled 96.9 percent of the time (Dwyer & LeCrom, 2013).

Dwyer and LeCrom (2013) found two interesting viewership patterns as it relates to this phenomenon: (1) participants watched games where the outcome was no longer in doubt and (2) participants cheered for in-game outcomes not tied to the pursuit of victory specifically for fantasy football reasons. For example, extreme blowouts are ripe for fantasy sport production as the team ahead often puts up little resistance. And while these actions do little to impact the outcome of the game, they have huge implications in fantasy. Likewise, fantasy participants have been known to cheer for injuries, turnovers, or even overtime to extend the opportunity to gain fantasy points. This leads directly the last sub-dimension of the stage of the FSCM, the creation of an all-day event.

As noted above, the phenomenon of fantasy participants having competitive interests in several professional contests each game day provides for additional opportunities to watch professional sport. In the case of football, fantasy shifted viewership from a 3.5 hour block when one's favorite team played to an all-day affair (Dwyer & LeCrom, 2013). The long-term impact of these new attitudes and behaviors is not yet known, but some would argue that incongruity and dissonance when thinking of a particular product or service is negative. In addition, others would argue a focus on outcomes not central to the overall goal of the team game may dissolve the overall equity of a brand. However, the short-run impact of these fantasy sport behaviors could not be any more opposite. Fantasy participation is up; television viewership is up, and the brand building opportunities associated with fantasy sport participation is at an all-time high. But, it does lead to a question of whether fantasy sport participation is a substitute to traditional sport fandom, or a complement?

The notion that fantasy sport participation may be substitute or complement for traditional sport fandom has been studied a number of times via several different samples and methods (Dwyer & Drayer, 2010; Dwyer et al., 2013; Dwyer et al., 2011; Shapiro et al., 2014). And while the results have provided preliminary evidence of some substitutional behaviors (Dwyer, 2011a), the majority of research supports the idea that fantasy sport complements traditional sport fandom. Most participants have indicated the ability to operate their favorite team fandom in chorus with their fantasy team. In addition, highly involved fantasy sport participants are most often highly-identified favorite team fans. This, once again, may be a function of how long participants have been involved with fantasy sports. It is certainly an area in need of additional exploration.

## FANTASY SPORTS AND MEDIA CONSUMPTION

Over the last decade professional sports leagues have seen revenue growth from broadcasting and media rights deals grow exponentially. The value of rights to air live broadcasts on television, radio, and mobile devices has increased 18.7 percent to $14.8 billion in approximately one year. Media rights for sport are forecasted to grow 9.1 percent annually to 19.3 billion by 2018 (Bond, 2014). This does not include revenue generated through mediated content not involving the live game. The growth of sport mediated consumption is significantly increasing revenue opportunities and increasing league and franchise values to new heights.

Based on the nature and format of today's fantasy sport, it seems logical participants are going to consume sport through mediated content. According to a 2013 study, fantasy sport participants spend significantly more time watching sports compared to traditional sport fans, up to eight more hours a week (Billings & Ruihley, 2013). Therefore, it could be argued that with the growth of fantasy sport participation, a considerable portion of the increased media rights revenue can be attributed to this segment of the sport consumer population.

How is this happening? Research suggests fantasy sport participants are not replacing traditional consumption behavior with fantasy consumption behavior. Fantasy participation is complementing, and in many cases expanding overall mediated consumption levels (Drayer et al, 2010). NFL *Monday Night Football* might be the best way to explain this behavior. Many fantasy participants find themselves tuning into the final NFL game of the week, and extending the amount of time consuming this game (understanding the game generally ends after midnight EST) for fantasy motivations. One player could change the outcome of a weekly fantasy matchup, magnifying the importance of the week's final contest. Could this phenomenon be increasing third and fourth quarter ratings for some *Monday Night Football* games where fans might have otherwise changed the channel? If this is the case, the value of advertising during the second half of this game may increase significantly. As mentioned in chapter 8, the role fantasy sport plays within the scope of television is considerable. The following section discusses this role within the context of Internet and mobile applications.

## Internet and Mobile Applications

The success of fantasy sport is based largely on the growth of technology through Internet and mobile applications. Explosion in fantasy participation can be linked directly to the development of online fantasy programs and the ability to provide scores in real-time. Therefore, Internet and mobile communication are the foundation for fantasy participation. Additionally, this has led to more general consumption of sport through these channels. Research has provided evidence that fantasy sport participation has influenced both Internet and mobile consumption (Dwyer et al., 2011; Dwyer & Kim 2011). It is common for fantasy players to follow their teams and consume general sport and fantasy-specific content on the Internet either as a substitution for or as a complement to traditional television viewership. In response, the number of websites dedicated to fantasy sport and the amount of resources traditional sport websites have dedicated to the activity had grown tremendously (see chapter 9, this volume).

Mobile consumption is one of the fastest growing sectors of mediated consumption. There has been a significant increase in Smartphone usage and being able to access content on the go is paramount for today's fast-paced consumer. Fantasy sport has been successful in providing mobile content to participants to allow for a more seamless consumption experience while they are away from the television or part of the second screen experience. This is most likely due to the development of mobile applications like Yahoo!, ESPN, and CBS Fantasy mobile applications that allow fantasy players to manage their teams and consume content as easy as they would from a home computer or laptop. These applications also allow fantasy players to stay engaged with their teams outside of the home, which includes at a stadium or in a sports bar. Prior to this technology (and enough broadband to support it) fantasy consumers may have had to make a choice between attending a game or consuming form home.

Additionally, there are hundreds of mobile applications designed to provide supporting material for fantasy participants. Applications such as Rotowire Fantasy Football Draft Kit provide content to help fantasy participants manage their teams successfully (Stella, 2014).

Fantasy sports will continue to play a significant role in how sport fans choose to consume mediated sport content. It is important to understand the impact of fantasy sport within this sector. Due to the significant revenue resulting from mediated consumption, sport managers must continue to develop new strategies for embracing the fantasy sport consumer as a valued (and growing) population of the sport consumer market.

## THE IMPACT OF FANTASY AND FAVORITE TEAM OUTCOMES

In the 1970s and 1980s, Robert Cialdini and his colleagues introduced the notion of "basking in reflected glory (BIRG)," where fans associate themselves more strongly with successful sport organizations, and "cutting off reflected failure (CORF)," where fans distance themselves with losing organizations (Cialdini & DeNicholas, 1989; Cialdini, Finch, & DeNicholas; Cialdini et al., 1976; Cialdini & Richardson, 1980). Based on this research, it is apparent that game outcomes are important to both sports fans' attitudes and their behaviors. With two sets of attitudes forming in the fantasy sports participant's mind as well as enhanced mediated and non-mediated consumption, it is critical to understand how game outcomes affect the fantasy sports participants' experience.

It has been well-documented that sports fans are among the most loyal of all consumers. Win or lose, most fans will remain faithful to their team and not defect to another. Further, the presence of a fantasy team does little to change this enduring loyalty to one's favorite team. However, if a fan's favorite team begins to lose, consumption of favorite team-related content through Internet and television will begin to decline (Dwyer, 2013). The NFL in particular has enacted league policies such as a strict salary cap and evenly-split revenue sharing among teams in order to ensure league parity so that more fans may remained engaged throughout each season. This parity is also particularly important at the beginning of the season, when team interest is often at its highest.

On the other hand, fantasy sports participants are much less loyal to their fantasy team. That is, if their fantasy team is not winning, participants will have less interest in the players that make up their team and also spend less time watching and researching those players. The individual sports leagues as well as the fantasy sports websites have a strong interest in making sure that their users remain competitive for as long as possible. This may include having more playoff teams in the standard fantasy formats or including other short season and daily fantasy options where participants can re-engage with the activity even if their initial fantasy team was not successful.

Interestingly, when a participant's favorite team and his or her fantasy team are successful, he or she will typically find time to consume both at high levels. Further, he or she will have strong positive attitudes toward both entities as well, even though there may be conflict between the successes of both. Sports fans may be conflicted when the success of their fantasy team comes at the expense of their favorite team; however, if both are successful, they will be highly involved in both. Ultimately, any organization with a vested interest in the success of a sports league, sports team, or fantasy sports-related company should be doing all they can to ensure that their consumers have a reason to continue to consume by giving them the best chance to experience some level of success through either or both their favorite or fantasy teams.

## CONCLUSION

In all, fantasy sports as an ancillary sport activity has exploded in participation in the last fifteen to twenty years. Currently, more than forty-one million Americans and Canadians play some form of fantasy sports (Fantasy Sports Trade Association, 2014), and the activity creates an annual economic impact estimated by Goff (2013) at $70 billion. As a result, broadcasters and media providers have taken notice. Mediated sport products and services have been amended to meet the evolving needs of this lucrative segment of sport fans. As a means to help administrators and media providers understand the changing nature of the contemporary sports fan, this chapter highlighted the empirical research done in this area. Specifically, it outlined the FSCM in hope of providing a clearer understanding of how fantasy sport participation directly and indirectly impacts sport media consumption.

## NOTE

1. The debate continues with regard to defining fantasy sports as a game of luck or skill; however, Holleman (2006) argued that "through research, intelligence, and skill, participants can control the outcome of the contests" (p. 79).

## REFERENCES

Billings, A. C., & Ruihley, B. J. Why we watch, why we play: The relationship between fantasy sport and fanship motivations. *Mass Communication and Society*, 2013; *16* (1): 5 doi: 10.1080/15205436.2011.635260

Bond, S. (2014, October 6). Value of US sports broadcast rights up 18.7 percent. *The Financial Times*. Retrieved from http://www.ft.com/cms/s/0/57def478-4b1c-11e4-8a0e-00144feab7de.html#axzz3IOWurtsg

Cialdini, R. B., Borden, R. J., Thorne, A., Walker, M. R., Freeman, S., & Sloan, L. R. (1976). Basking in reflective glory: Three (football) field studies. *Journal of Personality and Social Psychology, 34,*366–375.

Cialdini, R. B., & DeNicholas, M. E. (1989). Self-presentation by association. *Personality and Social Psychology, 57,*626–631.

Cialdini, R. B., Finch, J. F., & DeNicholas, M. E. (1989). Strategic self-presentation: The indirect route. In M. J. Cody & M. L. McLaughlin (Eds.), *The psychology of tactical communication (pp.* 194–206). London: Multilingual Matters.

Cialdini, R. B., & Richardson, K. D. (1980). Two indirect tactics of image management: Basking and blasting. *Journal of Personality and Social Psychology, 39,*406–415.

Drayer, J., & Dwyer, B. (2013). Perception of fantasy is not always the reality: An exploratory examination into Blacks' lack of participation in fantasy sports. *International Journal of Sport Management, 14,* 81–102.

Drayer, J., Dwyer, B., & Shapiro, S. L. (2013). Examining the impact of league entry fees on online fantasy sport participation and league consumption. *European Sport Management Quarterly, 13,* 339–357. DOI:10.1080/16184742.2013.783605

Drayer, J., Shapiro, S. L., Dwyer, B., Morse, A.L., & White, J. (2010). The effects of fantasy football participation on NFL consumption: A qualitative analysis. *Sport Management Review, 13,* 129–141.

Dwyer, B., Drayer, J., Greenhalgh, G. P., & LeCrom, C. W. (2013). Substitute or complement? Fantasy football and NFL fandom. *Marketing Management Journal, 23*(2), 71–85.

Dwyer, B. (2011a). Divided loyalty? An analysis of fantasy football involvement and fan loyalty to individual National Football League (NFL) teams. *Journal of Sport Management, 25,* 445–457.

Dwyer, B. (2011b). The impact of attitudes and fantasy football involvement on intentions to watch NFL teams on television. *International Journal of Sport Communication, 4,* 375–396.

Dwyer, B. (2013). The impact of game outcomes on fantasy football participation and National Football League media consumption. *Sport Marketing Quarterly, 22,* 33–47.

Dwyer, B., & Drayer, J. (2010). Fantasy sport consumer segmentation: An investigation into the differing consumption modes of fantasy football participants. *Sport Marketing Quarterly, 19,* 207–216.

Dwyer, B., & Kim, Y. (2011). For love or money: Developing and validating a motivational scale for fantasy football participation. *Journal of Sport Management, 25,* 70–83.

Dwyer, B., & LeCrom, C. W. (2013). Is fantasy trumping reality? The redefined National Football League experience of novice fantasy football participants. *Journal of Contemporary Athletics, 7*(3).

Dwyer, B., Shapiro, S. L., & Drayer, J. (2011). Segmenting motivation: An analysis of fantasy baseball motives and mediated sport consumption. *Sport Marketing Quarterly, 20,* 129–137.

Fain, I. (2013, February 4). Displaced fans remain connected—and valuable—to teams. Sports Business Daily. Retrieved from http://m.sportsbusinessdaily.com/Journal/Issues/2013/02/04/Opinion/From-the-Field-of-Fan-Engagement.aspx

Fantasy Sports Trade Association (2014, July 1). FSTA highlights record fantasy sports growth at summer conference! *FSTA.org.* Retrieved from http://www.fsta .org/news/180147/ FSTA-highlights-record-fantasy-sports-growth-at-summer -conference.htm

Farquhar, L. K., & Meeds, R. (2007). Types of fantasy sports users and their motivations. *Journal of Computer-Mediated Communication, 12,* 1208–1228.

Fazio, R. H., Powell, M. C., & Herr, P. M. (1983). Toward a process model of the attitude-behavior relation: Accessing one's attitude upon mere observation of the attitude object. *Journal of Personality and Social Psychology, 44,* 723–735.

Funk, D. C., & James, J. (2001). The psychological continuum model: A conceptual framework for understanding an individual's psychological connection to sport. *Sport Management Review, 2,* 119–150.

Festinger, L. (1957). *A theory of cognitive dissonance.* Evanston, IL: Row, Peterson.

Funk, D. C., & James, J. D. (2004). The Fan Attitude Network (FAN) Model: Propositions for Exploring Identity and Attitude Formation among Sport Consumers. *Sport Management Review, 7,* 1–26.

Goff, B. (2013, August). The $70 billion fantasy football market. *Forbes.* Retrieved from http://www.forbes.com/sites/briangoff/2013/08/20/the-70-billion-fantasy-football-market/

Howard, D. R., & Crompton, J. L. (2014). *Financing sport* (3rd Edition). Morgantown, WV: Fitness Information Technology.

King, P. (2013, November 6). Fantasy football now . . . and forever? *The Monday Morning Quarterback.* Retrieved from http://mmqb.si.com/2013/11/06/fantasy-football-now-nfl-midseason-report/

Lee, J., Ruihley, B. J., Brown, N., & Billings, A. C. (2013). The effects of fantasy football participation on team identification, team loyalty and NFL fandom. *Journal of Sports Media, 8*(1), pp. 207–227.

Madrigal, R. (1995). Cognitive and affective determinants of fan satisfaction with sporting event attendance. *Journal of Leisure Research, 27,* 205–227.

New DirecTV fantasy zone channel is a one-stop NFL Sunday afternoon experience for fantasy players. (2014, July 7). *DirecTV.com.* Retrieved from http://news.directv.com/2014/07/07/new-directv-fantasy-zone-channel-is-a-one-stop-nfl-sunday-afternoon-experience-for-fantasy-players/

Robinson, M. J., & Trail, G. T. (2005). Relationships among spectator gender, motives, points of attachment, and sport preference. *Journal of Sport Management, 19,* 58–80.

Trail, G. T., Fink, J. S., & Anderson, D.F. (2003). Sport spectator consumption behavior. *Sport Marketing Quarterly, 12,* 8–17.

Savage, B. (2011). The Cubs fan paradox: Why would anyone root for losers? Society for American Baseball Research. Retrieved from http://sabr.org/research/cubs-fan-paradox-why-would-anyone-root-losers.

Shapiro, S. L., Drayer, J., & Dwyer, B. (2014). Exploring fantasy baseball consumer behavior: Examining the relationship between identification, fantasy participation, and consumption. *Journal of Sport Behavior, 37*(1).

Shipman, F. M. (2001). Blending the real and virtual: Activity and spectatorship in fantasy sports. In *Proceedings from DAC'01: The Conference on Digital Arts and Culture. Retrieved on April* (Vol. 8, p. 2007).

Spinda, J. S. W., (2011). The development of Basking in Reflected Glory (BIRG-ing) and Cutting off Reflected Failure (CORFing) measures. *Journal of Sport Behavior, 34*, 392–420.

Spinda, J. S. W., & Haridakis, P. M. (2008). Exploring the motives of fantasy sports: A uses-and-gratifications approach. *Sports mania: Essays on fandom and the media in the 21st century*, 187–199.

Stella, R. (2014, July 7). Win your fantasy football league with the help of these An-droid and iPhone apps. *Digital Trends*. Retrieved from http://www.digitaltrends .com/mobile/best-fantasy-football-apps/

Wakefield, K. L. (1995). The pervasive effects of social influence on sporting event attendance. *Journal of Sport and Social Issues, 19*, 335–351.

Wann, D. L., & Branscombe, N. R. (1993). Sports fans: Measuring degree of iden-tification with their team. *International Journal of Sport Psychology, 24*, 1–17.

Woo, B., Trail, G. T., Kwon, H. H., & Anderson, D. (2009). Testing models of motives and points of attachment among spectators in college football. *Sport Marketing Quarterly, 18*, 38–53.

Yi, J. (2011, January 25). The value of the loyal fan. Sports Networker. Retrieved from http://www.sportsnetworker.com/2011/01/25/value-sports-loyal-fan/

# "IT WAS ALL YOUR FAULT"

Identity and Fan Messaging to Athletes at the
Intersection of Fantasy Sport and Social Media

*Jimmy Sanderson*

The fantasy sports industry has mushroomed into a billion dollar enterprise (Goff, 2013) that is comprised of millions of players who passionately manage rosters in diligent efforts to win matchups against other fantasy competitors. The Fantasy Sports Trade Association (2014) reports that in 2014, there were over forty-one million people playing fantasy sports in the United States and Canada, a figure that has steadily increased each year. For example, in 2007, there were 19.4 million people playing fantasy sports; thus, in only seven years, the number of participants has more than doubled. Social media technologies, such as Facebook, Twitter, Instagram, and Snapchat also have experienced a corresponding growth during the past decade. For instance, as of June 30, 2015, Facebook reported 1.49 billion monthly active users, with 968 million daily active users (Facebook. com, 2015). Twitter reports 302 million monthly active users, who collectively send 500 million tweets per day (About Twitter, 2015). In December 2014, Instagram announced they had surpassed 300 million users (300 Million: Sharing Real Moments, 2014) and as of January 2015, Snapchat was estimated to be approaching 200 million active users (Shontell, 2015).

Given the rapid growth of both fantasy sports and social media, it is not surprising that these two areas have integrated. To be certain, fantasy sports participation has involved the Internet for quite some time, and the fantasy sports industry is often at the forefront in providing interactive platforms that offer vast amounts of data to fantasy sports participants (Kwak, Lee,

& Mahan III, 2013). As social media and fantasy sports grow increasingly entwined, it is important that researchers explore the intersection of these two areas. However, to date, there has been little research done. Although scholars have examined topics such as the adoption of fantasy sports websites (Kwak & McDaniel, 2011); types of online fantasy sports players and their motivations (Farquhar & Meeds, 2007); and how fantasy sports league participation reifies hegemonic masculinity through online conversations (Davis & Duncan, 2006), there is a noticeable gap in the literature when it comes to fantasy sports and social media.

The interactive features provided by social media open up important avenues for study of fantasy sport. One notable example centers on fans sending messages to athletes via social media (primarily Twitter) when athletes fail to "deliver" a satisfactory number of points for a fantasy sports participant. Consider the following examples from the National Football League (NFL):

- In October 2013, New York Giants running back Brandon Jacobs posted two tweets he received from a fan with the caption "Look at what we deal with." The tweets he received stated, "@gatorboyrb ON LIFE [sic] BRANDON IF YOU DON'T RUSH FOR 50 YARDS AND 2 TOUCHDOWNS TONIGHT ITS OVER FOR YOU AND YO FAMILY;" and "@gatorboyrb FULFILL MY ORDERS STATED IN PREVIOUS TWEET OR THATS YOU LIFE BRUH AND IM NOT PLAYING" (Samuel, 2013).
- In September 2013, after receiving tweets criticizing him for his performance and it impact on fantasy football participants, Baltimore Ravens running back Ray Rice (2013) tweeted, "I was a fan of fantasy football until today so many spiteful words. I still love you all God Bless great win today #Ravens."

As illuminating as these examples are, they stand as just one potential area in need of research attention. The purpose of this chapter is to outline a trajectory for studying social media and fantasy sports that will hopefully spur more work examining the intersection of these two areas. Specifically, this chapter addresses the following trajectories for fantasy sports and social media research: (a) identity expression; (b) fan-athlete interaction; and (c) fantasy sports experts. In doing so, the chapter offers potential theoretical frameworks that can be applied to the study of fantasy sport and social media that will hopefully prompt researchers to pursue this line of inquiry.

## IDENTITY EXPRESSION

Scholars have investigated various ways that social media are used to express identity with a variety of sport constituents (Lebel & Danylchuk, 2012; Sanderson, 2014; Weathers, Sanderson, Matthey, Grevious, Tehan, & Warren, 2014). Additionally, for many people, sport fandom is an essential identity component (Wann, Royalty, & Roberts, 2000) and highly identified fans engage in a variety of both positive and negative behaviors reflecting how their identity is affected by sport teams winning and losing (Gibson, Willming, & Holdnak, 2002; Wakefield & Wann, 2006). With fantasy sports, identity functions as a two-pronged approach. Specifically, identity can be expressed through the names that fantasy sports players assign to their fantasy sports team, as well through the dialogue that occurs between fantasy sports participants.

Fantasy sports endow people with the capability to assume the role of team "manager" or "owner," a transition that potentially enhances identity (and which they are unlikely to obtain in the actual professional sports context). For example, when constructing a fantasy team, individuals must name their team and generally have the ability to create mottos or taglines that describe it. Potential directions for identity and fantasy sport research here include, what are the motivations for a player to name a fantasy team in particular ways? And, how might those names be related to identity expression? Do players focus on sport-themed names (e.g., BearsFan4Life) or more personality-based traits (e.g., NeverSatisfied)? How does the community of fantasy sports competitors interpret and react to these identity expressions?

Moreover, is there a relationship between team name and social capital in the fantasy sports community? For example, a fantasy sports participant could utilize sarcasm and puns to enhance his/her likelihood of getting praise for the uniqueness of his/her team name. Also, fan identity may influence the naming process. For example, a highly identified fan of the Dallas Cowboys may be more likely to reflect that in his/her team name (e.g., Cowboys4Life) than a lowly identified Cowboys fan. Fan identity level also may contribute to the roster construction process. More specifically, will fan identification preclude a fantasy sports participant from selecting players from a rival team, and instead trying to "stack" his/her fantasy team with players from his/her favorite team? One could see a scenario playing out where a fantasy baseball player who is a passionate New York Yankees fan, avoids selecting any players from the Boston Red Sox. In that vein, Dwyer (2011) found that highly identified fantasy sports participants showed lower behavioral loyalty to their favorite NFL team, but also showed higher attitudinal loyalty. Building on this research and accounting for how team and individual identity are affected will be an important direction for future researchers to pursue.

Many hosting sites for fantasy sports (e.g., Yahoo!) offer participants the ability to converse with other league participants via discussion forums. In addition to these dedicated forums, fantasy sports participants also can interact with one another in more public social media forums. These interactive spaces also offer a rich opportunity to examine identity expression in the context of fantasy sports. Some research has traversed down this path (Davis & Duncan 2006). Davis and Duncan (2006) studied three male fantasy sports leagues, one aspect of which centered on the league message board (discussion forum). They found that via the language in these forums, fantasy sports participation (re)produced problematic ideology in sport culture.

One such aspect of sport culture is hegemonic masculinity—a very narrow version of masculinity that champions violence, aggression, and playing through pain (Anderson & Kian, 2012). Hegemonic masculinity is perpetuated through sport participants taking great pains to avoid being seen as weak, feminine, and/or homosexual (Anderson & Kian, 2012). Not surprisingly, then, sports participants reinforce hegemonic masculinity through discourse that marginalizes others by feminizing them or insinuating their homosexuality (Sanderson, 2013a). Such misogynistic and homophobic expressions play out in fantasy sports message forums and via social media further reifying the hegemonic masculinity in sport culture. In Davis and Duncan's (2006) study, examples of this discourse included (unedited), "Hey fuck faces hey I couldn't play Garnett because he wasn't on my team until after I left for the cruise so fuck off. Now, you're all in big, big trouble;" and "I got you this week. I'm gonna beat your stacked team with my pussy team. I'm gonna bite your ear off and eat your children. Remember when Evander had two ears??" (p. 255).

While such discourse may seem harmless, and merely reflect, "boys being boys" it may serve to both further perpetuate problematic areas of sport culture such as hegemonic masculinity, and make it difficult for those outside preferred sport identities (e.g., male, heterosexual) to participate in fantasy sports. Indeed, Kassing and Sanderson (2015) discussed how social media works to both confirm and disconfirm participation in the community of sport, and through such discourse as noted in the Davis and Duncan (2006) study, certain individuals may be dissuaded or driven away from fantasy sports participation. In that vein, researchers could explore the motivations around the "performance" of identity expression through participants' discourse. For instance, how does the language used by and among fantasy sports participants enhance their masculine identity and/or strip it from other participants? Many researchers have examined the motivations for playing fantasy sports (Billings & Ruihley, 2013; Brown, Billings, & Ruihley, 2012; Farquhar & Meeds, 2007; Lee, Won, & Green, 2013; Ruihley & Billings, 2013; Spinda & Haridakis, 2008), however, the motivations underpinning the performance of identity as a result of fantasy sports participation remains underexplored.

While individual identity expression is an important facet for investigation, there are group identities that also must be considered when discussing fantasy sports and social media. Most fantasy sports participants operate a team under the auspices of a league "commissioner" who has administrative capabilities to approve trade requests between players, and the actions of the commissioner can greatly affect both individual and collective identity. For example, with those individuals who assume the "commissioner" role, what strategies do they use to demonstrate this identity with other group members via mediated communication platforms? Additionally, through social media, how do group members manage identity threats arising from group members deviating from established norms and rituals? Identity, both at the individual and collective level, is fluid for many fantasy sports participants, particularly in the realm of social media where selective self-presentation is often employed (Lebel & Danylchuk, 2014; van Dijck, 2013).

## Theoretical Approaches to Fantasy Sports, Identity, and Social Media

Through discourse between fantasy sports participants as well as the construction of team names, identity plays an integral role in the fantasy sports experience. In that vein, participant interaction and team naming constitute two viable areas where scholars can focus their efforts. For scholars who pursue this inquiry, there are several fruitful theories that can be drawn upon to examine the intersection of fantasy sports and identity. Social identity theory (SIT) (Tajfel & Turner, 1986) is one particularly useful lens for these undertakings. SIT posits that people have both individual and social identities and that social identity is largely derived from group membership (Turner, 1982). People tend to gravitate toward groups that they perceive to hold value for their individual identity (Spitzberg, 2014). However, group membership is not without turbulence. Group members can experience threats to their perceived social standing, or which can diminish the value of the group (Major & O'Brien, 2005). Branscombe, Ellemers, Spears, and Doosje (1999) posited that social identity threats manifested as either: (a) value threats—which undermine the value of group membership and attack group norms, rituals, and beliefs; or (b) distinctiveness threats— which alter perceptions of the group's uniqueness and place the group in the same standing as out-groups. When social identity threats occur, they create feelings of vulnerability for members, which can lead to rallying and elevated in-group identification (Brown & Ross, 1982; Maass, Ceccarelli, & Rudin, 1996; Sanderson, 2013a).

With respect to fantasy sports and social media, SIT could shed light on how group identity threats are managed via social media. For instance, threats may arise from a group member deviating from group rules (e.g., acquiring a player after a deadline, not actively attending to roster management) or from interactions between group members. Moreover, identity also could be a function of other social classifications. That is, many people play fantasy sports with members of their families and/or their co-workers and in these situations, which group identities become more/less salient? How does fantasy sports participants' identity hierarchy affect their communication with other participants, both inside and outside of the fantasy sports league itself? Scholars investigating the aforementioned areas could add both to the fantasy sport and the family and organizational communication literature. In these instances (as well as others) SIT would illuminate the ways that group members manage both their individual identity and the collective group identity when it is threatened.

Strategies for managing threats will surely vary, but also could provide an impetus to examine the perpetuation of problematic sport ideology (e.g., hegemonic masculinity). Consider the research that Sanderson (2013a) conducted on University of Cincinnati fans use of Facebook to manage a social identity threat arising from head football coach Brian Kelly leaving the school to accept the head coaching position at the University of Notre Dame. One of his findings was that fans mitigated the identity threat by framing Kelly with homophobic and misogynistic terminology. Similarly, Davis and Duncan (2006) found the presence of this language in their study of fantasy sports league message boards. Nevertheless, research in this area has not remained on course with the accelerating consumption of fantasy sports. However, given the popularity of fantasy sports, and how integral digital and social media platforms are to fantasy sports participation, understanding the ways that both individuals and groups manage identity threats through online discourse is an important avenue to pursue. This work also would need to concurrently examine the ways that social identity threat management strategies contribute to the perpetuation of problematic aspects of sport culture and attend to ways that such discourse excludes people from participation in the community of fantasy sport (Kassing & Sanderson, 2015).

Self-presentation (Goffman, 1959) has been a seminal framework in identity research for decades. In particular, with the advances of the Internet, self-presentation has become more strategic as individuals exert more control over their portrayal in digital spaces (Walther, 1996). In the sport arena, researchers have examined how social media provides benefits for athletes to construct their self-presentation in ways that allow them to counter media portrayals (Sanderson, 2008a) and to showcase more of their personality, thereby cultivating identification and parasocial interaction with fans (Sanderson, 2013b). Other researchers have looked at gender differences in both athletes (Lebel & Danylchuk, 2012) and sport media personalities (Weathers et al., 2014).

Fantasy sports provide a multitude of opportunities to enact self-presentation, including the naming of teams, selecting avatars to represent one's team, and creating bylines or mottos that shape how the team is represented to other league members. Potential research questions in this realm include: Do team names and biography information relate to a player's affiliation for the sport, a sport team, or personal character traits? Given differences in self-presentation by gender, it also would be fruitful to look at ways that female and male fantasy sports participants self-present. Do these strategies fall along traditional gender lines? If so, how might they reinforce ideology that women are novices when it comes to sports knowledge and information (Davis & Duncan, 2006)? Conversely, does self-presentation demonstrate more equality when it comes to gender roles in sport? Consider the work of Vann (2014) who found that social media facilitated opportunities to increase coverage of women's sports by circumventing traditional media structures and its historical unwillingness to devote more than marginal attention to women's sport. Could the self-presentation enacted by female fantasy sports participants have a similar effect? The link between identity expression and fantasy sports has many applications beyond the boundaries of the league in which a player is participating. Indeed, as mentioned earlier, this behavior may underpin one of the more visible trends to arise at the intersection of social media and fantasy sports—problematic messages from fantasy players to athletes for their perceived failure to deliver a fantasy league victory.

## FAN-ATHLETE INTERACTION

As social media has become more embedded in sport, researchers have advanced understanding of fan-athlete communication through messages exchanged via social media between these two groups (Cleland, 2014; Frederick, Lim, Clavio, & Burch, 2014; Kassing & Sanderson, 2010; Sanderson, 2014). Some work has examined such communication through the lens of parasocial interaction (Sanderson, 2008b; Kassing & Sanderson, 2010; Sanderson & Emmons, 2014), or the one-sided, mediated interaction that occurs between an audience member and a media figure (Horton & Wohl, 1956). Yet, as the first part of the term social media suggests, interaction is not always one-sided between these two groups. In fact, there are a growing number of incidents where fans and athletes interact.

For example, Frederick et al. (2014) found that athletes were using Twitter both in parasocial and social ways and that when athletes elected to be social, they were predominantly communicating with laypeople and other athletes. Kassing and Sanderson (2015) observed that interaction between athletes and fans on social media constituted more of a "circum-social" interaction as the communication between these groups rotated between social and parasocial interaction. Thus, as athletes have perhaps become more digitally accessible, sharing aspects of their identity and persona and crowdsourcing fans for information (Sanderson, 2013b), fans may perceive that athletes want to have conversations with them, prompting fans to initiate communication. With respect to the circum-social interaction described by Kassing and Sanderson (2015), fans may respond to an athlete's social media overtures multiple times before actually having interaction. The interaction may then revolve back to parasocial interaction, and fans may go back to initiating predominantly one-way communication with athletes, in the hopes that one of their messages will persuade the athlete to respond.

While there certainly have been positive interactions between fans and athletes on social media, there also have been plenty of problematic interactions, ranging from messages criticizing an athlete's performance to hostile messages that invoke hateful language as well as death threats. Kassing and Sanderson (2015) classified this behavior as maladaptive parasocial interaction and this type of parasocial interaction (as the examples earlier indicate) tends to predominate fan messaging to athletes about fantasy sports. Social media, in particularly Twitter, presents a unique and convenient avenue for fans to respond to athletes instantaneously and impulsively. Given the turbulence that accompanies sports contests, it is not surprising that fans have taken to Twitter and other social media channels to voice their displeasure with athletes through censure and more hostile verbal aggressiveness such as death threats.

As one example of how maladaptive parasocial interaction plays out, Sanderson and Truax (2014) examined Twitter messages to University of Alabama placekicker Cade Foster after he struggled in a game against Auburn University that Alabama ultimately lost. They found that maladaptive parasocial interaction manifested through: (a) belittlement; (b) mocking; (c) sarcasm; and (d) threats. Belittling was defined as comments that were overtly demeaning and critical and consisted of examples such as, "@Foster_43 when I find you on campus I'm gonna show you how to kick—with a swift one to the nuts. Jackass thought you would learn after LSU;" and "@Fostser_43 you fucking suck" (p. 340). Mocking was conceptualized as statements grounded in ridicule and involved comments such as, "@Foster_43 Better stay 4 years and get that degree, you're obviously not getting drafted;" and "@Foster_43 tried to hang himself but he couldn't kick the chair out from under him" (p. 341).

Sarcasm involved more lighthearted statements such as, "@Foster_43 congrats on the great game dude!" and "@Foster_43 has already blacked out his [Twitter] account out. He finna go missing like Lebron's hairline" (p. 341). Threats consisted of hateful and derogatory statements toward Foster, such as "@Foster_43 YOU FUCKING SUCK BITCH YOU COST US A FUCKING NATIONAL CHAMPIONSHIP I HOPE YOUR MOM GETS RAPED BY A BLACK MAN FUCK YOUR FAMILY" and "@Foster_43 hey kill yourself. Seriously. Do it" (p. 341–342). Perhaps because of these statements, Sanderson and Truax (2014) found that other fans came to Foster's defense and supported him, conveying that those individuals who expressed critical and hateful commentary were not "true" Alabama fans. Examples included, "@Foster_43 Thank you for all the hard work you have put in over the years. I am proud to say you are the kicker for #Bama" and "@Foster_43 Sorry to hear about the threats. This Alabama fan stands with you! The others aren't true Bama fans. Roll Tide" (p. 342).

With respect to fantasy sports, it is not uncommon (particularly with football) to see fans messaging athletes on Twitter to censure them for their perceived role in costing a fantasy sports participant a victory. While news accounts often focus on the sensational nature of these remarks, it would be interesting to explore if fans come to the defense of those who are rebuking athletes. In their study, Sanderson and Truax (2014) found that the supportive comments overwhelmed the maladaptive comments, and it would be worthwhile to see if similar behaviors manifested with fans messaging professional athletes about fantasy sports.

## Theoretical Approaches to Fantasy Sports, Fan-Athlete Interaction, and Social Media

Parasocial interaction offers a viable framework for studying fan-athlete interaction on social media in the context of fantasy sports. For example, how do messages from fans toward athletes vary? Are they general critiques? Or do they invoke hateful language and terminology that reflect problematic aspects of sport culture? Given the mobile capabilities that social media provides, it is very easy to send these messages to athletes at any time during an athletic contest. Thus, it would be fruitful to explore the juncture at which these messages are sent and how they change in frequency after the end-game result. In other words, while an athlete may make a mistake during a game that costs a fantasy player points, the athlete may atone for this mistake at a later point in the game (conceivably helping the fantasy player win his/her matchup), and how might that change the messaging? Do fans send an apology message? Or is there evidence of support and praise for the athlete helping the player in their fantasy contest? Connecting this strand back to Dwyer's (2011) study of identity with one's favorite team and fantasy team, how might team identification affect a fantasy sports participant's willingness to engage in this behavior? Conceivably, a fan may be more likely to send critique to a player that costs them fantasy points who is not affiliated with the fan's favorite team, but that remains for research to confirm.

Additionally, what about the athlete side of the equation? The trend of fantasy sports participants sending athletes messages via Twitter and other social media platforms is not lost on athletes, and there have been many who have spoken out about this behavior and even retaliated toward fans. One notable example of this occurred with San Francisco 49ers player Stevie Johnson in September 2014. On September 24, Johnson tweeted, "I drafted many of you to my fantasy work team so make sure and grab me some points today at your workplace. Don't let me down." Several individuals tweeted at Johnson describing the tasks they had accomplished at work and Johnson humorously interacted with some of them (Petchesky, 2014). Previous research has explored how athletes use social media as an identity protection mechanism (Sanderson, 2008a, 2014), and it would be interesting to explore how athletes are using social media to combat attacks from fans for their performance. This line of inquiry also could shed light on how circum-social interaction (Kassing & Sanderson, 2015) between athletes and fans manifests across social media. Such work also could incorporate the initial message from the fantasy sports participant to better understand what kinds of messages prompt athletes to respond. Another variable to consider here, although not specifically related to parasocial interaction, would be the average number of fantasy points that players who received these messages accumulated. Adding this component may shed light on possible correlations between fantasy scores and responsiveness to fan critiques. In other words, perhaps the athlete recognizes that she/he did not perform and therefore is more/less likely to respond?

Of course, as fantasy sports have grown in popularity and become increasingly commodified, this outcome also accounts for the rise in messages from fans to athletes about fantasy consequences. This may, in part, stem from the expectations that a fan holds for an athlete's performance, and these perceptions may be attributed to the growth of a cottage industry of fantasy sports "experts" who continually provide participants with fantasy advice and implications based on actual transactions and other events actually taking place in a particular sport. Consequently, this leads to the final area discussed in this essay, the role of social media as it pertains to fantasy expert advice.

## FANTASY SPORTS "EXPERTS"

It is not uncommon, especially when football is the sport being discussed, for news items relating to sport to contain an element focused on the "fantasy implications." Sport media outlets such as talk radio and online sport domains parade out a plethora of "experts" who claim to help fantasy participants capitalize on all the minutiae of information so as to help them gain an advantage in their fantasy league (see also chapter 14, this volume). Many of these experts maintain active profiles on social media, most notably Twitter, which they use to disseminate information to sizable audiences. For example, Matthew Berry, ESPN's senior fantasy analyst, has as of this writing, over 742,000 followers on Twitter (https://twitter.com/matthew-berryTMR). Considering the size of these audiences, it is not inconceivable to think that the advice and information emanating from these "experts" could significantly impact fantasy sports transactions and movements.

Whereas there are a number of fantasy sports "experts" who reside within legacy media such as ESPN, Yahoo! (and it is worth noting that when media entities such as ESPN hire individuals such as Matthew Berry, that act, in and of itself, shape the notion of expert), there are fantasy sport experts who exist outside the domain of legacy media. For example, FanDuel, an emerging fantasy sports platform that offers one-day fantasy sport leagues, provides participants with accessibility to daily fantasy sports experts. These individuals operate outside the mainstream media and appear to be site users who have accrued a considerable track record in various aspects of fantasy sports (FanDuel NBA Expert Series: A Couple of Minutes with dean78904, 2014). As fantasy sports participation has increased, so too have the number of "experts" and "insiders" who have what appears to be a never-ending supply of data to help satiate the cravings of fantasy sports participants. Accordingly, examining this emerging genre of individuals is another worthwhile endeavor for fantasy sport and social media research.

## Theoretical Approaches to Studying Fantasy Sports, Experts, and Social Media

One theoretical framework that would be useful for this particular line of inquiry is agenda-setting. Agenda-setting (McCombs & Shaw, 1972) posits that there is a relationship between the topics the media covers and the salience of these items with audience members. As Cohen (1963) observed, the media "may not be successful in telling its readers what to think, but it is stunningly successful in telling its readers what to think about" (p. 177). While agenda-setting was initially developed to study voter perceptions of issues based on the salience of media coverage around those issues (McCombs & Shaw, 1972), it has been applied to various aspects of the sport media agenda (Billings & Angelini, 2007; Billings, Angelini, MacArthur, Bissell, & Smith, 2014). While some researchers have examined agenda-setting and social media (Jacobson, 2013; Meraz, 2011), little work has examined social media agenda-setting in the context of sport. In one study, Frederick, Burch, and Blaszka (in press) examined tweets from the official account of the 2012 London Summer Olympics (@London2012) and tweets using the hashtag #London2012. They did not find an agenda-setting effect, but beyond this initial study, there has essentially been no work done in this area. With fantasy sports experts and social media, researchers could examine a group of "influential" fantasy sports experts and analyze the information they post about fantasy sports transactions (e.g., dropping/adding players) and then investigate roster movements across fantasy sports leagues to ascertain if there is an agenda-setting effect.

Moreover, with the rise of fantasy sport "insiders" and "experts" who operate outside the purview of legacy media, researchers could examine what might be termed "bottom up" agenda-setting as the bevy of fantasy sport participants exercise agency by selecting news, not on the basis of the reputation of the media outlet, but rather through the value offered by the individual. Accordingly, a person who has achieved success on a site such as FanDuel, may be looked to as a savant in the daily fantasy sports genre, whereas a mainstream media organization may not possess someone that fantasy sports participants view as having the requisite credibility to navigate the nuances of these leagues. Thus, as fantasy sports participants consume specific types of fantasy sports information, those actions might dictate the content that is then produced by both mainstream and independent fantasy sports outlets, rather than the reverse scenario.

Another framework that could be employed in this area of inquiry is identification. Identification occurs when media users perceive that they possess similarities with a celebrity or media figure (Fraser & Brown, 2002; Soukup, 2006). Given the investment that many people have with sport, and the many hours they spend consuming sport information, it is not surprising that identification would occur with sport participants, sport media personalities and even sporting venues (Trujillo & Krizek, 1994; Wann, 2006; Wann & Branscombe, 1993). In a study of user-generated websites, Flanagin, Hocevar, and Samahito (2014) found that people were more likely to find information to be more credible when it was submitted by someone they perceived to be similar, and as a result, people were more likely to take action based on that information.

Researchers could take a similar approach to explore the relationship between fantasy sports experts and participants as it pertains to the advice that these experts share on social media. Does perceived similarity prompt a fantasy sports participant to perceive the advice to be credible and to subsequently act upon it? How might this change based on variables such as identification with the sport, experience with fantasy sports, number of fantasy sports teams being managed, and willingness to seek information? Such investigations could shed light on the types of people who both seek out and act on information related to fantasy sports. Researchers could further add to this line of work by then investigating the actual performance of the fantasy sports participant to discover if there is a relationship between advice-seeking, following that advice, and the fantasy participant's actual performance.

## CONCLUSION

The adoption of, and participation in, both fantasy sports and social media has been impressive and these two areas offer compelling opportunities for study. However, to date, there has been relatively little work that has explored their integration. This article outlined several areas wherein scholars can examine this intersection: (a) identity expression; (b) fan-athlete interaction; and (c) fantasy sports "experts." Fantasy sports and social media have become increasingly interlocked, opening up fertile areas for investigation. Certainly, there are other directions where social media and fantasy sports research can traverse, and the literature in this area is in its relative infancy, which should be encouraging to scholars interested in these areas. It also is worth noting that fantasy sports and social media show no signs of slowing and as each becomes increasingly commodified, it will be imperative for researchers to examine how the monetization of these topics affects their usage and the interaction occurring around them. Fantasy sports are powerful, in that they endow participants with the ability to experience the highs and lows of managing a sport team, a reality that is unlikely for most participants. Yet, this "fantasy" becomes a vivid reality for many fantasy players who subsequently engage in a number of "actual" behaviors that provide rich opportunities to grow an emerging body of literature.

## REFERENCES

300 Million: Sharing Real Moments. (2014, December 10). Retrieved from http://blog.instagram.com/post/104847837897/141210-300million

About Twitter (2015). Retrieved from https://about.twitter.com/company

Anderson, E., & Kian, E. M. (2012). Examining media contestation of masculinity and head trauma in the National Football League. *Men and Masculinities, 15,* 152–173.

Billings, A. C., & Angelini, J. R. (2007). Packaging the games for viewer consumption: Gender, ethnicity, and nationality in NBC's coverage of the 2004 Summer Olympics. *Communication Quarterly, 55,* 95–111.

Billings, A. C., & Ruihley, B. J. (2013). Why we watch, why we play: The relationship between fantasy sport and fanship motivations. *Mass Communication & Society, 16,* 5–25.

Billings, A. C., Angelini, J. R., MacArthur, P. J., Bissell, K., & Smith, L. R. (2014). (Re)calling London: The gender frame agenda within NBC's primetime broadcast of the 2012 Olympiad. *Journalism & Mass Communication Quarterly, 91,* 38–58.

Branscombe, N. R., Ellemers, N., Spears, R., & Doosje, B. (1999). The context and content of social identity threat. In N. Ellemers, R. Spears & B. Doosje (Eds.), *Social identity* (pp. 35–59). Oxford, UK: Blackwell.

Brown, N., Billings, A. C., & Ruihley, B. (2012). Exploring the change in motivations for fantasy sport participations during the life cycle of a sports fan. *Communication Research Reports, 29,* 333–342.

Brown, R. J., & Ross, G. F. (1982). The battle for acceptance: An investigation into the dynamics of intergroup behaviour. In H. Tajfel (Ed.), *Social identity and intergroup relations* (pp.155–158). Cambridge, UK: Cambridge University Press.

Chen, B. (2014, September 24). Stevie Johnson tweets he has "fantasy work team," fans have hilarious responses. Retrieved from http://bleacherreport.com/articles/2210082-stevie-johnson-tweets-he-has-fantasy-work-team-fans-have-hilarious-responses

Cleland, J. (2014). Racism, football fans, and online message boards: How social media has added a new dimension to racist discourse in English football. *Journal of Sport & Social Issues, 38,* 415–431.

Cohen, B. C. (1963). *The press and foreign policy.* Princeton, NJ: Princeton University Press.

Davis, N. W., Duncan, M. C. (2006). Sports knowledge is power reinforcing masculine privilege through fantasy sports league participation. *Journal of Sport & Social Issues, 30,* 244–264.

Dwyer, B. (2011). Divided loyalty? An analysis of fantasy football involvement and fan loyalty to individual National Football League (NFL) teams. *Journal of Sport Management, 25,* 445–457.

Facebook.com (2015). Key facts. Retrieved from http://newsroom.fb.com/Key-Facts

FanDuel NBA Expert Series: A Couple of Minutes with dean7804. (2014, November 3). Retrieved from https://www.fanduel.com/insider/2014/11/03/fanduel-nba-expert-series-a-couple-of-minutes-with-dean78904/

Fantasy Sports Trade Association Industry Demographics (2014). Retrieved from http://www.fsta.org/?page=Demographics

Farquhar, L. K., & Meeds, R. (2007). Types of fantasy sports users and their motivations. *Journal of Computer-Mediated Communication, 12,* 1208–1228.

Flanagin, A. J., Hocevar, K. P., & Samahito, S. N. (2014). Connecting with the user-generated Web: How group identification impacts online sharing and evaluation. *Information, Communication, & Society, 17,* 683–694.

Fraser, B. P., & Brown, W. J. (2002). Media, celebrities, and social influence: Identification with Elvis Presley. *Mass Communication and Society, 5,* 183–206.

Frederick, E. L., Burch, L. M., & Blaszka, M. (in press). A shift in set: Examining the presence of agenda setting on Twitter during the 2012 London Olympics. *Communication & Sport.*

Frederick, E. L., Lim, C. H., Clavio, G., Pedersen, P. M., & Burch, L. M. (2014). Choosing between the one-way or two-way street: An exploration of relationship promotion by professional athletes on Twitter. *Communication & Sport, 2,* 80–99.

Gibson, H., Willming, C., & Holdnak, A. (2002). We're Gators . . . not just Gator fans": Serious leisure and University of Florida football. *Journal of Leisure Research, 34,* 397–426.

Goff, B. (2013, August 20). The $70 billion fantasy football market. Retrieved from http://www.forbes.com/sites/briangoff/2013/08/20/the-70-billion-fantasy-football-market/

Goffman, E. (1959). *The presentation of self in everyday life.* New York: Doubleday.

Horton, D., & Wohl, R. R. (1956). Mass communication and para-social interaction. *Psychiatry, 19,* 215–229.

Jacobson, S. (2013). Does audience participation on Facebook influence the news agenda? A case study of the Rachel Maddow Show. *Journal of Broadcasting & Electronic Media, 57,* 338–355.

Kassing, J. W., & Sanderson, J. (2010). Tweeting through the Giro: A case study of fan-athlete interaction on Twitter. *International Journal of Sport Communication, 3,* 113–128.

Kassing, J. W., & Sanderson, J. (2015). Playing in the new media game or riding the virtual bench: Confirming and disconfirming membership in the community of sport. *Journal of Sport & Social Issues, 39,* 3–18.

Kwak, D. H., & McDaniel, S. R. (2011). Using an extended technology acceptance model in exploring antecedents to adopting fantasy sports league websites. *International Journal of Sports Marketing & Sponsorship, 12,* 240–253.

Kwak, D. H., Lee, J. S., & Mahan III, J. E. (2013). Ad-evoked illusory judgments in fantasy sports participation: Effects of customization and expert information. *Journal of Sport Management, 27,* 393–406.

Lebel, K., & Danylchuk, K. (2012). How sweet it is: A gendered analysis of professional tennis players' self-presentation on Twitter. *International Journal of Sport Communication, 5,* 461–480.

Lebel, K., & Danylchuk, K. (2014). Facing off on Twitter: A generation Y interpretation of professional athlete profile pictures. *International Journal of Sport Communication, 7,* 317–336.

Lee, S., Won, J., & Green, C. B. (2013). Understanding why people play fantasy sport: Development of the fantasy sport motivation inventory (FanSMI). *European Sport Management Quarterly, 13,* 166–199.

Maass, A., Ceccarelli, R., & Rudin, S. (1996). Linguistic intergroup bias: Evidence for in-group protective motivation. *Journal of Personality and Social Psychology, 71,* 512–526.

Major, B., & O'Brien, L. T. (2005). The social psychology of stigma. *Annual Review of Psychology, 56,* 393–421.

McCombs, M. E., & Shaw, D. L. (1972). The agenda-setting function of mass media. *Public Opinion Quarterly, 36,* 176–187

Meraz, S. (2011). Using time series analysis to measure intermedia agenda-setting influence in traditional media and political blog networks. *Journalism & Mass Communication Quarterly, 88,* 176–194.

Petchesky, B. (2014, September 25). Stevie Johnson drafted a really great fantasy you team. Retrieved from http://deadspin.com/stevie-johnson-drafted-a-really-great-fantasy-you-team-1638997432

Rice, R. [Ray Rice]. (2013, September 15). I was a fan of fantasy football until today so many spiteful and hateful words I still love you all God Bless great win today #Ravens [Tweet]. Retrieved from https://twitter.com/RayRice27/status/379346797971640321

Ruihley, B. J., & Billings, A. C. (2013). Infiltrating the boys' club: Motivations for women's fantasy sport participation. *International Review for the Sociology of Sport, 48*, 435–452.

Samuel, E. (2013, October 24). NY Giants Brandon Jacobs slams fantasy football after getting death threat on Twitter. Retrieved from http://www.nydailynews.com/sports/football/giants/jacobs-rips-fantasy-football-owners-death-threats-article-1.1494661

Sanderson, J. (2008a). The blog is serving its purpose: Self-presentation strategies on 38pitches.com. *Journal of Computer-Mediated Communication, 13*, 912–936.

Sanderson, J. (2008b). "You are the type of person that children should look up to as a hero": Parasocial interaction on 38pitches.com. *International Journal of Sport Communication, 1*, 337–360.

Sanderson, J. (2013a). From loving the hero to despising the villain: Exploring sports fans social identity management on Facebook. *Mass Communication and Society, 16*, 487–509.

Sanderson, J. (2013b). Stepping into the (social media) game: Building athlete identity via Twitter. In R. Luppicini (Ed.), *Handbook of research on technoself: Identity in a technological society* (pp. 419–438). New York: IGI Global.

Sanderson, J. (2014). Just warming up: Logan Morrison, Twitter, athlete identity, and building the brand. In B. Brummett & A. W. Ishak (Eds.), *Sport and identity: New agendas in communication* (pp. 208–223) New York: Routledge.

Sanderson, J., & Emmons, B. (2014). Extending and withholding forgiveness to Josh Hamilton: Exploring forgiveness within parasocial interaction. *Communication and Sport, 2*, 24–47.

Sanderson, J., and Hambrick M. E. (2012). Covering the scandal in 140 characters: A case study of Twitter's role in coverage of the Penn State saga. *International Journal of Sport Communication, 5*, 384–402.

Sanderson, J., & Truax, C. (2014). "I hate you man!": Exploring maladaptive parasocial interaction expressions to college athletes via Twitter. *Journal of Issues in Intercollegiate Athletics, 7*, 333–351.

Shontell, A. (2015, January 3). Snapchat is a lot bigger than people realize and it could be nearing 200 million active users. Retrieved from http://www.businessinsider.com/snapchats-monthly-active-users-may-be-nearing-200-million-2014-12

Soukup, C. (2006). Hitching a ride on a star: Celebrity, fandom, and identification with the world wide web. *Southern Communication Journal, 71*, 319–337.

Spinda, J. S. W., & Haridakis, P. M. (2008). Development and construct validation of a fantasy sports motivations scale: A uses and gratifications approach (pp. 187–202). In P. M. Haridakis, L. W. Hugenberg, & A. C. Earnheardt (Eds).

*Sports Mania: Essays on fandom and media in the 21st century.* Jefferson, NC: McFarland & Company.

Spitzberg, B. (2014). Toward a model of meme diffusion. *Communication Theory, 24,* 311–339.

Tajfel, H., & Turner, J. C. (1986). Social identity theory of intergroup behavior. In W. Austin & S. Worchel (Eds.), *Psychology of intergroup relations* (2nd ed., pp. 33–47). Chicago: Nelson-Hall.

Trujillo, N., & Krizek, B. (1994). Emotionality in the stands and in the field: Expressing self through baseball. *Journal of Sport & Social Issues, 18,* 303–325.

Turner, J. C. (1982). Towards a cognitive redefinition of the social group. In H. Tajfel (Ed.), *Self, identity, and intergroup relations* (pp. 15–40). Cambridge, UK: Cambridge University Press.

van Dijck, J. (2013). "You have one identity": Performing the self on Facebook and LinkedIn. *Media, Culture, & Society, 35,* 199–215.

Vann, P. (2014). Changing the game: The role of social media in overcoming old media's attention deficit toward women's sport. *Journal of Broadcasting & Electronic Media, 58,* 438–455.

Walther, J. B. (1996). Computer-mediated communication: Impersonal, interpersonal, and hyperpersonal interaction. *Communication Research, 23,* 3–44

Wakefield, K. L., & Wann, D. L. (2006). An examination of dysfunctional sports fans: Method of classification and relationships with problem behaviors. *Journal of Leisure Research, 38,* 168–186.

Wann, D. L. (2006). The causes and consequences of sport team identification. In A. A. Raney & J. Bryant (Eds.), *Handbook of sports and media* (pp. 331–352). Mahwah, NJ: Erlbaum.

Wann, D. L., & Branscombe, N. R. (1993). Sports fans: Measuring degree of identification with the team. *International Journal of Sport Psychology, 24,* 1–17.

Wann, D. L., Royalty, J., & Roberts, A. (2000). The self-presentation of sports fans: Investigating the importance of team identification and self-esteem. *Journal of Sport Behavior, 23,* 198–206.

Weathers, M., Sanderson, J., Matthey, P., Grevious, A., Tehan, M., & Warren, S. (2014). The tweet life of Erin and Kirk: A gendered analysis of sports broadcasters' self-presentation on Twitter. *Journal of Sports Media, 9,* 1–24.

# THE INSTITUTIONAL PERSPECTIVE

**12**

# FANTASY SPORT AND WORLD CUP VIEWERSHIP

*Pamela Wicker, Nicholas M. Watanabe, and Grace Yan*

The Fantasy Sports Trade Association (FSTA) research studies have found that around 41.5 million people play fantasy sport in North America (Fantasy Sports Trade Association, 2014). These numbers coupled with growing trends of fantasy use in areas around the globe are part of increased participation and development of products and services which revolve around fantasy sport (Montague, 2013). Despite this growth, fantasy sport is considered to be a product that many consumers are not familiar with conceptually (Levy, 2009), and this lack of participation is even more evident in countries outside of North America (Billings & Ruihley, 2013a; see also chapter 3 of this volume).

At the same time, fantasy sports has presented itself as an important tool for leagues, teams, players, media companies and other stakeholders involved in the industry. Estimates of the fantasy sport industry have found that the amount of expenditures alone in North America has exceeded $10 billion (U.S.). The growth in fantasy sport participation as well as expenditures, products, and value continues to grow at an exponential rate from the 1980s, when only half a million people were playing fantasy sport in North America (Fantasy Sports Trade Association, 2014). Academic research into fantasy sport has found that it has played a role in changing the consumption patterns and attitudes exhibited toward sport leagues and products (Hansen & Gauthier, 1989; Kwon, Trail, & James, 2007). Furthermore, the activity of participation in fantasy sport has also been linked to the consumption of traditional sport products (Karg & McDonald, 2011), use of various types of media (Ruihley & Hardin, 2011), as well as being of importance for marketing and branding activities (Dwyer & Drayer, 2010). Research has also shown that a normal consumer who goes to ESPN's website will spend about three times more time on ESPN media in a week if they are a fantasy sport participant (Billings & Ruihley, 2013b). It is exactly because of the ability for fantasy sport services to generate traffic and viewership that media has focused on becoming heavily involved with fantasy sport. Considering the importance of the interconnection between the consumption of traditional forms of sport products/media and fantasy sport, this chapter attempts to further the discussion of sport viewership and fantasy sport participation. Specifically, the examination presented within this chapter focuses on understanding the similarities and differences which exist between individuals who view sporting events and play various forms of fantasy sport around the world. The purpose of this analysis is to help serve as a bridge to provide better understanding for practitioners, academics, and organizations to enhance participation in fantasy sport alongside television viewership in a global context. Furthermore, this chapter also provides important implications for sport organizations and media providers in building an understanding of the value fantasy sport can have in attracting consumers. In this way, the findings presented can help to inform the practices of managing both fantasy sport products and related products, services, and media.

From a contextual standpoint, this chapter focuses on viewership of the Fédération Internationale de Football Association (FIFA) 2014 World Cup, and how it relates to participation in fantasy sport in countries on both sides of the Atlantic Ocean. The FIFA World Cup, which is hosted every four years, is widely thought to be one of the biggest media spectacles and sporting events in the world. Reports generated by FIFA consulting companies indicated that the 2014 World Cup was the most watched sporting event ever, including the staggering number that an average of around a billion people watched each of the sixty-four matches during the tournament (Resnikoff, 2014)—that is, nearly one in seven humans living today tuned in to World Cup. The World Cup also serves as an ideal setting for researchers and practitioners looking at fantasy sport participation and television viewership across many countries, as it is a natural conflux of individuals from a variety of countries and backgrounds. Against this backdrop, not only does this study contribute to the literature through a multinational study of sport viewership and fantasy sport participation, it is also is one of the first studies to provide an in-depth examination of fantasy sport in the context of the World Cup. Furthermore, the results of this study provides important information in regards to the management of sport organizations in understanding the value that fantasy sport products have in generating interest in their sport. That is, the findings hint at the potential that can come from getting consumers to engage in fantasy sport, especially to help promote the brands of corporations, competitions, and other related sport organizations. In other words, the results can thus be applied to real-world contexts in order to enhance how fantasy products and services are managed.

## FANTASY SPORT RESEARCH

To properly investigate television viewership of sport alongside fantasy sport, it is necessary to consider the theoretical basis and body of literature which has focused on the motivations of consumers in sport, with specific emphasis placed on the context of fantasy sport. While the examination of fantasy sport in academic research can be traced back to early work on role-playing games and scenarios (Andes, 1983), proper focus on sport specific fantasy games did not really emerge until later when researchers began considering the importance of fantasy sport as a tool for teaching decision-making to students and managers (Gillentine & Schulz, 2001; London, 1970). Additionally, while there is a growing line of research studies which are focused on many aspects of fantasy sport, the analysis of participation, motivations, services, marketing, and business of the industry is still relatively new.

## SPORT SPECTATORSHIP BEHAVIORS

Examination of consumer behavior in sport has been one of the oldest and most researched areas in the field of sport management (Keaton, Watanabe, & Gerhart, 2015; Shilbury, Quick, & Westerbeek, 2003). Furthermore, consumer behavior research has been noted as fostering important connections between practice and the examination of sport by academics, especially in creating knowledge focused on developing a more nuanced understanding of sport consumers (Sutton, McDonald, Milne, & Cimperman, 1997). In order to develop this knowledge base, consumer behavior patterns, motivations, and antecedents (which influence the choices made by individuals) in sport have been specifically examined (Stewart, Smith, & Nicholson, 2003). Through this work, there is clearly a need to understand the consumer from an organizational standpoint, as it allows for more strategic management of resources and marketing in order to develop better relations with consumers. Of specific importance in recent years for sport organizations has been the balancing of both live attendees to sporting events, as well as drawing fan interest to digital products and television broadcasts (Budzinski & Satzer, 2011). Budzinski and Satzer (2011) specifically argue that with multiple streams of products in the sport market, it has become especially relevant for organizations to try to manage these products and their interconnections to create benefits.

To date, research has shown that there is great importance in analyzing motivations, antecedents, psychological factors, and other variables in understanding how fans are driven to consume sport products. This line of research has not only examined individual fan groups, but differences which exist between them, as well as consumption of different sport products. One of the growing lines in this area of research has been analyzing the consumption of fantasy sport, especially as participation in fantasy leagues has grown in recent years. At the same time, it is important to remember that while there is an intersection between examining fantasy sport and consumer behavior, the two lines of research do not always fully overlap. Thus, while one must consider the theoretical and empirical understandings of consumer behavior research in examining fantasy sport, there is also need to consider how fantasy sport studies have evolved and are interrelated to other research. Finally, this chapter also considers the relationship between fantasy sport and a variety of factors. One relation which is worth noting is the linkage between television viewership by consumers, and their participation in fantasy sport, which serves as a focal point of interest, especially in considering the nexus of fantasy sport and broadcasts of competitions.

## CONSUMPTION OF FANTASY SPORT

The fantasy sport industry evolved from small groups of individuals playing in leagues where they would draft players and compile their statistics over a season to see whose fantasy team performed the best (Hu, 2003). Specifically, these early leagues which were often called roto leagues (short for rotisserie) were the ones which helped to build the industry and get recognition of the activity (see also chapter 1, this volume). Because of the nature of simulation, the academic literature which discussed fantasy sport often approximated to other chance based simulation games, such as roleplaying games (e.g., Dungeons & Dragons, Star Wars, Pathfinder), and considered participants as having to make similar decisions in these activities (Hu, 2003; London, 1970). It was the influx of technology into fantasy sport leagues which revolutionized the way the game was played, and opened access to individuals across the globe. Through this, it is argued by Hu (2003) that the growth of the Internet did not just help boost participation in fantasy sport leagues, but also the creation of new platforms to access leagues, websites dedicated to the analysis of statistics and players, as well as other services which consumers could spend their time focused on. Thus, it is only natural that media and Internet corporations became involved in the production and development of fantasy sport products and services, as it allowed them to capitalize on a growing market segment which would continue to consume their media as they participated in leagues.

Beyond examination of the development of the fantasy sport industry, the predominant focus for fantasy sport literature has examined the different motivations for individuals to participate in fantasy sport. Farquhar and Meeds (2007) attempted to bring together motivations literature from communication and media studies, which focused on things such as why people have used the Internet (Green 1996; Leung 2001), and the aforementioned sport consumer behavior research. This early work specifically analyzed the importance of uses and gratification theory (Ruggiero, 2000) alongside the motivational scales for sport consumers developed by Trail and James (2001). Following the work of Hu (2003) and Farquhar and Meeds (2007), sport focused researchers also began more detailed examination of participation, motivations, antecedents, and consumption of fantasy sport. Specifically, Drayer, Shapiro, Dwyer, Morse, and White (2010) propose a conceptual framework through which to understand fantasy football participation. In this, it is believed that fantasy football participation can help individuals connect to various aspects of the sport industry, such as players, teams and other fans, and helps to potentially move them toward the consumption of merchandise, attendance at events, or sport media (Drayer et al., 2010). The theoretical backing for this framework makes important connections between future consumption behaviors and relationships that sport consumers may have with either a team or individual athlete. From this, it is believed that identification and loyalty can help to draw fans to various properties in the sport world (such as televised sporting events), and thus the ability to interact and manage some of these properties allows further connections to be developed in fantasy sport.

Furthermore, Dwyer and Drayer (2010) placed further focus on segmenting the different modes of consumption which is displayed by individuals who participate in fantasy football. To try to examine the differences between groups, the research divided individuals into four segments based on heavy or light consumption of fantasy participation, as well as NFL team consumption (here, watching games on television). Results from the study indicated the fans that were fantasy dominant (those who tended to consume more fantasy sport) tended to watch more NFL sporting events than someone who was favorite team dominant (those who focus on a specific team). That is, while an individual with a favorite team will often spend the time to watch their own team play, those involved with fantasy have the tendency to watch more of the games which are broadcast by the NFL. In this manner, the participation in fantasy sport can be considered as having a positive effect on the ratings and consumption of NFL games. Dwyer and Drayer (2010) noted that because of consumption patterns and behaviors exhibited by various individuals, that the fantasy-dominant consumers are who should be targeted by bars, football related media sites, and other football/fantasy related products, because of the higher level of consumption behavior shown by these people. This line of research is also worth noting, as it begins to draw together the relationship between fantasy sport participation and media. As fantasy sport leagues and platforms are often connected to media organizations that heavily cover sporting events (e.g., ESPN, Yahoo.com, CBS, etc.), it is necessary to consider this relationship from both a consumer behavior and a media perspective.

## FANTASY SPORT AND MEDIA

Media specific examinations of fantasy sport participation have also considered the relationship between various types of mass media and involvement in fantasy sport. Randle and Nyland (2008) examined sport fans that used message boards on the Internet, and surveyed them on both the use of media types and fantasy sports participation. This research also considered the importance of fantasy sport in getting individuals to use a myriad of media channels to try to find information in regards to performance and outcomes of games. Results from this study indicated that individuals who played in interactive fantasy sports leagues had more consumption of newspapers, television, and radio. Randle and Nyland (2008) argue that media groups should continue to build fantasy sports leagues to enhance the consumption of the various forms of media which are provided to consumers. Another study in this lineage examined both traditional and fantasy consumers, where motivational scales were employed to look at connections between being a fan of watching sport and being involved in fantasy sport (Billings

& Ruihley, 2013b). The findings noted that there were not many differences in regards to motivations between the two groups; however, it was shown that individuals who participated in fantasy sport had higher levels of fanship motivations than individuals who did not play fantasy sport. In this case, it was shown that when considering the difference between just fans who watched sport, and fans that watched and played fantasy sport, the fantasy sport participants displayed higher levels of fanship motivation. This research again backs the findings which have been consistent in the research noting that those involved in fantasy sport may exhibit higher levels of connection, fanship, or even consumption of sport products and media.

However, Billings and Ruihley (2013b) point out that it is important to continue investigation of the modern sport fan, especially due to the complexities involved in the environment because of access to multiple teams, leagues, products, fantasy sport, and other related services. These complexities come in the form of the many channels through which sport can be consumed (such as live attendance, television, mobile devices, and other modes), as well as the existence of a variety of related ancillary products, merchandise, and media. In the modern sport environment, it has become vital for sport organizations to try to manage all of these channels, and try to find ways to maximize overall benefits, and not necessarily seek maximum gains from any single channel/product. Thus, fantasy sport participation can be understood as being one important component of an overall sport product system that an organization manages to try to draw greater demand and interest from fans.

Considering the greater body of sport motivation, antecedent, and consumption literature, there has been a wide range of methods through which to investigate sport consumers, especially in the context of participating in fantasy sport. To date, research has focused on developing theory and empirical understanding of the motivations and antecedents which may draw individuals to participate in fantasy sport, while also considering the importance of media in this dynamic. It is worth noting that the majority of studies are not only couched in examining North American consumers, but that a great number of these studies have focused on fantasy football participation. Though it is understandable that great focus should be placed on the region where fantasy sport is most popular, and the type of fantasy sport participation which is most popular in the United States, there is also a need to consider the international importance of fantasy sport. Thus, this chapter attempts to provide further understanding to the literature focused on fantasy sport participation by examining individuals living in both the United States and Europe to analyze specific similarities and differences which may exist in their viewership of sporting events as well as their participation in fantasy sport. By conducting such examination, the present study not only builds this cross-cultural understanding, but also helps to enhance the knowledge of how fantasy sport leagues can be used to enhance consumer interaction and interest with both core and ancillary sport products. From such examination, fantasy sport stakeholders can build further practices and strategies to better attract consumers to these products and services.

## ANALYSIS OF INTERNATIONAL FANTASY SPORT DATA

### Data Collection

In this chapter, the key research question we asked was: "Is there a difference in the relationship between fantasy sport participation and World Cup viewership among individuals living in different countries?" This question was developed in order to gain a better understanding of the demographics and behaviors of individuals who watched the FIFA World Cup and participated in fantasy sport. In order to examine this relationship, an online survey was developed, administered, and released in Germany and the United States. The online questionnaire contained questions about World Cup viewership, general fantasy sports consumption, fantasy sports consumption in the context of the World Cup, general media and communication behavior, and socio-demographics of the respondents. The survey specifically asked questions examining how many matches of the 2014 FIFA World Cup that participants watched in order to provide detailed examination between fantasy sport participation and sport viewership. The surveys were approved by institutional research review boards in both countries, and directed at individuals aged sixteen years and older. At the beginning of the survey the respondents were asked to state whether they would like to complete the survey in English or in German.

In the United States, the survey was distributed through a listserv at a large public Midwestern university. Students, faculty, and staff were given the opportunity to complete either an online survey or a paper version. All paper surveys were collected and inserted into the online questionnaire by the researchers. In Germany, the survey link was distributed by postgraduate students and faculty of a graduate program at a university in North Rhine Westphalia. The link was mainly distributed via social media websites like Facebook and Twitter. The survey was available online from July 22 to October 6, 2014. Altogether, 413 individuals participated in the survey. Out of these, a total of 348 cases are used for the analysis. Of all survey respondents, 54.6 percent were from the United States and 45.4 percent from Germany. Most respondents were male (76.4%), with an average age of 23.86 years old.

## EMPIRICAL FINDINGS AND DISCUSSION

In this section the empirical results for the examination of World Cup viewership, general fantasy sport consumption, and fantasy sport consumption during the Football World Cup are presented. The results for World Cup viewership—both for the total sample and the two sub-samples United States and Germany—are summarized in table 12.1.

**Table 12.1. Football World Cup (WC) viewership**

|  | Total Sample (n=348) | United States (n=190) | Germany (n=158) |
|---|---|---|---|
| Share of people who watched WC games | 96.3 | 93.2 | 100 |
| Number of games watched (mean) | 25.2 | 15.2 | 35.3 |
| Spending on WC related merchandise (mean in US$) | 17.97 | 20.31 | 15.34 |
| Share of people who gambled on WC games (in %) | 33.4 | 18.6 | 50.0 |
| Betting agency (in %) | 12.5 | 5.1 | 20.9 |
| Number of games gambled on at betting agency (mean) | 2.02 | 0.25 | 4.00 |
| Spending on gambling at betting agency (in US$) | 8.48 | 5.70 | 11.57 |
| Private setting (in %) | 29.0 | 15.8 | 43.7 |
| Spending on gambling in private setting (mean in US$) | 9.20 | 12.54 | 5.45 |

The results show that most respondents (96.3%) watched games of the Football World Cup. In the United States, 93.2 percent watched games, while all of the German respondents stated that they watched games. Soccer is the most popular sport in Germany and the German team ended up winning the title, so it is not surprising to see that the figure is so high. Germans also watched more games than Americans. Interestingly, although the interest of North Americans in the World Cup seemed lower, they spent more money on World Cup related merchandise indicating that they also visually supported their team when watching games. Of those respondents who watched the World Cup, 18.6 percent of the Americans and 50.0 percent of the Germans gambled on World Cup games. The latter figure is surprisingly high for a nation not known to be affiliated with gambling on sports events. While most of the Germans (43.7%) gambled in a private setting (e.g., a betting round with co-workers or friends), 20.9 percent also gambled at betting agencies. The figures are lower for the United States: 5.1 percent of the Americans gambled at a betting agency and 15.8 percent in a private setting. While Germans spent more money on gambling at a betting agency, the North Americans spent more when they gambled in a private setting.

Table 12.2 presents the general fantasy sport consumption pattern of the total sample and also by country. The share of people playing fantasy sport is higher in the United States than in Germany: 68.9 percent of the North American respondents play fantasy sport, while only 33.5 percent of the Germans do so. While the share of people playing fantasy sport is higher, the North Americans have not played substantially longer than the Germans (5.74 years on average vs. 5.09 years). Yet, they owned more teams during the last twelve months (3.62 vs. 2.04) and played against more opponents (23.99 vs. 11.13). The higher involvement of North Americans in fantasy sport is also reflected in the number of hours per week dedicated to playing fantasy sport, the higher spending on fantasy sport, and the number of hours per week spent on sport statistics websites. Not surprisingly, North Americans won their fantasy league more often. The figures support the

**Table 12.2. General fantasy sport consumption**

|  | Total Sample | United States | Germany |
|---|---|---|---|
| Share of people who play fantasy sport (in %) | 52.9 | 68.9 | 33.5 |
| Number of years fantasy sport has been played (mean) | 5.55 | 5.74 | 5.09 |
| Number of teams owned during the last 12 months (mean) | 3.16 | 3.62 | 2.04 |
| Number of friends, family members, and/ or co-workers the person played against during the last 12 months (mean) | 20.29 | 23.99 | 11.13 |
| Number of hours per week spent on playing fantasy sport during the last 12 months (mean) | 3.82 | 4.37 | 2.45 |
| Spending on fantasy sport during the last 12 months (mean in US$) | 34.57 | 46.03 | 6.23 |
| Number of hours per week spent on sport statistics websites during the last 12 months (mean) | 3.10 | 3.68 | 1.68 |
| Number of times of winning the fantasy league (mean) | 1.55 | 1.69 | 1.21 |

reviewed literature indicating that the interest in fantasy sport is higher in the United States than in Europe.

The questionnaire also asked for the types of sport where people play fantasy sport and the providers where people play. The types of fantasy sports that are played most often in the United States are American football (90.8%), followed by baseball and basketball (each 38.9%), soccer (13.0%), and hockey (10.7%). In Germany, most fantasy sport participants play soccer (96.2%). Only a few people play other, mainly U.S. based sports like American football (5.7%). The fantasy sport providers that are used most often in the United States are ESPN (87.0%) and Yahoo! Sports (46.6%). In Germany, most respondents play fantasy sport (i.e., soccer) at Comunio (81.1%) and Kicker (18.9%).

Table 12.3 summarizes fantasy sport consumption during the 2014 Football World Cup. It shows that the percentages of people playing fantasy sport during the World Cup are much lower compared with World Cup viewership and general fantasy sport consumption. In Germany, 12.0 percent of the respondents played fantasy sport during the World Cup, while only 5.3 percent of the Americans did so. Thus, it seems that neither fantasy sport consumption nor World Cup viewership adequately translates into playing fantasy sport during the Football World Cup. Although the share of North Americans playing fantasy sport during the World Cup is smaller, they owned more teams than the Germans, played against more opponents, spent more hours playing fantasy sport, spent more money on fantasy sport,

**Table 12.3.  Fantasy sport consumption during the 2014 Football World Cup**

|  | Total Sample | United States | Germany |
|---|---|---|---|
| Share of people who played fantasy sport during the Football WC (in %) | 8.3 | 5.3 | 12.0 |
| Number of soccer teams owned during the Football WC (mean) | 1.21 | 1.30 | 1.16 |
| Number of friends, family members, and/or co-workers the person played against during the Football WC (mean) | 8.62 | 12.60 | 6.53 |
| Number of hours per week spent on playing fantasy sport during the Football WC (mean) | 2.03 | 2.40 | 1.84 |
| Spending on fantasy sport during the Football WC (mean in US$) | 0.51 | 1.50 | 0.00 |
| Number of hours per week spent on sport statistics websites during the Football WC (mean) | 2.03 | 3.10 | 1.47 |
| Number of teams of winning the Football WC (mean) | 0.21 | 0.30 | 0.16 |

and dedicated more time to sport statistics websites. Accordingly, North Americans won their fantasy sport competitions at the World Cup with 0.30 teams on average; the Germans only with 0.16 teams.

In the United States, people played fantasy sport during the World Cup at McDonalds FIFA World Cup Fantasy (30.0%), followed by fantasyleague and World Cup Manager (each 20.0%). In Germany, again Comunio (52.6%) and Kicker (36.8%) were the main providers of fantasy sport. Thus, the leading providers for general fantasy sport consumption are also the main providers for fantasy sport during the World Cup. This seems different in the United States where at least one new provider (McDonalds), which is not known for league based fantasy sport, has made its way into the list. This indicates that McDonalds has used its sponsorship contract with FIFA to increase its popularity among fantasy sport players.

When comparing tables 12.2 and 12.3, it stands out that the figures are lower for fantasy sport consumption during the World Cup compared with general fantasy sport consumption which is typically league based. To add some inferential statistics to the descriptive overview, we ran three correlation analyses between World Cup viewership, general fantasy sport consumption, and fantasy sport during the World Cup (table 12.4). They show that in the total sample general fantasy sport consumption and fantasy sport during the World Cup are significantly and positively correlated. Yet, a detailed analysis shows that this result can be attributed to the German subsample where the correlation is also significant and even higher. No significant relationship can be found for the United States. Interestingly, there is a significant positive correlation in the United States between World Cup viewership and general fantasy sport consumption: People playing leaguebased fantasy sport are significantly more likely to watch World Cup games. Yet, this general interest in playing fantasy sport does not translate into an interest to play fantasy sport during the World Cup.

**Table 12.4.   Relationship between fantasy sport consumption and World Cup viewership (correlation analyses)**

| Correlation between . . . | Total Sample | United States | Germany |
|---|---|---|---|
| WC viewership and general fantasy sport consumption | 0.057 | 0.179** | / |
| WC viewership and fantasy sport during the WC | 0.059 | 0.064 | / |
| General fantasy sport consumption and fantasy sport during the WC | 0.243*** | 0.056 | 0.520*** |

Note: ***p<0.01; **p<0.05; *p<0.1. The first two correlation analysis for the German subsample could not be run due to missing variation in the variable WC viewership (100 percent of all German respondents watched World Cup games).

To further examine the phenomenon of playing fantasy sport during the World Cup, a logistic regression analysis was estimated where the dependent variable was coded as "1" when the individual stated that he/she has played fantasy sport during the World Cup and "0" otherwise. The aim of this analysis is find out what people are significantly more likely to play fantasy sport during the World Cup. A set of independent variables capturing World Cup viewership and general fantasy sport consumption are included in the regression model. Also, a set of socio-demographic variables are entered as control variables. The model also controls for general media and communication behavior which could also affect fantasy sport consumption.

The results of the logistic regression analysis are summarized in table 12.5. Looking at the model fit parameter ($R^2$) indicates that the independent variables explain 55.8 percent of the variation in the dependent variable. Interestingly, when controlling for other factors there is no significant

**Table 12.5. Determinants of playing fantasy sport during the Football World Cup (logistic regression analysis; displayed are the unstandardized coefficients)**

|  | Total Sample |
|---|---|
| Nation (0=United States; 1=Germany) | 1.880 |
| Number of WC games watched | 0.032 |
| Number of years fantasy sport has already been played | 0.384** |
| Fantasy sport American football (1=yes) | 0.653 |
| Fantasy sport baseball (1=yes) | −0.144 |
| Fantasy sport basketball (1=yes) | 0.633 |
| Fantasy sport soccer (1=yes) | 3.103** |
| Fantasy sport hockey (1=yes) | 1.278 |
| Number of fantasy sport teams owned during the last 12 months | 0.174 |
| Number of fantasy sport opponents during the last 12 months (family members, friends, co-workers) | −0.051 |
| Number of hours per week spent on playing fantasy sport during the last 12 months | −0.243 |
| Spending on fantasy sport during the last 12 months (in $) | 0.017** |
| Number of hours per week spent on sport statistics websites during the last 12 months | 0.167 |
| Number of times of winning the fantasy league | −0.226 |
| Number of hours per week spent on the Internet for non-working purposes | 0.001 |
| Number of hours spent per week on social media websites | −0.079 |
| Gender (1=female) | −2.380* |
| Age | −0.064 |
| Relationship (1=yes) | −0.011 |
| Number of school years completed | 0.003 |
| Monthly net income (in $) | −0.001 |
| Constant | −3.501 |

Note: −2LL=81.304; Chi²=68.286***; $R^2$ (Nagelkerke)=0.558; ***p<0.01; **p<0.05; *p<0.1.

difference in playing fantasy sport during the World Cup between the two nations; the effect is not significant. Similarly, the number of World Cup games watched on television has no significant effect on the probability of playing fantasy sport during the Football World Cup. Thus, the significant positive correlation from table 12.4 does not hold anymore when other influencing factors are included in the model.

On the contrary, general fantasy sport consumption matters: The more years people have played league-based fantasy sport, the more likely they play fantasy sports during the World Cup. It is likely that experienced players search for a new sport and/or a different context like a major event (as opposed to a league) to play fantasy sport. Out of all the sports people play through fantasy sport providers, only the soccer effect is significant. People who play fantasy soccer in general (league based) are also more likely to play fantasy sport during the World Cup. Playing other fantasy sports does not translate into playing fantasy sport during the World Cup. While many other characteristics of fantasy sport participants do not play a significant role (e.g., number of teams owned, number of opponents, and number of hours spend), spending on general fantasy sport has a significant positive effect. The more people spend on general fantasy sport, the more likely they play fantasy sport during the World Cup. The socio-demographic control variables are not significant with the exception of gender: Males are more likely to play fantasy sport during the World Cup, probably because they are also more likely to play league based fantasy sport.

## CONCLUSION

This chapter looked at fantasy sport consumption and the characteristics of fantasy sport participants. The spread and growth of fantasy sport was documented and the literature on consumer behavior, fantasy sport consumption, and the relationship between fantasy sport and the media was examined. The empirical section of this chapter was dedicated to one specific topic: the relationship between FIFA World Cup viewership, general fantasy sport consumption, and fantasy sport during the 2014 Football World Cup. An online survey was administered at two universities in the United States and in Germany. Altogether, 348 people completed this survey and represent the basis for the empirical analysis. The empirical results showed that nearly all respondents watched games of the Football World Cup. As expected, league-based fantasy sport consumption was higher in the United States than in Germany. Yet, neither World Cup viewership nor league-based fantasy sport seemed to adequately translate into playing fantasy sport during the World Cup. Thus, huge market potentials on the side of football viewership as well as on the side of general fantasy sport consumption are left out. The results of a logistic regression analysis indicates that particularly males who are experienced in playing fantasy, who spent a lot of money on fantasy sport, and who play fantasy soccer are significantly more likely to play fantasy sport during the World Cup.

Although the present sample is not representative of the general population of both countries, it may capture well the profile of fantasy sport participants who are usually young, male adults. Thus, the present study has the potential to make some recommendations for the fantasy sport industry. Considering the results from this study, there seems to be a disconnect between the consumption of watching televised matches from the World Cup and participation in fantasy sport. Given the huge interest in watching World Cup games and the regular fantasy sport consumption of many people, the fantasy sport industry may not be capitalizing on these interests during major events like the Football World Cup. It is astonishing to see that one provider (McDonalds) has easily made its way into the list of providers where people played fantasy soccer during the World Cup, but that there is not any statistical linkage between the World Cup and fantasy participation. One first step for fantasy organizations could be to target those people who were shown to be more likely to be interested in fantasy soccer. The next step would be to examine how people interested either in soccer or in fantasy sport could be inspired to play fantasy sport in the context of major sport events like the Football World Cup. Since this research was among the first to examine fantasy sport participation in the context of a major sport event, future studies should pursue this avenue further by looking at different sports, events, and countries.

Considering overall implications for sport organizations, the results of this chapter help to build a better understanding of the linkage which exists between participation in fantasy sport and the viewership of sport competitions. While the results of the survey found no direct link between World Cup viewership and fantasy sport participation, part of this may have come about because of FIFA's lack of interest and emphasis in fantasy sport. That is, because the organization in charge of the World Cup was willing to allow other corporations and media companies to take charge of fantasy competitions during the tournament there was likely less promotion of them, and hence consumers were not as familiar with the existence of most leagues. However, as the research has shown, the value of fantasy sport in driving the interest of consumers to the viewership of sport competitions, it would seem that it would be beneficial for FIFA to further their marketing and promotion of fantasy sport at future tournaments. This recommendation can also be extended to other organizations involved in producing sport competitions and fantasy products, as other studies presented in this chapter indicate a relationship between viewership and fantasy sport participation.

Additionally, the findings of this study displays that individuals who were interested in other types of fantasy sport products were more inclined to be involved with World Cup fantasy sport competitions. This indicates that those who play one type of fantasy sport league are likely interested in playing in different fantasy competitions in other sport settings. From this, it is possible that there could be further potential for the development of the fantasy sport consumer base by enhancing the ability for individuals to crossover from one fantasy league to the next. Employed in a strategic manner, this type of cross-promotion could not only be beneficial for large media companies that offer a variety of fantasy sport products, but could also help to bring financial benefits and further interest to a range of sport leagues and competitions.

A final implication which can be drawn for this chapter are the findings in regards to demographic differences between individuals from different countries in choosing to participate in fantasy sport leagues. While these differences were relatively small, they do indicate that consumers in various regions of the world may engage and participate in fantasy sport in different manners. As organizations and sport leagues/competitions continue to try to build the interest in their products through fantasy sport, there will be a point where they will begin to look toward global audiences to garner larger audiences. The results of the survey provided in this chapter hint that it is important for those involved with the production, marketing, management, and creation of fantasy sport leagues to try to understand the subtle differences which may exist with international audiences. By developing such understanding, these organizations could potentially be more successful in trying to grow fantasy sport in markets around the globe in the years to come.

## REFERENCES

Andes, J. (1983). The use and development of simulation in educational administration. Unpublished Manuscript.

Billings, A. C., & Ruihley, B. J. (2013a). *The Fantasy Sport Industry: Games within Games*. Routledge.

Billings, A. C., & Ruihley, B. J. (2013b). Why we watch, why we play: the relationship between fantasy sport and fanship motivations. *Mass Communication and Society, 16*(1), 5–25.

Budzinski, O., & Satzer, J. (2011). Sports business and multisided markets: towards a new analytical framework?. *Sport, Business and Management: An International Journal, 1*(2), 124–137.

Drayer, J., Shapiro, S. L., Dwyer, B., Morse, A. L., & White, J. (2010). The effects of fantasy football participation on NFL consumption: A qualitative analysis. *Sport Management Review, 13*(2), 129–141.

Dwyer, B., & Drayer, J. (2010). Fantasy sport consumer segmentation: An investigation into the differing consumption modes of fantasy football participants. *Sport Marketing Quarterly, 19*(4), 207–216.

Farquhar, L. K., & Meeds, R. (2007). Types of fantasy sports users and their motivations. *Journal of Computer Mediated Communication, 12*(4), 1208–1228.

Gillentine, A., & Schulz, J. (2001). Marketing the fantasy football league: Utilization of simulation to enhance sport marketing concepts. *Journal of Marketing Education, 23*(3), 178–186.

Green, L. (1996). Technology and conversation: Construction and destruction of community. *Australian Journal of Communication, 23*(3), 54–67.

Hansen, H., & Gauthier, R. (1989). Factors affecting attendance at professional sport events. *Journal of sport management, 3*(1), 15–32.

Hu, J. (2003). *Sites see big season for fantasy sports.* Retrieved November 1, 2014, from http://news.com/2102-1026_3-5061351.html

Karg, A. J., & McDonald, H. (2011). Fantasy sport participation as a complement to traditional sport consumption. *Sport Management Review, 14*(4), 327–346.

Keaton, S. A., Watanabe, N. M., and Gearhart, C. C. (2015). Comparison of college football and auto racing fan profiles: Identity formation and spectatorship motivation. *Sport Marketing Quarterly, 24*(1), 43–55.

Kwon, H. H., Trail, G., & James, J. D. (2007). The mediating role of perceived value: Team identification and purchase intention of team-licensed apparel. *Journal of Sport Management, 21*(4), 540.

Leung, L. (2001). Gratifications, chronic loneliness, and Internet use. *Asian Journal of Communication, 11*(1), 96–119.

Levy, D. P. (2009). Fanship habitus: The consumption of sport in the US. In *Quantifying Theory: Pierre Bourdieu* (pp. 187–199). Springer Netherlands.

London, H.J. (1970). The futility of testing: Simulation as a "test" case. *Educational Leadership*, October, 93–95.

Montague, J. (2010, January 20). The rise and rise of fantasy sports. *CNN.com.* Retrieved from: http://www.cnn.com/2010/SPORT/football/01/06/fantasy.football.moneyball.sabermetrics/

Randle, Q., & Nyland, R. (2008). Participation in internet fantasy sports leagues and mass media use. *Journal of Website Promotion, 3*(3–4), 143–152.

Resnikoff, T. (2014, June 21). Brazil 2014 World Cup breaks TV records says FIFA. Retrieved 2014, November 3 from http://edition.cnn.com/2014/06/21/sport/foot ball/world-cup-broadcasting-stats/

Ruggiero, T. E. (2000). Uses and gratifications theory in the 21st century. *Mass communication & society*, 3(1), 3–37.

Ruihley, B. J., & Billings, A. C. (2013). Infiltrating the boys' club: Motivations for women's fantasy sport participation. *International Review for the Sociology of Sport*, 48(4), 435–452.

Ruihley, B. J., & Hardin, R. L. (2011). Message boards and the fantasy sport experience. *International Journal of Sport Communication*, 4(2), 233–252.

Shilbury, D., Quick, S., & Westerbeek, H. (2003). *Strategic sport marketing*. Allen & Unwin.

Stewart, B., Smith, A. C., & Nicholson, M. (2003). Sport consumer typologies: a critical review. *Sport Marketing Quarterly*, 12(4), 206–216.

Sutton, W. A., McDonald, M. A., Milne, G. R., & Cimperman, J. (1997). Creating and fostering fan identification in professional sports. *Sport Marketing Quarterly*, 6, 15–22.

Trail, G., & James, J. (2001). The motivation scale for sport consumption: Assessment of the scale's psychometric properties. *Journal of Sport Behaviour*, 24(1), 108–127.

# 13

# FANTASY SPORTS LAW

## A Primer

*Mark Grabowski*

**M**any fantasy sports businesses and participants may be surprised to learn that there is an array of state and federal laws affecting them. Although fantasy sports-type games have existed for more than seventy years, it is only relatively recently that laws and regulations have been enacted to specifically address such contests. While some critics consider any games that involve the exchange of money a form of gambling that should be outlawed, it is generally legal to operate and participate in fantasy sports games in the United States. However, a handful of states prohibit pay-for-play fantasy games. In addition, popular new types of short-term games, such as the daily contests offered by FanDuel, are legally murky. Where there are legal issues involved, businesses that operate fantasy sports contests face far more risks than individuals who participate in the games.

Beyond the permissibility of playing fantasy sports, other legal issues can arise, such as intellectual property infringement, cheating scandals, and defamation lawsuits. In addition to those who play fantasy sports or operate gaming sites, businesses offering ancillary services, such as insurance or advertising, must be mindful of laws. While this chapter provides a primer on fantasy sports law, it should not be construed as legal advice. As fantasy sports lawyers caution, laws are in a state of flux and subject to change, therefore those who plan on engaging in or operating a fantasy sports venture should retain competent legal counsel. Despite some legal obstacles, the future of fantasy sports looks bright, given that many professional sports and lawmakers seem to be warming up to the idea. Fantasy sports help generate both increased interest in the actual games on the field and tax revenues for the government off the field. Those benefits may just be enough to overcome efforts to outlaw it.

## GAMING LAWS

In the current sports landscape, fantasy sports law is a hot topic, as evidenced by the growing number of attorneys who specialize in the area, the law schools offering courses on it, and blogs devoted to its latest developments. Almost none of this existed at the turn of the twenty-first century. But, by 2012, there was so much information about fantasy sports law that it prompted law professor Marc Edelman to publish a *Harvard Law Review* journal article summarizing the many and varied legal issues. Despite being 54 pages, he dubbed it, "A Short Treatise on Fantasy Sports and the Law." While many of the laws regulating it are fairly new, fantasy sports have been played for several decades. Fantasy sports can trace its roots back to 1941, when Major League Baseball player Ethan Allen designed a board game for Cadaco-Ellis called, "All Star Baseball," which allowed baseball fans to play simulated games with an imaginary team created from a collection of player cards (Sielski, 2011).

The 1980s brought the introduction of "Rotisserie Leagues," in which participants drafted teams from active Major League Baseball players and tracked their statistics during the season to tally their scores (Tozzi, 1999). Fantasy games involving other professional sports soon emerged. Still, fantasy sports were mostly a fringe hobby. That dramatically changed with the Internet boom in the 1990s, which transformed it into a popular mainstream activity. The new technology lowered the barrier to entry for fantasy sports as stats could quickly be compiled online and news and information became readily available (Clapham, 2012). Fantasy sports rapidly became a lucrative business for dot-com entrepreneurs, who were looking to cash in on a growing consumer market, and an obsession for participants, many of whom began playing for more than just bragging rights (Chakraborty, 2013). Today, America's fantasy sports industry attracts more than forty million participants and is estimated to generate billions of dollars, according to the Fantasy Sports Trade Association's website (2015b). Some participants wager tens of thousands of dollars on a single contest and some leagues offer million dollar payouts, which has caused concern among anti-gambling groups, prompting calls for more stringent regulation (Dahlberg,

2014). As with all things related to technology, the law invariably lags behind and online fantasy sports games were largely unregulated until 2006. With so much money at stake, lawyers and lawmakers are now taking an increasing interest in fantasy sports. Significant new legal developments happen so regularly that Edelman often updates his popular fantasy sports law blog on Forbes.com multiple times a week.

Although the law is in a state of flux, the general rule for fantasy sports remains this: With some exceptions, it is perfectly legal to be involved in fantasy sports games in the United States. According to Richard Lee (2014), a partner at the Los Angeles-based litigation firm Salisian Lee, who specializes in sports, gaming and entertainment law:

> Some people think that it is legal to bet on fantasy sports—i.e., contribute entrance fees to the fantasy football league pool, with the winner to take the jackpot. Others think it is illegal because it constitutes, in their view, prohibited organized gambling. To clarify, the bottom line is this: It is legal.

Fantasy sports games that do not involve money and prizes are completely legal nationwide. Contests that require an entry fee or wagers and that pay out cash prizes are generally legal as well, but it depends on the state.

In 2006, Congress enacted Title VII of the Security and Accountability For Every Port Act of 2006, also known as the Unlawful Internet Gaming Enforcement Act (UIGEA), to prevent gambling over the Internet. But the act contains specific language stating that participation in fantasy sports does not constitute gambling. Lawmakers rationalized that winning fantasy sports games primarily requires knowledge and skills to win, as opposed to card games and slot machines, which largely require luck or chance (Lee, 2014).

Specifically, the UIGEA makes legal:

> participation in any fantasy or simulation sports game or educational game or contest in which (if the game or contest involves a team or teams) no fantasy or simulation sports team is based on the current membership of an actual team that is a member of an amateur or professional sports organization and that meets the following conditions: (I) All prizes and awards offered to winning participants are established and made known to the participants in advance of the game or contest and their value is not determined by the number of participants or the amount of any fees paid by those participants. (II) All winning outcomes reflect the relative knowledge and skill of the participants and are determined predominantly by accumulated statistical results of the performance of individuals (athletes in the case of sports events) in multiple

real-world sporting or other events. (III) No winning outcome is based on the score, point-spread, or any performance or performances of any single real-world team or any combination of such teams; or solely on any single performance of an individual athlete in any single real-world sporting or other event.

In layman's terms, the law requires the following: First, payouts must be established up front before the season begins. According to David O. Klein (2014a), managing partner at Klein Moynihan Turco, a New York City law firm specializing in fantasy sports and gaming law, "While it might be tempting as an operator of a pay-for-play fantasy sports contest to treat the purse for each contest like a lottery pool—the more players that enter, the greater the prize—such a scenario would be in violation of applicable law." Second, the scoring system must be based on a collection of individual player statistics in actual games played, not just one individual player in one game. And, third, the scoring system must not be based on team results (e.g., the wins and losses of the New York Yankees). Klein (2014a) also recommended, "Accordingly, at a minimum, fantasy sports contests should require contestants to assemble a roster consisting of several athletes from more than one team and participating in more than one game."

Generally, paid fantasy sports contests that meet the UIGEA's requirements and that last an entire—or at least most—of a season are permissible because they are deemed to require a sufficient level of skill. That is because winners are not determined by the outcome of a single game or the performance of a single player. "Managers must take into account a myriad of statistics, facts and game theory in order to be competitive," according to the Fantasy Sports Trade Association's website (2015a). However, this legal exception "does not necessarily insulate all forms of fantasy sports games that currently appear on the Internet," advised Edelman (2014). Edelman (2014) also noted, "Each fantasy game must be reviewed separately under the carve-out." For example, the new breed of fantasy sports websites—which allow users to wager thousands of dollars on an athlete's daily performance—invites legal challenges comparable to the now-banned online poker sites. These short-term fantasy games are booming because season-long leagues can become stagnant and many participants want instant gratification (Brustein, 2013). However, many gaming law experts say it is unclear whether or not they involve enough skill in order to pass muster under federal law (Klein, 2014b). Critics contend such games primarily require luck to win because, on any given day, an injury or bad officiating call could affect the outcome. "It becomes akin to a flip of the coin, which is the definition of gambling," noted Robert Bowman, the chief executive of Major League Baseball Advanced Media, the league's Internet company (Brustein, 2013). Officials at such sites contend that what they are doing is legal because better players consistently beat weaker players over time. Darren Heitner (2014), a sports lawyer with an emphasis on gaming-related issues, agrees that short-term games

> should be deemed legal, at least under the Dominant Factor test, which deems an activity to be of chance if greater than 50 percent of the result is derived from chance. The games require a level of knowledge, expertise and research of the individual performers, existing injuries, weather conditions, etc.

While it is well-established that longer duration fantasy sports games (e.g., full season) involve the levels of skill and knowledge necessary to meet the UIGEA's requirements, no court has directly addressed whether the much shorter in duration daily fantasy sports games meet this test. A 2012 lawsuit challenged the legality of short-term fantasy sports contests. Since that federal court case, *Langone v. Kaiser & Fan Duel*, was ultimately dismissed on procedural grounds, the underlying legal question remains unresolved (Masters & Rose, 2014). Interestingly, this lawsuit was initiated by a private plaintiff, rather than the government, and experts believe more of these suits will be filed (Masters & Rose, 2014). However, if courts do not put an end to these daily sites, lawmakers could. The games are raising eyebrows because of guilt of association with illegal gambling:

> [P]eople who know the industry also acknowledge some troubling aspects of daily fantasy. Many sites are run by people with backgrounds in online poker or sports betting, activities that have run afoul of government regulators. For the top players, mostly young men, daily online fantasy sports are a full-time job in which they can win six figures annually (Brustein, 2013).

Joseph Romano (2014), an attorney who is chief operating officer of fantasy sport dispute resolution site SportsJudge.com, agrees such sites will face legal battles:

> I think the biggest, newest frontier that will find its way in front of the courts or controlled by legislation are the daily fantasy leagues, such as FanDuel. With revenue generation similar to the house take at a poker table, they will make easy targets. They really represent the first way a host site makes money beyond classic revenue streams, such as advertising, hosting fees and premium content. I think there will be a close parallel with the early poker websites that were ultimately outlawed.

Some argue that daily fantasy sites would significantly benefit if their legal status remains cloudy. "Start-ups are able to take the lead in the industry in part because the competition is limited by legal ambiguity" (Brustein, 2013). Heitner (2014) disagrees:

> Clarity will ensure longevity of the industry and sub-sectors. It should be much preferred that operators are investing money into developing platforms and user bases attached to legally sound concepts. It will cost much more money to re-work the system later on should legal status be jeopardized.

In addition to the potential limitations at the federal level, individual states may ban any and all games involving money or prizes. The laws relating to gambling vary by state, but the vast majority of states consider fantasy sports a game of skill and therefore view them as legal (Edelman, 2012, p. 26–33). In the states that allow fantasy sports to be played for money, the contests are essentially unregulated (Brustein, 2013). But playing fantasy sports for money could lead to legal trouble in a minority of states. In Montana, residents are allowed to wager on fantasy sports only through state government-run contests (State of Montana, 2014). Other states have banned all pay-to-play fantasy contests. In Arizona, operators of such contests may face felony charges (McClay, 2013). And, in some states, the law is ambiguous about the legality of playing fantasy sports for money. Kansas officials, for example, have given "conflicting" accounts on whether fantasy sports wagering is illegal (Edelman, 2014b).

Gaming attorneys say other potential trouble spots include: Arkansas, Iowa, Louisiana, North Dakota, Washington, Tennessee, and Vermont (Edelman, 2014c; Heitner, 2014). Heitner (2014) adds, "State laws are fluid and subject to change. Further, many states have simply not provided their explicit opinion on the legality of fantasy sports within their borders. Expect that to change in the coming years." While some fantasy-friendly states may begin imposing regulations, other states that currently ban the games may soon embrace them. For example, Kansas lawmakers said they plan to propose legislation in the 2015 session that would formally legalize fantasy sports. "It is an innocent, entertaining pastime enjoyed by thousands of Kansans that have now been made criminals by burdensome regs," State Representative Brett Hildabrand observed (Rothschild, 2014).

The online nature of fantasy sports also can raise unexpected jurisdictional issues. Even though host sites may be located in a safe state, they could still run into legal issues with authorities in states that ban fantasy games since the Internet is borderless. "Even if a particular fantasy sports game seems to comply with federal law, it is not advisable to allow participants to enter if they are located within these [risky] states," Edelman (2014d) cautions. Host sites, therefore, should implement Internet protocol tracking technology to block their website from users in impermissible states, thus preventing any mistake or confusion from residents of those states. Some host sites have rolled the dice and continue to operate in states with laws against fantasy sports (Chakraborty, 2013). While most state laws against fantasy sports tend to target sites offering pay-for-play games, participants also could face prosecution:

> Host sites have more to be concerned about at the moment. However, it is not inconceivable that a state with strict prohibitions goes after individuals who overtly violate the restrictions and earn a significant amount of money in the process. Such people would be used as an example to deter others from willfully violating the law (Heitner, 2014).

Florida, for example, has specific statutes outlawing the paying of entry fees into fantasy leagues—and participants risk being charged with misdemeanors (Lamar, 1991).

Of course, even if playing fantasy sports is legal, Lee (2014) said, "The question of whether betting on fantasy sports should be legal . . . is a different one altogether." Ethics and law are separate spheres after all. In theory, ethics justifies laws and legal practices. Given that, opponents argue that fantasy sports betting should be outlawed because it threatens the moral fabric of sports and society. John Kindt, an emeritus professor of business and legal policy at the University of Illinois who is a leading national gambling critic, stated:

> Societal goals should be directed toward protecting the integrity of sports and the next generation. When you're talking about people who think they can actually make a living off of fantasy sports, that's also when it veers into problematic gambling. Playing fantasy sports shouldn't be a year-round occupation, but, when it is, that makes it more like bookmaking. . . . It's a multibillion dollar industry, and all of that money is disposable income that could otherwise have been diverted to constructive contributions to our economy, like education and health care, as well as consumer goods like cars and appliances (as cited by Ciciora, 2013).

The Fantasy Sports Trade Association (2015a), however, opines that lucrative jackpots are a secondary consideration for participants: "Fantasy sports players are motivated to enter the hobby for reasons that have nothing to do with money or prizes."

## INTELLECTUAL PROPERTY LAWS

Aside from gambling laws, fantasy game operators have to contend with intellectual property issues in connection with the information they provide to participants. Intellectual property law can be both friend and foe for fantasy game websites. While the law protects businesses against the unauthorized use of their content, it also limits their ability to reproduce the works of others. Those running websites related to fantasy sports must be careful to respect laws governing copyright, trademark, patent, and personality rights.

Copyright is of primary concern to fantasy sports sites. It is a set of federal laws that grant content creators the exclusive right to benefit from their work. There are three main requirements for content to be protected by the U.S. Copyright Act. First, it must be original. Material that already exists or that belongs to someone else cannot be copyrighted without the original creator's permission. Second, creators must have shown at least a small spark of creativity when they made the work. The result does not have to be good and the standard is not an especially high one, but there must be some creativity. For example, courts have ruled that simply alphabetizing a list of names lacks the creativity necessary to qualify for a copyright (U.S. Supreme Court, 1991). Finally, the work must be "fixed in any tangible medium of expression." This fixation requirement means that only works preserved in a tangible form, such as a photo, book, blog, or website—as opposed to those existing entirely in a creator's mind—will receive copyright protection (U.S. Copyright Office, 2012a, pp. 3–4). Just because it is now possible to find and download almost any image, text passage, or video that exists with one click of the mouse button does not mean it is legal to do so (Student Press Law Center, 2006a, pp. 5–18). As long as a work satisfies these three requirements, the list of fantasy sports material eligible for copyright protection is a long one. For example, commentary and articles about fantasy sports, photos of players, computer programs and templates used for websites are protected. Original works are protected by copyright the moment they are "fixed" in a tangible medium of expression. From that moment forward, no one else has the right to use, alter, or sell a creator's photos or papers in any way without her express permission. A copyright notice is not required (Student Press Law Center, 2006a, p. 28).

Still, while the copyright eligibility list is extensive, it is not unlimited. There are certain things that copyright does not protect. Copyright does not prohibit the use of ideas. Similarly, only the expression of facts—not the facts themselves—are subject to protection (Student Press Law Center, 2006a, pp. 20–21). Of particular importance to fantasy sports is the use of statistics, which has been contested by some professional sports leagues. Courts have ruled that statistics are considered facts that can be freely used by the public, and as a result, do not warrant protection under copyright law. Therefore, fantasy leagues are free to copy athletes' statistics and display them on their websites, no permission or license is needed (Hambleton, 2014). For instance, while ESPN will have a copyright on the exact words and arrangement of an article about fantasy sports, the facts and statistics included in ESPN's reporting belong to no one and can therefore be used as a source for other fantasy sports reporters, advisors, and websites. Entrepreneurs also are free to look to other host sites for ideas of their own or for facts to use in creating their own fantasy sports game.

Although generally, permission is required to use someone's copyrighted work, there are important exceptions. The Fair Use Doctrine allows for the use of limited amounts of copyrighted works for important purposes such as reporting, commentary, critiques, research, education, and Internet search engines so long as the use does not significantly cut into the commercial value of the original copyrighted work (U.S. Copyright Office, 2012b). No permission is needed if fair use applies. For example, short quotations will usually be considered fair use, not copyright infringement. So, a blogger can generally reprint a short passage from a new book to accompany a book review and a podcast is usually safe to include a short clip from a game to illustrate its recap. Unfortunately, determining what qualifies as fair use can often be a tough call. There is no simple formula or clear-cut threshold. Fortunately, fantasy sport websites and blogs need worry only about the content their employees post. Webmasters and bloggers who allow users to submit comments or post content can avoid being held responsible for copyright infringement enacted by readers. The federal Digital Millennium Copyright Act (1998) provides a limited safe harbor allowing online publishers to escape liability for copyright infringement if they promptly remove infringing material posted by outside parties after receiving notice of the infringement. To secure protection, the website operator must register with the federal copyright office and pay a fee.

Second, patent law protects technological inventions, such as computers and software. Under Article 1, Section 8 of the U.S. Constitution (1788), inventors can obtain patents from the U.S. government "to promote the Progress of Science and useful Arts, by securing for limited times to Authors and Inventors the exclusive Right to their respective Writings and Discoveries." Courts have ruled that certain aspects of fantasy sports games are patentable. For example, in *Fantasy Sports Properties, Inc. v. SportsLine.com, Inc.*, a federal circuit court found SportsLine (now part of CBSSports.com) infringed on a patent relating to "a method of and apparatus for playing a 'fantasy' football game on a computer," by which players earned "additional points awarded beyond those given in an actual football game for unusual scoring plays, such as when a player scores in a manner not typically associated with his position." Based on the court's reasoning in that 2002 case, Edelman (2012) stated:

> all fantasy sports host sites need to ensure that their products do not allow users to exploit scoring methods that have already been patented. In addition, fantasy sports games that adopt unusual methods of scoring may wish to seek patent protection for their own methodologies as a way to secure a comparative advantage over competitor host sites (p. 39).

Third, trademark law protects the symbols and slogans that identify businesses with their consumers. Trademarks—for example, the Minuteman logo used by the New England Patriots or the brand name "Roto-Wire"—and service marks—for example, the blue bird used to identify Twitter—are unique symbols, names, or other "marks" that companies use and consumers rely upon to distinguish one product or service from another. Under Section 32 of the Federal Lanham Act (1946), trade infringement occurs when:

> a person uses (1) any reproduction . . . of a mark; (2) without the registrant's consent; (3) in commerce; (4) in connection with the sale, offering for sale, distribution or advertising of any goods; (5) where such use is likely to cause confusion, or to cause mistake or to deceive.

Trademark law is generally only problematic when a trademark or service mark is used in a way that would confuse a potential consumer. If there is no likelihood that a consumer would be confused by the use of a trademark, there is generally no violation. That is why, for example, there would be no problem with a blog publishing a team's logo when discussing which defense is best to play in a fantasy NFL game. There is, obviously, no likelihood that a reasonable blog visitor would read the blog post thinking it was an official team blog. According to the Official Review (2013), a sports law blog published by the New York Law School:

> The sports leagues for the most part have no enforceable IP rights here—any use of their marks and logos is incidental to the news reporting function of the fantasy data site and so falls under the First Amendment 'fair use' defense to a trademark infringement claim (para. 7).

On the other hand, a fantasy sports game that is branded in such a way that it prominently features professional sports logos could cause confusion among participants and open the site to a trademark infringement lawsuit. In branding and promoting their game, host sites should avoid use of actual sports teams' logos without a license (Edelman, 2012). If a fantasy sports host site wants to identify a professional sports team by name, the host site should either obtain a license or reference the team's name in small print, while having its own site's name and marks appearing far more conspicuously. Additionally, businesses must be careful when registering domain names, the unique name that identifies the cyberspace address or URL of a website. If they register a URL that is identical or confusingly similar to a protected trademark or service mark, they could be forced to surrender ownership of the domain (Internet Corporation for Assigned Names and Numbers, 2009).

Finally, fantasy sports sites must be careful not to violate athletes' "personality rights," also known as the right of publicity. Most states have laws providing the right of athletes to control use of their names and identifying characteristics for promotional purposes. Typically, if a website wants to use anything identified with a person's likeness—such as a picture of someone or someone's voice—they first have to get their permission (Bobbitt, 2007). But, merely using players' names and statistical information without authorization would likely not violate state right of publicity laws. Suits have been brought against fantasy sports providers, claiming they were misappropriating player names and likenesses to gain a commercial advantage. However, fantasy news and stats suppliers have won all suits brought to date (Balsam & Kozhevnikov, 2013). In a ground-breaking case, *C.B.C. Distribution and Marketing v. Major League Baseball Advanced Media*, a federal Circuit Court of Appeals ruled in 2006 that the information provided to baseball fantasy sports participants is information in the public domain and constitutes informative speech entitled to protection under the Fair Use Doctrine. The court also found that fantasy sites' use of player names and likenesses presents no danger that participants will be misled to believe any particular player is endorsing the site. The U.S. Supreme Court declined MLB's request for an appeal hearing, which means the ruling stands. In 2009, another federal court extended this ruling to football. In *CBS Interactive v. National Football League Players Association*, the court characterized the manner in which fantasy sites present player information as "akin to newspapers and magazines, which routinely display pictures and information about . . . professional athletes." These precedents have deterred lawsuits by other sports, but, with fantasy sports' profits growing, players may want a piece of the action and renew their publicity rights claims in the future. Additionally, courts are more likely to rule against sites that run fantasy games involving college athletes. This is because, "unlike professional athletes, who are rewarded separately for their labors, collegiate athletes are not otherwise compensated based on their fame" (Edelman, 2012, p. 43). Edelman (2012) further observed, "Thus, the American legal system has an especially strong interest in protecting the proprietary nature of the collegiate athlete's right to publicity" (p. 43).

## ADDITIONAL LEGAL ISSUES

While fantasy sports lawyers spend most of their time handling issues involving gaming and intellectual property laws, some less common problems may arise as well. Allowing minors to play fantasy sports can open game operators to liability. Host sites must be careful not to allow minors to participate in games involving money, which is illegal. Age limits vary by state, with some states requiring that participants be eighteen and others setting the minimum age as high as twenty-one. Even sites offering games that do not involve money or prizes must take precaution with minors. The federal Child Online Privacy Protection Act requires any website that allow users under thirteen to take extra steps to protect children's privacy, such as securing parental consent. In addition to crafting terms of service that bar underage participants, site operators also may want to consider borrowing some of the age verification technologies currently utilized by adult entertainment sites (Edelman, 2014a).

Site operators also must take steps to protect participants' privacy and data. Undisclosed tracking of customer activities online poses class action risk. The use of tracking mechanisms, such as cookies, should be fully disclosed in a fantasy sports website's privacy policy (DLA Piper, 2014). California is particularly strict on this issue. Under the state's Online Privacy Protection Act, sites that collect any data from its residents are required to conspicuously post and comply with a privacy policy that meets certain requirements. The privacy policy must detail what kind of information is gathered by the website, how the information is shared with other parties, and, if such a process exists, it must describe how users can review and make changes to their stored information. It also must include the policy's effective date and a description of any changes made through revision (Jolly, 2014). Fantasy sports websites would be wise to invest in cyber security. In the event that a website is hacked and customers' information is stolen, nearly every state has laws requiring data breaches be reported to affected parties (Greenberg, 2014).

Playing fantasy sports also can lead to troubles at work. For example, with studies showing that fantasy sports can cost billions of dollars in lost productivity, some workplaces forbid it (Burkes, 2014). An employer may fire an employee found to be soliciting other employees to participate in their fantasy sports games during work hours, in violation of company policies against solicitation or gambling at work. On the flip side, many offices sponsor fantasy sports leagues as a way of building employee morale. However, an employer may be exposed to a potential hostile work environment claim if an employee does not participate in gambling activities due to religious beliefs, but receives pressure to do so from other coworkers (McDonough, 2013).

Playing fantasy games also can lead to legal troubles in participants' personal lives. High-stakes fantasy sports participants run a heightened risk of bankruptcy based on their financially risky behavior. Like compulsive poker players and slot machine users, they can become addicted to the gambling aspects of fantasy sports and gamble incessantly on short-duration fantasy sports contests (Edelman, 2012). Consequently, some lawmakers and anti-gambling groups oppose fantasy games on morality grounds.

However, participants must watch more than just their wallet. They also must watch their mouths—and keyboard. Words matter deeply, and when used carelessly, words can cause harm and lead to defamation lawsuits. Defamation, also known as slander and libel, is the broadcasting or publication of false statements of fact that seriously harms someone's reputation (Student Press Law Center, 2006b, pp. 5–7). Participants in fantasy leagues often bash players and coaches on Internet message boards and in the comments section on websites (also see chapter 11, this volume). Fortunately for participants, players and coaches are generally considered public figures to whom one can direct a wide variety of invective without being liable for defamation. Public figures who claim that they have been defamed must prove that the person who made the comments knew what they wrote was false or acted with reckless disregard for the truth. Trickier, though, is the situation in which participants in a league start verbally attacking one another and getting personal, even making vulgar references and insults. When disputes get too heated, and the comments are made publicly, such as on a website that is accessible to many people, the rules of defamation apply. If a statement contains only opinion, it cannot be defamatory. So, if a participant posts a comment saying that someone is "an idiot" or that someone's fantasy team is "awful," it cannot really be proven true or false and would be protected in a defamation lawsuit. On the other hand, if a participant posts a comment that says, "Our fantasy league commissioner rigged the fantasy draft so his friend would get the best players," that claim better be accurate. If it is not, the participant has probably seriously harmed and defamed the commissioner. Lee (2014) notes:

> I have never seen situations in which people threatened to sue one another, but I have observed situations in which a supposedly problematic participants gets expelled from the league. And there is the danger of rubbing a particularly litigious person the wrong way.

Defamation is primarily a concern for those who play fantasy sports. Those who operate a fantasy sports blog, discussion board, social media platform, or website that allows users to comment are not legally responsible for defamatory comments made by outsiders. The federal Communications Decency Act should shield them and their website, though the authors of such comments can and do get sued. The reason for this is that Congress did not want to stifle web development by placing an enormous burden on website owners to screen every comment for defamation. Without such a law, massive online discussion boards such as Reddit—which includes a section devoted to fantasy sports—would likely not be possible. Bloggers and websites can retain legal immunity even if they voluntarily screen profane or defamatory comments. But if they start rewriting comments to "improve" them, then they may become responsible as a co-creator.

Cheaters must beware as well. As with any type of competition, cheating sometimes occurs in fantasy sports—and this may lead to a lawsuit. For example, cheating may occur through owner collusion in lopsided trades, participants dumping their star players into the free agent pool after they realize there is no chance at the playoffs, a commissioner vetoing trades that will hurt the commissioner's team but allowing their own questionable trades to go through, or a participant setting up fake teams to operate simultaneously and gradually siphon players to one super-team. Lee (2014) noted:

> Normally, this is just part of the landscape. But when the amount of money at stake in a fantasy league gets too high, cheating that affects the outcome of the league standings could lead to real monetary disputes. And where there are monetary disputes between people, litigation—even if it is in small claims—is sure to follow at some point.

To reduce the temptation to cheat, fantasy sports leagues should consider adopting policies such as early trade deadlines.

Attempting to cheat the government will also bring trouble for business and individuals alike. Fantasy sports businesses are required to follow the same federal, state, and local tax laws as regular businesses. Sites operating in a state that charges a sales tax or levies a gross receipts or excise tax on businesses may have to apply for a tax permit or otherwise register with their state revenue agency. Fantasy sports businesses are responsible for collecting state and local sales taxes from their customers when applicable, and paying these taxes to state and local revenue agencies (U.S. Small Business Administration, n.d.). Likewise, fantasy sports participants must report their earnings to their state revenue agency along with the Internal Revenue Service. The rules for fantasy football fortunes are the same as those for gambling income. Even winnings for those who win a private fantasy league among friends are considered taxable. Participants can deduct their losses, such as entry fees in leagues they did not win, against their gains, as long as they occurred in the same year (Block, 2014).

Finally, various ancillary fantasy sports actors—including league officers, arbitrators, advisors, insurers, and advertisers—also may risk legal liability for fraud or negligence. First, there are some potential risks for officials who handle disputes among participants, such as commissioners and fantasy dispute resolution services. In recent years, there has been movement in both commercial and private fantasy leagues to outsource some of the commissioner's responsibilities to a third-party dispute resolution business, such as SportsJudge.com. Any decision provided by in-house officials or outside consultants may be challenged in the courts, on the basis that the dispute arbitrator acted arbitrarily, capriciously, fraudulently or in violation of public policy. But plaintiffs face a high burden in proving their claims (Edelman, 2012).

The treasurer is another league official who also must be careful. Those who collect money at the beginning of the season and distribute it to the winners at the season's end may face suits from fantasy sports participants for failure to turn over contested winnings to the proper league participant. According to Edelman (2012), "This is because the treasurer/participant relationship is comparable to one of bank and customer, in which the bank is indebted to the customer and promises to debit his account only at the customer's direction" (pp. 48–49). Next, those who make their living by providing advice or analytical tools to other fantasy sports participants risk liability if they negligently supply misinformation that is used in a business transaction or if they fail to perform services as warranted. Given these contract law risks, fantasy sports advisors should minimize their potential liabilities by drafting clear disclaimers that require all users to bear all risks associated with the use of the advisor's services or tools (Edelman, 2012).

Similarly, legal issues can arise for businesses that provide insurance to protect fantasy sports participants from monetary loss in the event of an injury to a player on one's fantasy sports team. Insurers must ensure that state law deems their services to be bona fide insurance contracts and not a disguised form of illegal gambling. For example, if a fantasy sports participant files a claim after their starting quarterback suffers a season-ending injury, an insurer must avoid overcompensating for the loss of potential winnings had the player remained healthy. Otherwise, the insurer would violate the doctrine of indemnity (Edelman, 2012). Lastly, advertisers and marketers must comply with certain laws. Fantasy sports advertisers who use false or deceptive advertising face prosecution and fines from the both state attorney generals and the Federal Trade Commission (Klein, 2014c). All businesses that send commercial e-mails to customers must avoid violating federal anti-spam laws by providing a way for recipients to opt-out of receiving future e-mails (Bureau of Consumer Protection, 2009).

## WHAT THE FUTURE HOLDS

Legal battles continue to wage and the legality of fantasy sports in some contexts is murky, therefore host sites would be wise to consult with attorneys before offering their services. Klein (2014a) notes:

> The interplay of business interests with the evolution of federal and state interpretations of fantasy sports gaming remains a significant topic. If you plan on engaging in, or operating, a fantasy sports venture, you should retain competent legal counsel to help you design the contests in a way that comports with applicable law.

Those offering new types of games should be especially careful. Edelman (2014d) noted, "New businesses should innovate with caution, as certain unique formats of fantasy sports are more risky." Existing fantasy leagues have some deep pockets and may even try to keep those start-ups out so they do not cut into their bottom line. Romano (2014) contended:

> It's worth keeping in mind that the professional leagues are unhappy about the upswing in daily leagues, or at least the inability to directly profit from it. Given the power each league maintains, they will have indirect input, at a minimum.

That said, fantasy sports continue to thrive. The vast popularity of fantasy sport may just keep them legally alive. Fantasy sports have increased fan interest and excitement in actual sporting contests (Fortunato, 2011). Consequently, professional sports leagues have become supportive of fantasy sports, recognizing these games as important drivers of fan interest in their respective offerings. For example, in 2014, the NBA signed a sponsorship agreement with FanDuel. In recent history, professional sports leagues professed zero tolerance for gambling (Golen, 2014). While their imprimatur does not guarantee that fantasy games will be deemed legal by governmental authorities, having such powerful and visible advocates can only help the cause. According to the New York Law School's sports law blog (2013):

> The leagues and the players have thrived with the rise of fantasy sports, as previously uninteresting match-ups get renewed hype when they feature certain fantasy players. Fans tune into games across the nation that normally would generate little interest to follow their favorite (and most hated) fantasy players. The increased revenue for all involved in sports may ultimately trump concerns about gambling or player publicity rights (para. 9).

## REFERENCES

Arizona State Legislature. (n.d.). Arizona Revised Statutes § 13–33. http://www.azleg.state.az.us/ArizonaRevisedStatutes.asp?Title=13

Balsam, J. & Kozhevnikov A. (2013, December 6). Are investors in fantasy sports gambling on their legality? *The Official Review.* Retrieved from http://www.theofficialreview.com/are-investors-in-fantasy-sports-gambling-on-their-legality/

Block, S. (2014, November). 9 surprising things that are taxable. *Kiplinger.* Retrieved from http://m.kiplinger.com/slideshow/taxes/T056-S003-9-surprising-things-that-are-taxable/index.html?page=5

Bobbitt, R. (2007). *Exploring Communication Law: A Socratic Approach.* Boston: Allyn & Bacon.

Brustein, J. (2013, March 11). Fantasy sports and gambling: Line is blurred. *New York Times.* Retrieved from http://nyti.ms/1zG5TCs

Bureau of Consumer Protection. (2009, September). *CAN-SPAM Act: A compliance guide for business.* http://www.business.ftc.gov/documents/bus61-can-spam-act-compliance-guide-business

Burkes, P. (2014, September 9). Fantasy football good for morale but maybe not so good for productivity. *Colorado Springs Gazette.* Retrieved from http://gazette.com/fantasy-football-good-for-morale-but-maybe-not-so-good-for-productivity/article/1537066

California Online Privacy Protection Act of 2003, Cal. Bus. & Prof. Code §§ 22575–22579 (2004), http://leginfo.ca.gov/cgi-bin/displaycode?section=bpc&group=22001-23000&file=22575-22579

Chakraborty, B. (2013, August 31). Gaming laws could pose risk for fantasy football craze. Fox News. Retrieved from http://www.foxnews.com/politics/2013/08/31/gaming-laws-pose-risk-for-fantasy-football-craze/

Children's Online Privacy Protection Act of 1998. 5 U.S.C. 6501–6505. http://www.ftc.gov/enforcement/rules/rulemaking-regulatory-reform-proceedings/childrens-online-privacy-protection-rule

Ciciora, Phil. (2013, July 29). John Kindt, legal policy expert and gambling critic. A Minute with . . . http://illinois.edu/lb/article/72/76010

Clapham, K. (2012, May 14). Fantasy sports becoming big business as popularity continues to rise. Medill Reports. Retrieved from http://news.medill.northwestern.edu/chicago/news.aspx?id=205473

Communications Decency Act. 47 U.S. Code § 230. http://www.gpo.gov/fdsys/pkg/USCODE-2011-title47/pdf/USCODE-2011-title47-chap5-subchapII-partI-sec230.pdf

Dahlberg, T. (2014, August 23). Fantasy explosion has some giving up day jobs. Associated Press. http://bigstory.ap.org/article/fantasy-explosion-has-some-giving-day-jobs

Digital Millennium Copyright Act. (1998). 17 U.S.C. §§ 512. http://www.copyright.gov/title17/92chap5.html

DLA Piper. (2014, November 30). Data protection laws of the world. http://www.dlapiperdataprotection.com/system/modules/za.co.heliosdesign.dla.lotw/functions/export.pdf?country=all

Edelman, M. (2014a, November 13). 7 legal risks of the NBA investing in FanDuel. Forbes. Retrieved from http://www.forbes.com/sites/marcedelman/2014/11/13/7-legal-risks-of-the-nba-investing-in-fanduel/

Edelman, M. (2014b, September 5). Kansas gaming commission backtracks after fantasy football faux pas; replaces claims of illegality with useless double-talk. Forbes. Retrieved from http://www.forbes.com/sites/marcedelman/2014/09/05/kansas-gaming-commission-backtracks-after-fantasy-football-faux-pas-replaces-claims-of-illegality-with-useless-double-talk/

Edelman, M. (2014c, July 22). NFL launches pay-to-enter fantasy football in 43 states. Forbes. Retrieved from http://www.forbes.com/sites/marcedelman/2014/07/22/nfl-launches-pay-to-enter-fantasy-football-in-43-states/

Edelman, M. (2014d, January 14). Fantasy sports legal issues will remain a hot topic in 2014. Forbes. Retrieved from http://www.forbes.com/sites/marcedelman/2014/01/14/legal-issues-in-fantasy-sports-will-remain-a-hot-topic-in-2014/

Edelman, M. (2012). A short treatise on fantasy sports and the law: How America regulates its new national pastime. Harvard Journal of Sports & Entertainment Law, 3, 1–54. http://harvardjsel.com/wp-content/uploads/2012/03/1-54.pdf

Fantasy Sports Trade Association. (2015a) Why fantasy sports is not gambling. http://www.fsta.org/?page=FSandGambling

Fantasy Sports Trade Association. (2015b). Industry demographics. http://www.fsta.org/?page=Demographics

Florida State Code. 849.14 Unlawful to bet on result of trial or contest of skill, etc. http://www.leg.state.fl.us/statutes/index.cfm?App_mode=Display_Statute& Search_String=&URL=0800-0899/0849/Sections/0849.14.html

Fortunato, J. (2011). The relationship of fantasy football participation with NFL television ratings. *Journal of Sport Administration & Supervision*, 3.1, 1–17. http://hdl.handle.net/2027/spo.6776111.0003.114

Golen, J. (2014, November 14). Pro sports leagues gradually embrace gambling. *Associated Press*. http://bigstory.ap.org/article/7b3cf67ab549418c87384c8c1b26c 15b/pro-sports-leagues-gradually-embrace-gambling

Hambleton, C. W. (2014). Are intellectual property rights in fantasy sports a reality? (2014). *Law School Student Scholarship*, Paper 490, 1–29. http://scholarship .shu.edu/student_scholarship/490

Heitner, D. (2014, November 24). E-mail interview.

Greenberg, P. (2014, September 3). Security breach notification laws. National Conference of State Legislatures. http://www.ncsl.org/research/telecommunications -and-information-technology/security-breach-notification-laws.aspx

Illinois Northern District Court. (2012). Langone v. Kaiser & Fan Duel. http:// documents.jdsupra.com/3ccb3b98-ecfc-46cc-b1f7-feda1e42cfe6.pdf

Internet Corporation for Assigned Names and Numbers. (1999). Uniform domain-name dispute-resolution policy. http://www.icann.org/resources/pages/udrp-2012 -02-25-en

Jolly, I. (2014, July 1). Data protection in United States: overview. *Practical Law*. http://us.practicallaw.com/6-502-0467

Klein, D. O. (2014a, May). Fantasy sports contests: Avoiding civil and criminal liability. [Blog post]. Retrieved from http://www.kleinmoynihan.com/blog/fantasy -sports-contests-avoiding-civil-and-criminal-liability/

Klein, D. O. (2014b, September). Legal challenges to daily fantasy sports games disappearing. [Blog post]. Retrieved from http://www.kleinmoynihan.com/blog/ legal-challenges-to-daily-fantasy-sports-games-disappearing/

Klein, D. O. (2014c, March). Online fantasy sports providers do battle. [Blog post]. Retrieved from http://www.kleinmoynihan.com/blog/online-fantasy-sports-pro viders-do-battle/

Lamar, L. (1991, January 8). Advisory Legal Opinion—AGO 91-03. http://myflorida legal.com/ago.nsf/Opinions/9ADEF3B402960199852562A6006FB71E

Lanham Act. (1946). 15 U.S.C. §1114(1). https://www.law.cornell.edu/uscode/ text/15/1114

Lee, E. (2014, September 12). E-mail interview.

Masters, D. N. & Rose, S. A. (2014, September 9). Are fantasy sports operators betting on the right game? *Chicago Daily Law Bulletin*. Retrieved from http:// www.loeb.com/~/media/Files/PDFs/Masters_Rose_ChicagoDailyLawBulletin _Sept2014.pdf

McClay, B. (2013, September 4). Fantasy football leagues considered illegal in Arizona. *KTAR News*. http://www.ktar.com/22/1659815/Fantasy-football-leagues-considered-illegal-in-Arizona

McDonough, T. (2013, September 16). Fantasy football leagues in the workplace. *HR Legalist*. http://www.hrlegalist.com/2013/09/fantasy-football-leagues-in-the-workplace/

Romano, J. C. (2014, November 13). E-mail interview.

Rothschild, S. (2014, August 28). Fantasy sports illegal in Kansas. *Lawrence Journal-World*. Retrieved from http://www2.ljworld.com/news/2014/aug/28/reality-bites-fantasy-football-illegal-kansas/

Sielski, M. (2011, July 18). Baseball's original nerd magnet. *Wall Street Journal*. Retrieved from http://on.wsj.com/1B2AUEE

State of Montana. (2014). Montana Code Annotated § 23–5. https://media.dojmt.gov/wp-content/uploads/Gambling-Statutes-and-Rules-as-of-August-19-20141.pdf

Student Press Law Center. (2006a). Copyright law. http://media.spl.s3.amazonaws.com/304_ppcopyrightlawfinal_noteso.pdf

Student Press Law Center. (2006b). Libel law. http://media.spl.s3.amazonaws.com/311_pplibellawfinal_noteso.pdf

Taylor, D. (2014, July 23). Is the NFL's new fantasy football league legal where you live? *FindLaw*. Retrieved from http://blogs.findlaw.com/tarnished_twenty/2014/07/is-the-nfls-new-fantasy-football-league-legal-where-you-live.html

Tozzi, L. (1999, July 5). The Great Pretenders. *Austin Chronicle*. http://weeklywire.com/ww/07-05-99/austin_xtra_feature2.html

Unlawful Internet Gambling Enforcement Act. (2006). 31 U.S. Code § 5362. http://www.gpo.gov/fdsys/pkg/USCODE-2008-title31/pdf/USCODE-2008-title31-subtitleIV-chap53-subchapIV-sec5362.pdf

U.S. Copyright Office. (2012a). Copyright basics. http://www.copyright.gov/circs/circ01.pdf

U.S. Copyright Office. (2012b). Fair use. http://www.copyright.gov/fls/fl102.html

U.S. Constitution. (1788). http://www.archives.gov/exhibits/charters/constitution_transcript.html

U.S. Copyright Act of 1976. (1976). 17 U.S.C. §§ 101—810. http://copyright.gov/title17/

U.S. Court of Appeals, Federal Circuit. (2002). Fantasy Sports Properties, Inc. v. Sportsline.com, Inc. http://caselaw.findlaw.com/us-federal-circuit/1411740.html

U.S. Court of Appeals, Federal Circuit. (2007). C.B.C. Distribution and Marketing v. Major League Baseball Advanced Media. http://media.ca8.uscourts.gov/opndir/07/10/063357P.pdf

U.S. Small Business Administration. (n.d.). Online businesses. http://www.sba.gov/content/start-online-business

U.S. Supreme Court. (1991). Feist Publications, Inc. v. Rural Telephone Service Co., Inc. https://supreme.justia.com/cases/federal/us/499/340/case.html

# FOR THE LOVE OF
# THE FANTASY GAME

**14**

# EXPLORING THE BRAINTRUST

The Evolution and Impact of the
Fantasy Sport Trade Association

*Brody J. Ruihley and Andrew C. Billings*

**V**ince Lombardi is credited as asserting that, "the achievements of an organization are the results of the combined effort of each individual." There is, perhaps, no greater fantasy-sport-oriented example of such co-ordinated efforts leading to robust success than the formation, expansion, and continued organized efforts of the Fantasy Sport Trade Association (FSTA). Founded in 1999, the FSTA was created to "provide a forum for interaction between hundreds of existing and emerging companies in a unique and growing fantasy sports industry" (Fantasy Sport Trade Association, 2014c, para. 1). This organization serves "the small, the large, the entrepreneurs, and the corporations" and provides networking and learning opportunities for "the visionaries, innovators, investors, advertisers, and sponsors that would like to network and learn more about the exciting fantasy sports industry" (para. 1). The fantasy sport industry has experienced several surges in participation (and is arguably experiencing another at the time of this writing), yet the mainstreaming of the Internet in the mid-1990s resulted in fantasy sport league migration—moving from using pens, paper, newspaper, and often snail-mail services to online league management, drafts, and statistical analysis. This essay will explore the conception, growth, threats, and opportunities related to the role of the FSTA within the multi-faceted fantasy sport industry, now boasting 56.8 million North American participants (Fantasy Sport Trade Association, 2015). It will utilize a series of interviews with FSTA professionals and board members to explore how the FSTA has organized a synergistic industry in place of a scattershot previous approach in which each part of the fantasy industry was an individual pioneer without focus or network.

## CONCEPTION AND GROWTH

### Beginnings

Conceived in 1997 and then informally meeting for the first time in 1998, the FSTA was born in Minneapolis, Minnesota, after a series of successful consumer-based functions at prominent locations ranging from the Mall of America to the Metrodome. Fanball founder and current FSTA president, Paul Charchian, notes the formation of the organization was an overt expression that the industry had arrived because they came to a collective "realization that we were big enough to have the need to speak as an industry" (personal communication, January 2013). The timing for such a formation of an organization was ideal, as mainstream fantasy online entities were forming, including Rotowire (then named Rotonews) in 1997 and Rotoworld in 1998. Rotowire founder Peter Schoenke summarizes the rapid growth of his own organization by noting: "About two years after we did it, we were the eighth-biggest sports site on the Internet; we were bigger than NBA.com. We couldn't keep the servers up. It was the rare Internet success story" (personal communication, January 2013).

Coupled with the information-based start-ups were the mainstream league management systems, each offering slightly different models ranging from free entries (e.g., Yahoo!) to structures requiring league origination fees (e.g., ESPN, CBS Sports). All needed a place to meet, share ideas, and jointly offer a strategized, unified voice. The emphasis seemed to be less on attaining business from other competitors in the industry and more on growing the size of the fantasy sport pie. Leaders in the FSTA felt that their current number of participants (roughly fifteen million) could be doubled or more in the coming years, leading to the focus on making the product less niche and more mainstream.

### Development

For obvious reasons, the evolution of the FSTA parallels overall fantasy industry development. With that, garnering the collective trust of administrators, decision-makers, and external stakeholders to understand the impact of fantasy was difficult. With this in mind, Charchian noted the need to combat certain preconceived images, such as countering "a certain social misconception that we are nerds who grew up playing *Dungeons and Dragons*" (Charchian, personal communication, January 2013). The FSTA needed to add credibility. In addition, organizations sought to ascertain the direction and administrative willingness over pursuing fantasy sport. When asked about who and how to reach audiences at ESPN, senior fantasy analyst Matthew Berry agreed that his goals were two-fold: (a) to reach the people that have an interest in fantasy and provide analysis and information on "how they can best win their fantasy leagues" (personal communication, January 2013) *and* (b) provide commentary that can be viewed by mass sport fans in a palatable way. He adds,

> The main points of resistance were—and to this day remain somewhat—is the belief that it's just a game. . . . I think that there was a failure on the part of some of the people that were in decision making roles--not just at ESPN, but just across the board. . . . There was a failure to recognize how passionate, and how large the fan base was (Berry, personal communication, January 2013).

In the same ways Berry attempted to straddle the line between serving highly-identified, already-established niche hobbyists while also offering mass appeal, others involved with FSTA had and were also trying to define their role in fantasy. *USA Today's* Steve Gardner and Howard Kamen elaborated on this perception problem. Gardner states:

> When *Baseball Weekly* was launched [in the 1990s], [USA Today executives] knew at the time that fantasy was one of the main reasons that people were buying it. But, fantasy was a dirty word, and if you said *fantasy*, you had already turned off 80 percent of your potential audience. So many of the things that were written, if you went back and looked at them now, you could see, playing time battles, pitching rotations, and things like that. A lot of injuries—a lot of those things were written to where you can get some serious fantasy information from this, but to label it fantasy was taboo. It was a big step to actually have a fantasy column (Gardner, personal communication, January 2013).

Kamen adds, "I really think what kind of happened with *USA Today* is that we collectively didn't realize the potential there for fantasy . . . and quite frankly we got passed there" (Kamen, personal communication, January 2013). He continues,

> There just was not an understanding by the management teams that this was something that could be a moneymaker. It was seen as "Oh, it's a little niche

thing that a few geeky guys are playing and that sort of thing." . . . I wrote this memo back in 1997 talking about "We need to be doing this and this and this with fantasy sports" . . . and nothing ever came of it. Slowly, we were able to get some content back into the paper, which turned into kind of a weekly NFL column (Kamen, personal communication, January 2013).

Charchian spoke of other struggles for legitimacy for the FSTA and members. For instance, credit card companies and banks refused to work with fantasy-oriented companies because of the misconception of the word *fantasy* and what the activity actually involved. Initially, the aim appeared to be marketing fantasy sport without using the word "fantasy," undoubtedly a difficult prospect.

## Mainstream Momentum

Over the course of a few short years, the FSTA and industry professionals acknowledged an exciting shift within mainstream sport: a momentum was building. Assisting in this shift were the efforts of people trying to make fantasy-related material more mainstream. Arguably the most visible fantasy sport media member in the world, Matthew Berry recounts trying to get fantasy content in a *SportsCenter* episode for the Worldwide Leader of Sports, ESPN.

> They've got to fit an entire day's worth of sports into forty minutes [once commercial breaks are removed from the equation]. I'm sitting there knocking on a producer's door and saying you've got to do more fantasy, and right after me it's the NASCAR guy saying you've got to do more NASCAR, and it's the soccer guy saying you've got to do more soccer. Then it's somebody from *30 for 30* saying, "We've got this great *30 for 30* coming up tomorrow. Can you do a minute-long segment from that?" They've got a million people knocking on their door saying, "Hey, my thing's important, too." It gets challenging (Berry, personal communication, January 2013).

Brandon Funston and Brad Evans of Yahoo! Sports, also discuss similar issues of promotion regarding website promotion within a multi-layered platform with many oft-conflicting informational interests. A crucial aspect of what they do involves the Yahoo! web presence and the importance of getting sport content or even fantasy-specific coverage on that front page as that significantly escalates web traffic. Funston states, "Yahoo.com's front page is a huge piece of real estate. It's one of the most visited sites on the Internet on a daily basis" (Funston, personal communication, January

2013). He continues to discuss the importance of writing "something that is unique, because they're always looking for unique spins" (B. Funston, personal communication, January 2013). Evans adds, "That's when we've gained our most traffic—whatever is in-season. When the NFL got revved up late this year, we made a huge push with front-page promotion" (Evans, personal communication, January 2013). Having data and other networks established through the FSTA was essential in these types of negotiations, establishing that fantasy sport was rapidly becoming a media game-changer.

In yet another example of trying to mainstream fantasy content, Jim Bernard of FOX Sports Interactive discusses how something as simple as altering the bottom-line scroll or halftime scores was a serious point of negotiation, because of the growth of the fantasy industry. He recalls some debates in the mid-2000s:

> I remember [the graphic designers] were just going to put just scores [in the scroll at the bottom of the screen]. And, we were like, "No, you can't. These guys care. You've got to say who scored that touchdown." Certain times, the graphics do have it, certain times they don't. The fantasy guy needs his info. So, we like to keep pushing it forward. You'll see in the halftime shows . . . they definitely have bullet points that are exactly directed to the fantasy guy. It's there (Bernard, personal communication, January 2013).

The fantasy sport industry also was a key advocate for the importance of radio. In 2010, SiriusXM announced it was launching a twenty-four-hour/seven day a week satellite radio station devoted entirely to fantasy sport. SiriusXM senior vice president of Programming, Steve Cohen, recounts the inception of this station.

> When we launched Sirius NFL Radio [in 2005], we launched a Friday night fantasy football show hosted by Adam Caplan and John Hanson. The show was a big hit on the channel. When the opportunity came for me to convince the folks here to launch a fantasy sport channel, I had quite a bit of documented research that I was able to bring to that meeting to convince them to allow us to launch this channel. So, we launched the [fantasy-exclusive] channel in the summer of 2010 (Cohen, personal communication, February 2013).

After the first two years filled with celebrity drafts, remote broadcasting from FSTA events, and steady listener participation and overall interest, SiriusXM's Fantasy Sports Radio became one of the most popular sports stations on the vast list of satellite radio offerings, receiving nearly 28,000 calls per day (Cohen, personal communication, February 2013).

The FSTA was born in the late 1990s, but grew into a group of organized individuals in those early advocacy years at the turn of the century. The FSTA was devoted to seeing the industry grow, prosper, and advance into the future with protection of the gains they had already secured and fresh ideas on how to expand the number of offerings and number of people interested in participating. As illustrated, there were problems with definition of the industry and misconceptions about the activity, and the FSTA assisted with a response to such claims, believing that with proper research, message, strategy, networking, and unification, fantasy sport play could move beyond stereotyped notions of lonely, anti-social males participating from their parent's basement. The strategy appeared to be less about being combative and instead to utilize growth data to advocate for more coverage and mainstream exposure, which only made the data more compelling for executives. The FSTA not only added the framework and credibility needed, but has continued to have a major influence on the industry as a whole to those currently working in it and those desiring to become a part of it.

## CURRENT INFLUENCE OF THE FSTA

The FSTA is influential in many different ways. From hosting industry meetings and awarding industry excellence, to assisting with the perception of newly-established daily leagues and providing research reports, the FSTA provides opportunities for networking, knowledge gathering, and support for a strong and vibrant future in the fantasy industry. The following paragraphs will outline several of the influential activities of the FSTA.

### Association Meetings

Following the first informal meeting in 1998, the FSTA held its first official conference in 1999. Since then, industry professionals have been meeting every year for the FSTA Winter Conference. In 2000 and 2001, the demand for more opportunities to share information and network resulted in the implementation of doubling the opportunities to meet by offering a winter and summer conference. Such conferences provide an opportunity for industry professionals to be in one place to share ideas, learn about innovative technological advancements, prepare for potential threats to the industry (e.g., league lockouts/work stoppages, gambling, or other legislation), and network with people with unique skills to help their part of the industry flourish.

Conference agendas are typically predominantly occupied by experts giving insight to the fantasy professional, whether that involves insight about overall fan or media trends or overarching psychological information about the nature of human behavior. This may include, but is not limited to, legal specialists, research professionals (industry and academic), professional and college sport administrators, technology innovators, and media professionals. These presentations are designed to stay current in a multi-pronged media reality to be leaders rather than followers for trends and advancements in technology and sport. Some of the most recent issues, having major industry consequences, dealt with (a) the potential lockout of National Football League (NFL) players and management and (b) the explosion of daily and weekly fantasy football sites, offering clarification and assurance that those organizations did not constitute gambling or other impermissible activities. Such specific topics—given their serious implications to the industry as a whole—are given priority attention at the annual conferences to assure everyone has the same mind-set, messaging, and overarching strategy moving forward.

## Elevator Pitch

One of the major ways the FSTA aids in shaping the industry is through the facilitation of an "elevator pitch" competition, which takes place during each of the annual conferences. Within this structure, fantasy-minded entrepreneurs are granted a period of time (usually between three to four minutes) to explain and pitch their company, product, or idea. Their audience consists of over 100 of the most influential people in the industry voting on the idea or concept that has the most promise. A prize is granted to the winner, but the true award is that the seeds have been planted for network connections from all participants. This is one of the most influential areas hosted by the FSTA because it gives fledgling organizations an opportunity to be heard in a crowded room of major players. For instance, several years ago, daily leagues were a new "elevator pitch;" they are now an established portion of the fantasy sports industry. These organizations are usually not able to contact and pitch their ideas to entities such as ESPN, FOX Sports, Rotoworld, or Yahoo!. However, with this type of session, they have an opportunity to share new ideas that are innovative, forward-thinking, and consumer-oriented. There is an inherent nature of extroversion involved in participating in the elevator pitch and that provides a vehicle for discussion and collaboration in the hours—and even years—to come.

## Research

One of the earliest and most resourceful areas the FSTA implemented, in its infancy as a trade organization, involved industry research. FSTA president, Paul Charchian, states that when it came to the industry and the people that were participating, "nobody knew" the depth and breadth of the participants within it (Charchian, personal communication, January 2013). By marshaling everything from college professors to major research collaboratives such as IPSOS, the FSTA was able to shape the conversation about the industry impact: "Through the mid-2000s, the only data that was out there was the data that we generated ourselves" (Charchian, personal communication, January 2013). Within this time frame, the academic community gained interest in fantasy sport and its impact on media and sport environments. As Charchian states:

> Research that's being done at the academic level is really, really detailed and you apply all kinds of scientific data mining that we don't necessarily have or understand ourselves. . . . That's really allowed us to go tap into all these other areas of research that we wouldn't necessarily have the means, interest, or capability to do (Charchian, personal communication, January 2013).

With access to third-party industry data and academic investigations, Charchian notes a serendipitous situation where the two types of experts can create knowledge bases that create a clearer view of the industry.

From industry newsletters and website communication to conference presentations and data collection, the commitment to research has always been evident within the overarching structure of the FSTA. On its website, research statistics outline industry demographics, including both standard participant information (e.g., age, sex, race, education, marital status) and also fantasy-specific profiles (e.g., number of sports per year, number of leagues per year, fantasy news consumption, use of mobile devices, daily games, and entry fees). In addition, purchasable research reports are available, focusing on areas of participation, non-participation, technology usage, demographic segmentation, and other consumptive behaviors.

## Fantasy Sport Writers Association

Another way the FSTA is having an impact on the fantasy sport industry is through its association with the Fantasy Sport Writers Association (FSWA), an organization designed to be a "voice for writers in the arena of fantasy sports . . . [and] promote and acknowledge the hard work and dedication shown by fantasy sports writers throughout the industry" (Fantasy Sport Writers Association, 2014). With many of the same consumers, association members, and overall stakeholders, the FSTA and FSWA are a great combination. The FSTA conferences provide meeting facilities and a stage to highlight the FSWA via the recognition of writing award winners. Such awards impact the industry via promoting many of the media companies that: (a) host fantasy games, (b) create fantasy content in writing, audio, or video, and (c) house fantasy experts. In turn, this creates more buzz, excitement, and consumption of fantasy content.

### Fantasy Sports Hall of Fame

Influencing the fantasy sport industry does not always necessitate supporting the present while preparing for the future; it can also include recognizing the past. With its first inductees in 2001, the FSTA created the Fantasy Sports Hall of Fame. The purpose is simply to "honor those individuals whose contributions have helped shape the fantasy sports industry" (Fantasy Sport Trade Association, 2014b, para. 1). The current criterion to be eligible for induction requires nominees to have been actively participating in the fantasy sport industry for a minimum of ten years and be considered as a "founder of the fantasy sports movement" (Fantasy Sport Trade Association, 2014a, para. 2). The importance of recognizing these people is not only to honor them, as they paved the way for current professionals in the field, but also to learn and hear about their experience starting in the industry. Hearing just one acceptance speech or reading a nomination biography about the struggles, difficulties, and strategies involved in working within the industry at its foundation can and has motivated many others in their own present endeavors. Knowing this, the FSTA honors not only the Fantasy Sports Hall of Fame inductees during a conference dinner, but they also allow for time to honor the FSWA Hall of Fame honorees. Presenting and accepting Hall of Fame honors in this type of setting amplifies the learning potential from all those that came before.

## POTENTIAL PITFALLS

Fairly consistently, three major pitfalls were identified by the FSTA, all of which have had considerable impact not just on growth, but also on basic viability of the industry. Those issues to explore and overcome consisted of: (a) beliefs that fantasy sport participation constituted gambling, (b) concerns over who owns the rights to statistics generated by professional sports league games, and (c) hindrances involved within any potential league stoppage through either strike or lockout (see also chapter 13, this volume).

## Gambling Ties

Pertaining to the first issue, the potential tie to gambling, correlates are known; causation is not. For instance, one decade ago, the amount wagered on sports each year was $380 billion (Levinson, 2006). Money has been found to be an incentive for playing fantasy sport (see Dwyer & Kim, 2011), yet does not appear to be a primary incentive (Billings & Ruihley, 2014). Radio has a terminology known as the "P1 listener," defined as the station a fan of radio spends its majority of the time consuming. For sports media, fantasy participants are the television broadcast equivalent of the "P1 watcher," consuming triple the media as a non-participating sports fan (Enoch, 2011) while money is presumed to be a factor for any form of overall consumption of products such as NFL games (see Drayer, Shapiro, Dwyer, Morse, & White, 2010).

Thus, inevitably, there is a notion of financial gain or loss percolating within overall sport consumption (see Lee, Kwak, Lim, Pederson, & Miloch, 2011) that likely seeps into motivations for play. Those overlapping circles can lead to conclusions that fantasy sport constitutes organized gambling (Moorman, 2008). The presence of high-stakes fantasy leagues seemingly confirms money can be a primary factor at least at the most competitive levels. As a high-stakes player indicated to Billings and Ruihley (2014): "It's all about the money for me. If anyone told you different, it's about the money. When you're playing these leagues for this deal, it's all about the money" (p. 99).

Thus, the FSTA had to make a case to state and federal courts that fantasy sport was primarily a game of skill rather than luck. Bernhard and Earle (2005) contend, "if we broadly define gambling as an activity that risks something of value (substantial amounts of money) on an event whose outcome is underdetermined (such as whims of a professional baseball season), fantasy [sport] clearly qualifies" (p. 29). Thus, the FSTA had to counter with logic and evidence. One strategy was to marginalize those motivated by money to depict them as outliers, a fairly sound strategy given that 90 percent of participants do so for $50 or less per league. Paul Charchian claims:

> You're dealing with probably in the neighborhood of a 1000th or a 10,000th. They're playing for only one reason: cash. They're playing with strangers, so

it's not camaraderie. There's so much money involved, it's not because they want to go to a draft party or something (Charchian, personal communication, January 2013).

Another strategy was to argue for the skills involved in playing. As Lenny Pappano (FSTA member and founder of a high stakes league) argued:

What I would say in front of judge is: "All right, if you think this is gambling, we'll take a cheat sheet, put it up on a wall. I'll put down my $1,000, you put down your $1,000. You throw darts and I'll pick players and we'll see who wins" (Pappano, personal communication, September 2013).

Ultimately, several rulings in different states, most notably Maryland in 2012 found that fantasy sports are not gambling because the ratio of skill to luck favored the experienced participant (Katz, 2012).

## Statistical Ownership

Given the rapidly growing number of people participating in fantasy sport, the FSTA has had to advocate for one core principle to be able to offer games with real-time scoring and league management: The statistics generated from the games are free and open to whoever wishes to use them without copyright. FSTA board member Howard Kamen notes the "precedent setting" first case of *NBA v. Motorola and STATS, Inc.*, that was settled in 1997. The case was ultimately decided at the Second Circuit Court of Appeals, arguing in favor of sharing of sports statistics in a plentitude of media platforms (Cornell Law Copyright Cases, 1997). However, the FSTA still needed to advocate in many courtrooms, arguing as a cohesive unit.

The second seminal case was a 2006 lawsuit filed by CBC Distribution and Marketing, Inc. (St. Louis, Missouri) against Major League Baseball (MLB). MLB denied a licensing agreement with CBC, believing that the entirety of the numbers arising from MLB games were exclusively theirs. Moreover, MLB claimed that fantasy sport leagues impinged upon player rights (Greenhouse, 2008). With aid from the FSTA, the court sided with CBC (Biskupic, 2008).

Despite winning two landmark cases, leagues continued to fight back, seeking revenue from the industry. Three years later, Yahoo! sued the NFL over whether they needed to pay for the rights to publish statistics generated from games (Ross, 2009). Again, courts sided with the FSTA. Thus, the FSTA is batting 1.000 in legal cases, yet remains vigilant because of the devastating effect a ruling against them would have in regard to the use of statistics. Most current lawsuits seem to have subsided because leagues were beginning to tie their increased revenues to increased fantasy play. As FSTA member Matthew Berry postulates: "Getting more people to play it and referencing it as something that everyone does helped move it more into the mainstream" (Berry, personal communication, January 2013).

## League Work Stoppages

The final major challenge to the growth of the FSTA is one they have little to no control over: the potential for a work stoppage for a major league, which would halt all fantasy league participation as well. At the time of this writing, no league has a collective bargaining agreement that is about to expire, leading the FSTA to feel positive about prospects for the immediate future, while always maintaining contingency plans that involve growth of ancillary fantasy sports (NASCAR, golf, hockey, etc.) Still, the FSTA seemingly feels good about long-term prospects even if a work stoppage occurred, mostly because the people participating in fantasy sport are core sports fans. As Kamen articulates:

> You cannot question the loyalty of the fantasy sport player. So, while there could be bumps in the road, it's not something that could wipe out the industry. Loyal fans will be back en masse from the start and the casual fan base will eventually come back, too (Kamen, personal communication, January 2013).

## GROWTH OPPORTUNITIES

One major limitation for growth of fantasy sport participation has been the role of nationalized sport and the difficulty of including international sport (also see chapter 3, this volume). While fantasy sport is played across the globe ranging from millions of fantasy soccer participants in the United Kingdom to fantasy cricket in India to fantasy horse racing in China and Australia (Mactarggart, 2008; Pfanner, 2004), most fantasy sport leagues are specific to one (perhaps two) countries and fail to garner truly startling numbers of participants found in North America. Part of these problems stem from language barriers, yet other issues impede progress in this regard, such as the lack of developed statistical mechanisms for some games (soccer has far fewer statistics generated than baseball, for instance), as well as the difficulty of watching one's fantasy players in action (time zone gaps can cause very bleary-eyed fantasy sports fans). Still, as Paul Charchian notes: "They're just as passionate about their sports [in other nations], if not more, than we are here in America and so many of the same things that we enjoy about fantasy sports could work on fantasy soccer in Argentina" (Charchian, personal communication, January 2013).

Another area of growth that is already occurring involves the recent escalation of daily league offerings, where people redraft a new team for a single day of competition. As Yahoo! senior writer and FSTA member Andy Behrens argues, "Play-to-play, quarter-to-quarter, moment-to-moment fantasy opportunities are out there now" (Behrens, personal communication, January 2013). Such leagues also represent a potential challenge for the FSTA, as a considerable amount of money is being wagered on sites such as FanDuel, which was already generating millions of profits based on thousands of daily players in 2012 (King, 2012). Instead of paying $20 for a league entry fee that encompasses several months, daily leagues can command such dollars on a daily basis, exponentially increasing profits for fantasy companies. However, such leagues also increase the dimension of luck at the expense of skill, as there are fewer repetitions in which one's superior knowledge can lead to fantasy victories.

Behrens notes that traditional season long leagues are less likely to garner heavy gambling interest than daily leagues are because of the immediacy of winning. He claims:

> All of my longtime fantasy leagues—nobody in them is a hard-core gambler. Nobody's betting games each weekend. I'm not betting games each weekend. I've known some guys with gambling problems, and they were not the fantasy audience. They had no interest. They were all about winning back their $1,500 *today*" (Behrens, personal communication, January 2013).

A final area of potential expansion and opportunity for the FSTA is present in the increased focus on mobile and second screen technologies. It could be argued that fantasy sport makes people less likely to attend games in person, as people are more interested in consuming a plethora of games that all have fantasy implications. However, attempts are being made to counter that problem, ranging from many new applications that allow for in-stadium wagers and fantasy bets along with the ability to consume fantasy sport while in the stadium, whether that is a Yahoo!-sponsored fantasy football lounge at San Francisco's new Levi's Stadium (Rosenberg, 2013) or an air-conditioned fantasy football area at Jacksonville's EverBank Field (Gardner, 2013). Technology has always seemed to aid the future of fantasy sport participation, and the FSTA continues to facilitate these advancements.

## CONCLUSION

This essay has outlined the manner in which the FSTA has facilitated tremendous growth. The role of the FSTA is to serve a wide-range of fantasy stakeholders, which sometimes can be conflicting, but most often are overlapping in a potentially synergistic fashion. Representing nearly 200 member companies, the FSTA is responsible for the current state and future progression of the fantasy sport industry, requiring prioritization, protection, and promotion. With regards to priority, the FSTA must place emphasis on current issues, trends, and problems facing the industry. Aforementioned examples included the rise of daily/weekly games and a possible player/management strike in major sports leagues, most notably the NFL. The FSTA brought those issues to the forefront at the association's conferences and aligned the appropriate experts and research to inform FSTA members of the severity of these issues. Assigning such priorities assures FSTA members that these issues are real, they have consequences, and if not prepared for or addressed, significant damage can result.

In a similar vein, the FSTA protects the industry. As outlined in the portion of this chapter dedicated to pitfalls, the daily/weekly fantasy leagues have the potential to skew toward a perception of fantasy being equated to gambling. The FSTA quickly ceased any language, publication materials, and other ideas that might falsely cause people to make such associations. In fact, the FSTA created a Daily Gaming Committee responsible for creating standards and policies for daily game companies. This protection not only outlines good business practice in the fantasy field, but also safeguards the entire industry from potentially industry-stifling legislation.

Promotion arises in a variety of ways. First, the FSTA has and continues to promote the activity and stakeholders surrounding it. From fantasy gaming hosts, writers, and media members, to technology innovators and graphic designers, the FSTA has been at the forefront of support for the activity. Second, the FSTA promotes its own people and products from within. Between conferences, newsletters, membership information access, and website information, the FSTA is promoting internally, allowing members to act as a community and, in some cases, not as competitors but rather as collaborators. Lastly, the FSTA promotes research. Professional industrial research, as well as academic research are highlighted and shared with fantasy professionals, highlighting true commitment to understanding the industry from a variety of angles while sharing the information to integrate knowledge into everyday practice.

This chapter adopts a tone that some could rightly characterize as positive and supportive. Without question, the FSTA has had occasional missteps in its attempts to achieve such lofty objectives. However, when considering this organization started as a group meeting in a shopping mall at the turn of the century and is now the central mouthpiece and networking structure for an industry involving 56.8 million participants, it is fair to characterize their work as successful. Coming years will likely involve major obstacles for fantasy sport, whether involving increasingly complex media platform structures or legislation that alters the role of finances within fantasy sport participation. Regardless of the issue, the FSTA is likely to be a primary figure in how these issues are negotiated and assembled for mass fantasy consumption.

## REFERENCES

Bernhard, B. J., & Earle, V. H. (2005). Gambling in a fantasy world: An exploratory study of rotisserie baseball games. *UNLV Gaming Research & Review Journal*, 9, 29–42.

Billings, A. C., & Ruihley, B. J. (2014). *The fantasy sport industry: Games within games*. London: Routledge.

Biskupic, J. (2008, June 3). Judges let stand fantasy use of stats. *USA Today*, p. 4C.

Cornell Law Copyright Cases (1997). NBA vs. Motorola and STATS, Inc. Retrieved at: http://www.law.cornell.edu/copyright/cases/105_F3d_841.htm.

Drayer, J., Shapiro, S., Dwyer, B., Morse, A., & White, J. (2010). The effects of fantasy football participation on NFL consumption: A qualitative analysis. *Sport Management Review, 13*, 129–141.

Dwyer, B., & Kim, Y. (2011). For love or money: Developing and validating a motivational scale for fantasy sport participation. *Journal of Sport Management, 25*, 70–85.

Enoch, G. (2011, October 3). Life stages of the sports fan. Lecture conducted from the University of Alabama, Tuscaloosa, AL.

Fantasy Sport Trade Association. (2014a). Fantasy sports hall of fame nomination and election procedures. Retrieved from http://www.fsta.org/?page=HOFProcess.

Fantasy Sport Trade Association. (2014b). Hall of fame. Retrieved from http://www.fsta.org/?page=HallofFame.

Fantasy Sport Trade Association. (2014c). What is the FSTA? Retrieved from http://www.fsta.org/?page=WhatisFSTA.

Fantasy Sports Trade Association (2015). Industry demographics. Retrieved from http://fsta.org/research/industry-demographics

Fantasy Sport Writers Association. (2014). Home page. Retrieved from http://www.fswa.org.

Gardner, S. (2013, July 27). Jaguars setting up in-stadium fantasy football lounge. *USA Today*. Retrieved at: http://www.usatoday.com/story/sports/fantasy/2013/07/02/jaguars-fantasy-football-lounge/2484375/

Greenhouse, L. (2008, June 3). No ruling means no change for fantasy baseball leagues. *New York Times*, p. 4.

Katz, D. (2012, October 3). New fantasy football law legalizes fantasy league prizes. Retrieved at: http://blogs.findlaw.com/tarnished_twenty/2012/10/new-fantasy -football-law-legalizes-fantasy-league-prizes.html

King, B. (2012, Feb. 6). Fan duel delivers daily dose of fantasy games. *Sports Business Daily*. Retrieved at: http://www.sportsbusinessdaily.com/Journal/Is sues/2012/02/06/In-Depth/FanDuel.aspx

Lee, W. Y., Kwak, D., Lim, C., Pederson, P., & Miloch, K. (2010). Effects of personality and gender on fantasy sports game participation: The moderating role of perceived knowledge. *Journal of Gambling Studies, 27*, 427–441.

Levinson, M. (2006). Sure bet: Why New Jersey would benefit by legalized sports wagering. *Sports Lawyers Journal, 13*, 143–178.

Mactaggart, G. (2008, September 12). Fantasy rides again. *Northern Territory News* (Australia), p. 26.

Moorman, A. M. (2008). Fantasy sports league challenged as illegal gambling. *Sport Marketing Quarterly, 17*, 232–234.

Pfanner, E. (2004, Oct. 30). Leagues may be fantasy, but revenue isn't; Sports fans worldwide flock to online games. *International Herald Tribune*, p. 13.

Rosenberg, M. (2013, June 17). 49ers, Yahoo team up for social media and fantasy football deal at new stadium. *San Jose Mercury News*. Retrieved at: http://www .mercurynews.com/ci_23478401/49ers-yahoo-team-up-social-media-and-fantasy

Ross, J. (2009, June 4). Who owns major league stats? Yahoo! sues NFL Players Association to get free access to players' statistics for the fantasy football leagues it runs on the Internet. *Minneapolis Star Tribune*, p. 1B.

**15**

# DAILY FANTASY SPORTS (DFS)

The Future of Fantasy Games

*Renee Miller*

This chapter deals with a relatively new form of fantasy sports—Daily Fantasy Sports (DFS). As the name suggests, DFS is a way to play fantasy sports with no long-term commitment. Players can draft a new fantasy team every day/week. Contests are run by websites specializing in daily games and may include anywhere from 2-500,000+ participants. There are several different options for contests, and nearly every major sport can be played in a daily format: NFL, NBA, MLB, PGA, NHL, European soccer, NASCAR racing, college football, and college basketball. Contest entry fees range from free to around $1,000, and prizes can go up to $2,000,000. The popularity and rapid growth of DFS has garnered much interest among season long fantasy players, the legal system, and potential investors.

## DIFFERENCES BETWEEN DFS AND SEASON LONG FANTASY GAMES

The biggest difference that DFS brings is the ability for players to start seasons over when something bad happens to their team. In season long fantasy leagues, the team that players draft is largely the team they are stuck with for the duration of the season. Of course, players can be added/dropped and traded to change the composition to some extent, but if the star point guard or running back gets hurt in Week 2, players will have a very hard time recouping value over the rest of the season. With DFS, if a player gets hurt, it only costs the squad for that one day or week. Players start anew when the next games start.

In season long fantasy, players compete against the same league opponent's week after week, (and year after year, for many of us). This structure brings a sense of camaraderie, familiarity, and bonds with fellow participants. Players get to know league members favorite fantasy players, their style, who they are likely to trade for and when they are likely to make these deals. League members share connections that binds them across seasons. If they are lucky enough to still have live, in-person drafts, it is one of the best days of the year. In DFS, players lose that constancy. Instead, they enter games where they will largely be pitted against strangers. Even if they know some opponents, the field will change from game to game, day to day, and sport to sport. This is both good and bad, as the chapter will discuss later.

Third, if players compete in season-long fantasy sports for money or prizes, they have to make it through long, challenging, bouts to claim prizes. Players need more high performance weeks than subpar performance weeks in a head-to-head style league to make the playoffs, and then they need to be at the top of their game to beat the "best of the best" to win the league. In DFS, prizes are paid out each day or week. Players can have a great week and win all the contests they entered and be immediately rewarded. Players also can have an off week and still receive immediate cash payouts in some of the contests. The flip side is that if players do have a terrible night, the money they invested in the contest is gone, and there is no chance to make it up with future performances. Strategies top players use to mitigate these losses will be discussed later.

## LEGAL ISSUES

Given that a great deal of money is at stake in DFS, one of the first things people wonder is how it can be legal. In fact, DFS has had its day in court and has been ruled a skill game, not gambling (https://www.govtrack.us/congress/bills/109/hr4411). Although, DFS falls under the 2006 Unlawful Internet Gambling Enforcement Act (UIGEA), it received an exemption because it is considered a game of skill. While any fantasy sport has an element of luck associated with it, the fact that the same players win so consistently in daily fantasy sports supports the idea that is the skill and knowledge of the participants that is driving win rates, rather than mere luck.

In order for DFS to be legal, several conditions must be met, according to H.R. 4411, passed by the 109th US House of Representatives (Internet Gambling Prohibition and Enforcement Act, 2006). First, at least two actual independent sporting events must be included in the gaming slate. Second, the prize pool must be specified ahead of time and not changed once registration for games has commenced (also see chapter 13, this volume).

It is not hard to meet the first criterion, except during the playoffs. In this case, a single "daily" contest may span two days to capture at least two different real games. It also means that sites can create their own clever gaming slates, such as only the Monday and Thursday Night Football games or only the 1:00 p.m. EST Sunday football games. Not all the games being played need to be included in the fantasy slate in DFS. The second criterion applies mainly to contests that are guaranteed to run by the site (see next section for contest descriptions). If the site guarantees a contest, it must pay out the prizes specified, even if the contest does not fill to capacity. In other words, the promised prizes cannot be changed for any reason after a contest is offered. Non-guaranteed games may be cancelled if they do not reach capacity.

Despite the passing of the UIGEA, residents of the states of Arizona, Iowa, Louisiana, Montana, and Washington are prohibited from playing fantasy sports such as DFS for money, though they can play in free contests. At the time of this writing, legislation is under consideration in Washington and Iowa to reverse this interpretation of the law.

## GAMES AND STRATEGIES

### Games

Contests offered by DFS sites can be broadly divided into tournaments and "cash" games. Tournaments are typically large field games with a top-heavy payout structure. They are higher risk, higher reward style games. Often, these games are guaranteed by the site to run and payout the top 10–15 percent of the entrants even if they do not fill up. When this is the case, they are known as guaranteed prize pools (GPPs). The buy in to participate can run from $1 to over $1,000, with prizes now routinely equaling $1,000,000 for the biggest contests. Cash games are those in which half of the participants will be paid. They range from head-to-head contests with two entrants to thousands of entrants who will be paid if they finish in the top 50 percent. With such good odds, this is where many regular and even professional DFS players put most of their money.

Daily fantasy sports sites are increasingly running exclusive live-event, large prize pool tournaments for a select few players that qualify by winning preliminary games. Examples of recent live events include those held at the Playboy mansion in Los Angeles, California; Las Vegas, Nevada; and Atlantis, Bahamas. Upcoming venues include Newport Beach, California and Miami, Florida. Qualifiers for these big tournaments range from low cost, high volume entries to high cost, low volume entries. Usually, only the top finisher wins entry to the big live tournament via a qualifier, but occasionally multiple seats are awarded in a single game. Qualifiers may run throughout the season, to build excitement and fill the finale slowly, while the live main event takes place toward the end of the sport's season.

In addition to direct qualifiers, sites also run satellite tournaments for entry tickets to qualifier games. Thus, I could enter a $1 satellite contest with thirty other people. If I came in first place, I would win a ticket to a $27 qualifier. If I won that contest, playing against perhaps 2,800 other entries, I would win a seat at the live event and an all-expenses paid trip to the location to compete for $1,000,000. Qualifiers represent the lowest rate of return in DFS—in other words they are the hardest to win. They offer exciting prizes though, so they are quite popular games.

## Strategies

The strategy for winning cash games differs from that used to win GPPs and larger tournaments. When the odds are good, it makes sense to play the most obvious highly skilled athletes. The goal is to maximize the fantasy score while maintaining a very safe floor. When the odds are against a DFS player, she/he has to be more flexible. It makes more sense to play more volatile players, those that either strike out four times or hit two homeruns, score two touchdowns or gain only sixteen yards, and can go on a three point shooting rampage at any time. GPP tournament lineups are typically more unique for this reason; searching out those volatile characteristics makes participants draw from a different pool of athletes than they would look at for cash games.

When DFS players face many opponents under conditions where only a few can be paid, it also makes sense to avoid players likely to be widely owned. This is known as being contrarian and is necessary in big GPPs and qualifiers. If a low-owned player does have a career night, the participant will be one of the few to benefit. If a highly owned player scores a ton of fantasy points, all players' lineups rise by the same amount. As previously mentioned, cash games have fairly good odds, players only need to beat 50 percent of the opponents to win double the entry fee (minus the site fee, or rake). To give participants the best chance to do just that, it makes sense to draw from a safe player pool, one where participants know what they are getting: a certain number of minutes, carries, or batting average that predicts a high scoring game.

## FACTORS USED IN DFS ROSTER CONSTRUCTION

Professional DFS players spend much of their time doing research about available players. For that matter, casual players do too! It's critical to track past performance across all the relevant statistics that contribute to overall fantasy score, monitor trends in usage, and evaluate individual matchups on a nightly basis. The ruling of fantasy sports as a skill game was no accident. It takes a wealth of knowledge, discipline, and hard work to win over time. Factors to research include the projected game score, team totals, defensive ranking against each position, player game logs and historical production and usage to name just a few. Participants will roster players much as they do for seasonal leagues, with some site to site variation. For example, participants may have one to two quarterbacks, two running backs, two to three wide receivers, tight ends, and one defense on their football roster, whereas some sites also use kickers or flex positions (an additional roster spot for any skill position player) in their football roster. For baseball, players use the typical nine-man rotation, and for basketball there is a lot of site-to-site variability. Some operate with general guard, forward, and utility designations, while others require strict adherence to established position listings.

After a participant decides who he or she might like to use in his or her roster based on the research that he or she conducted, there is another hurdle to pass: the salary cap. All the major sites impose a salary cap on participants' daily fantasy roster. Participants have to fill the roster while staying within the cap they are allotted. The total amount of the cap varies between the sites, but the player salaries are adjusted accordingly. That is where research will come in handy. Participants' will not be able to afford all the best players so they need to focus on finding value: Who will produce the best for their salary costs? The added element of a salary cap in daily fantasy games leads to much more roster diversification than would be expected by research alone, as it is impossible for participants to use all the best players because they're all expensive. It's also the case that personal preference and even fandom can influence lineup choices. The decision of how to divide the salary cap is the most important one participants make in DFS. Many people, myself included, write regularly on the subject of strategies that might be best for any given MLB/NBA/NHL night or NFL week.

## DAILY FANTASY SPORTS SITES

FanDuel Inc. was founded in 2009 and is the largest site in the industry. Five co-founders formed the idea that has grown to a multi-national corporation led by CEO Nigel Eccles. FanDuel began offering a six figure top prize for the NFL in December 2011. Their first million dollar first prize was won for MLB in August 2013. They now award more than $10,000,000 every week in prizes. FanDuel claims to control 70 percent of the market share and has raised $88 million in capital investments.

DraftKings, Inc was founded in 2012 by Jason Robins, Matt Kalish, and Paul Liberman and has seen the fastest rise in popularity of any DFS company to date. DraftKings brought a more advanced platform to the field, is the site most responsive to player demand for changes in the games, and pushed the envelope by offering a $1 million first prize every week for the NFL in 2014. They have built their reputation on these factors and continue to aggressively expand their reach through an intensive advertising campaign to attract new users. Most recently, DraftKings obtained a license to operate in the United Kingdom and plans to open an office in Europe soon.

DraftDay Inc. was founded in 2011 by Andrew Wiggins and Taylor Caby under the name of CardRunners Gaming Inc. The two brought their professional poker backgrounds to the DFS arena, recognizing correctly that many of the same skills would apply to DFS. From the beginning, DraftDay focused on the user experience, customer service, education and entertainment creating a smaller, but loyal customer base. The company sold to MGT Capital Investments Inc in April of 2014[1] and remains a niche DFS site.

In the contemporary landscape, new start-up DFS sites are appearing regularly. Fantasy Aces and Fantasy Feud are probably the next most popular sites, with newcomers Victiv, Swoopt, SportsTradex, Ballr, Star Fantasy Leagues (who also run season long leagues), and Fantasy Draft (employing a novel multi-level marketing plan to attract new users) aiming to get in on the action.[2] The biggest newcomer is sports giant Yahoo.com, who began offering MLB DFS games in the summer of 2015.

Several of the early sites such as beloved DraftStreet and StarStreet (both bought by DraftKings in 2014) as well as Daily Joust (acquired by MGT in 2013) are no longer running. The landscape continues to evolve, and no one is certain where the ultimate balance between size and number of DFS sites will land.

## THE PLAYER COMMUNITY OF DFS

While no academic research currently exists on DFS play motivations, the same reasons people give for playing fantasy sports (cf. Farquhar & Meeds, 2007; also see chapters, 1, 4, and 10, this volume) are not so different as the ones they give for DFS—the games are fun, players can win money, it makes the games more interesting, and they can keep in touch with friends they would not perhaps otherwise. Although players enter contests on websites and compete against strangers most of the time, the DFS community is very social and friendly.

## CHATS

In the past, the major DFS sites all used to encourage participants to talk to one another about players, salaries, games, and anything else under the sun in the site sponsored chat rooms. Some still have a chat, though major sites like FanDuel eliminated it due to widespread abuse (FanDuel.com, 2014), and DraftKings launched without it. DraftDay maintains within game chats for entrants into a specific contest, which are rarely used. The demise of the DFS chat rooms can be attributed to the abuse of a few insensitive, angry, and outspoken users (see also chapter 5, this volume).

## DFS HELP/ADVICE SITES

The growing popularity of DFS sites like FanDuel and DraftKings has created the demand for supplemental advice and social/community businesses. As much as ESPN and Yahoo! write and produce content geared toward helping the players in their season long leagues succeed several sites exist exclusively to provide DFS advice. Starting with the 2014–15 NBA season, ESPN began to provide content directed specifically at DFS players on FanDuel and DraftKings.

### RotoGrinders

One of the first and largest of the DFS advice sites is RotoGrinders. com—thought to be the most popular. RotoGrinders provides registered users with daily articles on strategic plays for every sport on every DFS site. They have research tools built in to the site, forums for users to discuss (responsibly) any DFS industry related issues, and depending on the season, live TV shows (also viewable on youtube) for multiple sports each day with accompanying chat rooms. RotoGrinders also tracks DFS player performance (with the player's consent) and keeps track of wins and winnings across all the different sites for its Grinder Rankings and ultimately to crown the DFS Tournament Player of the Year. Their Grinders University section aims to help people learn DFS philosophy and good practices in bankroll management and lineup strategy in general. The award winning RotoGrinders podcast, hosted by Dan Back, is the industry standard in DFS news. Beginning with the 2014 NFL season, RotoGrinders partnered with RotoWorld (NBC Universal Inc.), which allowed selected RotoGrinders strategy articles to appear in the Daily Fantasy section of RotoWorld.com.

## Fantasy Insiders

Another social advice site in the industry is Fantasy Insiders Inc, or FI (www.fantasyinsiders.com). FI produces DFS strategy and player advice articles for all of the main DFS sports plus NCAA college football and basketball, and European soccer with "cheat sheets" emailed to subscribers' inboxes daily. They've also used the best projection systems in the business, such as the BAT, designed by Derek Carty for MLB, to develop user-friendly applications that help you create optimal lineups based on the factors the projections feel most accurately predict player performance each day. The lineup optimizer tools require some user input; the exact amount is up to the player. For example, in MLB DFS, the user has to minimally specify a starting pitcher. The optimizer tool will then subtract his salary from the cap and use the athlete projections for that day to recommend the best five combinations of catcher, first base, second base, third base, shortstop, and three outfielders to round out the lineup with the remaining the salary cap. Users can eliminate athletes on cold streaks (defined mathematically by a deviation from their career average performance), weather, and can even exclude certain games completely with a click of a button.

FI hosts a daily fantasy podcast by Dave Loughran and Dan Strafford, and a seasonal live TV show with accompanying chat to further support their subscribers. They recently implemented a free educational feature aimed to teach new DFS players how to have fun and succeed long term in this industry. The multi-media LEARN tab includes webinars, articles, interviews with professional DFS players, and a virtual encyclopedia of DFS.

## DailyRoto

The acquisition of the LuDawgs community site (www.ludawgs.com, which redirects to www.dailyroto.com) by RotoExperts to form the new DailyRoto site joined a DFS "social club" with some of the best daily fantasy advice in the business. They offer incentives and special contests for new players, sell and give out gear, and award entry tickets to various contests run by sites who sponsored them. DailyRoto produces a daily podcast and appears regularly on Sirius/SM radio. They have active member forums and a blog, with information and analysis focused on every major DFS sport. Professional DFS experts Drew Dinkmeyer and Michael Leone, along with others, will continue to provide daily fantasy analysis to subscribers in a setting that enhances the community building and social aspects of DFS.

## Daily Fantasy Bootcamp

Founded by Al Zeidenfeld, Daily Fantasy Bootcamp is a subscription based content site with a twist. In addition to daily articles on a variety of sports, they offer live, in person training seminars for people looking to become better DFS players. Each training session is a single day, with four to five expert presenters speaking on various topics (from important wide receiver characteristics to Milly Maker strategy to bias in decision making (me)). The seminars feature multiple small group breakout sessions for participants to get direct interaction with the speakers and work on building lineups together.

## Fantasy Labs

A collaboration between professional DFS players Peter Jennings, who won a million dollars in DraftKings King of the Beach MLB DFS final in 2014, and Jonathan Bales, author of the Fantasy Football for Smart People series of books, has led to the development of Fantasy Labs. If it sounds experimental, well, it kind of is. Subscribers can adjust the weight of multiple parameters (statistics and contextual factors) in order to generate fantasy point projections for players in the given slate of games (a week of NFL or a night of baseball). They can then use those projections to aid their lineup construction process. The site also offers data driven strategy and advice articles for users.

## DK (DraftKings) Pros

DraftKings itself has embraced the social component of DFS in a unique way that also complements its aggressive advertising campaign. DraftKings Pros is comprised of industry leaders (DFS user names in parentheses): David Kitchen (SocrDave), Peter Jennings (CSURAM88), Drew Dinkmeyer (Dinkpiece), Al Zeidenfeld (Al_Smizzle), and Jonathan Bales (BalesFootball). All top players in multiple sports, and with combined winnings that exceeded $5 million in 2014 on DraftKings, this team provides fantasy advice and entertainment on DKTV several times a week. Their popular "Sweat Show" during *Monday Night Football* tracks the movement in the week's biggest NFL contests, including the Millionaire Maker and Atlantis qualifiers. They started providing professional quality coverage at live DraftKings finals in 2015. The chat is full of players asking questions, making jokes, and submitting answers to trivia questions in order to win prizes.

Countless other fantasy sports sites now have DFS sections that employ countless writers to opine on which players are the best to use in any given day's/sport's/contest's lineup. The amount of information available to DFS players is staggering. It makes the whole enterprise operate at a higher knowledge level, increases engagement, and provides the basis for consumer/provider interactions.

## Twitter

The bulk of the social interactions in the DFS community happen on Twitter. Twitter is where participants hear the latest player injury, starting lineup, or weather news that affects how they will build their lineup. Following DFS accounts such as @InsidersDFS, @RotoWorldDaily, and @RotoGrinders clue users to new articles and opportunities to interact with site experts. Following beat writers of all the teams in sports that you play DFS in is the single best way to get injury and lineup news as soon as it is available. Most professional DFS players have Twitter lists of such writers for each major sport. There are automated "Twitter bots" that tweet things like home runs, stolen bases, and touchdowns as they happen, making it easy to find the big scores that affect your DFS lineup . . . or your opponent's.

Twitter is where DFS players can ask questions of the people who wrote the advice articles they read. It is probably the preferred place by most writers, myself included, to answer lineup or strategy questions. It is where they can eavesdrop on the strategy or scouting conversations between the experts they follow. Twitter is where DFS players congratulate each other, encourage each other, commiserate with and even poke fun at each other. A few examples:

- #skateboardlostawheel: The Pittsburgh Pirates were playing at Coors Field in July 2014, a dream scenario for MLB DFS players. Davis Mattek (DFS expert and writer at Fantasy Insiders and RotoViz), having stacked several of the Pirates hitters in his lineups that night in what ended up as a 8–1 loss for Pittsburgh, tweeted something to the effect that he didn't think his night could get any worse but then his skateboard lost a wheel. Ever since, it's the go to line whenever something goes wrong in the lineup or life of regular DFSers.
- #smizzlife: Referring to DraftKings Pro and DFS expert, DFS Bootcamp founder, and Twitter personality Al Smizzle (@alzeidenfeld), or more accurately to his life of impossibly extravagant luxury that most of us can only aspire to. When you want to denote the best of the best, this is the hashtag.
- #dadlife is the go-to excuse for missing last minute lineup news, entering the wrong game, etc. or simply refers to the skill in balancing Sesame Street, dirty diapers, and FanGraphs research. There are a fair number of stay at home dad DFS professionals including long time experts and FI founders @socrdave and @mrtuttle05.
- #dessertlife is for those who love their sweets enough that the right mousse or piece of cake can ease even the worst lineup disasters. Ask @kcannonDFS, @alzeidenfeld, @2hats1mike, @brit_devine, or @DHP to name just a very few of the partakers of this delicious hashtag.
- #tilt: Tilt is what one feels when the best laid plans and soundest lineup decisions go awry. It's a mixture of regret, astonishment, and pure unadulterated anger, at oneself, one's players, and frankly, at everyone not tilting the poor outcome. Sharing the misery with this hashtag helps a little bit.
- #dinksmillion: Ever wonder what would Drew Dinkmeyer's million dollar prize money do? Not just a hashtag anymore, but owner of its own twitter account (@dinksmillion), this money weighs in on all kinds of topics. Everyone has ideas for how best to spend it, that's for sure.

## DFS AND LIVE EVENTS

Live finals for DFS tournaments are a place where players that have qualified for these exclusive events come together to "sweat" out the games together, very similar to eSports and video games (Taylor, 2012) or more specific to sports, the annual Madden video game tournaments hosted by EA
Sports (Gaudiosi, 2011; also see chapter 2, this volume). Former DFS site
StarStreet ran live event finals at the Playboy Mansion, a venue that now
belongs to FanDuel. The 2014 FanDuel PlayBoy Football Championship
awarded over one million dollars in prizes while competitors who qualify
enjoy a weekend at the luxurious estate. FanDuel also ran a live final with
a two million dollar first prize for NFL in Las Vegas in 2014, and started a
new trend of smaller live final events around the country in cities such as
Boston and San Francisco during the 2015 MLB season. DraftKings hosted
a luxurious live final at the Atlantis Resort in the Bahamas for MLB DFS
in August 2014, which was followed up with its King of the Beach NFL live
final in December 2014 at the same venue. Fantasy Aces entered the live
final arena with events in Newport, California, for NFL and MLB. Qualifying for live events not only gives players a chance for a huge top prize, but
the chance to interact with top DFS players and site personnel. The luxury,
social aspect, and of course high stakes DFS appear to make these tournaments among the most popular emerging contests on the major sites.

## THE FUTURE OF DFS

The number of users enjoying DFS is growing fast, yet is estimated to
include only about 5 percent of season long fantasy players. Sites like Fan
Duel and DraftKings launched aggressive advertising campaigns in 2014,
which we should expect to continue. Television advertising focuses on the
opportunity to turn a small initial investment into a huge prize. In support
of their claims, both big sites run small buy-in tournaments ($25–27) where
the first prize is $1,000,000–$2,000,000. Data is not available as to how
many new users come to play in these games, nor how many continue to
play—such data in fact should be the focus of future academic and market
research into DFS. Retention is obviously a huge goal for any site, but for
the near future, attracting new users will remain the priority.

Advertising on season-long fantasy web sites has increased awareness
among users, as has exposure on Twitter, Facebook, and simple word of

mouth. A new era in DFS began in 2014 with FanDuel and DraftKings partnering with professional sports franchises to promote DFS. FanDuel initially announced a partnership with the Orlando Magic, with the permission of the NBA (NBA.com, 2014). This led to agreements with other teams in the fall of 2014, ultimately resulting in an official partnership between FanDuel and the NBA (Rovell, 2014). In the deal, the NBA becomes a part owner of FanDuel, and gives FanDuel the exclusive rights to advertise on official NBA sites. Fantasy sports greatly increases television viewership (cf. Fortunato, 2011; see also chapters 9 and 10, this volume), and DFS might amplify that effect since all the action takes place during a few short hours. In the same week of November 2014 as FanDuel announced their NBA deal, competitor DraftKings announced an exclusive partnership with the National Hockey League (NHL.com, 2014) and is now the MLB's official daily fantasy game according to an April 2015 partnership extension (Heitner, 2015) These mutually beneficial deals with professional sports organizations legitimize DFS, and have the potential to increase awareness, and acknowledge that fantasy games are a major factor in driving sports viewing.

Challenges remain for DFS. There are still five states that do not recognize the legality of DFS: Washington, Arizona, Iowa, Louisiana, and Montana (see also chapter 13, this volume). On a site-by-site level, player retention is a concern, as there seems to be a huge disparity between the top two sites and everyone else in terms of the number of registered users—actual numbers are a bit difficult to come by. Small sites with a good product will attempt to lure new players with deposit bonuses, free games for prizes, and novel contests, but they are largely at the mercy of the whims of their customers, many of whom are drawn to DFS because of their short-term commitments. Even the large sites have to plan for players leaving after losing money or their favorite sport's season ends. Ultimately, the appeal of fresh start fantasy, immediate prize payouts, and the lure of a social experience to boot will likely continue to attract and retain new DFS players. The legal and technical challenges, should they persist at all, will almost certainly find amicable solutions. Partnerships with professional sports leagues are a big step in legitimizing DFS, while the widespread advertising campaigns are attracting new customers. Excellent customer service, unique and engaging games and user platforms, and the availability of education tools will retain those new users. This industry is poised to explode, bringing the new wave of fantasy sports experience to the world.

## REFERENCES

Cardano, M. (2015, January 14). Anthem Media acquires LuDawgs.com, a sprawling daily fantasy community. *SportsGrid.com*. Retrieved from http://www.sports grid.com/fantasy/anthem-media-acquires-ludawgs-com-sprawling-daily-fantasy -community/

Fantasy Insiders, Inc. (n.d.). Fantasy Insiders: www.fantasyinsiders.com

FanDuel.com (2014, January 21). Side-wide chat has been removed. FanDuel.com. Retrieved from http://www.fanduel.com/insider/2014/01/21/site-wide-chat-has -been-removed/

Farquhar, L. K., & Meeds, R. (2007). Types of fantasy sports users and their motivations. *Journal of Computer-Mediated Communication, 12*, 1208–1228.

Fortunato, J. A. (2011). The relationship of fantasy football participation with NFL television ratings. *Journal of Sport Administration and Supervision, 3*(1), 74–90.

Gaudiosi, J. (2011, February 2). EA Sports' Madden Bowl XVII video game tournament goes live on ESPN3.com. Retrieved from http://www.hollywoodreporter .com/news/ea-sports-madden-bowl-xvii-95812

Heitner, Darren (2015, April 2) DraftKings and Major League Baseball extend exclusive partnership. Retrieved from http://www.forbes.com/sites/darrenheitner/ 2015/04/02/draftkings-and-major-league-baseball-extend-exclusive-partnership/

Internet Gambling Prohibition and Enforcement Act (2006). H.R. 4411—109th Congress.

National Basketball Association (2014, August 19). FanDuel joins the Magic as a Champions of the Community Sponsor. *NBA.com*. Retrieved from http://www .nba.com/magic/fanduel-joins-magic-champions-community-sponsor

National Hockey League (2014, November 10). NHL announces partnership with DraftKings. *NHL.com*. Retrieved from http://www.nhl.com/ice/news.htl?id =738520

RotoGrinders.com (n.d.). RotoGrinders.com: The Daily Fantasy Authority: www .rotogrinders.com

Rovell, D. (2014, November 12). NBA partners with FanDuel. ESPN.com. Retrieved from http://espn.go.com/nba/story/_/id/11864920/nba-fanduel-reach-4 -year-exclusive-daily-fantasy-deal

Taylor, T. L. (2012) *Raising the stakes: E-sports and the professionalization of computer games*. Cambridge, MA: MIT Press.

# CONCLUSION

## Projecting the Next Round: Scouting the Future of Fantasy Sports

*Nicholas David Bowman, John S. W. Spinda,*
*Jimmy Sanderson, and Shaun M. Anderson*

Since their earliest formalized roots in the 1960s, fantasy sports contests have grown and matured from an isolated hobby to an activity embraced by the larger MediaSport enterprise (to borrow from Wenner, 1988). The chapters offered in this volume—at least to us—provide definitive evidence that fantasy sports contents have emerged from (imagined) dark and dank basements of a few fervent baseball and football fans feverishly following their favorite (or at least, the best performing) players, and they have blitzed the mainstream of professional sports both in the United States and abroad.

As with most innovations, the impact of fantasy sports play has been at once immediately realized (in terms of increased fandom and sports consumption) and is still being felt (concerns about gambling and demographic inequity in fantasy sports play) as the contests evolve. In reflection of our fifteen chapters, we offer a summary of their main points below.

## FANTASY SPORTS AND SPORTS CULTURE

### More Avid Sports Fans

Perhaps one of the more emergent themes from this volume is the role that fantasy sports plays as an individual's expression of his or her fandom. The earliest games were started by avid fans of MLB and the NFL, and a common theme and motivation for fantasy sports play is the games' ability to help the fans connect to their favorite players, teams, franchises, and leagues. DeSarbo and Madrigal (2011) would likely refer to such activities as off-field fan participation, similar to fans expressing their fandom by attending tailgates, theme parties, and engaging in other sports-themed social activities. As fans have become more avid, however, fantasy sports has prompted some compelling challenges for fans, which are addressed by Dwyer, Shapiro, and Drayer in chapter 10. For example, how does a fan manage his/her fandom in relation to his or her fantasy sport enterprise? Consider a fantasy football participant who is a fan of the Dallas Cowboys and yet has players from rival teams such as the Philadelphia Eagles and New York Giants. Does this fantasy sports player try to unload these players prior to when they play the Cowboys? Or does the fan experience some sort of fractured experience wherein she/he roots for the Cowboys to win the game, but hopes the Eagles receiver on his or her fantasy football roster has a banner game? Whereas football has a much shorter season and fans might be able to manage the cognitive dissonance resulting from having rival players on their fantasy sports team, a fantasy basketball or baseball player may have a harder time doing so, given the length of those seasons. Moreover, does a New York Yankees fan draft any Boston Red Sox players, even if a Red Sox player could provide a competitive advantage? How fans might navigate these dualities is one area addressed in this volume.

## Fantasy Sports and Social Media

Several of our authors demonstrated the largely positive role that fantasy sports play has had for the sports media industry. Perhaps one of the most apparent examples of this complementary relationship can be found during the 1981 MLB players' strike—with little other baseball action to cover during the '81 season, many baseball journalists turned their attention to Gamson and his group's Rotisserie League Baseball (see chapter 1 for more details). As Bien-Aimé and Hardin suggest in chapter 9, traditional news outlets such as *USA Today* were some of the earliest adopters of constant fantasy sports coverage, both in print and in their online operations. Major broadcasters such as NBC, CBS, FOX, and even cable networks such as ESPN all have regularly scheduled programming dedicated to fantasy sports, and fantasy sports players self-report being regular consumers of sports media in general. Given the well-documented discussions regarding shrinking editorial staffs at many newspapers and other legacy media outlets, fantasy sports coverage has the potential to provide content for sports departments at traditional sports media as well as fuel the creation of start-up operations wholly devoted to fantasy sports coverage.

One area of particular growth regarding fantasy sports and sports media is the area of social media. Whereas fantasy sports has initiated some potential fractures for fandom, fantasy sports has led to some more overt expressions of fandom via social media. It is not uncommon, particularly during football season, to see fans lashing out at players via Twitter who they perceive to have "cost" the fantasy sports player a victory, which Sanderson addresses in chapter 11. These expressions, while perhaps reflective, underscore larger implications stemming from the financial growth of the fantasy sports industry. Moreover, often these critiques are underpinned with misogynistic language that in one sense, almost seems to be normalized in online fantasy sport banter. Thus, it may be difficult for female participants to gain long-term access to fantasy sports, despite this being a potentially underserved market for the fantasy sport industry, a topic that Lavelle attends to in chapter 7. Additionally, social media also has become a space for fantasy sports experts to build identity and demonstrate it through the host of advice that is solicited from them during the course of a fantasy season. Many fantasy sports "experts" have significant followings on Twitter, and Sanderson considers whether these individuals have agenda-setting power when it comes to dictating fantasy sports transactions.

## FANTASY SPORTS AS COMPUTER-MEDIATED COMMUNICATION

Several authors, such as Boyan, Westerman, and Daniel (chapter 5), Sanderson (chapter 11) and Miller (chapter 15) discussed how fantasy sports play can be understood as a rather unique arena for social interactions—in some ways, conceptualizing fantasy sports contests as computer-mediated communication spaces. While Sanderson's work focused more on the interactions between fantasy sports players and the professional athletes themselves (previously discussed), one relatively unexplored area of fantasy sports is how they might function as spaces for understanding (competitive) human communication.

On the one hand, fantasy sports competitions can elicit rather toxic behaviors among participants—the sort of hypernegative commentary addressed by Boyan et al. (chapter 5) that might naturally emerge from anonymous environments with high levels of competition and intense levels of loyalty to particular groups (such as players and teams). Many fantasy sports forums attempt to control such behavior in their terms of service, and as mentioned by Miller (chapter 15), one of the largest Web sites FanDuel.com actually disabled all player chat in early 2014, for a variety of reasons:

- At peak times chat scrolled so fast it was not readable or usable
- It had become a support channel that was a challenge to serve due to its speed during peak times and site issues
- It was used for frequent abuse and inappropriate comments that offended a large number of our players
- People were sharing real and misleading player updates which spoiled the gameplay and were against our rules
- It was a significant drain on our customer support team who could be helping with legitimate support issues elsewhere instead of monitoring and moderating chat
- Our data showed that only a small minority of people used it, and surveys showed significantly more players were in favor of removing it than keeping it (FanDuel.com, 2014, para. 2)

While it is unclear if this list was meant to be hierarchal in nature, a quick browse of FanDuel user comments on this story (ironically?) reveals those players' frustrations with toxic language in the forums. For example (unedited):

> I visited the room only once and it reminded me of my teenage days watching people make fun of others. I was trying to see if there was any serious discussion about games, players, etc but was disappointed. No real value added for most I'm sure.

> I can understand why you took the chat room down its to bad a few PUNKS!who no nothing about the game of football and sports in general. Or sportsoolmanship they see morons on tv say stupid things and think that's coo lmyself love the fanduel site and will continue to play and respect what changes may come.

> I will miss the fun banter with all the good guys on Fan Duel, I will not miss all the trolls that tried to derail any civil conversation on chat . . . It was fun while it lasted, but it was abused all too often. Kinda sucks not being able to talk to all the guys anymore, but it is what it is . . . (forum comments, FanDuel.com, 2014)

At the same time, it might be possible that some of this intense fantasy (sports) competition can be healthy for interpersonal relationships—particularly those with established friendships and relationships. As an analogy, there is research on video games and cooperation suggesting that playing competitive video games can result in higher levels of cooperative behavior afterwards (Ewoldsen et al., 2012), suggested by Bowman, Kowert, and Cohen (in press) to be in part a function of the inter-relatedness created by the gameplay environment. That is, while the players are actively competing with one another, they are also sharing and engaging in relational maintenance with one another during the experience (cf. Stafford, Dainton, & Haas, 2000).

## FANTASY SPORTS AS BIG BUSINESS

Fantasy sports also has grown from something often ridiculed as being done in "mom's basement" to a very lucrative business enterprise. Ruihley and Billings, in chapter 14, discuss the growth of the Fantasy Sports Trade Association from an ad-hoc group to an industry powerhouse that has taken great pains to overcome potential legal hurdles and challenges. The legitimization of the fantasy sports industry can be seen in the surge of partnerships between fantasy sports leagues and professional sports leagues. The legal implications arising from fantasy sport, particularly as the industry strives to maintain its assertion that fantasy sports is not "gambling," is covered by Grabowski in chapter 13. Grabowski recounts how the fantasy sports industry has navigated this hurdle as well as discussing the growth of independent dispute resolution services such as SportsJudge.com that handle fantasy sports conflicts. Grabowski outlines a number of compelling legal challenges that could emerge within both micro-level (i.e., individual leagues) and macro-level for the industry at large.

## BARRIERS TO FANTASY SPORTS GROWTH

### International Appeal

In chapter 3, Nicholas Watanabe and his colleagues gave a comprehensive analysis as to the U.S. roots of fantasy sports, suggesting that while the games have begun to spread internationally—in particular, to Europe and Asia—

that their growth and popularity in these regions pales in comparison to the United States. Of course, this pattern can largely be attributed to the fact that fantasy sports have their roots in the United States, but a closer inspection of the culture and practice of fantasy sports seems to reveal two other notable characteristics, specifically in relation to the more established fantasy sports contest based around MLB and the NFL. First, both of these sports dominate the larger American sports scene, with Rovell (2014) reporting that both leagues have occupied the top spot for U.S. sports fans since the first Harris Polls on the subject taken in 1985; both leagues have consistently comprised nearly 50 percent of all fans responding to their favorite sport (notably, U.S. college football occupies the third spot on this list). American-rules football and baseball are sports that do not have as much international appeal—one reason cited for their exclusion in the Olympic Games (along with concerns about MLB's reluctance to allow players to participate in the Summer Olympics as the games often take place during the league's regular season of competition; cf. Michaelis, 2005), although we should note that professional baseball does enjoy a place of cultural prominence in Japan as well as many Latin American countries. Second (and related to the first), the more popular fantasy sports leagues are often those that provide players with a good deal of statistics and other rubrics for which to compete—understand that fantasy sports at its core (simulation games, excluded) is a competition of actual professional player performance. Much of this competition is centered around comparisons of a dizzying array of statistics, such as (to use baseball as an example) a player's batting average, stolen bases count, home runs, doubles, triples, walks drawn, on-base percentage, total bases reached, runs batted in (RBIs), runs scored, and any combination of these metrics as well as others. For baseball (as well as football, which also produces a similarly rich set of sabermetrics with which to evaluate players), fantasy sports competitions can be as simple or complex as the players wish, but the sport itself provides a number of different comparison points that players can use to evaluate whose team wins and loses a given competition. In contrast, sports such as soccer (football in most every nation outside of the United States) have a much broader international appeal—soccer is widely accepted as the most popular spectator sport in the world, as well as the most played according to FIFA (played by over 265 million people; Kunz, 2007). However, Simkins (2015) explains that "while soccer statistics are not quite yet to the level of MLB or the NFL, the interest in analytics and gaming engagement appears to be growing" (para. 3). Some such as Bialik (2008) argue that the fluid and holistic nature of soccer emphasizes aesthetics for statistical acumen, although he relents that the emergence of sabermetrics a sport called "The Beautiful" by footballer Pele is part of a natural evolution toward maximizing and understanding performance. Notably, Watanabe and his colleagues (in chapter 3 of this volume) present a compelling case for the internationalization of fantasy sports play, which largely seems to be overcoming these barriers.

Beyond the nature of the sports that lend themselves to fantasy sports competition, there are other barriers that limit the popularity of fantasy outside of the United States. As outlined in chapter 3 as well as by Grabowski in chapter 13 (focused primarily on the United States), there are legal barriers to the expansion of fantasy sports in some countries—many of which have attempted to regulate the games as form of (sometimes, illegal) gambling. Although not covered in any great detail in the current volume, the systematic gap in technology (and specifically, Internet) access known as the Digital Divide (Chinn & Fairlie, 2004) might greatly impact fantasy sports play. Given that most popular fantasy sports games are played via the Internet either directly (fantasy sports leagues hosted online) or indirectly (players using the Internet to access information), disparities in technology access could stifle attempts to connect with and cultivate new fantasy sports players. Moreover, even if those non-connected individuals did engage in analog fantasy sports play, they might not benefit from the social interactions enjoyed by online contestants (see Westerman and colleagues' work on this in chapter 5 of this volume) and they would be unable to use social media tools as part of their fantasy sports play (see Sanderson, chapter 11 of this volume).

## Lack of Participatory Diversity

Both Anderson and Bowman (chapter 1, this volume) and Lavelle (chapter 7, this volume) highlight one rather stark reality of fantasy sports in terms of player demographics: They are overwhelmingly white and male. Comedian Chris Rock was a featured guest on Real Sports with Bryant Gumbel. With his appearance, he lamented on the lack of diversity in sports, specifically Major League Baseball. He claimed that the MLB's main issue is its poor efforts to stay current with how our society is becoming more diverse. Further, he explained that the MLB has made poor efforts to reach out to individuals from diverse backgrounds.

Considering that the four major American professional sports leagues (i.e, National Football League, National Hockey League, Major League Baseball, National Basketball Association) have earned an estimated revenue of approximately $500 billion dollars (Pieters, Knoben, & Pouwels,

2012), it makes sense to examine the positive impact diversity has on both traditional sports and fantasy sports. Demographic figures from the FSTA's 2014 report suggest players to be from this one population segment, which might counteract efforts by most major league franchises to encourage diversity within their fan bases. Although many sport organizations are making the efforts to market to more diverse fan bases, many like Chris Rock, feel that these efforts are falling on deaf ears. On the one hand, it could be that many sport organizations are not taking the time to properly research the communities in their respective cities. On the other hand, it could be that these organizations are not knowledgable on how to connect with these communities.

Beyond general concerns about diversity, such a demographically heterogeneous player base might make it difficult for those few minority players to find like-minded communities online. While not addressed specifically by Boyan and colleagues in chapter 5, concerns about hypernegative (their language) comments in online fantasy sports spaces might be magnified when considering the potential for racial or gender disparities. Lavelle (chapter 7) already highlights some of the hypermasculine messaging and commentary contained on some fantasy sports sites, and contrasts this with the fact that females and males differ very little in terms of their motivations for playing the games in the first place (citing Billings & Ruihley, 2014). At the same time, it might be possible that given the similar motivations that fantasy sports players seem to give for engaging in the activity—regardless of their gender and likely regardless of their race and ethnicity—these spaces might exist somewhat as post-racial activities, although research on this point is needed.

While demographic diversity might emerge as a primary concern for many, another concern—somewhat highlighted above when discussing the international appeal of fantasy sports—is the relative lack of professional sports that can be played. MLB and NFL games along with the other dominant U.S. sports such as the National Basketball Association (NBA) and the National Hockey League (NHL) seem to dominate the larger fantasy sports landscape, although there is an influx of games related to the English Premiere League (EPL) and other international soccer leagues (Cardillo, 2014). Notably, growth of the EPL's branded (and even non-branded) fantasy sports competition appears highly correlated with the league's rise to prominence in the larger U.S. sports culture, including the signing of a three-year, $250 million live broadcasting deal with NBC Sports at the start of the 2013 season (Associated Press, 2012). This deal came at a time at which other major U.S. sports media outlets such as *USA Today* and

ESPN were already devoting coverage to EPL (and other European soccer leagues), which serves to provide soccer fans with a ready space to track their favorite (or at least, drafted) players' and teams' fantasy performances. As previously discussed both in chapter 3 and in the current chapter, one barrier to the expansion of fantasy sports models to other sports involves the unique role that statistics play in other sports, but fantasy contents have begun to emerge for a variety of sports, including cricket (sponsored by ESPN), horse racing (sponsored by the Breeders' Cup) as well as a number of hobbyist pages, such as the fantasy volleyball page (based on player performance from U.S. National Collegiate Athletic Association Division 1 players) found at http://www.straightfromdehart.com/fantasy-volleyball-information-page/. Given that the only base requirements for fantasy sports are (a) players whose performance can be tracked and (b) meaningful comparisons that can be drawn between those performances, it would seem that most any sport could be "fantasized" by those determined to do so. Moreover, Internet technologies greatly enhance the potential for any number of these leagues to grow, as they make it feasible for a comparatively small number of interested players to gather and compete in digital spaces with few encumbrances—this small group representing the statistical "long tail" of intensely interested fans of an otherwise marginalized sport (Anderson, 2008; Manovich, 2009). As technologies develop, so should their applicability to enhancing the fantasy sports experience.

## CONTEMPORARY ISSUES IN FANTASY SPORTS

### Debate about Gambling vs. Gaming

An enduring argument proposed in several of our chapters—most succinctly by Grabowski in chapter 13—is whether or not fantasy sports content can be considered competitions and simply games, or should be regulated as forms of gambling. As of 2014, Yahoo! Finance's Pras Subramanian has identified contests with payouts as high as $1 million (the NFL's Fantasy Perfect Challenge, a free game available to anyone over the age of eighteen), and high-stakes leagues with players "usually paying more than $1,000 as a buy-in" (para. 5). Some argue that the increasingly high buy-ins and payouts suggest that fantasy sports should be regulated in a similar way that we might regulate online poker and gaming, whereas others consistently argue—in line with the Unlawful Internet Gambling and Enforcement Act of 2006 (UIGEA)—that fantasy sports are games of skill, with fantasy players who know more about sports outperforming players who know less. Such laws protect the growth of fantasy sports in the United States, although Watanable and colleagues (chapter 3, this volume) explain how the classification of such games as gambling internationally has had a drastic impact on their development—often stifling their growth. Outside of legal briefs on this "gaming vs. gambling" debate, however, there is scant research on the potential uses or effects of fantasy sports play on the players themselves—specifically related to notions of gambling or financial loss. Berdhard and Eades (2005) offer exploratory research into the self-titled "gambling" behaviors of fantasy rotisserie players, but conclude their essay by suggesting that fantasy sport are a rather benign social activity; however, they do note:

> . . . as our understanding of gambling behavior matures, it makes sense to examine 'gambling acts' that are not confined within the walls of traditional gaming establishments, in order to more fully understand the complex wagering passions of the masses (p. 41).

Of course, it should be noted that of the potential negative impacts reported in that study, none were related to financial loss and all were anecdotal in nature. Nonetheless, even if some of the legal positions regarding fantasy sports gaming vs. gambling classification are protected, little published research—outside of a plethora of legal briefs—has endeavored to specifically explore the extent to which some of the same behaviors and consequences associated with gambling might also be analogous with excessive fantasy sports play, which leaves open questions related to the impact of fantasy sports wagers on those playing (cf. Smith, 2012). Thus, while we acknowledge that legal journals and judgments are the most proper place to address the gaming vs. gambling debate, such arguments might not advance our scientific understanding of fantasy sports play's potential consequences (both intended and unintended) on the players themselves.

## Fantasy or Labor?

A rather illuminating critique of fantasy sports was offered by Baerg in chapter 6—the notion that fantasy sports play might serve to reinforce neoliberal approaches to risk management by their very nature: Fantasy sports players are essentially good risk management officers, which seems to reduce the fantasy and play elements of the competitions to a series of carefully constructed and crafted strategy moves performed not out of some divine or idiosyncratic intervention or playfulness on behalf of the individual competitor, but rather as nearly autonomous (and perhaps mindless) reactions to a litany of statistical information. One interpretation of Baerg's research is that a curious paradox might exist for the fantasy sports players in which they are engaging the activity as a leisurely escape into their favorite sports league, but consequently end up engaging in a rather laborious surveillance of objective data in order to craft pre-set risk management plans rather than engaging the games as spaces for play. Somewhat related to this is the emergence of the professional fantasy sports player—some who can earn as much as $100,000 U.S. or more in annual prizes (cf. Mandell, 2013). On this point, and related to the notions of gaming vs. gambling above, future work might consider the lived experience of fantasy sports play in terms of being a leisurely pursuit or a professional one, and how these different motivations might drastically alter how the contests are taken up, experienced by, and influence the players. Related to this, fantasy sports companies might more closely examine potential differences and similarities between these (likely) very divergent play styles—somewhat following the example of DraftKings Pro as discussed in brief by Miller (chapter 15, this volume).

## CONCLUSION

Fantasy sports are an important and relevant part of the larger Media-Sport scene—they are a fan-initiated activity that has become enmeshed, for better or worse, into the larger cultural and economic reality of professional sports. The fifteen chapters of the current volume attempt to provide a comprehensive look at the impact and role of fantasy sports play on itself, as well as the many shareholders—the fans, the sports leagues and teams, and the sports media—that all constitute the larger MediaSport entity. While there are many debates as to the present and future of fantasy sports, there can be no doubt that the contests are, and will continue to be, a legitimate aspect of professional sports. Indeed, fantasy sports appears to be thriving and practices that would have, several decades ago seem absurd, such as sport news organizations providing fantasy sport hosting services, have arguably become economic necessities in an industry that has seen a seismic digital transformation.

The fifteen chapters provided in this text, while providing a foundation upon which future inquiries can build, illustrate what is perhaps the biggest misnomer of fantasy sports. That is, "fantasy" sports is anything but "fantasy." Participants invest significant time, energy, and in some cases, financial resources to demonstrate their superiority over their friends and co-workers in sports roster construction and management. The diligence and dedication exerted by users feeds the larger SportMedia complex, who provides a host of experts who offer sophisticated analysis that helps participants reduce risk and maximize return. The sport media entities that employ these experts and provide the platforms for participation generate sizable revenue from the audiences they are able to market to advertisers. As these factors coalesce, athletes find themselves inserted in media narratives about the "fantasy impact" of various issues both on and away from competition. Such is the reality of fantasy sports.

## REFERENCES

Anderson, C. (2008). *The long tail: Why the future of business is selling less of more.* New York: Hyperion.

Associated Press. (2012, October 28). NBC secures English Premier League broadcasting rights. USAToday.com. Retrieved from http://www.usatoday.com/story/sports/soccer/2012/10/28/nbc-secures-english-premier-league-soccer-rights/1664681/

Bernhard, B., & Eade, V. (2005). Gambling in a fantasy world: An exploratory study of rotisserie baseball games. *UNLV Gaming Research & Review Journal, 9*(1), 29–42.

Bialik, C. (2008, June 24). Can statistics explain soccer? *Wall Street Journal.* Retrieved from http://blogs.wsj.com/numbers/can-statistics-explain-soccer-363/.

Billings, A. C. & Ruihley, B. J. (2014). *The Fantasy Sport Industry: Games within games.* New York: Routledge.

Bowman, N. D., Kowert, R., & Cohen, E. (in press). When the ball stops, the fun stops too: The impact of social inclusion on video game enjoyment. Manuscript forthcoming in *Computers in Human Behavior.*

Cardillo, M. (2014, August 13). EPL fantasy: Maybe it's up to America to bring it out of the Dark Ages. thebiglead.com. Retrieved from http://thebiglead.com/2014/08/13/epl-fantasy-maybe-its-up-to-america-to-bring-it-out-of-the-dark-ages/

Chinn, M. D., & Fairlie, R. W. (2004). *The determinants of the global digital divide: A cross-country analysis of computer and Internet penetration.* Santa Cruz, CA: University of California Working Papers. Retrieved from https://escholarship.org/uc/item/6hz053p3#page-1

DeSarbo, W. S., & Madrigal, R. (2011). Examining the behavioral manifestations of fan avidity in sports marketing. *Journal of Modelling in Management, 6*(1), 79–99. doi:10.1108/17465661111112511

Ewoldsen, D. R., Eno, C. A., Okdie, B. M., Velez, J. A., Guadagno, R. E., & DeCoster, J. (2012). Effect of playing violent video games cooperatively or competitively on subsequent cooperative behavior. *CyberPsychology, Behavior, and Social Networking, 15*(5), 277–280. doi:10.1089/cyber.2011.0308.

Kunz, M. (2007). 265 million playing football. *FIFA Magazine*, July 2017, pp. 10–15.

Mandell, N. (2013, October 29). Dream job? Fantasy sports players turning game into six-figure career. USAToday.com. Retrieved from http://ftw.usatoday.com/2013/10/dream-job-fantasy-sports-players-turning-game-into-six-figure-career

Manovich, L. (2009). The practice of everyday (media) life: From mass consumption to mass cultural production? *Critical Inquiry, 35*, 319–331. doi:10.1086/596645

Michaelis, V. (2005, July 8). Baseball, softball bumped from Olympics. USAToday.com. Retrieved from http://usatoday30.usatoday.com/sports/olympics/2005-07-08-baseball-softball-dropped_x.htm

Pieters, M., Knoben, J., & Pouwels, M. (2012). A social network perspective on sport management: The effect of network embeddedness on the commercial performance of sport organizations. *Journal of Sport Management, 26*, 433–444. doi:

Rovell, D. (2014, January 6). NFL most popular for 30th year in row. ESPN.com. Retrieved from http://espn.go.com/nfl/story/_/id/10354114/harris-poll-nfl-most-popular-mlb-2nd

Simkins, T. (2015, January 29). For fantasy, is soccer the next football? BusinessOfSoccer.com. Retrieved from http://www.businessofsoccer.com/2015/01/29/for-fantasy-is-soccer-the-next-football/

Smith, C. (2012, September 19). Why is gambling on fantasy football legal? Forbes.com. Retrieved from http://www.forbes.com/sites/chrissmith/2012/09/19/should-gambling-on-fantasy-football-be-legal/

Stafford, L., Dainton, M., & Haas, S. (2000). Measuring routine and strategic relational maintenance: Scale revision, sex versus gender roles, and the prediction of relational characteristics. *Communication Monographs, 67*(3), 306–323. doi:10.1080/03637750009376512.

Subramanian, P. (2014, August 29). The 3 biggest prizes in fantasy football. Yahoo! Finance. Retrieved from http://finance.yahoo.com/news/the-3-biggest-prizes-in-fantasy-football-174712081.html

Wenner, L. (1998). *MediaSport*. New York: Routledge.

# INDEX

# ABOUT THE EDITORS
# AND CONTRIBUTORS

## ABOUT THE EDITORS

**Nicholas David Bowman** (Ph.D., Michigan State University) is an Associate Professor of Communication Studies at West Virginia University, where he is the founding research associate in the Interaction Lab (#ixlab). His research examines the role of communication technology in the uses and effects of media on human communication, and he has published in *Media Psychology* and *Journal of Media Psychology* as well as *New Media & Society, Computers in Human Behavior,* and *Journal of Communication.* Prior to his academic work, he was a sports writer in St. Louis and taught courses on sports writing and radio broadcast in northern Georgia.

**John S. W. Spinda** (Ph.D., Kent State University) is an Assistant Professor in the Department of Communication Studies at Clemson University. His research focuses largely on the roles that fans play in the consumption and perception of sport, especially mediated effects as well as technology uses and effects. His teaching is specifically focused in the newly established Sport Communication major at Clemson University. Dr. Spinda currently serves on the International Association for Communication and Sport (IACS) Board of Directors.

**Jimmy Sanderson** (Ph.D., Arizona State University) is Director of Marketing, Communications, and Faculty Relations for Clemson Online at

Clemson University. He maintains an active research agenda that explores the influence of social media on sports media, sports organizations, athlete and fan identity, and social/parasocial interaction in sports. He is the author of *It's a Whole New Ballgame: How Social Media Is Changing Sports* (Hampton Press). You can find him on Twitter @Jimmy_Sanderson.

## ABOUT THE CONTRIBUTORS

**Shaun Anderson** (M.S.M.C., Arkansas State University) is a Ph.D. Candidate in Communication Studies at West Virginia University. His primary areas of research are in organizational communication and mass media. His research interests are in diversity and sport. Prior to his doctoral studies, he worked as a sports journalist and sport producer in Arkansas. Currently, he consults with various youth, college, and professional sport organizations on diversity initiatives and the social well-being of athletes.

**Andrew Baerg** (Ph.D., University of Iowa) is an Associate Professor of Communication at the University of Houston—Victoria. His primary research interest involves the relationship between sport and the media with a specific focus on the cultural and social significance of the medium of the sports video game. His prior research has focused on the relationship between sport and culture in sports games.

**Steve Bien-Aimé** (B.A., Penn State University) is a doctoral candidate in Penn State's College of Communications. Steve's research interests include race and gender portrayals in news and sports media. He has also co-authored an article in the *International Journal of Sport Communication*. Before entering graduate school, Steve worked as a copy editor at both the *News Journal* in Delaware and the *Baltimore Sun*, and served in a variety of functions at FOXSports.com in Los Angeles, departing as deputy NFL editor.

**Andrew Billings** (Ph.D., Indiana University) is the Director of the Alabama Program in Sports Communication and Ronald Reagan Chair of Broadcasting in the Department of Telecommunication and Film. His research interests lie in the intersection of sport, mass media, consumption habits, and identity-laden content. He is the author and/or editor of ten books, including *The Fantasy Sport Industry: Games within Games* (Routledge, 2014); his writings have been translated into five languages.

Additionally, he is also the author of over 110 refereed journal articles and book chapters in outlets such as the *Journal of Communication, Journalism & Mass Communication Quarterly*, *Mass Communication & Society*, and *Journal of Broadcasting & Electronic Media*.

**Andy Boyan** (Ph.D., Michigan State University) is an Assistant Professor of Communication Studies at Albion College. His scholarly research focuses on the impact of new technologies on communication contexts including sports, digital and traditional games, as well as studying communication as a process. He has taught Sport Communication, Social Media, and Entertainment Media courses.

**Emory S. Daniel Jr.** (M.A., Virginia Tech) is a Doctoral Student and Graduate Teaching Assistant at North Dakota State University. His scholarly research focuses on advertising, entertainment media, and parasocial interaction/relationships.

**Joris Drayer** (Ph.D., University of Northern Colorado) is an Associate Professor in Sport and Recreation Management at Temple University. His research interests include ticketing and pricing strategies in both primary and secondary ticket markets, as well as consumer behavior.

**Brendan Dwyer** (Ph.D., University of Northern Colorado) is an Associate Professor and the Director of Research and Distance Learning for the Center for Sport Leadership at Virginia Commonwealth University. His research interests include sport consumer behavior with a distinct focus on the media consumption habits of fantasy sports participants.

**Christopher Gearhart** (Ph.D., Louisiana State University) is an Assistant Professor in the Department of Communication Studies at Tarleton State University in Stephenville, Texas. He has completed several research projects focused on sport fan identification, including a 2015 article published in *Sport Marketing Quarterly*. He is the father to two wonderful sons, Christian and Luke.

**Mark Grabowski** (J.D., Georgetown University) is an Associate Professor of Communication at Adelphi University in Long Island. He previously worked as a lawyer and a sports journalist. He holds a J.D. from Georgetown Law. His most recent publication, "Both Sides Win: Why Using Mediation Would Improve Pro Sports," was published in the Spring 2014 volume of the *Harvard Journal of Sports & Entertainment Law*. Grabowski won the 2015 James Madison Prize for Outstanding Research for First Amendment Studies.

**Marie Hardin** (Ph.D., University of Georgia) has studied gender, sport journalism, and newsroom norms. Some of her more recent research has focused on social attitudes and values of sports journalists and bloggers and on the experiences and career paths of women in sports journalism. She has been the associate director of the Curley Center for Sports Journalism at Penn State University and has taught about issues in sports communication at the graduate and undergraduate levels. Hardin received her Ph.D. in 1998. Before completing her Ph.D., she worked as a newspaper reporter and editor; she has also worked as a freelance magazine writer.

**Cody T. Havard** (Ph.D., University of Northern Colorado) is an Assistant Professor of Sport Commerce at The University of Memphis. His research interests involve fan perceptions of rival teams, fan behavior, and the use of online social networking by athletes and sport organizations.

**Cory Hillman** (Ph.D., Bowling Green State University) is currently a Lecturer at Central Michigan University. He has published in *Communication and Sport* as well as the upcoming anthology on sports and video games entitled *Playing to Win: Sports, Video Games, and the Culture of Play*, edited by Thomas Oates and Robert Brookey.

**Shaughan A. Keaton** (Ph.D., Louisiana State University) is Assistant Professor of Communication Studies at Young Harris College. Shaughan grew up in Ohio and follows the Browns, Cavaliers, and Buckeyes, although he also cheers for his alma maters, UCF and LSU. He is an ardent fantasy sport participant, having been in the same league for twelve years (three time champion). Shaughan has co-edited *The Influence of Communication in Physiology and Health* (Peter Lang, 2014), in which he authored a chapter dealing with the physiological effects of sport fandom.

**Katherine L. Lavelle** (Ph.D., Wayne State University) is an Assistant Professor of Communication Studies at the University of Wisconsin-La Crosse, in the Advocacy and Communication Criticism Emphasis Area. Her primary research interest is in the representation of gender, race/ethnicity, and nationality in professional and college basketball.

**Renee M. Miller** (Ph.D., University of Rochester) is a Lecturer in the Department of Brain and Cognitive Science at the University of Rochester. Her scholarly research focuses on the genetic basis for sex differences in behavior. She writes for numerous fantasy sports web sites including ESPN.com, ProFootballFocus.com, RotoViz.com, and FantasyInsiders.com. Miller is also author of the eBook, *Cognitive Bias in Fantasy Sports: Is Your Brain Sabotaging Your Team?* (Xlibris, 2013).

**Brody J. Ruihley** (Ph.D., University of Tennessee) is an Assistant Professor of Sport Administration at the University of Cincinnati. His primary research interest lies in the area of fantasy sport consumption and motivation, and he is the co-author of *The Fantasy Sport Industry: Games within Games* (Routledge, 2014). He earned his bachelor's degree in Communication from the University of Kentucky, master's degree in Sport Administration from the University of Louisville, and doctoral degree in Sport Studies from the University of Tennessee.

**Stephen L. Shapiro** (Ph.D., University of Northern Colorado) is an Associate Professor of Sport Management at Old Dominion University. His research focuses on ticket pricing in the primary and secondary markets and consumer behavior as it relates to both purchase and charitable contribution decisions.

**Nicholas Watanabe** (Ph.D., University of Illinois) is an Assistant Teaching Professor in the Department of Parks, Recreation and Tourism at the University of Missouri, working in the sport management emphasis. His main research interests are: sport management, economics, finance, communications and development.

**David Westerman** (Ph.D., Michigan State University) is an Assistant Professor in the Department of Communication at North Dakota State University. His research focuses on computer-mediated communication. Specifically, he focuses on how people utilize technologies to accomplish their communication goals. He has taught a variety of CMC courses and is coauthor of the recent book *Computer Mediated Communication: A Functional Approach* (released Fall 2014). His recent research has been published in outlets such as *Journal of Computer Mediated Communication*, *Computers in Human Behavior*, and *Cyberpsychology, Behavior, and Social Networking*.

**Pamela Wicker** (Ph.D., German Sport University Cologne) is a Senior Lecturer at the Department of Sport Economics and Sport Management, German Sport University Cologne. Her main areas of research are development of non-profit sports clubs, financing sport, and economics of sport consumer behavior. She is Associate Editor (Economics) of *Sport Management Review* and on the board of another four academic journals (*Journal of Sport Management, International Journal of Sport Finance, Managing Sport and Leisure*, and *Journal of Sport & Tourism*).

**Grace Yan** (Ph.D., University of Illinois) is an Assistant Teaching Professor in the Department of Parks, Recreation and Tourism at the University of Missouri, working in the sport management emphasis. Her main research interests are: communications in sport and leisure as well as socio-cultural aspects of sport, leisure, and tourism.